Effective Teaching of Reading

Effective Teaching of Reading

by

Albert J. Harris
and
Edward R. Sipay

SECOND EDITION
Revised and Enlarged

DAVID McKAY COMPANY, INC.
New York

Effective Teaching of Reading

LIBRARY OF CONGRESS CATALOG CARD NUMBER: 72–134804

MANUFACTURED IN THE UNITED STATES OF AMERICA

To Edith and Betty

Preface to the Second Edition

In preparing this revised edition we have given primary consideration to the needs of students who are taking a first course that deals with the teaching of reading in the elementary school; either a separate course, or part of a course on teaching the language arts. We have tried to keep the language clear, the treatment concise, the point of view objective, the focus on practicality. We hope that the book will be useful also to teachers and supervisors who want an up-to-date description of good elementary-school reading practices.

The 1960's were years of innovation in reading instruction. This was especially true in programs for beginning readers. Accordingly, while the entire book has been up-dated and every chapter changed somewhat, the greatest changes will be found in Chapter 2, which deals with reading readiness, and Chapter 3, which describes beginning reading methods and materials. The newer phonic, linguistic, and programmed approaches are described, in addition to the eclectic basal reader programs which retain widespread popularity.

The basic organization of the book is unchanged. The first five chapters cover the total elementary reading program in a sequential way. The first chapter reviews relevant aspects of child development, describes and defines reading, and lists the objectives of a comprehensive reading program. The next four chapters cover reading readiness, beginning reading instruction, and reading instruction in the primary, middle, and upper grades.

The remaining chapters are arranged topically, each covering one important area of reading instruction. Chapter 6 deals with formal and informal methods for evaluating reading skills and discovering instructional needs. Chapter 7 deals with differentiated reading instruction, individually and in groups. Chapters 8 through 10 cover word recognition, word analysis and phonics, and meaningful vocabulary. Chapter 11 is concerned with development of basic comprehension skills. Chapter 12 is about functional reading and study skills, and Chapter 13 takes up reading interests and recreational reading. Finally, in Chapter 14 there are concise treatments of the reading needs of the mentally slow, the educationally disadvantaged, the disabled reader, and the potentially superior reader. Each of these chapters has been revised and brought up to date.

The illustrative material has been more than doubled in amount, and has been chosen for its practical value. Pages reproduced from many kinds of reading materials give added meaning and vividness to the verbal descriptions in the text. Sample one-week plans at several grade levels provide models that show how individualized and group procedures can fit together in well-planned instructional sequences. Many aids are provided which teachers can copy and use: informal tests of oral and silent reading, word recognition, and phonic knowledge; rating scales, check lists, questionnaires, and summary forms.

While we have read assiduously in the research on reading to give us the background for preparing this revision, we have purposely kept the number of footnotes small. Those who wish for more extensive, selective annotations may find them in the senior author's *How to Increase Reading Ability*, Fifth Edition. The annual reviews of reading research that appear in *Reading Research Quarterly* and *Journal of Educational Research*, and the special bibliographies prepared by ERIC/CRIER (Educational Resources Information Center for Reading, located at Indiana University, Bloomington, Ind.) make it possible to locate the relevant research on a special topic fairly easily.

The appendixes have also been substantially revised. Appendix A provides concise information about published tests mentioned in the book. Appendix B summarizes information about phonics for the teacher. Changes have been made to bring this into better agreement with linguistic terminology. Appendix C gives names and current addresses for the publishers.

To the many publishers who have graciously given permission to reproduce copyrighted material we extend our thanks. Specific ac-knowledgments are given in the legends that accompany the reproductions. We also wish to thank Professor Frank Hodge of the State University of New York at Albany for his valuable assistance in revising Chapter 13.

Finally, to our wives we owe deep gratitude for their patience, for their taking over many responsibilities so that we could have uninterrupted time to write, and for their support and encouragement.

ALBERT J. HARRIS
EDWARD R. SIPAY

June, 1970

knowledgments are given in the legends that accompany the reproductions. We also wish to thank Professor Frank Hodge of the State University of New York at Albany for his valuable assistance in revising Chapter 13.

Finally, to our wives we owe deep gratitude for their patience, for their taking over many responsibilities so that we could have uninterrupted time to write, and for their support and encouragement.

Albert J. Harris
Edward R. Sipay

June 1970

Contents

Chapter		Page
	Preface to the Second Edition	v
1	What Is Reading?	1
2	Readiness for Learning to Read	23
3	Beginning to Read	57
4	Reading in Grades Two and Three	101
5	Reading in the Middle and Upper Grades	128
6	Determining Learning Needs in Reading	152
7	Providing for Individual and Group Needs	184
8	Learning to Recognize Words	207
9	Developing Independence in Word Recognition	231
10	Fostering Vocabulary Development	265
11	Developing Comprehension in Reading	294
12	Developing Efficiency in Functional Reading	333
13	Improving Reading Interests	365
14	Achieving Maximum Reading Goals for Every Child	394
	Appendix A. Resources for Teachers of Reading	433
	Appendix B. A Concise Summary of Phonics	444
	Appendix C. List of Publishers and Their Addresses	461
	Index	467

Illustrations

Figure   *Page*

1   Diagram showing how eye-movement characteristics are represented in a photograph   15

2   Items from a test of visual discrimination   38

3   Items from tests of auditory discrimination   39

4   Items from a test of word meaning   40

5   A reading readiness rating scale   43

6   Part of a lesson to develop left-to-right progression and language skills   52

7   A page from a second preprimer (*A Magic Box*)   68

8   A page from a second preprimer (*Fun with the Family*)   71

9   A three-group plan for the first grade   76

10   Page from a first reader-workbook   86

11   A page from the second book of a phonic-linguistic series   87

12   A page from an audio-readiness book and preprimer   88

13   A page from the second book in a linguistic series   91

14   A page from Book 2, *A Game of Ball* (Spelled in i/t/a)   93

15   A page from a programmed reader   94

16   A page from a second reader (*Enchanted Gates*)   107

17   A page from a second reader (*Fields and Fences*)   108

18   A three-group plan for the second grade   114

19   A three-group plan for the fourth grade   136

20   A child's performance on an individual textbook test as recorded on a mimeographed copy   157

21   The record of an individual textbook test   160

22   A set of graded words for testing word recognition   172

23   A check list for concise recording of a large amount of information about a child's reading   178

24   Samples of material which may be used for developing
        a sight vocabulary   224
25   A page from a phonics workbook (*Phonics We Use*)   240
26   A page from a phonics workbook (*Building Reading
        Skills*)   242
27   Utility of phonic generalizations as determined by
        applying commonly taught generalizations to words
        encountered by children in their reading material   247
28   A page from a first-grade dictionary   255
29   A page from a picture dictionary   256
30   An exercise to develop the ability to select the correct
        dictionary definition   283
31   A practice exercise on interpreting idiomatic language   286
32   A page from a children's thesaurus   289
33   Example of the use of a word's origin to develop a
        clear and vivid meaning   290
34   An exercise intended to develop efficient phrase reading
        and to diminish frequency of regressions   297
35   An exercise to develop the ability to understand main
        ideas   308
36   Part of an exercise to develop the ability to recognize
        sequence   312
37   An exercise to develop the ability to follow printed
        directions   314
38   Part of an exercise to develop the ability to predict
        outcomes   316
39   An exercise to coordinate rate with comprehension   324
40   Life uses of reading classified according to rate   326
41   Part of a workbook exercise on outlining   351
42   Two one-week time plans   357
43   A simple interest questionnaire   374
44   A bookcase chart for recording independent reading   379
45   A form for recording independent reading   380
46   Individual progress charts   410
47   Page from a high interest-low vocabulary load book   412

Tables

Table   *Page*

I   Ages at Which Children of Varying I.Q.'s Reach the Mental Age of Six Years   27

II   Distribution of Reading Grade Scores on the Stanford Reading Test, Intermediate I, at the Beginning of the Fourth Grade   133

III   Approximate Mental Grade for Children of Different I.Q.'s at Chronological Ages Eight to Thirteen   397

Effective Teaching of Reading

1

What Is Reading?

Reading plays an indispensable role in our lives. Few of us stop to think just how different, and perhaps difficult, our lives would be if we were not able to read. Even if one does not read newspapers, magazines, or books, reading still is important in our daily lives. For example, in the course of a day, people are likely to read such things as street or traffic signs, advertisements, food or medicine labels, directions for cooking or repairing an appliance, and business or social letters. Reading is so much a part of everyday living that one can hardly imagine modern life without it.

Many of life's needs may be fulfilled through reading. Children, adolescents, and adults may read to meet the practical demands of everyday living; to carry on occupational activities; to further their recreational interests; to satisfy intellectual curiosity; to understand current events; to gain desired information; and to satisfy spiritual and emotional needs. Yet we often fail to develop a lasting interest in reading. The percentage of adults who read books regularly is far smaller in the United States than in a number of countries, particularly some in Europe. Since unused skills are of little value, we need to instill in children a love of reading.

Reading is uniquely individual and flexible. With no other form of mass communication can a person control the content and rate of presentation of the material. A reader can not only select his reading material from an almost limitless variety; he can also read where,

1

when, and as he pleases. He sets his own pace, pausing to reflect or reread, taking an intermission, skimming or taking careful notes. Reading is a pre-eminently private, personal, and self-controlled activity.

The attainment of reading competence is a major educational objective that must be accomplished if the rest of the academic program is to be effective. Until children are able to use the tools of learning (e.g., textbooks, reference books, and library books), their educational opportunities are limited. The child whose reading skills are inadequate is necessarily handicapped in many curricular areas, not just one. Of course, children must learn to read before they can read to learn. Reading is therefore both a major part of the elementary-school curriculum and an essential tool for mastering subject matter.

Reading and Child Development

DEVELOPMENT IS CONTINUOUS

From infancy to maturity children are always growing and changing. Abilities of all kinds that can be measured show continuous progress, although not necessarily at a uniform speed. The development of children is gradual and progressive.

The child in the elementary school tends to develop at a fairly uniform rate. After the very rapid growth of infancy, development settles down during the preschool years, and from kindergarten through the sixth grade steady increase is usual. The accelerated growth that is part of early adolescence tends to start around the age of eleven in girls and a year or so later in boys, so that most of it takes place in the junior high school years.

The majority show fairly regular and steady growth, but some children have individual growth curves or cycles that are untypical. When children have been examined year after year, some are found who start rapidly but slow down later; others are slow starters but show accelerated growth later on. The majority tend to continue at a consistent rate; the ones who seem slow in the first grade and bright in the sixth, or are short at one age and tall at another, are definitely exceptions. Many children grow at about the same rate in most significant characteristics, while some show marked disparities, being accelerated in some aspects of growth and retarded in others.

DEVELOPMENT INVOLVES BOTH MATURATION AND LEARNING

Maturation refers to the aspects of development which are part of the biological make-up of the organism and which inevitably take place if the environment is reasonably suitable. Learning is change in the individual as a result of experience. In the development of children the two are intimately interwoven. Without maturation the child cannot learn; without experiences he has nothing to learn.

Psychologists and educators differ among themselves about the relative importance of maturation and learning, and about the implications to be drawn for education.

Those who stress maturation tend to believe that what and how a child will learn depends primarily on his own growth characteristics and that not much can be done educationally to modify this developmental pattern. They stress the importance of adapting school expectations and practices to the growth rate of each child. They advocate waiting until the child shows that he is ready and then allowing him to set his own pace of learning. Theirs is a largely laissez-faire program in education.

Those who stress learning believe that children are adjustable creatures whose outstanding characteristic is their ability to profit from experience. They believe that what seems like a lack of readiness to learn is often either a lack of motivation or a failure to devise the best possible learning situation, and that both of these difficulties can usually be overcome. They believe in building readiness for learning rather than waiting for it.

In the teaching of reading it is desirable not to overstress either maturation or learning. Strong reliance on maturation may lead teachers to wait years for a child to develop readiness when he could have responded to effective instruction much earlier. Ignoring maturation, on the other hand, leads teachers to overlook marked differences in ability to learn, and to strive in vain for uniform achievement. This puts undesirable pressure on the slow and tends to be deadening and unstimulating to those capable of rapid progress.

PHYSICAL DEVELOPMENT AND READING

Sensory handicaps can make it difficult for a child to learn the perceptual tasks in reading. In vision, the common defects that are correctible with glasses should of course receive attention, but they are less likely to interfere with progress in reading than difficulties in the aiming, focusing, and binocular coordination of the eyes. School eye examinations are usually not able to detect the latter kinds of visual problems. Since young children tend to be farsighted, periods requiring close vision should not be prolonged in the first grade, and much of the reading practice should be at a distance of several feet.

A partial hearing loss may make it hard for a child to discriminate between sounds that are somewhat alike, such as /t/ and /d/, or /sh/ and /ch/, and if he cannot hear the difference he will have trouble learning to associate the printed symbol with its sound. Children with hearing defects are, therefore, likely to benefit from a reading program in which phonics is not emphasized.

Brain functioning is certainly very important in reading. When the quality of brain functioning is generally poor, the child is mentally retarded, and learning to read is delayed and difficult. Brain functioning can also be somewhat impaired in children who are not mentally retarded. When there is an injury to the brain at birth, or from a head injury, or as an occasional result of a feverish disease such as scarlet fever, the damage may affect only part of the brain, and some functions may develop normally while others are severely affected. It is also thought that the brains of some children do not develop at a uniform rate, so the child is normal in some ways and in others there is a marked delay; when there is delayed and irregular brain maturation, marked difficulty in learning to read is liable to occur. Finally, the brain is a functioning organ which is influenced by drugs, endocrine secretions, excessive fatigue, etc. Anything that has an adverse effect on brain functioning can, if prolonged, interfere with learning to read.

MENTAL DEVELOPMENT AND READING

There is a substantial relationship between a child's general mental development and his success in learning to read. In young children perceptual, reasoning, verbal, and numerical aptitudes are all inter-related, so that the idea of general intelligence has considerable value. As children near adolescence, these abilities may develop at varying rates.

The intelligence tests commonly used in elementary schools are usually scored in terms of mental age (M.A.) and intelligence quotient (I.Q.). To the teacher of reading, the child's present mental age gives an idea of the degree of maturity he is likely to show in understanding, reasoning, explaining, and remembering. Thus a bright eight-year-old and a dull twelve-year-old who both have M.A.'s of ten years are more like typical fifth graders in their ability to understand what they read than they are like typical third graders or seventh graders.

The I.Q. is a measure of the rate of mental development which indicates in a rough way what the child's future rate of mental growth is likely to be. The more the I.Q. is above 100, the faster is the probable rate of progress; the more below 100, the slower.

There is a substantial relationship between reading scores and I.Q., which tends to increase as children get older, perhaps because the tests are measuring very similar skills. However, children who are poor readers should not be tested with I.Q. tests that require reading skills.

Reading ability and I.Q. have about the same correlation with general scholastic performance. Although both are far from being perfect predictors, one can predict the average marks children will earn about as well from reading test scores as from I.Q.'s.

If well taught, reading provides both a wide variety of information and varied practice in thinking and reasoning. If a child misses these experiences because he cannot read well, he will be handicapped on I.Q. tests and his tested I.Q. is liable to get lower as he grows older.

LANGUAGE DEVELOPMENT AND READING

The baby begins to build his understanding of speech when he is able to notice and remember the sounds, produced by an adult, that accompany a specific experience such as feeding. During the second year, children become able to reproduce many of these sounds and achieve satisfaction from doing so. From the second year on, speech develops rapidly.

Typical children entering the first grade have already achieved considerable mastery in speaking and listening. They understand the meanings of thousands of words. They tend to speak in simple but complete sentences, averaging about six words in length. Most of them have outgrown baby talk and can pronounce most words correctly. They can understand, remember, and carry out a short series of instructions, and can enjoy the plot of a story that is read or told to them. They understand quite well the meanings of words that refer to specific objects, actions, or sensory qualities, but have only a limited comprehension of words that stand for abstract ideas or relationships. Their concepts dealing with time, quantity, and cause-effect relationships tend to be vague and inaccurate. In general their mastery of spoken language is quite adequate to provide a basis for beginning reading experiences.

Improvement in all aspects of language development proceeds steadily and rapidly when a favorable elementary-school program is reinforced by home conditions that give many opportunities for conversation and new experiences. Since children develop language skills by practicing them, an environment that provides many opportunities for listening and speaking promotes language development better than one in which children are "seen but not heard."

Comprehension in reading is closely related to ability to understand spoken language because both involve the understanding of concepts and sentence patterns, regardless of whether they are represented by printed or spoken symbols. Children whose knowledge of English, or standard English, is limited because they speak and think in a foreign language or a different dialect or because they come from language-impoverished homes (some children have both handicaps) need a program rich in all aspects of language development rather than one that concentrates mainly on reading skills.

SOCIAL AND CULTURAL DEVELOPMENT
AND READING

The progress that children make in reading is related to home and neighborhood conditions as well as to schooling. Homes in which the parents value education, enjoy reading themselves, have good books in the home, read to their children and tell them stories, converse with them, take them on trips and outings and vacations, encourage them to watch television programs of educational value—homes like these make it easy for children to become good readers. They help children to develop the linguistic skills and the background of concepts and ideas on which good reading skills can be built. They encourage the child to read through providing adult models to imitate and through their expressed interest in the child's reading. They keep watch over his progress and confer with the teacher if any difficulty seems to arise.

Many children, however, come from homes in which the parents are either indifferent to the school or actually antagonistic. Parents whose own educational experiences were unsatisfying and whose work demands little or no education tend to place little importance on education in general or reading in particular. Often they live in a neighborhood in which general attitudes are anti-intellectual. This is especially true when child society is organized along gang lines, as it is in many educationally disadvantaged areas. In such a neighborhood, conformity to an antieducational pattern may be necessary for social acceptance.

Teachers whose schools are located in such neighborhoods can succeed when they make the learning situation in the classroom vital enough to arouse interest and effort. Unfavorable socioeconomic conditions do not make it impossible to teach well, but they do make extra effort necessary.

CHILD DEVELOPMENT THROUGH READING

In the preceding discussion it has been pointed out that progress in reading is related to many phases of child development. Now we may well ask, what does reading do for child development?

For the child who becomes a reader, reading is an open road into an ever-expanding, multidimensional world. It provides new ideas and images for his thirsty mind. It offers answers to his hundreds of questions about the nature of the world and its contents. It transports him to distant places and other times. It allows him to live vicariously in the lives of all kinds of people: kings and princesses, soldiers and beggars, Cinderella and Napoleon and Joan of Arc. It acquaints him with many phases of human behavior: nobility and baseness, greed and generosity, arrogance and humility, courage and cowardice. Its heroes and heroines provide models for him to admire, emulate, and imitate.

Reading is, then, a way of living many lives in one. Through reading, the reader extends his knowledge far beyond the boundaries of his own limited experience.

The Nature of Reading

COMMUNICATION AND READING

Language is a process of communication between someone who has something to express and someone who receives the message. Speakers and writers attempt to communicate ideas; listeners and readers try to get the appropriate meanings. Speaking and writing are expressive and active. Listening and reading, while receptive, cannot properly be called passive because the listener or reader must create his own meaning by seeking to understand, by using his past experiences and the vocabulary and ideas he has gained before, and by thinking about the speaker's or writer's ideas and reacting to them. Reading and writing (or spelling) have in common the representation of words by written or printed symbols. All of the "language arts" are interrelated. The beginning reader does not start from zero, but rather builds on a language foundation which he has been developing since infancy.

READING IS SENSING

The act of reading starts with the focusing of the two eyes so that they center on particular symbols. Light reflecting from the page into the eyes forms patterns of light and dark on the retina (the sensitive screen at the back of the eyeball), and these patterns are carried by the thousands of nerve fibers in the optic nerve to the brain. "Although the initial photochemical processes occurring in the retinal receptors have been largely worked out, we still do not know how these biochemical reactions are translated into the nerve signals which are channelled to the brain." [1] This is the sensory aspect of reading. At this level, reading requires that the symbols be legible, the light be adequate, and the eyes able to focus clear patterns on the retina.

READING IS PERCEIVING

When a child looks at an orange, he does not see it just as an orange-colored disc, but rather as a juice-filled fruit. The sensory impulses coming to the brain arouse traces formed during previous experiences with oranges. Part of this experience is the sound of the word *orange,* and as he looks at the orange he is likely to "think" the name, as if hearing the word inwardly. The memory traces of hearing the word and saying it are closely associated with the idea or concept of what an orange is, which includes notions of its size, weight, feel, the taste of its juice, the feel of orange pulp in the mouth, the experience of peeling an orange, etc.

Although it depends on the method employed, when a young child

---

[1] Jay M. Enoch, et al., "A Review of Research in Vision," *Vision and Its Disorders,* NINDB Monograph No. 4, Public Health Service Publication No. 1688 (Washington, D.C.: U.S. Government Printing Office, 1967), p. 9.

is learning to read the printed word *orange,* he is likely to see it next to the picture of an orange while the teacher pronounces *orange.* The visual sensations aroused by the printed symbols become associated with the already existing memory traces of the visual appearance of the fruit, of the spoken word, and of its meaning. After a sufficient number of repetitions, the number of which varies greatly from child to child, the printed word arouses the memory traces of the spoken word and meaning just as the sight of a real orange, or a picture of one, does.

What happens when we perceive a word is therefore dependent both on the pattern of symbols on the page and on the reader's previous experience with the word and its meaning. One perceives the present stimulus in terms of one's past experience.

Perceiving a printed word means seeing it with an awareness of the sound and meaning it represents. When a printed word has more than one sound or more than one meaning, its context—the sequence of words preceding it and following it—tends to help the reader to make the right choice automatically. Thus the word *lead* may, in different settings, have the sound of *led* and mean a heavy metal or part of a pencil, or have the sound of *leed* and mean to precede, or an open space in arctic ice. Which pronunciation and which meaning would come to mind would depend on the context.[2]

READING IS ACHIEVING MEANING

Although perceiving single words accurately is a minimum essential for reading, the emergence of combined meaning as a whole series of perceptions taking place in rapid succession gives reading a distinctive character. Recognizing a triangle is perception and recognizing *dog* is perception, but recognizing *dog* is reading when *dog* is part of a sequence of words in which a writer has expressed an idea and a person is attempting to re-create that idea.

[2] For more information on perception, refer to Helen K. Smith, ed., *Perception and Reading,* Vol. 12, Part 4, Proceedings of the 12th Annual Conference of the International Reading Association (Newark, Del.: International Reading Association, 1968).

As words are recognized, the eyes move forward from left to right. The pattern of the ideas represented by the sequence of words builds up an expectation of what is likely to come next. If this anticipation is correct, the recognition of the word is made easy; if incorrect, one is likely to misread a word or two before going back and getting on the right track. The concepts represented by single words fit together into a meaningful unit that we call the sentence. Sentences fit together into larger units called paragraphs. Reading is a process in which meaning builds up as the concepts aroused by the printed words become organized into larger and more comprehensive ideas.

In one's own experience it is impossible to distinguish between sensing the word, perceiving the word, being aware of its meaning, and fitting it to the preceding concepts. One is simply aware of the word as a unit in a sequence that conveys meaning. This awareness of meaning is the heart of reading.

READING IS REACTING

When the printed word has been learned, the young child tends to say the word aloud. If encouraged to read silently he is likely to go through the motions of saying the word, but without audible sound. Since the spoken word is so closely tied to the meaning, at this stage the child can hardly "think" of the meaning without going through the motions of saying the word, and hearing the word inwardly as if he were saying it out loud. Gradually the child becomes able to think the word with less and less motor accompaniment, so that he can get along without lip movements or tongue movements; tiny changes in the muscles of the larynx and imagery of hearing the word as if spoken by an inner voice are likely to continue. This kind of reading is called *subvocal* reading, since it is noiseless but involves some of the movements of speaking. Most people continue to read subvocally all their lives. Only the superior reader achieves truly silent reading with no accompanying changes in the speech muscles; to be able to think meanings without any accompanying inner speech is achieved by relatively few, if any.

For most readers, and for all beginners, achieving meaning is inseparably tied to inner speech and to the muscular activity of saying the word, whether that is out loud, or silent but with obvious lip movement, or reduced to tiny changes in muscular tension. Achieving meaning is, therefore, part of the total reaction in reading.

There is always some muscular activity in reading. Usually the reader is physically quiet and the main muscular response is moving the eyes to the next sensory unit, but sometimes reading involves greater muscular activity. When an experienced driver sees a STOP sign his foot starts for the brake. Some readers actually feel themselves performing the acts of characters with whom they identify, and an observer can see twitchings and changes of posture which are tiny representations of the actions described.

Reaction in reading also means reacting evaluatively as one reads. Sometimes the reader stops to think about the ideas; more commonly he makes a running commentary as he goes along. Some of the comments this reader has noticed himself making in the past day or so include: "Cleverly put!" "That's really important." "A really funny one; I'll try to remember it." "What rubbish!" We accept and reject, we praise and we criticize, we delight in and can be made furious by what we read.

Other reactions are going on also. Perhaps as the hero is threatened with imminent death the reader's pulse quickens, his breathing becomes more rapid, and he feels tension and some anxiety or apprehension. When the hero triumphs in the end, the reader feels relief, gratification, and a relaxation of tension. Feelings and emotions and their physical accompaniments are important parts of the reader's reaction when he is really stirred by what he reads.

READING IS LEARNING

Whenever a person has a new experience, he emerges from it a slightly changed individual. What we can remember, in the sense of recalling a specific experience or chain of events, is only a small part of what we learn. Through experience (and learning) we become better able to differentiate and perceive; we acquire new concepts and expand and modify old ones; we form new habits and improve and refine old skills; we develop tastes and aversions, attitudes and ideals.

Reading provides vicarious, or substitute, experience. Through reading, new words and ideas are learned; concepts are enlarged and clarified; information is digested and combined with what was known before; feelings of many kinds are intensified, weakened, or changed. When a boy or girl reads *Lad: a Dog,* there is, of course, the pleasure and excitement of having an absorbing story unfold. In addition the child's concept of *dog* undergoes many changes, and almost certainly the child's feelings about dogs, and collies in particular, become warmer and friendlier.

Reading is, then, a way of learning, changing, and developing. Reading can enrich and ennoble; it can also delude and debase. The act of reading is itself neutral, but the ideas and feelings aroused while reading become part of the person's total background of experience; they become integrated with the traces of all related previous experiences. Reading allows individuals to learn from the experience of others and permits human knowledge to become cumulative.

DEFINITION OF READING

For the purpose of this book, *reading is the meaningful interpretation of printed or written verbal symbols.* As we have seen, reading is a very complex process that involves sensing, perceiving, achieving meaning, and reacting in a variety of ways; and through reading much important learning takes place. Reading is accurate when the reader perceives the words as the author wrote them and the meaning he achieves corresponds closely to what the author intended; to this are added the reader's motor responses, his feelings, and his evaluative reactions.

Reading is sometimes used broadly in the sense of interpretation. Thus, an Indian can "read" a footprint or a lover can "read" his beloved's countenance and determine her feelings. One can also read mathematical symbols and musical notations, and in all probability many of the principles of verbal reading apply to the interpretation of these other kinds of symbolic systems.

EYE MOVEMENTS IN READING

When a person reads, his eyes do not move steadily along the line of print, but progress in a series of alternating pauses and quick, jerky movements. The pauses, which are called *fixations,* last only a fraction of a second each, and the eyes see in reading only during the fixations. The efficient reader does not look at each letter separately, but usually sees one or more words at each fixation; the more he can see at one fixation the fewer fixations are necessary. At the end of each line a *return sweep* is made to the beginning of the next line. Sometimes the eyes move backward to get a second look at something; this is called a *regression.* The amount seen in an average fixation is called the *recognition span.* Good reading is characterized by a wide recognition span, a small number of fixations per line, and a small number of regressions.

Useful information has been obtained by photographing the eyes during reading. The special camera (a commercial version is called *The Reading Eye*) uses motion-picture film which moves at a steady speed. Each eyeball reflects a tiny beam of light onto the film, producing a vertical line when the eye is still during a fixation, and a nearly horizontal line when the eye moves sideways. As the two eyes move together, the lines on the film appear parallel. A diagram illustrating the characteristics of eye-movement photographs is shown in Figure 1.

Analysis of thousands of eye-movement photographs has shown that on the average there is steady progress in reading efficiency grade by grade. This is indicated in several ways. (1) The average number of fixations per word decreases from 2.2 at the end of the first grade to about 1.2 in the sixth grade. By then the average span of recognition is less than one word (.88), but that average is held down by regressions and by occasional unfamiliar words that require several fixations. (2) Regressive movements decrease from about one every two words to one every five words. (3) The average duration of fixations changes only slightly, becoming about one quarter of a second by the end of the sixth grade. (4) Rate of reading on standardized passages increases rapidly in the first and second grades and then improves at a progressively slower rate, averaging 80 words per minute at the end of the first grade, 115 at the end of the second grade, 158 at the end of the fourth grade, and 185 at the end of the sixth grade.[3]

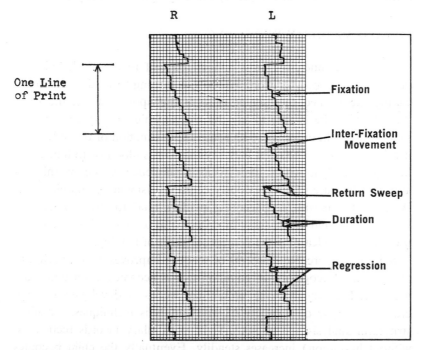

FIGURE 1. Diagram showing how eye-movement characteristics are represented in a Reading Eye II recording. Reproduced with the permission of Educational Developmental Laboratories, Inc., Huntington, N.Y.

What the eyes do while reading is controlled by the brain. When a word is not recognized at once, extra fixations occur as the reader takes another look or inspects the word part by part. Long fixations, extra fixations, and regressive movements are not faulty eye move-

[3] Stanford E. Taylor, Eye Movements in Reading: Facts and Fallacies, EDL Reading Newsletter 30 (Huntington, N.Y.: Educational Developmental Laboratories, November 1963).

ments or causes of poor reading ability. They are usually indications of some difficulty with either perception or interpretation. In the elementary school it is usually better to work on improvement of word recognition and comprehension than to try to train such eye movements. As reading skills improve, these symptoms usually disappear.

TOWARD MATURITY IN READING

For the beginner, the most difficult part of reading is learning to perceive and remember word symbols. Learning to read means associating the printed representation with the spoken word; the child "reads" when he is able to say the words which the symbols represent, in the right order and with some approximation of the inflections used in speaking. The child may say the words aloud or to himself; if he says the right words, they form a sequence whose meaning is apparent because of his previously acquired listening comprehension. Writers of material for beginning readers tend to stick to familiar words, ideas, and expressions in order to allow the child to concentrate mainly on learning the perceptual skills of reading.

Skill in the perceptual aspects of reading improves over a period of many years. Recognition of common words becomes faster and more accurate. Skill in attacking unfamiliar words is developed through gradual learning of a variety of word analysis techniques, including structural analysis and phonics. Sight vocabulary (words recognized without hesitation) increases steadily. Eventually the child becomes able to recognize many short, familiar phrases as perceptual units. The subvocal elements in word recognition diminish gradually.

As the perceptual tasks are mastered, the achievement of meaning tends to become a more challenging problem. The reading material used becomes more complicated, and unfamiliar words and new ideas are encountered. Sentences become longer, more complex, and less like everyday speech. To continue to comprehend well the child must keep on enlarging his vocabulary, expanding and refining his concepts, and becoming familiar with adult forms of expression.

The ways in which reading is employed gradually become more varied. In recreational reading a variety of interests emerge, with tremendous differences in what individual children choose for themselves. Fiction tends to be chosen for excitement or humor; appreciation of characterization and literary style develops slowly. Many children prefer interestingly written and well-illustrated factual books for their recreational reading.

Learning how to read effectively in factual material requires special reading techniques. Children should be taught how to skim, to read for main ideas, to note details, to follow directions, to grasp cause-effect relationships and time sequences. Training should be given in the location of information and use of reference books. Summarizing and outlining are skills that are often taught in the intermediate grades.

In a democratic society it is not enough just to read; an enlightened citizen should be able to read critically, to evaluate what he reads, and to distinguish between factual reporting and biased propaganda. The mature reader relates new material to what he knows from the past and compares one author's presentation with another's. The beginnings of training for careful evaluation of what one reads belong in the reading program of the elementary school.

Objectives of Reading Instruction

What we aim for determines to a large degree what we achieve. If our goals are vague, we are unlikely to get clean-cut results. Since reading is a highly complex activity involving the learning of many specific skills, instruction should be planned with highly specific outcomes in mind. Two teachers can achieve the same planned objective by using different teaching approaches; but without the same objective, similar outcomes could occur only by sheer accident. Objectives determine procedures.

Some teachers of reading follow a printed set of instructions day by day, without thinking much about the meaning and purpose of the procedures. An intelligent teacher cannot long remain satisfied, however, with the blind carrying out of a ritual, or following a recipe as in a cookbook. He wants to know *why* and *what for*. When he understands the purpose for which a procedure is planned, he can decide whether or not it is needed by his pupils and can modify it to fit the circumstances. He appreciates and utilizes specific suggestions, but employs them in a selective and purposeful way.

The teacher needs, therefore, to have an understanding of the goals of the reading program as a whole. Each of the broad purposes needs to be made clearer by developing it in detail. The detailed objectives can then be made specific in the planning of lessons.

The total reading program of the elementary school has three broad purposes or goals. The first is to develop the ability to read. *Developmental reading* activities are those in which the teacher's primary general aim is to bring about the improvement of reading skills, and the materials and procedures are selected accordingly. The second broad purpose is to help children to use reading as an efficient tool of learning. *Functional reading* includes those uses of reading in which the primary purpose is to gain information or understanding; in other words, in which reading functions as a tool of learning. It is sometimes called work-type reading, or study-type reading, or is referred to as the work-study skills. *Recreational reading* is the part of the reading program which is concerned with the development of liking for reading as a voluntary activity, and with the raising and refining of taste and appreciation. An outline of what is included under these main headings is as follows:

I. Developmental reading
   A. The mechanics of reading
      1. Development of a large sight vocabulary
      2. Development of skill in identifying unfamiliar words, through the use of
         a. Context
         b. Phonics
         c. Structural analysis
         d. Dictionary
      3. Development of good eye-movement habits
      4. Development of good postural habits while reading
      5. Development of oral reading skills
         a. Phrasing and expression
         b. Volume, pitch, and enunciation
      6. Development of speed and fluency in silent reading

B. Reading comprehension
  1. Acquisition of a rich, extensive, and accurate vocabulary
  2. Learning to interpret thought units of increasing size
     a. The phrase
     b. The sentence
     c. The paragraph
     d. The story
  3. Learning to read for specific purposes
     a. Finding and understanding main ideas
     b. Locating answers to specific questions
     c. Noting and recalling details
     d. Grasping the sequence of events
     e. Anticipating outcomes
     f. Making inferences
     g. Following directions
     h. Grasping the author's plan and intent
     i. Evaluating and criticizing what one reads
     j. Remembering what one reads
  4. Coordinating rate with comprehension
II. Functional reading
  A. Learning to locate information
     1. Mastering alphabetical order
     2. Using an index
     3. Using an encyclopedia
     4. Using other reference works
  B. Developing functional comprehension skills
     1. Learning specialized vocabularies
     2. Applying comprehension skills in content areas
        a. Learning to read textbooks in content subjects
        b. Learning to read independently in content subjects
     3. Developing specialized reading skills needed by special subject matter, e.g.,
        a. Reading arithmetical problems
        b. Interpreting maps, charts, graphs, and diagrams
        c. Reading about scientific experiments
     4. Learning to organize and record what one reads
        a. Outlining
        b. Summarizing
        c. Note-taking
     5. Learning to remember what one reads
        a. Previewing
        b. Reciting to oneself
        c. Reviewing

III. Recreational reading
  A. Development of interest in reading
    1. Enjoyment of reading as a voluntary leisure-time activity
    2. Skill in selecting appropriate reading matter for oneself
    3. Satisfaction of present interests and tastes through reading
  B. Improvement and refinement of reading interests
    1. Development of more varied reading interests
    2. Development of more mature reading interests
    3. Achievement of personal development through reading
  C. Refinement of literary judgment and taste
    1. Establishment of differential criteria for fiction and non-fiction, prose and poetry, and drama
    2. Development of appreciation for style and beauty of language
    3. Learning to seek for deeper symbolic meanings

Reading activities should be planned, when possible, to satisfy more than one objective at a time. For example, in selecting material for developing specific skills one seeks for enjoyable stories and interesting factual selections which will suit the purpose. A strong emphasis on repetitive drills, on the detailed analysis of a "masterpiece," or on written book reports can kill the desire to read for pleasure.

STAGES IN READING INSTRUCTION

The emphasis on one or another objective changes as children's skills improve. In beginning reading instruction nearly all reading activities are developmental. Recreational reading becomes significant when children become able to do some independent reading. Functional reading increases in importance as one goes up the grades, and from the fourth grade on is likely to occupy a larger share of the school day than developmental reading. The needs and abilities of a particular group of children or child also influence the teacher's decisions about the weight to be given to different objectives.

The reading program has been considered for more than thirty years to have five main stages or periods. These are as follows:

Stage 1. Development of reading readiness. This stage, which begins before children enter school, includes kindergarten and a variable period in the first grade.

Stage 2. Beginning reading. Overlapping the readiness period somewhat, this stage usually occupies most of the first grade but may extend beyond it.

Stage 3. Period of rapid skills development. Continuing on from beginning reading, this stage, which usually occupies the second and third grades, is one of major attention to developmental reading and rapid growth in reading skills.

Stage 4. Period of wide reading. During the fourth, fifth, and sixth grades developmental reading continues, but functional and recreational reading activities take the center of the stage and children read many different kinds of materials.

Stage 5. Refinement of reading. During high school and college there is increased recognition that reading skills need to be developed further to meet the requirements of longer and more taxing reading assignments.

The four chapters which come next take up the first four of these stages in order and describe successful teaching practices, giving an overview of the entire reading program during each of the stages. The later chapters each take up one important phase of the reading program and consider it in detail.

Summary

1. Reading is a vital and essential activity that permeates civilized life.
2. Learning through reading is essential for educational success.
3. Reading growth conforms to the general pattern of child development, which is one of continuous and sequential progress.
4. Both maturation and well-planned learning activities are necessary for growth in reading skills.
5. Certain kinds of health problems, particularly sensory defects and relatively uncommon brain dysfunctioning or defects, can interfere with success in learning to read.
6. Progress in reading is closely related to the child's intellectual development and linguistic maturity, and is also strongly influenced by the child's family and neighborhood.

7. The act of reading is a very complex process involving sensing, perceiving words as meaningful symbols, achieving meaning from a succession of perceptions, and reacting with appropriate thoughts, feelings, and motor reactions.
8. Reading may be defined as the meaningful interpretation of printed or written verbal symbols.
9. Well-planned learning activities can result when the teacher's objectives are clearly formulated and developed in detail.
10. The three main areas or types of reading are developmental, functional, and recreational reading. These change in relative importance as one goes from readiness, through beginning reading, into the primary, middle and upper grade reading programs.

Recommended Reading

BARBE, WALTER B. *Teaching Reading: Selected Materials.* New York: Oxford University Press, 1965. Ch. 1.
BEERY, ALTHEA, BARRETT, THOMAS C., and POWELL, WILLIAM R., Eds. *Elementary Reading Instruction: Selected Materials.* Boston: Allyn and Bacon, Inc., 1969. Ch. 1.
CLYMER, THEODORE. "What is 'Reading'?: Some Current Concepts," in *Innovation and Change in Reading Instruction.* 67th Yearbook of the National Society for the Study of Education, Part II. Chicago: University of Chicago Press, 1968. Ch. 1.
HARRIS, ALBERT J. "Reading and Human Development," in *Development in and Through Reading.* 60th Yearbook of the National Society for the Study of Education, Part I. Chicago: University of Chicago Press, 1961. Ch. 2.
POOLEY, ROBERT C. "Reading and the Language Arts," in *Development in and Through Reading.* 60th Yearbook of the National Society for the Study of Education, Part I. Chicago: University of Chicago Press, 1961. Ch. 3.
RUSSELL, DAVID H. *Children Learn to Read.* 2nd ed. Boston: Ginn and Co., 1961. Chs. 1–4.
SMITH, NILA B. *Reading Instruction for Today's Children.* Englewood Cliffs, N.J.: Prentice-Hall, 1963. Pp. 3–50.
STAUFFER, RUSSELL G. *Directing Reading Maturity as a Cognitive Process.* New York: Harper & Row, 1969. Ch. 1.

2

Readiness for Learning to Read

Even if you have only casually observed a class of first-grade children, you are aware of the wide range of physical differences present. For example, young children vary greatly in size. In a typical first grade, you probably will find at least one child who looks too small even to be in kindergarten, and another who looks like an average third-grader. Less obvious, but educationally much more significant, is the wide range of differences in the characteristics that are related to readiness for learning to read. These characteristics or factors, such as mental maturity, language facility, and perceptual development, are at least as important as the method and quality of instruction in determining the progress to be made in reading by each child during the year. This chapter is concerned with the factors that contribute to reading readiness, how readiness can be measured, and ways of developing readiness.

The Meaning of Reading Readiness

Reading readiness may be defined as the state of general maturity that allows a child to learn to read without great difficulty. It is a complex concept involving many interrelated factors. Although we currently do not fully understand how these factors interact for each

23

child, generally readiness develops through the interplay between biological growth, which is considerably influenced by heredity, and the learning environment to which the child is exposed at home and in school.

Readiness is not an all-or-none characteristic, but one with many degrees of variation. How ready a child seems to be depends not only on his development but also on the instructional program. Thus, a child with low general readiness is likely to learn slowly and with much effort if the instructional program is nicely adapted to his limited capabilities, while he may be completely unable to make progress in an inflexible program that is geared to an average or above average rate of learning. A child with well above average general readiness is likely to succeed with any of a variety of instructional procedures and rates.

Since readiness is a composite characteristic involving many different kinds of abilities and many previous learnings, it is possible for a child to be advanced in some aspects of readiness and to be average or retarded in others. In such a case, how he will succeed depends on how well the instructional situation is adapted to his particular needs. The content and pacing of the program will greatly influence a child's success or failure. His initial success or failure in learning to read will have a lasting effect on the child.

The different aspects of development that have an important bearing on readiness for reading are discussed below. It should be noted that no one factor by itself is the key to readiness.

CHRONOLOGICAL AGE

Although most school systems in the United States set a minimum entrance age for first grade (usually five years nine months), chronological age in itself is not an important factor in readiness. It is of significance, however, because of the rapid developmental changes that usually take place in children in this age category. Older children tend to be more advanced in readiness than younger children, not just because they are older but because they have usually learned more and have reached a higher level of general development. No matter at what age reading instruction is initiated, there are wide differences in achievement at the end of the year. An intelligent, mature five-year-old may learn faster and achieve more than a dull youngster of seven. Chronological age is a convenient but very inaccurate measure of reading readiness.

SEX DIFFERENCES

Generally, one might expect girls to be ready to learn to read sooner than boys. Girls usually mature faster physiologically, tend to develop language facility earlier, and spend more time in sedentary activities that help to develop skills related to schoolwork. Primary-grade girls tend to score higher on reading achievement tests, and fewer girls than boys are reported to be reading disability cases.

The research concerning sex differences in readiness, however, indicates that differences tend to be small and that on the average, girls do not always score higher. Perhaps sex differences in reading achievement are more influenced by environmental than by biological factors. In addition to the possibilities mentioned above, among the hypotheses offered for the superior achievement of girls are: (1) early reading materials are geared to the interests of girls; (2) almost all primary-grade teachers are women who may have a better understanding of the needs of girls and may be less tolerant toward the boys' behavior; and (3) boys are less motivated to learn to read. The latter may be more true of certain subcultures where reading is not considered to be a masculine activity.

Regardless of whether mean differences favor boys or girls, the range of individual differences within each sex in any readiness factor is far greater than the overall difference between the groups; many boys are above the average girl, and many girls are below the average boy.

INTELLECTUAL FACTORS

General Intelligence. General intelligence is the most important single factor related to reading readiness. Both mental age (M.A.), a measure of the level of mental maturity, and intelligence quotient (I.Q.), a measure of the rate of mental growth, are related to ease in learning to read. Mental age tends to be a slightly better indicator of what the child is likely to be able to learn in the near future, while the I.Q. is a better long-range predictor for groups. Studies indicate that the reading scores of individual children cannot be predicted with a great deal of accuracy from I.Q. scores.

Despite frequent mention in the literature, a mental age of six years, or six years and six months, is *not* a prerequisite for success in learning to read. It is desirable, but not essential, for a child to have a mental age of six or over at the beginning of reading instruction, because most children who fail to learn to read in first grade have a mental age below six years. All else being equal (and it rarely is), the higher the mental age for those children with M.A.'s between five and seven, the easier and more successful the first steps in reading are likely to be.

Many factors besides general intelligence are involved in reading readiness; therefore, it is impossible to set a definite minimum mental age. In addition to the factors discussed in this chapter, the progress a child makes in reading will be influenced by such things as the instructional method employed, the pace of instruction, the difficulty of the material used, and the quality and individualization of instruction. Many children with mental ages below six can and do learn reading skills. Even dull five-year-olds can be taught the beginning reading skills, but to do so is a long, slow, difficult process with no apparent lasting advantage. On the other hand, some children with mental ages way above six have specific handicaps that lower their readiness.

Although there will be variations due to the lack of complete accuracy of tests, the ages at which children with different I.Q.'s generally reach a mental age of six years are shown in Table I. About 25 percent of all children have I.Q.'s above 110. These bright children are above the M.A. of six before they enter first grade. Those with I.Q.'s above 130 reach it before they are in kindergarten. This does not mean, however, that every child with an I.Q. of 130 or above *should* learn to read before he enters kindergarten.

About half of all children have I.Q.'s between 90 and 110; these are referred to as having "average intelligence." Since the average chronological age of first graders when school opens is about six years and three months, most of the "average" children are at the six-year mental

TABLE I. Chronological Ages at Which Children of Varying I.Q.'s
Reach the Mental Age of Six Years

Above Average I.Q.	C.A.	Average I.Q.	C.A.	Below Average I.Q.	C.A.
130	4–8	110	5–6	85	7–1
125	4–10	105	5–9	80	7–6
120	5–0	100	6–0	75	8–0
115	5–3	95	6–4	70	8–7
		90	6–8		

level; the younger children with I.Q.'s in the 90's reach this status during the year.

Approximately one-quarter of all children have I.Q.'s below 90 and tend to have difficulty with academic tasks. As seen in the last column of Table I, most of these children are at least seven years old before they reach the mental age of six, and they are likely to be slow in learning to read. If the child is dull (great faith should not be placed in a single test score, especially if it is derived from a group intelligence test), realistic goals should be set for him. It is just as wrong to expect little or nothing from a dull child as it is to set unatttainable goals for him. Children with below average intelligence can learn to read, admittedly not as fast nor to as high a level as other children, but they can attain success if rigid grade standards are not mandated and proper material is presented at a pace that will allow assimilation of skills. Teachers should not just wait for the child to attain a mental age of six and expect that at that point the child will miraculously learn to read.

The majority of first-grade children are, therefore, *intellectually* ready for the beginnings of reading instruction at the beginning of the school year or soon thereafter. For a minority, intellectual readiness was attained before they entered school; for others such readiness may be delayed substantially.

Specific Mental Abilities. Traits such as memory and attention are closely interrelated and in young children are not clearly distinguishable from general intelligence. Yet it is possible for a child with average or better intelligence to have a specific deficit, such as poor visual or auditory memory, or inability to concentrate and to attend to the task at hand. These and other deficits in specific mental abilities may adversely affect a child's progress in learning to read.[1]

VISUAL AND AUDITORY SKILLS

In order to be able to associate a printed symbol with its spoken equivalent, it is necessary to be able to perceive visually and auditorily well enough to make the necessary discriminations.

Visual Skills. Most first-graders are far-sighted and it is often suggested that they should not be given close work requiring near-point vision for extended periods of time. As for other visual problems, it is impossible to state their exact relationship to reading ability. Although some studies have found little or no relationship, there also is evidence of a relationship between certain types of visual defects and reading difficulties. Furthermore, some children apparently have the ability to compensate for visual problems, provided that they are not too severe and are not accompanied by other problems. There is little the classroom teacher can do to overcome most visual difficulties except to refer the child for a thorough examination when a visual problem is suspected, and help to compensate for such problems by procedures such as the use of books with large print or by preferential seating.

Although a child may be able to see clearly, he may be weak in visual discrimination. That is, he may have difficulty noticing the similarities and differences between printed symbols. Many young children do not pay much attention to the details of visual stimuli. Visual discrimination skills are very important in reading readiness because before a child can learn to recognize a word like *house* he must be able to distinguish it not only from words of different length and configuration (e.g., *handkerchief, be,* and *party*) but also from words that resemble it much more closely (e.g., *horse* and *mouse*). Some children tend to

---

[1] For a discussion of such problems and their treatment refer to Albert J. Harris, *How to Increase Reading Ability,* 5th ed. (New York: McKay, 1970), Chs. 9 and 10.

look only at the initial letter or letters of a word and to ignore the rest of it.

Since many first-grade children are not yet sensitive to directional orientation, there is a tendency for them to make reversal errors. Reversals may be made with letters (*b, d, p, q*) or with words (*saw-was; on-no*). Most of these children overcome the problem with suitable instructional emphasis on the left-to-right direction.

Auditory Skills. As in the case of defective vision, the extent to which partial hearing losses interfere with reading ability varies from child to child. Again, the role of the teacher is to refer suspected cases for a thorough hearing examination and to assist the child by preferential seating, making certain he has understood oral instruction or directions, and perhaps by using a method for reading instruction that does not place great emphasis on an oral-phonic approach. Poor auditory acuity or discrimination is suggested by the persistence of infantile pronunciation (*bruvver* for *brother*) into the first grade.

Although their auditory acuity (keenness of hearing) may be normal, some children, particularly the culturally different, may have difficulty discriminating auditorily between speech sounds and between the sounds in words. The child may be unable to distinguish between words with gross differences (*cat-dog*), between words that have minimally contrasting sounds (*cat-cot, ran-rain*), or be unable to tell whether two words start with the same sound or rhyme.[2] If a child has difficulty distinguishing between spoken words, he is apt to have difficulty in learning sound-symbol relationships and in consistently associating spoken words with their printed counterparts.

RELEVANT KNOWLEDGE

Most first-grade children have had experiences that are useful in preparation for reading. The many hours they have spent watching television have provided useful training in visual skills and in listening

---

[2] The teacher should always be certain the children understand the terms he uses. For example, a child may not give a correct response when asked if two words rhyme, not because he doesn't hear the rhyme but rather because he doesn't know what "rhyme" means.

comprehension. They may have already learned to recognize a variety of advertised products from the actual packages or from pictures in magazines, on billboards, or on T.V. While most of these children rely on the total appearance of the container or some conspicuous feature of it, some of them have learned to recognize brand names of much-advertised products; they have already started to read without formal instruction. These children usually do not require the typical readiness program.

Many of the children will have had the advantage of a home that provides opportunities for favorable development and intellectual stimulation. Their parents foster a sense of responsibility and self-direction, present good models for language and speech development, provide them with picture books and magazines, read to them allowing the children to interpret the illustrations, tell them stories that help the children to learn what stories are like, and take them on trips that have provided broadening experiences.

Children who come from disadvantaged urban or rural homes may not have had many of the experiences mentioned above. Effective compensatory preschool and school programs that contain specific and well-planned activities to develop intellectual and perceptual skills can bring about significant gains in factors related to reading readiness.

From their experiential backgrounds children acquire a storehouse of concepts. A rich background of concepts and ideas is obviously helpful to reading since it provides the basis that makes meaningful interpretation and reaction possible. Writers of material for beginning readers tend to use a limited vocabulary of familiar words and to employ concepts that are within the experiences of most six-year-olds, to allow major attention to be devoted to the new and difficult perceptual and associative tasks. Background concepts become more important when one gets beyond the beginning stage of reading. Even so, marked differences in clarity of ideas and grasp of meanings show up early in reading instruction.

Research has shown that in general children who know alphabet letters by name when they enter the first grade tend to do better in reading than children who do not know them. This does not mean, however, that teaching children the letter names will necessarily enable them to achieve better in reading.[3] It may simply mean that those children who can learn letter names by themselves already possess skills that are important in learning to read.

LANGUAGE DEVELOPMENT

As indicated in Chapter 1, all aspects of communication are inter-related. The child's ability to understand spoken language (his receptive language ability) provide a framework for the development of his speaking or expressive language ability, both of which in turn provide a basis for reading ability.[4] As the child recognizes the printed symbols, saying or thinking the words that are in his vocabulary arouses the meanings for which these words are labels.

The aspects of language development that are most significant for reading readiness are vocabulary, maturity of sentence structure, and clarity of pronunciation. Because first-grade reading materials use only a few hundred words that are understood by most children, sentence structure and clarity of speech are more likely to be problems. The more immature the child's oral use of sentence structure, and the greater the difference between his oral language pattern and that used in the reading material, the more likely it is that he will have difficulty in learning to read. Children whose speech development is retarded are also likely to be slow in learning to read.

Although the mastery of language depends on many factors, the most important are intelligence, hearing, and home environment. The relationship with intelligence is obvious because language is a highly

[3] Two studies reported at the 1970 American Educational Research Association Convention did not find that such training produced higher reading achievement: S. Jay Samuels, "Letter-Name Versus Letter-Sound Knowledge as Factors Influencing Learning to Read"; and Ronald J. Johnson, "The Effect of Training in Letter Names on Success in Beginning Reading for Children of Differing Abilities."

[4] For further information on the relationship of language and reading ability refer to:

James Walden, Ed., *Oral Language and Reading* (Champaign, Ill.: National Council of Teachers of English, 1969).

Kenneth Goodman and James T. Fleming, Eds., *Psycholinguistics and the Teaching of Reading* (Newark, Del.: International Reading Association, 1969).

intellectual acquisition. Retarded language development in children of at least normal intelligence is usually caused by defective hearing, an educationally disadvantaged background, or a neurological problem.

Children who come from a very low socioeconomic level usually have not had adequate opportunities to develop the language skills that are required in school. They may find such a marked difference between the speech of their parents and peers and that of the teacher that the teacher almost seems to be speaking a foreign language. If the child comes from a home in which little or no English is spoken, he is even more handicapped. For such children it is very important to develop oral language skills before and while reading skills are taught. When children cannot express their ideas in words and sentences and when they cannot understand the language used by the teacher, communication and therefore education is almost impossible.

PHYSICAL DEVELOPMENT

There is little value in attempting to estimate reading readiness by any index of physical maturity that can be observed or measured by teachers because there is little relationship between success in reading and such factors as height and weight.

Defects of vision and hearing can interfere with the perception of words, printed or spoken, and the early detection of such defects is important. Teachers should be alert to such signs as excessive tearing, redness of the eyes, frequent rubbing or blinking, frequent headaches, and comments that the print or pictures look blurred.[5] The possibility of a hearing loss may be suggested in indistinct speech, difficulty in comprehending directions, cocking of the head to one side or forward, or an appearance of dullness.

The kind of neurological immaturity that produces delay in readi-

---

[5] Many schools use only a Snellen-type vision test, which is inadequate for detecting the kinds of visual problems that are most likely to affect reading ability adversely. Such tests fail to detect moderate degrees of farsightedness or astigmatism and even severe cases of poor fusion and eye-muscle imbalance. Furthermore, a test administered at a distance of 20 feet cannot detect some kinds of visual problems that may occur at reading distance, which is approximately 12 to 18 inches.

ness for reading cannot be diagnosed by teachers. It can be suspected, however, if a six-year-old who shows normal general intelligence has very poor finger dexterity in such tasks as tying knots and cutting with scissors, cannot copy a drawing of a square, seems to have poor visual and auditory discrimination, uses both hands about equally, has marked motor incoordination as indicated by general clumsiness, seems unable to learn a consistent left-to-right sequence, is overactive, and has a very short attention span. No one of these symptoms alone indicates a neurological deviation. The child should be referred to a pediatric neurologist, however, when the symptoms are severe, occur in combination, and persist.

The general health of the child affects reading indirectly. If the child is frequently absent because of illness, his learning may be disrupted by the many interruptions, and he may fall behind if attempts are not made to teach him the skills he missed. If he is tired and sleepy because of watching T.V. until late at night, his alertness for any learning is liable to suffer. Any chronic health condition that impairs strength and vitality may diminish the child's ability to expend effort in a learning situation.

Lateral Dominance. Directional confusion, shown by the inability to consistently identify left and right correctly, and delay in establishing a consistent preference for one hand, appears to be significantly related to difficulty in learning how to read. There seems to be little relationship, however, between crossed dominance (the child's preferred hand and preferred eye being on opposite sides of his body) and success in reading.

Learning the left-to-right sequence needed for reading is easiest for consistently right-handed children, a little harder for the definitely left-handed, and hardest for those who have not yet developed a consistent preference for either hand. Children who have trouble in distinguishing right from left and in following the correct directional sequence are likely to have reversal difficulties in reading and writing.

EMOTIONAL AND SOCIAL MATURITY

Children differ as much in their personality traits as they do in their intellectual and physical characteristics. Immaturity in social adjustment and emotional development helps to explain why some quite bright children get off to a disappointing start in reading.

Self-reliance is a highly desirable characteristic. Children whose parents have wisely encouraged them to try to feed, wash, and dress themselves, and to show initiative in choosing their play activities and in solving their little problems, are likely to carry this self-reliance over into the schoolroom. They can be started on an activity and can continue with it on their own. Children who are extremely dependent upon their mothers often make excessive demands for the teacher's attention and may stop trying as soon as the teacher pays attention to another child.

Emotional self-control also is important. Some first-grade children still display the volatility and emotional instability that are characteristic of preschool children. The child who cries or who has a temper tantrum in the classroom on slight provocation disrupts the learning situation for everyone, and most of all for himself.

The ability to participate actively and cooperatively in group activities is important in the first grade because a great deal of instruction is done in groups. The child needs to be able to pay continuing attention in a group situation, to listen attentively when directions are given and be able to follow them, to act in unison with the other group members, and to take his turn and allow others to take theirs. Some practice in learning these social skills is desirable before reading instruction is begun. Kindergarten experience tends to be helpful in this regard.

Children who are socially or emotionally immature can be taught readiness skills and to learn to read. However, it is much more difficult to do so (e.g., a child who cannot function in a group can be tutored individually) especially if there are several such children in the class or if the class size is large.

INTEREST IN LEARNING TO READ

Most first graders are eager to start reading. They have spent many pleasurable hours listening to stories read from books by their parents and in looking at picture books and illustrations. Many of them have memorized favorite selections and can recite them when the book is opened to the page with the corresponding illustration, or even when the book is closed. But they know that this is not real reading and are impatient to get started.

If this eagerness were universal, teaching beginning reading would be easier than it usually is. There are some children who would rather run, play, or fight than sit still and take part in a listening or reading activity. Others may be afraid that if they learn to read by themselves their parents will stop reading and telling stories to them. Still others may fear to enter the learning situation because they have been told by other children how hard it is to learn to read. When some children do not seem to be interested in learning to read, it is a challenging part of the teacher's job to arouse and nourish their interest in reading.

READINESS FOR HIGHER LEVELS OF READING

The general idea of readiness applies at every level of reading development, not just at the beginning. The teacher who takes care to think about the pupil's readiness for a particular learning activity will ask questions like the following:

(1) What ideas or concepts in this lesson are likely to be unfamiliar or strange to the children? Should these be introduced and explained before reading, or can they be absorbed during reading? The answer to the latter question will often depend on the teacher's purpose for the lesson.

(2) What words in the selection to be read are likely to be new to the children? (When a word is called "a new word" in a basal reader or similar material it simply means that it has never been used in that series before. Some "old" words are less well understood than some "new" words.) Do their meanings have to be explained? Should they be pretaught, or will the children be able to figure them out? The answers to the last two questions will be influenced by the teacher's purpose, the level of ability of the children, and whether or not (in such cases as the use of context clues) the material is written so as to allow the child to apply his skills.

(3) Are the children already interested in the topic or is it

desirable to spend a little time in arousing curiosity and interest? (4) Are special skills needed to read this kind of material efficiently? If so, have the children mastered those skills or do they need some further help with them?

(5) Is the difficulty of the material suitable for the children? If it seems too difficult and alternative materials are not available, what else can be done to help the children cope with it? Material selected for instructional purposes should be neither too difficult nor too easy for the children. Considering readiness is a part of lesson planning at all levels.

How to Evaluate Readiness for Beginning Reading

Readiness for successful learning in the early phases of reading instruction can be evaluated by using intelligence tests, reading readiness tests, and teacher observations and judgments.

USE OF INTELLIGENCE TESTS

Many schools administer group intelligence tests that do not require any reading ability to children in kindergarten or in the early part of first grade.[6] The scores provide useful information about the child's general intelligence, which is the most important single factor in reading readiness. If some children obtain very low scores, or are thought to be brighter than the test indicates, they should be retested individually or in a small group with an alternate edition of the test first administered, or with a different group test (intelligence tests do not all measure the same factors). If a child still tests very low, he should be referred for individual testing by a qualified psychologist.

As pointed out earlier, success in the beginning of reading is only partly dependent upon mental ability, and while bright children who fail and dull children who succeed in reading are the execptions, they do occur in significant numbers. A high M.A. or I.Q. alone does not assure success. Nevertheless, the teacher may use the following as a

---

[6] A descriptive list of all types of tests mentioned in this book is given in Appendix A.

guide: children whose mental ages are already six and a half years are probably ready; and those with mental ages below six may be somewhat delayed in achieving readiness.

USE OF READING READINESS TESTS

Reading readiness tests are intended to be used near the end of kindergarten or the beginning of first grade and to provide some measure of children's readiness to learn to read. They attempt to measure particular abilities that are related to success in beginning reading. To some extent they resemble the group intelligence tests used at the same level, but they deliberately include certain types of acquired knowledge.

Although the content of the reading readiness tests varies considerably, the abilities tested include the following: (1) ability to recognize and interpret pictures; (2) knowledge of word meanings; (3) comprehension of spoken directions as shown by success in carrying them out; (4) visual discrimination of similarities and differences in pictures, geometrical designs, letters, and words; (5) ability to copy visual designs; (6) auditory discrimination involving recognition of rhyming words and of similarities and differences in the initial sounds of words; (7) visual memory as shown by the ability to match visual stimuli with similar stimuli that are presented only briefly and then removed from sight; (8) ability to name letters of the alphabet (or mark a letter when its name is given orally by the examiner) and Arabic numerals; and (9) ability to identify words that have been taught during a standardized lesson that is part of the test; such a test may help to indicate whether a whole-word approach is advisable. Of these different kinds of testable abilities, the only one that occurs in all published reading readiness tests is visual discrimination.

As shown by the preceding list, readiness tests do not measure all of the factors associated with success in learning to read. Although correlations between total readiness test scores and reading scores at the end of first grade are high enough to allow good prediction for a group, they are not high enough to allow accurate predictions for individuals. These two facts indicate that a high degree of faith should not be placed in readiness test scores when making decisions about individuals.

Not all reading readiness tests are equally valid in predicting success in reading, nor are they equally reliable. Furthermore, it is quite possible that two subtests which supposedly measure the same skill (e.g., auditory discrimination), in fact measure different skills. Selecting the best test for a particular school involves careful study and tryout.[7] Some readiness tests provide only a total score while others provide separate norms for each part of the test. The latter procedure is preferable because, although the subtests are usually not highly reliable, an examination of each child's performance on the subtests should assist the teacher in determining if he shows particular strengths and weaknesses.

Among the latest or more widely used reading readiness tests are: *Clymer-Barrett Prereading Battery; Gates-MacGinitie Reading Tests: Readiness Skills; Macmillan Reading Readiness Test; Metropolitan*

5				
B	D	P	R	B

7				
p	b	d	q	p

9				
me	boy	main	me	tree
10				
ball	bike	get	play	ball

FIGURE 2. Items from a test of visual discrimination. Taken from the *Macmillan Reading Readiness Test,* rev. ed. © 1970 by The Macmillan Company, New York. Reproduced by permission of the publisher and reduced in size. In each row the child is to put a cross on the item that is the same as the one in the box.

[7] Expert opinion regarding reading readiness and reading achievement tests may be found in Oscar K. Buros, *Reading: Tests and Reviews* (Highland Park, N.J.: Gryphon Press, 1968); and in Roger Farr and Nicholas Anastasiow, *Tests of Reading Readiness and Achievement: A Review and Evaluation* (Newark, Del.: International Reading Association, 1969).

Reading Readiness Test; and *Murphy-Durrell Reading Readiness Analysis.* Figures 2–4 illustrate the ways in which various skills are measured.

Attention should be given to the following points in selecting a

FIGURE 3. Items from tests of auditory discrimination. Items A and B are reproduced from the *Murphy-Durell Reading Readiness Analysis: Phonemes Test,* copyright 1964, 1965 by Harcourt Brace Jovanovich, Inc. Reproduced by special permission of the publisher. Item C from the *Gates-MacGinitie Reading Tests: Readiness Skills,* © 1968 by Teachers College Press, Columbia University, New York. Reproduced by permission of the publisher and reduced in size.

In Item A, the child is to put a cross on the pictures (all are previously named by the examiner) that begin "with s-s." In Item B, he is to mark the picture that "has the 1-1 sound at the end." In Item C (note the difference between how the skill is measured on the *Murphy-Durrell* and *Gates-MacGinitie*), for the first box the child is to put an X on "tie" (vs. "tea"; both items are previously named by the examiner); for the second, on "anchor" (vs. "ankle") and for the third, on "marks" (vs. "march").

FIGURE 4. Items from a test of word meaning. Reproduced from *Metropolitan Readiness Test,* Copyright 1965 by Harcourt Brace Jovanovich, Inc. Reproduced by special permission of the publisher and reduced in size.
In the first row, the child is to mark the moose (the word is pronounced by the examiner), in the second, the globe; and in the third row, the collie.

readiness test, and other tests as well: (1) How well does the test predict reading achievement? The manual should indicate the test's predictive validity. (2) Does the test have adequate reliability (a measure of the consistency with which a test measures given factors)? For satisfactory measurement of individual children the reliability coefficient should be at least .90. The standard error of measurement is a good indicator of how reliable a test is for individuals; the lower the standard error, the more reliable the test. (3) Are the norms based on a sufficiently large and representative sampling population? Are norms provided for the separate parts as well as for the total score? (4) How clear and complete are the directions for administering and scoring the test? (5) How long does it take to administer and score the test? If parts must be administered individually, is it worth the time required? (6) Does the test help to indicate a child's specific strengths and weaknesses? A subtest that contains only a few items cannot provide a reliable measure of a specific ability.

In most cases it is advisable to administer a readiness test in the first grade two or three weeks after school begins. The delay allows the children time to become accustomed to school, yet testing comes early enough to allow the teacher time to make use of the test results. Some schools give readiness tests near the end of kindergarten.

USE OF TEACHER OBSERVATION AND JUDGMENT

Teacher observations and judgments are important not only because they are needed to assess factors such as attitudes, which are not measured by standardized tests, but also because there is a need for a continuous on-going evaluation of the progress a child is making.

Competent first-grade teachers who have had experience that can be used as a basis for comparison can size up most of their children fairly well after two or three weeks. The accuracy of teacher estimates of learning ability tends to improve as the year progresses and the teacher can base judgments on more and more observations.

The most experienced teacher can, however, sometimes be wrong about a child. Talkative youngsters often seem brighter than they are; superior children who are shy and self-effacing are easy to overlook. Bright eyes may signify good health rather than a bright mind. A girl who behaves in class is more likely to receive favorable attention than a boy who acts out. What children are able to do is a safer basis for judgment than how they look or behave. The open-minded teacher who jots down notes and impressions about children is less likely to be misled than the teacher who is content to form a quick general impression of the child.

The progress children make in readiness activities and in the very beginnings of reading instruction can provide some of the best evidence the teacher has available. Thus a "sample lesson" in which a simple reading chart is read to the children, where the individual words are pointed out and the children are given opportunities to point to particular words, can help the teacher to note which children easily learn the words and which ones seem to be untouched by the experience.[8]

Accuracy of prediction is increased when teacher judgment is supplemented by the scores on an intelligence test and a readiness test. When teacher judgment and test scores agree about a child, the rating is very likely to be correct. When the teacher rates the child high and his test scores are low, or *vice versa,* either one can be correct and further study of the child is needed. For example, perhaps the child did poorly on the test because he did not understand the directions, or is unable to work on his own. There are many reasons why a child may attain a poor test score other than real inability to perform the tasks required.

A READING READINESS RATING SCALE

When teachers use a device like the Reading Readiness Rating Scale shown in Figure 5 or a rating scale that is part of a test such as *The Macmillan Reading Readiness Test,* they are helped to clarify their judgments and to make them specific. The items on which the child is to be rated have been discussed in the first part of this chapter. In making the ratings, the teacher should rely mainly on the accumulated information that builds up in daily observation of the child in the classroom. Teacher judgments should be reevaluated periodically because original opinions may not have been correct, and if the instructional program is effective there should be improvement and growth noted.

Each characteristic is rated on a scale from $+2$ to -2 by making a check in the appropriate place. The number of checks in each column is multiplied by the value of the column, so that if the "-2" column has two checks, as in Figure 5, it has a total of -4. The

---

[8] Semi-standard lessons accompanied by structured observations have been developed commercially to be used as a basis for rating readiness. Two such test lessons are the *Kindergarten Evaluation of Learning Potential: KELP* published by the California Test Bureau, and *Let's Look at Children* published by Educational Testing Service.

READING READINESS RATING SCALE
Devised by
Albert J. Harris

Date _Oct. 3_

Rated by _____

Name _Frederick_   Date of birth _Nov. 26_   Total Score _-5_

Characteristic	Low -2	-1	Average 0	+1	High +2
Intellectual development					
General mental maturity (MA)	••••	••••	✓	••••	••••
Brightness (IQ)	••••	••••	••••	✓	••••
Visual Perception	✓	••••	••••	••••	••••
Auditory perception	••••	✓	••••	••••	••••
Listening comprehension	••••	••••	✓	••••	••••
Knowledge and concepts	••••	••••	••••	✓	••••
Language development					
Vocabulary	••••	••••	••••	✓	••••
Sentence structure and length	••••	••••	••••	✓	••••
Maturity of pronunciation	••••	✓	••••	••••	••••
Physical development					
Vision	••••	••••	?	••••	••••
Hearing	••••	••••	?	••••	••••
Muscular coordination	••••	✓	••••	••••	••••
General health and vigor	••••	✓	••••	••••	••••
Consistent hand preference	✓	••••	••••	••••	••••
Home background					
Cultural-education level	••••	••••	••••	••••	✓
Richness and variety of experience	••••	••••	✓	••••	••••
Parental interest in schooling	••••	••••	✓	••••	••••
Emotional and social development					
Self-reliance and independence	••••	✓	••••	••••	••••
Emotional maturity, self-control	••••	••••	✓	••••	••••
Group participation	••••	✓	••••	••••	••••
Interest development					
Knowledge of alphabet, words	••••	✓	••••	••••	••••
Attention during story reading	••••	••••	✓	••••	••••
Expressed desire to read and write	••••	••••	✓	••••	••••
Column totals:	-4	-7	0	+4	+2

FIGURE 5. A reading readiness rating scale.

algebraic sum of the column totals gives the Total Score, which is above average if plus and below average if minus.

The ratings given to a first grader named Frederick are shown in Figure 5. Freddie's I.Q. on a test given late in September was 114, rating as bright; but since he was one of the youngest in the class (five years ten months at the time of the rating) his mental age was no higher than average. In the few reading readiness exercises involving visual perception that he had done, he had seemed confused and had shown a marked reversal tendency. He understood rhymes but had not yet caught on to making comparisons of beginning word sounds. He seemed to understand directions and stories, and in "Show and Tell" he displayed a range of information, vocabulary, and language usage that was above average. He spoke with a lisp and had a little difficulty with the sounds of /l/, /r/, and /w/.

His vision and hearing had not been tested but seemed all right. He did not seem particularly strong, vigorous, or well coordinated. He used his left hand a little more than his right, but often shifted from one hand to the other.

Freddie's parents were known to be college graduates, but since they had not yet been to the school, the ratings under "Home background" were very tentative. Freddie seemed to need a little more help and direction than many of his classmates, and in a group he would participate but not volunteer. He did not cry or lose his temper and was not aggressive. He could name about five capital letters, and seemed to have a normal degree of interest in stories and reading.

The Total Score, −5, indicated that Freddie was a little below the class average in readiness. The specific ratings pointed out to the teacher where he needed specific help. His inconsistent handedness seemed probably related to the reversals and confused perception. Since he showed some preference for the left hand, the teacher decided to encourage him to concentrate on the left hand and to give him extra training in the left-to-right direction, as well as extra practice in visual discrimination. None of the other ratings was so low as to be a cause for special concern, and since Freddie's immaturity was natural for a child who was about the youngest in the class, it would probably improve as the year progressed.

Testing and rating children for reading readiness is useful when it helps the teacher to discover the specific needs of children. The teacher can then concentrate on overcoming specific weaknesses, and in that way can make reading readiness activities functionally useful.

TESTS OF SPECIFIC ABILITIES

In addition to the factors already discussed, others may have some bearing upon the child's readiness for reading. It is sometimes suggested that the child be tested for color-blindness. There is, however, little relationship between color-blindness and reading achievement. Yet, color-blindness may create a problem if coloring pictures is stressed in early reading instruction.

Tests of psycholinguistic ability, visual perception, and perceptual-motor skills are available.[9] Many of these tests must be administered individually or require special training in their administration and interpretation. Furthermore, the exact relationship of the skills measured to reading readiness has not been clearly established. Likewise the effect on reading readiness of programs designed to overcome the weaknesses uncovered by such tests is still in need of further research.

Developing Reading Readiness

Many children will make easier and faster progress in learning to read if they are given a systematic readiness training program prior to the beginning of reading instruction, but not all children should be given the same readiness program as to content or length. For children who enter first grade with highly developed readiness or even knowing how to read, a very brief readiness program should be sufficient, mainly to give the teacher time to identify them. Children who are ready to learn advanced skills should not be held back. Other children will need a concentrated and extended period of readiness training. Even for the majority of children, the success of the program will depend to a great extent on how well the teacher individualizes instruction. Strengths and weaknesses will vary greatly from child to child even in "average" groups. Much time and effort are wasted either when children are required to perform tasks that require skills

[9] For a comprehensive discussion of such tests and special teaching procedures, refer to Albert J. Harris, *How to Increase Reading Ability,* 5th ed. (New York: McKay, 1970), pp. 218–223.

they have already attained to a high degree, or when they are given tasks for which they do not possess the necessary prerequisite skills. It is important that the child neither be bored nor fail repeatedly in his first experiences in learning to read.

Although maturation does play an important role, the teacher should not just wait for readiness to develop. When specific weaknesses are noted, she should make specific efforts to improve those skills and attitudes which can be developed, and should adjust her teaching procedures and the child's program to assist the child to compensate for those problems that cannot be overcome by direct teaching.

Readiness skills are not of equal importance and therefore need not all be developed to the same extent before reading instruction is begun. Specific types of readiness training can be continued after reading instruction has started.

DEVELOPING BACKGROUND ABILITIES

Kindergarten programs should include activities that are directly related to the later development of reading skills which will be taught in the particular reading methodology employed in the first grade. Perceptual skills and hand-eye coordination can be developed in play with blocks, clay, crayons, paint, weaving, cutting, and pasting. Range of knowledge can be expanded through well-planned trips, "show and tell," stories, and the use of audio-visual aids. Language can be developed through a wide range of activities, among the most useful being: listening to stories, dramatizing stories, conversation, discussion, "show-and-tell," and listening to rhymes and poetry. Interest in alphabet books can also be fostered. Social maturity can be enhanced as children learn to abide by classroom regulations, to listen to directions and carry them out, to attend to the task at hand, to curb one's temper, to take one's turn and let others take theirs, and to respect the rights of others. There are many other ways a well-structured prereading program can contribute to the development of reading readiness.

During the past few years some specialists in the education of mentally retarded and brain-damaged children have emphasized the importance of certain types of physical training in enhancing readiness for school learning.[10] The value of such training in improving reading readiness for most young children has not yet been established.

For many children it may be advisable to move the readiness program from the beginning of first grade to the latter part of kindergarten. Whether or not reading should actually be taught in kindergarten is a matter that should be decided for individual children. If a child is ready and eager to read, it probably will do no harm to let him try, but forcing an unready child to read will only create immediate and later problems.

When first graders do not appear to be ready, it may be wise to start the year with a few weeks of a kindergarten-type program. During this time the children can get accustomed to the classroom situation, and the teacher has an opportunity to study them before starting systematic instruction. If a class as a whole seems quite low in readiness, such a program can be continued, supplemented by activities planned to build up specific abilities that are involved in readiness.

Most of the activities mentioned in the first paragraph continue as part of the first-grade program after reading instruction has been started. Activities that involve practice in listening and speaking, that build new ideas and concepts, that sharpen perceptual skills, and that provide training in independent action and group participation continue to be beneficial to the reading program.

THE GENERALLY IMMATURE CHILD

Although the number may vary greatly depending upon the area in which the school is located, in a fairly typical first-grade class of about twenty-five children one can expect that six or seven will have I.Q.'s below 90; two or three of these probably will be below 80 I.Q.; and on the average, one will fall below 75 I.Q. These children are

[10] Marianne Frostig and Phyllis Maslow, *Movement Education: Theory and Practice* (Chicago: Follett Educational Corp., 1970).

Newell C. Kephart, *The Slow Learner in the Classroom* (Columbus, Ohio: Charles E. Merrill Books, 1960).

also likely to be retarded in language development, low in perceptual abilities, and immature emotionally and socially. They are apt to need more than the usual few weeks to get ready, and when they do start on reading their rate of learning is likely to be slow. We do not have any educational magic that can transform naturally slow children into normal learners, but we can provide them with appropriate readiness and reading programs.

We must recognize that we cannot measure the intelligence and other aspects of readiness with high accuracy, and that the relation between any test and success in beginning reading is far from perfect. We should, therefore, give every first grader, *regardless of test scores,* an opportunity to take part in beginning reading activities. This can be done most easily with the "language-experience" method described in Chapter 3. The children who show little or no progress with this approach can be continued with simple but appropriate beginning reading activities long after the other children have started to use preprimers and primers. The possibility also should be considered that some children find it difficult or impossible to learn through the use of a "whole-word" approach; a "phonic" approach may be more appropriate for some of them. The teacher who prefers to get into preprimer material early can move along very slowly with the immature children and can keep them in material of similar difficulty until they are ready to move ahead. Activities designed to build readiness can go on while the children are in the earliest stages of reading.

When sufficient numbers of children who are low in readiness are present, it may be advisable to have a transition class or reading-readiness first grade. In such classes a specially trained teacher works to develop readiness with a smaller number of children than are usually found in the first grade.

THE GENERALLY MATURE CHILD

When the idea of reading readiness was first developed in the 1920's, it was customary for 20 to 40 percent of the first-grade children to fail in reading and repeat the year. The readiness idea was advanced to save these children from having to try to keep up with the others and to give them an opportunity to start gradually and slowly, experiencing success instead of failure. It was never intended to justify a reading readiness program for all children.

By the time children have been in the first grade three or four weeks, the teacher usually has identified several children who seem quite ready for reading. The sooner these children start to read, the better. No good purpose is to be served by requiring all children to complete a certain amount of readiness work, such as finishing a reading readiness workbook, when some of them have nothing to learn from it.[11]

Some children may already have started to read before receiving any instruction in school. The alert teacher will spot these children quickly and help them to develop more advanced reading skills. They should be allowed to participate in reading group activities if they wish, but they should not be held down to the pace of the group.

THE CHILD WITH SPECIAL WEAKNESSES

There are many children who, like Freddie, are ready in many respects but have one or two special problems that may create real difficulty in learning to read. Often there are a few children who can benefit from the same kind of help and it is economical of teacher time and effort to work with them in a group. The teacher usually will start this kind of work before reading instruction is begun, and if it is still needed can continue it as a supplementary activity after the children have started to read. More detailed activities for developing readiness can be found in the references listed at the end of this chapter and in the teacher's manuals that accompany the readiness and preprimer materials of most reading series.

Training in Visual Discrimination. When children need help in visual discrimination, most of the practice should deal with letters and words. Improvement in ability to match pictures of animals, or of

---

[11] Although reading readiness workbooks can be useful to assist in developing some of the objectives of a good readiness program, the teacher should not over-rely on them.

geometric designs, seems to have little to do with reading. For this reason much of the practice in visual discrimination provided in many readiness workbooks is of doubtful value. Some useful exercises can be found in published readiness workbooks, but teachers may have to devise and duplicate additional exercises or purchase duplicating masters that contain sheets for specific skill development.

There are many kinds of exercises that are useful in developing discrimination of letters and word forms. They include:

1. Practice with single letters
   a. Indicating if two letters are the same or different [12]
      t t ; f s ; r n ; b d ; e e ; m m
   b. Marking all the letters that are the same as the first letter
      m : m n m m w
   c. Marking the one letter that is the same as the first letter
      k : h f t k l
   d. Marking the one letter that is not like the others
      b b d b b
2. Practice with word forms
   a. Indicating if two word forms are exactly alike
      rag bone ; tip tip ; miss mess ; rat tar
   b. Marking the one word that is not exactly like the others
      bell bell bet bell
   c. Marking the one word that is just like the first word
      make : fine mite make fake
3. Practice with letters within words
   a. Marking the words that begin with the same letter as the first word
      take : two have run top fine tell
   b. Marking the one word that begins like the first word
      draw : prow brat quick dress
   c. Marking the one word that ends with the same letter as the first word
      run : come fan tar bit

Each of the illustrations given above is a one-line sample of a kind of exercise of which several pages can be prepared, starting with very easy and obvious comparisons and gradually getting harder.

---

[12] The concepts "same," "different," "begins," "ends," etc., must be understood by the child before he can do such exercises.

The more closely the distractors (wrong answers) resemble the correct answer, the more difficult the item. In using exercises like these for developing readiness, the aim is to help the children to perceive the visual similarities and differences, not to teach them to identify the letters or words by name.

Training in Auditory Discrimination. Skill in auditory discrimination also can be improved by training. The kinds of discrimination that need to be developed are very much like those needed in visual discrimination. The child needs to be able to distinguish whether two sounds are exactly alike or somewhat different; whether two spoken words are exactly alike or somewhat different; and to notice and compare particular sounds within words. If an emphasis is not placed upon teaching phonics in beginning reading instruction, most of this training can be given after the children have begun to read.

During the readiness period, the attention of children can be called to the rhyming words in poems and jingles, and some practice can be given in listening to and comparing beginning sounds of words. The kinds of games and exercises that are useful in improving auditory discrimination for reading are described on pages 236–239.

Training in the Left-Right Direction. Some languages are read from right to left (Hebrew), some from top to bottom (Chinese), and at one time ancient Greek was written from left to right on one line and from right to left on the following line. The left-to-right direction we employ is arbitrary but, like driving on a one-way street, failure to observe the rule can cause a great deal of trouble.

Teachers can do many things to help children learn the left-to-right sequence.

1. Teach children who don't know which is their left hand and which is their right. If necessary let a child use a reminder such as wearing a ring, a string, or a rubber band on a finger of his left hand.
2. Find out for each child which hand seems to be the naturally dominant one. Encourage children who do not use either their right or left hand consistently always to hold a crayon, pencil, scissors, etc., in their dominant hand.

3. When reading material to children from the chalkboard or a chart, run the hand or pointer smoothly and slowly under the words from left to right.
4. Encourage children to look at words by starting at the left and going steadily to the right, when careful inspection is needed.
5. Provide practice in discriminating between words that have reversed letter sequences, such as on-no, of-for, rat-tar, and saw-was.

Many reading readiness workbooks contain exercises for developing left-to-right progression as well as other pre-reading skills. Figure 6 shows an example of a workbook page that combines the development of left-to-right direction, picture interpretation, and oral language skills (speaking in complete sentences).

FIGURE 6. Part of a lesson to develop left-to-right progression and language skills. Taken from *Picture Stories,* Preparatory Book 1 (Sheldon, William D., Mills, Queenie B., and Mower, Rosalie). © Copyright 1968 by Allyn and Bacon, Inc., Boston. The original is in color. Reproduced by permission of the publisher and reduced in size.

Through questioning, the teacher encourages the child to interpret the pictures from left to right.

BUILDING INTEREST IN LEARNING TO READ

Kindergarten and first-grade teachers can do many things to get children to want to read for themselves.

1. Signs and labels around the room excite curiosity, but be careful not to overdo them because it may overwhelm distractible children. Practically every child wants to be able to identify his name above his coat hook and to know what the other signs and labels mean. Playing store often requires the "clerk" to obtain a labeled package, or a "customer" to determine if a brand-named product is on the shelf.
2. When the teacher reads interesting stories and poems to the children, shows them illustrations, and then leaves the book on the library table, children like to go to the book and look at the pages and pictures.
3. Notices, rules, weather charts, committee lists, experience charts, and many other kinds of reading matter, placed on the board or charts and read to the children by the teacher, convey the idea that it is necessary to read in order to find out many things for oneself.
4. Perhaps most important is making sure that the earliest reading experiences are relatively easy and satisfying. It may be an old cliché but, nothing succeeds like success.

THE TEACHER'S RESPONSIBILITY FOR HEALTH PROBLEMS

The teacher is often better able to notice and interpret the signs of a physical problem than are parents. The question can be referred to the school nurse for further investigation. Providing medical care is the responsibility of the parents. When there is a physical problem the teacher and the school nurse should make certain that the parents are informed of any recommendations. If the parents are slow to follow a recommendation, such as getting eyeglasses for the child, the teacher's job is one of persuasion by explaining the importance of correcting the difficulty. On such issues as excessively late bedtime or a poor diet, teachers have no authority. The best they can usually do is to explain to the parents the relationship that they see between the particular problem and the child's performance in school. Sometimes the teacher can take the initiative to see that the child receives free milk or meals in school and can provide information about medical and other services that are free or low in cost. A competent social worker can be very valuable in some school situations.

COPING WITH EMOTIONAL MALADJUSTMENT

Many children take a while to adjust to living in the first grade. One of the teacher's main objectives during the first few weeks is to help them to settle down and get adjusted to classroom routines. If time passes and a particular child remains so restless, so timid, so helpless, or so aggressive that he seems to be making little or no progress in becoming able to participate effectively in group activities, this has to be regarded as a serious problem.

Timid children often need extra time and patience before they get used to school. If the child seems very much upset by the mother's leaving, it is sometimes advisable to allow the mother to stay in the classroom for part of the morning and to make the weaning process a gradual one. When children become overexcited, rebellious, stubborn, or angry, it is usually advisable to remove them from the group temporarily and to provide them with quiet individual activities.

Maladaptive behavior that persists beyond the first couple of months should be discussed with the parents. They may be able to provide some of the corrective procedures that are necessary. If the problem continues unimproved, the teacher should not hesitate to discuss it with the school principal, guidance counselor, or psychologist. The problem may require a kind of diagnostic study and treatment that no teacher can provide.

Summary

1. Readiness for beginning reading instruction is a composite trait that includes many aspects of both maturation and learning.

a. The intellectual characteristics of general mental maturity and brightness, visual and auditory discrimination, and acquired knowledge are very important.

b. Language is the framework on which reading is built, and therefore listening and speaking skills are highly relevant.

c. Home background, emotional and social development, and the child's degree of interest in learning to read are all involved.

d. Health handicaps can interfere with progress.

2. In the evaluation of readiness, the combined use of teacher ratings with both an intelligence test and a reading readiness test is recommended.

a. Intelligence and reading readiness tests provide useful information, but they do not measure all the factors related to readiness for reading, and are never perfect predictors of later reading success.

b. Observations and judgments by the teacher provide the best evidence about some aspects of readiness, and can be improved by using an appropriate rating scale and by being alert to the implications of children's day-to-day behavior and performance.

3. Even though the teacher may group children for readiness activities, she should give attention to the wide range of individual strengths and weaknesses found in each group and in each child.

a. After a relatively brief orientation period, those children who seem quite ready should be introduced to reading without further delay.

b. Children who seem generally immature should be given a somewhat longer period of prereading activities, but it seems more practical to give them a very slow-moving reading program than to give them no reading activities at all.

c. Regardless of whether they are quite mature, average, or generally immature, children who have special weaknesses should be given specific kinds of practice and experiences. This can begin in the prereading period and can continue after they have started to read.

d. When there are physical problems or persistent emotional

56 · EFFECTIVE TEACHING OF READING

difficulties, the cooperation of the parents, other members of the school staff, and perhaps appropriate outside agencies is often necessary.

RECOMMENDED READING

ANDERSON, VERNA D. *Reading and Young Children.* New York: The Macmillan Co., 1968.

BEERY, ALTHEA, BARRETT, THOMAS C., and POWELL, WILLIAM R., EDS. *Elementary Reading Instruction: Selected Materials.* Boston: Allyn and Bacon, Inc., 1969, Ch. 9.

BOND, GUY L., and WAGNER, EVA BOND. *Teaching the Child to Read,* 4th ed. New York: Macmillan, 1966. Ch. 2.

DURKIN, DOLORES. *Teaching Them to Read.* Boston: Allyn and Bacon, Inc., 1970. Chs. 3–5.

FROST, JOE L. *Issues and Innovations in the Teaching of Reading.* Glenview, Ill.: Scott, Foresman, 1967. Pp. 57–100.

HARRIS, ALBERT J. *Readings on Reading Instruction.* New York: McKay, 1963. Ch. 3.

HEILMAN, ARTHUR W. *Principles and Practices of Teaching Reading,* 2nd ed. Columbus: Charles E. Merrill, 1967. Ch. 2.

TINKER, MILES A., and McCULLOUGH, CONSTANCE M. *Teaching Elementary Reading,* 3rd ed. New York: Appleton-Century-Crofts, 1968. Chs. 3–5.

3

Beginning to Read

Opinions differ as to when it is advantageous to start systematic reading instruction for all children. In some countries, teaching reading begins at age five, while in others it begins at six or even seven years of age. Such decisions are arbitrary and deny the fact of individual differences. Ideally each child should start when he is ready and interested. If chronological age, or any other single factor, is used as the criterion, some children will be unnecessarily delayed and others will fail in their initial attempt in learning to read. Some children have learned to read before entering school. There is little evidence that this may be harmful unless pressures have been exerted, and it may even be helpful for some children. On the other hand, a delayed start apparently does not harm children with at least average intelligence.

From Readiness into Beginning Reading

Actually there is no exact point at which reading readiness ends and systematic reading instruction begins. Many of the activities undertaken by teachers during the reading readiness period, in order to arouse and strengthen interest in learning to read, actually form a natural transition into reading.

One of the first of these activities is providing each child with a large card on which his name has been printed. Cards can be used to identify the child's desk and his locker or clothes hanger. Early in the year children can wear name cards. Most children quickly learn to identify their own names. They can draw self-portraits and print their names below their pictures.

First-grade children generally like repetition. When they enjoy a story they may ask to have it read to them again and again, and some of them memorize it word for word. When a child goes to the library table and looks at a book that has been read to him many times he may or may not look at the printed words in sequence as he recites the story to himself; if he does, he will gradually become able to recognize some of the words.

Notices of many kinds can be placed on the chalkboard and read to the children by the teacher. A weather report can be posted each day, and some children will come to distinguish "Today it is sunny," from "Today it is raining." Committee assignments can be posted, and children will look eagerly for their names. Special events, such as trips and holidays, can be the basis of notices placed on the board and read to the children. Messages for individual children can be given to them in written form, even though teacher has to tell the child what the message says. Labels can be placed on important objects in the room, such as the door, chalkboard, closet, window, or fish tank. The children learn in many ways that reading is a form of communicating, and that when they learn what the words say they will be able to find out many things for themselves.

After children have started to read, the kinds of functional reading described above should be continued and bulletin boards, committee and individual messages and assignments, special notices, weather report, absence list, and many other temporary items can be used to continue and expand the role of reading as a form of communication.

A Brief Historical Overview

Children can learn to read, and have been taught to read, in many different ways. Until a little more than a century ago the prevailing method was memorizing the spelling of words: see—ay—tee says cat.

The word method, sponsored by Horace Mann, became well known around 1850 and was popular for about a generation. It was supplanted by intensive phonic methods which held sway from the 1890's to the 1920's. They were followed by a period of extreme emphasis on silent reading for meaning. Each of these trends was a protest and revolt against the increasingly obvious shortcomings of its predecessor and each, in its turn, was found to have its own weaknesses. As new methods became fashionable, many teachers resisted change and clung to their established procedures, so that older methods have continued to be used long after newer procedures have become popular.

The trend during the past twenty or so years has been to try to develop a balanced method of instruction that incorporates most of the good features of the older one-sided approaches and avoids their shortcomings. Perhaps the most significant feature of current procedure is the real effort that has been made to bring methods of teaching reading into agreement with the psychological development of children and with the psychology of learning.

New methods and revivals of older methods in modified form continue to be advocated, and what is fashionable today may perhaps be out of style twenty years from now. In the past, changes have usually come about mainly through enthusiastic salesmanship; the weaknesses of the currently popular method were exaggerated, and the claims for the new idea were often based more on faith than on facts.

Recent large-scale research projects have compared the merits of different approaches to teaching beginning reading. These findings are discussed near the end of the chaper following descriptions of the various approaches to teaching children to read.

Differences Among Approaches to Teaching Beginning Reading

In general, there are wide differences among approaches to teaching beginning reading in regard to story content, scope and sequence of skills taught, the emphasis placed on skills, materials for use by the child, and instructional guides provided for the teacher. Even within a given approach, there are wide variations. There is no such thing as *the* basal reader approach, *the* phonic approach, or *the* linguistic approach. Rather, there are basal reader programs, phonic programs, etc. For example, basal reader programs vary greatly in the emphasis placed on word-identification skills, especially phonics, in the initial stages of instruction. Phonic programs differ in the manner in which a child is taught to make symbol-sound associations and the pace at which phonic generalizations are introduced.

There are, however, two basic differences among most approaches; (1) the way in which the child is first taught to read words, and (2) the initial emphasis placed upon either decoding (the ability to work out the pronunciation of words) or comprehension (the ability to read for meaning). It should be noted that whatever the emphasis in the initial stages, in later stages the instructional program almost always includes factors that were not initially emphasized (e.g., programs that emphasize comprehension include later instruction in decoding).

Some methods (programs) begin by having the child learn small parts such as letter sounds or names (*c a t*), or letters and letter combinations (*c at*) which are used to form words, which in turn are used in sentences. These are called synthetic methods because they start with small parts and build into larger units. In such methods, as well as in phonic and linguistic programs that employ a whole-word phonics or word-to-sounds method, the early emphasis is upon the decoding process.

Methods that start with whole words and move to the study of word parts are generally referred to as analytic methods. In most "whole-word" or "look-say" [1] methods, the early emphasis is placed upon obtaining meaning with little or no attention given to the decoding process. Children are shown a word, and through various procedures learn to associate the printed word with its oral counterpart and the meaning that it represents. Words that are in most children's vocabularies are selected for use, so that the child's effort can be focused upon making the association between the printed word

[1] A more appropriate term would be "look-while-you-say" because the task is to make an association between the printed word and its oral counterpart. Unless the child is attending to the printed symbol while he is saying the word, the association will be weak or will not be made at all.

and its oral equivalent. At one time, almost all basal reader programs employed a "whole-word" method. Recently, however, some basal reader programs have placed more emphasis upon phonics in the initial stages of instruction and have increased the pace at which phonic skills are introduced. In one basal series, phonics instruction and meaningful reading start simultaneously.[2] Rather than teaching words as wholes, the teacher helps the children to identify each new word through a combination of phonic and context cues.

Basal Reader Approaches

A set of basal readers provides the framework for the major part of reading instruction in the first grades of most schools in the United States. A basal reader series is not just a set of books, but rather is an organized method for the development of reading skills, preplanned down to tiny details, in which the materials have been written to conform with the method, and the details of method are planned for use with these specific materials.[3]

Basal reader series provide a vehicle primarily for the teaching of developmental reading skills (see p. 18). They should not be thought of as being the *total* reading program in a school, because functional and recreational reading are important components of any good total reading program.

BASAL READER MATERIALS

Most basal reader series include the following materials usually intended for use in the first grade: (1) a series of books, starting with one or two readiness workbooks and including two to four pre-primers, a primer (1^1)[4] and a first reader (1^2); (2) a teacher's guide

[2] *The Macmillan Reading Program,* rev. ed. (New York: Macmillan, 1970).
[3] "Basal" reader and "basic" reader have been used interchangeably. Since several series use "basic" as part of the name of the series, "basal" is used throughout this book to avoid ambiguity.
[4] Markings on the texts such as 1^1 may be used to help identify the level of the material. Such designations do not indicate that the material should be used during a certain time during the school year (e.g., 1^2 does not mean the

or manual for each book, and (3) workbooks correlated with the readers. In addition, the materials may include: (4) large word, phrase, and story cards for group instruction; (5) a very large reproduction of the first preprimer that can be used to introduce books at that level; (6) related exercises on stencils; (7) related filmstrips and recordings; (8) dictionaries; and (9) supplementary paper-bound story books.

Preprimers are paper-bound booklets averaging about sixty pages in length. Most basal series have three of them. They can be used right after the readiness period as the first reading materials, or can be used after a period of experience story reading (see p. 80). Reading material frequently starts with the introduction of the names of the characters (in some series this occurs in the readiness workbooks) and the amount of reading goes from one word per page to a maximum of about eight lines, with each line usually being a complete sentence. The stories are told largely by the pictures and much of the reading matter represents what the characters say to one another. Despite the restrictions imposed by the limited vocabulary, which often is introduced at a rate of not more than one or two new words per page and abundantly repeated, well-written preprimer stories have interest, suspense, and even humor for first-grade children. When the story is developed as recommended in the teacher's manual, the language does not seem to the children to be as stilted and repetitious (especially with the recent trend to make the language patterns more natural) as it does to an adult who looks at it without reference to the teaching method.

The name "primer" means first book, but now that the preprimers

---

text should be used from February to June, the second semester), nor do they mean that the text should be used only in that grade. Such designations should be thought of as indicating *levels of difficulty* rather than *grade* levels. For example, a first reader may be appropriately used with a child in the second grade, and conversely a second reader may be used with a first grader who has acquired all the skills usually taught in the first grade. Several recently published basal reader programs no longer employ grade-level designations, but rather have numbered the texts in sequence. For example, a first reader, which follows two readiness books, three preprimers, and a primer, might be labeled "Book 7."

come first, the primer is the first hard-covered book. A typical primer of the early 1960's started with the sixty or so words used in the pre-primers and gradually added about a hundred new words [5] in its approximately 175 pages. There has been a trend toward richer vocabularies in primers published very recently. As the vocabulary expands, the language becomes more varied and natural and conveys more of the story, while the illustrations become somewhat less important, although still copious.

Analyses of seven basal reader series published between 1960 and 1963 show that they varied in the number of different words used in preprimer, primer, and first reader texts. The total preprimer vocabulary ranged from a low of 54 words to a high of 83 words; primer vocabularies ranged from 113 to 173 words; and the first reader vocabularies from 285 to 340 words.[6] In general, the easier series may be more appropriate for slow learners and the more challenging books for bright children.

Stories in the first preprimer through the first reader often center around a single family and are based largely on activities that are familiar to most children, involving playing with each other and with pets, celebrating birthdays and holidays, and going on trips and visits. The characters usually include a brother and sister old enough to go to school, a younger child, parents, a dog, and a cat or kitten. Other characters, such as friends, grandparents, the postman, and the policeman, are gradually introduced. Most of the more recently published basal series have introduced ethnic and cultural pluralism, with a few stressing multi-ethnic characters and urban settings. However, regardless of the ethnic or cultural background of the characters and

[5] The term "new word" means that the word is introduced for the first time in that basal series. Some children may already be able to identify it in its printed form, and its particular meaning may be already known by most of the children. There is a trend in recently published series to distinguish between words which most children probably will not be able to identify independently and those which many children should be able to identify, with varying degrees of assistance from the teacher, by using previously taught word-identification skills.

[6] Arthur V. Olson, "An Analysis of the Vocabulary of Seven Primary Reading Series," *Elementary English*, 42 (March 1965), 262.

whether the setting is suburban or urban, the families are most often of the middle class.[7] Occasionally, the one-family theme is dropped or diminished at or near the end of the primer, and replaced by old folk tales, factual stories, fanciful stories, space-age stories, and poetry.

There are usually teacher's manuals for each of the preprimers, the primer, and the first reader. The manual may be bound with a copy of the reader (perhaps annotated) in a teacher's edition, or it may be a separate soft-covered book. In the latter case, the reader page is reproduced with the teaching plans below or to the side of it. Most manuals have more pages than the readers they accompany, explaining the general methodology in introductory chapters and then giving detailed specific lesson plans for each story.

There is usually one workbook to accompany the preprimers, one for the primer, and one for the first reader. Since some teachers use the workbooks and others do not, most manuals are so organized that doing one or more pages in the workbook is an optional supplementary activity following the reading of the related pages in the reader. A few current series are so organized so that some of the workbook's pages are preparatory; they can be used to introduce new words and ideas before the child encounters them in his reader. Workbooks vary greatly in the amount of attention given to word recognition, phonics, comprehension, and other reading skills, and in their adaptability for independent use. At the first-grade level most workbook activity has to be guided and supervised. The added repetition of the basic vocabulary provided by a workbook is often helpful to slow learners, while good readers may become annoyed and impatient with workbook practice. There is no need for every child to do every page in a workbook. When used, workbook pages should be promptly corrected, returned, and discussed as needed. The errors children make on workbooks, or in any lesson, can provide valuable diagnostic information for the alert teacher. Rather than writing such

[7] There is little evidence regarding the extent to which children identify with story characters, and the effect that identification or lack of it has upon the acquisition of reading skills.

statements as "Do this page over" on the top of a page, the teacher should attempt to determine why the child performed poorly in order that plans can be developed for overcoming specific weaknesses.

INSTRUCTIONAL PROCEDURES

Each basal reader series has an instructional plan which is a little different from the others, but when variations in terminology are set aside it is evident that the similarities are much greater than the differences. There are, in general, four major divisions to the general plan, and these are repeated with minor variations in story after story. These four divisions are: (1) preparing for the reading, or establishing readiness; (2) guided reading and rereading, silent and oral; (3) developing specific reading skills; and (4) enrichment or supplementary activities. The last two divisions may be considered as one step and entitled "Follow-up Activities."

Preparing for the Story. Getting ready for a new story involves three different kinds of purposes. The first is motivation and arousal of interest, usually necessary when a new unit or group of stories is being introduced. The second is the introduction and explanation of new concepts, ideas, and meanings. The third is oral and visual presentation and preteaching of new words, often accompanied by some review of words previously taught. The new concepts and new words are often taught together.

The extent to which interest need be aroused, the necessity for and depth of concept development needed, and the extent to which "new" words are already known and "old" words unknown will vary from child to child. Therefore, each teacher should know as well as possible the backgrounds, interests, strengths, and weaknesses of each child in the class.

Guided Reading and Rereading. Before starting to read, there is usually some discussion of the first picture and the title of the story, with guesses about what may happen in the story. The teacher then asks a question that provides a motive for reading ahead, and the children read silently to find the answer. Then they discuss the answer, and perhaps read orally the sentence or two that contains the answer. The amount read may vary from one line at a time in the earliest preprimer reading to a page or more at a time.

Rereading is usually oral, sometimes silent, and manuals provide a variety of purposes for rereading: to clear up a disputed point, to find out how different characters feel, to find the happy parts or sad parts, to prepare to draw an illustration, to make it sound as if the characters are really speaking, to prepare a puppet show or dramatization of the story, etc. Rereading comes after skills development in some sequences, before it in others. The number of times a story should be reread also shows differences of opinion.

Developing Specific Reading Skills. Under this heading one finds suggestions for exercises to develop various comprehension skills, word recognition practice, training in auditory and visual discrimination, training intended to develop independence in word attack through use of context and the learning of phonics and structural analysis, and the use of workbook exercises to provide additional practice in these various skills. The relative importance given to these skills and the amounts and kinds of practice provided vary considerably in the different series.

Enrichment. Many kinds of suggestions are included under the general idea of enrichment or extension or supplementation. Language practice can include jingles and rhymes intended to improve clarity of enunciation. Suggestions are made concerning stories which the teacher can read to the children, songs that can be sung, and poems with related themes. As children become able to do some independent reading, suggestions are also given about books and stories that children may like to read for themselves.

EXAMPLES OF PREPRIMER METHODOLOGY

In *A Magic Box,* the second preprimer of the Macmillan Reading Program, a story entitled "Mike Rides the Bike" occupies pages 9–12. On page 9, pictures of the children's bicycles are shown, and the title appears near the bottom of the page.

On page 10 Mike, the youngest child, states that he can't get on his bike. He is encouraged to do so by his brother and sister. On page 11

Mike gets on his bike, and Jeff and Mary plan to get on their bikes to join him. On page 12, all three children are riding and Mike is pleased to be able to ride his bike. Each page has a large colored picture, with from five to seven short one-line sentences beneath representing what the characters are saying.

The accompanying manual devotes thirteen pages to this lesson. The new vocabulary consists of two words, *He* and *go*. The three steps suggested in the manual are summarized below.

Preparation. Through questioning the children are led to understand that Mike's new bike is a two-wheeler with training wheels. Next the children are encouraged to tell about their own experiences with two-wheelers.

An introductory story card (reproduced in the manual) is then displayed. The sentences are read by the children and the new words are identified and underlined. For each new word, a pupil is asked to tell how he knew what the word was (e.g., *He*—it makes sense in the sentence; it begins like the known word *here*). A game is then played using the initial consonant sound. Independent work in the workbook or in a Practice Exercise (reproduced from the manual) is suggested. Finally the teacher supervises the pupils in locating *he* and *go* in the brief picture dictionary included in the preprimer.

This section also includes a subsection "Let Their Errors Tell You" which suggests ways for using pupil errors constructively.

Reading the Story. The preceding story is briefly reviewed and the teacher provides three motivating questions, after which the children read the entire story silently and independently. Then the teacher asks the pupils to tell what happened when Mike tried to ride the bike. This is followed by oral rereading for specific purposes. For example, the following is suggested for the page shown in Figure 7:

PAGE 12. "Read to yourself the three lines that tell what Mike said." (Show the exact lines with your own book facing the group.) . . . "How do you think Mike felt when he said that?" (He was excited.) . . . "Who can find the little mark—the exclamation point—which shows us that he was excited?" "Sue (name a pupil), read what Mike said, and make him sound happy and excited." . . . "Read the four lines that tell what Mary said." . . . "Do you think Mary was really asking anyone *Who can*

Mike said, "I can get on the bike!
I can ride with Mary and Jeff.
I can go and go."

Mary said, "Who can ride?
Who can ride a bike?
Mike can ride.
I can ride with Mike."

FIGURE 7. A page from a second preprimer. From Mae Knight Clark, *A Magic Box*, revised ed., p. 12. The Macmillan Reading Program. New York: The Macmillan Company, © 1970. The original is in color. Reproduced by permission of the publishers and reduced in size.

ride?" (No, Mary could see that for herself.) . . . "Mary was making a little rhyme. Read aloud the little rhyme that Mary made." . . . "What word did Mary rhyme with *bike?*" . . . "I like to make rhymes, too:

Mary can ride
By Jeff's side.

What word did I rhyme with *ride?*" . . . "Can you think of another word that rhymes with *ride?*" (Possible words are *hide, tide,* and *wide.* If the pupils give a rhyme word with a different spelling, such as cried, accept it. Say that it doesn't have the same letters in it, but it does rhyme.)[8]

Follow-up. A correlated practice exercise (duplicated from the manual or from a spirit duplicating master) and workbook pages are suggested. This is followed by suggestions for teacher-directed activities for reviewing known word analysis skills: (1) using context; (2) using beginning sound; (3) looking on through the word. Suggestions are then provided for helping individuals who may have had difficulty with acquiring the skills developed in this lesson. Finally, related activities in literature, poetry, and music are suggested.

In *Fun With the Family,* the second preprimer of the New Basic Readers, a story entitled "Father" occupies pages 15–18. On page 15, Father is shown throwing a football to Dick. The story title appears below the picture.

On page 16, Dick calls to his father to watch him run as Spot chases Dick. On page 17, Father runs after Dick; and on page 18 Spot jumps at Father who tells him to get Dick. Each page has a large colored picture, with from three to four short one-line sentences beneath it representing what the characters are saying.

The accompanying manual devotes eight pages to this lesson. The new words are *Father, I,* and *no.* The three steps suggested in the manual are summarized below.

Establishing Background. The manual suggests that if most of the children have never handled a football, that one be brought into the room before the story is read. The teacher tells the children the name of the book and after the story title page is displayed, the children are encouraged to discuss boy's games. A picture card is displayed and the teacher says "This is a picture of Dick's father," after which she places the word *Father* under the picture and comments "This is the

---

[8] Mae Knight Clark, *Teacher's Annotated Edition and Guide to Accompany Opening Books, A Magic Box, Things You See* (New York: The Macmillan Company 1970), p. 198. Copyright © The Macmillan Company 1965, 1970. Quoted by permission of the publishers.

word *Father.*" The words *I* and *No* are presented by having the teacher tell a story and displaying the words every time she says them. Next the boys are encouraged to relate their experiences in playing football.

Guiding Interpretation. Questions are suggested to guide line-by-line reading of the text which is followed by the reading of the whole page. Children take the roles of the characters or take turns reading aloud certain parts of the page. The suggested questions for page 18 which is shown in Figure 8 are: "Why do you suppose Spot jumped at Father?," "How can you tell Father was not angry at Spot?" and "What did Father do when Spot leaped at him?" [9]

The children are then helped to see the relationship of this story to the title of the book, and the entire story is read silently, then orally. This section also contains suggestions concerning the use of markers under a line of print and the transition from oral to silent reading.

Extending Competence. A workbook page that reviews the form and purpose of capitals in sentences is suggested. This is followed by a teacher-directed activity designed to use three approaches, auditory, visual, and kinesthetic, in teaching the /f/ sound. The lesson also contains exercises in auditory discrimination and discriminating meanings on the basis of the difference in one sound. Finally, a workbook page on which the child is to encircle pictures representing words beginning with /f/ is suggested.

VARIATIONS IN BASAL READER METHOD

In order to really understand how reading is taught with basal readers one should make a careful study of representative lesson plans, using the manual, the reader, and the workbook, and going step by step through the complete instructional sequence. If one samples the teaching method in this way at preprimer, primer, and first reader levels for two or three of the currently popular series, the procedures

[9] Helen M. Robinson, *et al. Guidebook for Second and Third Pre-Primers* (Chicago: Scott, Foresman, 1965), p. 47. Quoted by permission of the publishers.

Father said, "No, Spot, no!
Look at Dick.
Get Dick.
Go and get Dick!"

FIGURE 8. A second preprimer page from *Fun with the Family*, by Helen M. Robinson, *et al.*, p. 18. The New Basic Readers. Copyright © 1965 by Scott, Foresman and Company. The original is in color. Reproduced by permission of the publishers and reduced in size.

that have been described in the preceding few pages will become vividly meaningful. It is still better if, after making such a study of the materials, one can observe a capable first-grade teacher conducting some reading lessons according to the manual.

The very specific directions given in the manuals are extremely useful to inexperienced first-grade teachers. As teachers grow in experience they become selective in what they take from the manual, using it as a resource with many useful ideas and suggestions rather than as a set of directions to be followed exactly. Certain skills may need more practice than the manual provides and other skills may require less practice or none at all. Teachers also learn to go through the manuals of other basal reader series for specific ideas that they may want to try.

In addition to differences in vocabulary load and story content, there are other variations among basal series. Although there is general agreement on the main steps in teaching from basal readers, the amount of emphasis given to different objectives varies considerably. The amount of systematic instruction in phonics is one question on which there is marked variation. In general, readers published since 1960 have tended to provide earlier and more intensive practice in word-identification skills than was common between 1930 and 1960. Some series attempt to assist the teacher in adapting instruction to individual differences in one or more of four ways: (1) providing different sets of lesson plans for fast, average, and slow learning groups; (2) offering suggestions for exercises for slow and accelerated groups that may be used in addition to the suggested lesson plan; (3) publishing two texts with basically the same content, but with one written at grade level and the other below grade level; and (4) publishing three different texts per grade level, one each for the above-grade level, the on-grade level, and the below-grade level groups. One series gives plans for both a "basic reader approach" and a "modified basic reader approach." The latter includes considerable emphasis on the use of experience stories and suggests using the pre-primers and primers for independent collateral reading. Another series has separate sets of materials (and programs) for developmental, functional, and recreational reading. The amount of oral reading and the place of skills development in the lesson plan are other issues on which reader systems disagree.

USING DIFFERENT BASAL SERIES

The question is often asked whether it is better to go straight through one series of basal readers or to read the materials of several series at one level before going on to books of the next level. Actually, either of these plans can work successfully, but first the teacher must decide what he hopes to accomplish by using materials from other series. In general, they may be used for three purposes, which are not mutually exclusive: (1) additional skills practice or teaching; (2) additional practice in establishing a sight vocabulary (words which are recognized almost immediately); and (3) independent reading.

If the objective is to develop or reinforce specific reading skills, then the teacher must select material on the basis of whether or not it lends itself to the teaching or practice of these skills; and if the child is to use the material independently, whether or not the vocabulary employed is suitable.

For the last two purposes listed above, much depends on the degree to which the vocabularies of books to be read in sequence correspond. A study reported in 1965 revealed that of 763 different words found in first-grade materials of seven basal series, only 92 appeared in five or more of the series. Thirty-two words were common at the preprimer level, 31 at the primer, and 30 at the first-reader level. The number of words unique to each series ranged from 59 to 159, with a median of 64.[10]

If two primers have 90 percent of their vocabularies in common, either can be read easily and quickly after the first has been mastered. If they have only 50 to 60 percent of their vocabularies in common, the second will not seem much easier than the one read first. There may be fewer unknown words per page in the next higher book in the series being used than in a book at the same level from a different basal series. Unless a teacher is willing to go to the trouble of com-

[10] Arthur V. Olson, *op. cit.*

paring the vocabularies of different books, the proper sequence in which books of the same level are easiest to read is a matter of guesswork.

For the inexperienced teacher, therefore, it is safest to proceed from the preprimers of one series into the primer of the same series, and from the primer into the first reader. In this way one can be sure of a coordinated vocabulary development. In addition, there will be consistency in the kinds of lesson plans in the manuals, and important skills are likely to be developed in a planned sequence. If a child is extremely slow in acquiring word recognition skills, the teacher should attempt to determine if another means of teaching a sight vocabulary is more appropriate. Poor reading skills may also result from moving too rapidly through the skill development program without allowing time for acquisition and assimilation.

When children are going through their basal primer systematically, they can read independently in the preprimers of other series and in other primers and books with closely corresponding vocabularies. While they are being given systematic instruction in a basal first reader they can read independently in primers of other series, in easy first readers, and in very simply written library books. A combination of systematic, sequential instruction with a considerable amount of individualized supplementary reading has much to commend it.

TIME ALLOTMENTS

Satisfactory teaching of reading in the first grade usually requires a minimum of an hour and a half of the teacher's time per day. Each group should have a daily instructional period of at least 20 minutes. In addition, time will be needed for developing and reading experience stories, for stories read and told by the teacher, for going through a weekly newspaper written for first grade, for a second group lesson for each group once, twice, or three times a week, for work with small groups that have special needs, and for individualized reading. Insufficient time allotments make it impossible for the teacher to cover the full instructional program. When this happens, the temptation is to get through the books somehow on schedule, at the expense of slighting the development of specific skills and of supplementary reading activities.

Some schools limit the first-grade schedule to a half day. When this is the case, it may be possible to invite a few children each day to come back for some extra individualized help after lunch. This can provide enrichment for the good readers and invaluable assistance to those who are making slow progress.

GROUP INSTRUCTION IN THE FIRST GRADE

Every first-grade teacher becomes aware early in the year of marked differences in readiness and rate of learning to read. These differences can be dealt with in three main ways: (1) The oldest method is to teach all the children together as one large group. The fast learners are held down to the pace of the average. The slow learners either get progressively more and more completely lost or are given substantial amounts of extra teaching by the teacher or the parents; even with this extra help, many of them go through the lessons without building adequate skills. (2) The class is divided into groups, each group containing children of reasonably similar learning ability. The most common number of groups is three, although teachers sometimes find that a particular class may require four groups. The groups begin book reading at different times as they become ready, and progress at different rates of speed. Despite many difficulties that are encountered by teachers in group instruction, this is the most common procedure at present. (3) A highly individualized method is used in which the teacher has a short session with each child two or three times a week. This kind of procedure is discussed later in this chapter (see page 95) and in greater detail in Chapter 7.

Before either group or individual reading instruction can be undertaken, the children must learn to carry on a variety of activities in independent fashion without calling on the teacher for help. While this learning is going on, the teacher is conducting readiness activities and developing experience stories mainly with the class as a whole.

Early in the fall, considerable emphasis needs to be placed on helping children to learn to plan their activities and to work independently. Activities of a nonreading character that can be carried on while the teacher is with another reading group should be relatively quiet ones, such as painting at an easel, drawing with crayons, coloring, looking at library books, cutting pictures out of old magazines and mounting them, doing puzzles, playing quietly with a doll house and dolls, working on a special project, caring for pets and plants in the classroom, and so on. The need for walking quietly, speaking softly, and getting and putting away equipment without fuss can be discussed with the children and they can help to define their own rules of conduct.

During a large part of the first grade, most children are not capable of doing much reading by themselves. The teacher needs to guide the reading step by step. While she works with one group, the other groups usually engage in nonreading activities. As the year progresses, the highest group becomes able to do some reading without the teacher.

A one-week plan that is representative of successful group instruction in the first grade is shown in Fig. 9. There are three reading

Low Group (preprimer)	Middle Group (primer)	High Group (first reader)
MONDAY		
Nonreading activities	T Preparation of new story	Individualized silent reading in supplementary preprimers and primers.
T Preparation for new story	Cut pictures from old magazines for a picture dictionary	Continue reading. Draw a picture about an event in the story
Nonreading activities	Nonreading activities	T Preparation for a new story
Whole Class: Initial consonant f, auditory discrimination, listing words beginning with /f/, underlining the f. Teacher reads a story to class.		

TUESDAY

Nonreading activities	T Guided reading and discussion	Silent reading of story. When finished, supplementary reading or nonreading activities, continuing through second period
T Guided reading and discussion	Nonreading activities	
Cut pictures from magazines	Mount and paste pictures	T Discussion and oral rereading of story

Whole Class: Teacher reads a poem. Children recite poems and rhymes that they know. Children listen for words that rhyme.

WEDNESDAY

Nonreading activities	T Reread story Guided use of workbook	Workbook, followed by nonreading activities or supplementary reading
T Reread story Guided use of workbook	Duplicated seat-work to reinforce workbook	
Nonreading activities	Nonreading activities	T Check and discuss workbook Preparation for new story

Whole Class: Review f, introduce another initial consonant as on Monday. Choral reading of duplicated poem read on Tuesday, or one group dramatizes a story from their reader.

THURSDAY

Nonreading activities	T Preparation for new story	Silent reading of new story When finished, supplementary reading or nonreading activities
T Preparation for new story	Playing word games Nonreading activities	
Mount and paste pictures	Nonreading activities	T Discussion and oral rereading of story

Whole Class: Develop experience story about some new experience, practice reading it. Introduce another
consonant as on Monday.

	FRIDAY	
Nonreading activities	T Guided reading of new story	Workbook pages. When finished, play word games, supplementary
T Guided reading of new story	Labeling pictures for picture dictionary	reading, or non-reading activi-ties
Nonreading activities	Nonreading activities	T Check and discuss workbook Preparation for new story

Whole Class: Review the three initial consonants of the
week. Group dramatization of stories, or
teacher reads a story.

FIGURE 9. A three-group plan for the first grade. T indicates the group
with which the teacher is working. The three periods each day
are approximately 20 minutes each, and the whole-class period
varies between 15 and 30 minutes.

periods daily, of about 20 minutes each (this time allotment may
vary), and each group has at least one period with the teacher. The
low and middle groups generally engage in nonreading activities
when not with the teacher, although simple activities such as cutting
out and mounting pictures for a picture dictionary and playing simple
games with word cards can be used somewhat. With these groups the
regular sequence includes preparation, guided reading and rereading,
and guided workbook activity that involves practice on specific skills.
Phonic skills and enrichment activities are provided during the daily
whole-class activities.

The high group at this time (February or March) are capable of
some independence. They have reached the point where they can do
individualized silent reading in supplementary primers, easy first readers, and library books. After a preparatory session they can read

ahead silently without teacher guidance, and after the story has been discussed and reread they can use the workbook with only preliminary directions. Toward the end of the year, the middle group in an average class may also be able to function in this way.

The use of the whole-class period in this plan represents a departure from the plans in most teacher's manuals. Phonic principles are taught to the whole class together, partly for economy of teacher time and effort but mainly because the fact that a child learns words slowly by whole-word visual study does not necessarily mean that he will also be slow in learning to use phonic principles. Enrichment activities of various kinds are also planned largely on a whole-class basis because the usual alternative is to neglect them, particularly with the slower groups.

In addition to the regular groups, the teacher will find it necessary from time to time to bring together a few children who need extra instruction on some particular reading skill; these children may come from two or even three of the regular groups. Some children should be moved to faster or slower groups. When children have been absent because of illness they need some special attention to help them to catch up with the group. One or two children may find the pace of even the slowest group to be too fast for them. Group instruction needs to be supplemented with alertness to the special needs of individual children and resourcefulness in finding the time to give them special attention.

Additional suggestions about ways of making group instruction efficient are given in Chapter 7.

Alternative Approaches

A number of approaches to reading that differ markedly from the basal reader approach are currently being advocated. Although some programs are difficult to classify and there is considerable variation within an approach, these approaches fall into six broad categories: language-experience; phonics; linguistics; special alphabet; programmed materials; and individualized reading.

THE LANGUAGE-EXPERIENCE APPROACH

Many teachers like to introduce children to reading in the setting of a total experience in which reading is closely related to speaking, listening, and writing. The children participate in an experience which is highly interesting to them. Under the guidance of the teacher they discuss the experience and formulate a title and a series of sentences that summarize the experience to their satisfaction. They watch intently as the teacher writes their group composition on the chalkboard and listen attentively as the teacher reads it to them. The story may be used for reading instruction, as described below, or its use may stop when the teacher has read it to the children.

Almost any event in the lives of first graders can be made the basis of an experience story. Many stories tell about pets which live in the classroom or are brought in to visit: goldfish, turtles, a kitten, a puppy, a parakeet, rabbits, hamsters, etc. Birthdays are frequent, and holidays have their special appeal. Seeds are planted, sprout, and grow. Simple scientific experiments are tried. A trip to the local fire station may provide material for one story about plans for the trip, another about what happened on the trip, and a third summarizing what was learned on the trip.

During the prereading period the teacher may use experience stories as part of the readiness program, rather than as material for teaching reading. Discussion about what should go into the story provides practice in thinking, speaking, and listening. Children can be helped to formulate their ideas in complete sentences and to compare alternative statements to select the best one. The written record enhances the importance of the experience for the children and helps to crystallize new concepts and word meanings. As the teacher reads the story to the children, running her hand under each line from left to right as she does so, the children learn that each line says something definite, that the line is made up of separate words, and that the left-to-right sequence is important. Even though the teacher does not try to teach the recognition of specific words at this stage, some of the brighter children may be starting to identify a word here and there.

After reading instruction has been started, not all experience stories are suitable for use in teaching reading. Some charts that are excellent experience records, good for language development and for recording an event or summarizing an experience, are much too complicated for effective use as beginning reading material. Their vocabularies may include too many unfamiliar words and their sentences may be too long. Such charts are read to the children, but teaching the recognition of all the unknown words and phrases is not advisable.

When the teacher intends to use an experience story for reading instruction, an effort is made to keep the sentences short and to employ words that will appear in the preprimers and primers to be read later in the year. The experience story is composed by the children, with help from the teacher. The teacher uses manuscript printing to place it on the chalkboard, and reads it to the children in the usual way. Later (usually after school) the teacher prepares two or three copies. One of them is made on a large sheet of newsprint or ruled paper. A second copy is made on a fairly stiff paper such as oak tag, which can be cut into line strips, phrase cards, and single word cards. Some teachers like to make two oak tag copies, one for line strips and one for phrase and word cards.

Using the newsprint copy, mounted on an easel, the teacher reads the story to the group line by line, using her hand to swing under the words as she reads them. The teacher may read the story in this way two or three times. Then children are given a chance to volunteer to identify lines. Guiding questions are asked, such as: "Who can read the sentence that tells what kind of pet we have?" "Who can read the sentence that tells us what our pet's name is?" "Who can read the sentence that tells us what kind of noise he makes?" The child has to identify the sentence silently. He then comes up to the chart and "frames" the line with his hands or runs his hand under it as he recites from memory what the line says. Some of the children are beginning to identify separate words; others are noticing only the general characteristics of the lines, such as their varying length.

An oak tag copy of the chart is read aloud by the teacher, compared with the original, and cut into line strips as the children watch. Various activities can be carried on with the line strips. For example, the strips can be placed in random order along the chalkboard ledge. The teacher asks, "Who can find the strip that tells the name of our story?" The title strip is found, read, and placed on the top level of a pocket chart or flannel board. The other lines are similarly located, read aloud, and placed in position. Another procedure is to ask for the sentences in scrambled order. Or, the sentence strips can be matched to the corresponding lines in the complete copy.

The line strips, or another oak tag copy of the chart, can next be cut into phrase units of two or three words each, and these can be matched to the original, identified, read aloud, and arranged into sentences on the pocket chart. The phrase strips can be cut into separate words, and these can be assembled into phrases and sentences. New sentences can be made with them, as well as sentences duplicating the original chart story.

It is generally preferable to ask questions that require a little thinking than to tell the children exactly what is on the line, phrase, or word card and ask them to find it. Thus it is better to ask, "What line tells us how our kitten looks?" than to ask, "Who can find the line that says 'Our kitten is black and white'?" In answering the first type of question the children read to themselves and have to think about meaning. When they select the correct line they can be asked to read it out loud and the teacher can correct inaccuracies.

Sometimes it is desirable to have the experience chart illustrated. This should be done by the children rather than by the teacher. When the topic is favorable, each child can draw or paint his own illustration and the teacher or the group can decide which to place on the chart. When sufficient progress in writing has been made, the children can make their own copies of the story below their pictures, or the teacher can provide duplicated copies which they can paste below their pictures.

Experience stories are widely used today. Their first use is as a bridge between the prereading period and reading in preprimers. The teacher, having the list of all the words that occur in the preprimers to be used, makes an effort to include as many as possible of these words in the experience charts. The children who learn and remember words from experience stories are easily identified, and when the teacher has several such children, they are brought together as a group and are started on the first preprimer. Progress is enhanced because some of the words are already familiar.

Meanwhile the teacher continues with experience stories with the rest of the class, and also gives special practice to improve readiness. As additional children show that they are ready for formal reading lessons, another group is formed and started with the preprimer, until all have been launched on book reading.

Experience charts continue to be used as part of the reading program long after children are reading books. They may be of a narrative type, recording a sequence of events. They may be descriptive. They may summarize plans or record outcomes. They may be of very temporary interest, gone forever when the chalkboard is erased, or they may be bound and kept for later rereading. As children reach more mature levels of reading, experience charts become records of group planning and of group and individual compositions. The experience story can, then, be a useful part of the total reading program throughout the elementary school.

During the early 1960's the use of experience stories was expanded and renamed the language-experience approach. In this approach, emphasis is placed upon closely correlating reading with the other language arts. In the early stages the pupil-dictated stories, sometimes on an individual basis, are used as the reading materials.[11] As the child's sight vocabulary and reading skills progress, he may be placed in a more structured program such as a basal series, or into an individualized reading program.

Although some commercial material is available,[12] a great deal of

[11] Dorris M. Lee and R. V. Allen, *Learning to Read Through Experience* (New York: Appleton-Century-Crofts, 1963).

For suggestions on using the language-experience approach, refer to:

MaryAnne Hall, *Teaching Reading as a Language Experience* (Columbus: Charles E. Merrill, 1970).

For a discussion of its possible use with educationally disadvantaged children, see Blanche L. Serwer, "Linguistic Support for a Method of Teaching Beginning Reading to Black Children," *Reading Research Quarterly,* 4 (Summer 1969), 449–467.

[12] R. Van Allen, *Language Experiences in Reading* (Chicago: Encyclopedia Britannica, 1966).

teacher initiative and planning is necessary to implement the language-experience approach successfully. The classroom atmosphere must be conducive to the development and expression of language skills and the teacher must allocate time to record and reproduce the stories. Phonic and other word identification skills are introduced as the teacher perceives the need, with the words found in the stories being used to develop these skills. Therefore, the teacher must be perceptive, have knowledge of the skills that need to be taught and a sequence for teaching them, and must have the ability to organize as well as be well-organized. It is often difficult to achieve control of vocabulary and sentence structure without lessening the children's verbal enthusiasm, or without editing the verbal expressions as they come from the children, or the written material after the initial discussion. The acquisition of a sight vocabulary may be a problem for some children because the words are not repeated frequently enough to allow for learning and review.

PHONIC APPROACHES [13]

Phonic programs place emphasis on the decoding process (translating printed forms into their spoken counterparts) through the learning of symbol-sound associations and the application of phonic generalizations. They differ, however, on many important points such as whether instruction begins with consonants or vowels or a combination; whether to take short or long vowel sounds first; how many and which rules to teach; the sequence of skills; and when and how to introduce meaningful material. Programs that emphasize phonics vary greatly as to content and methodology.

Phonic programs are of three kinds: those intended for use before basal readers, those intended for use instead of basal readers, and

[13] *Phonetics* and *phonics* are two words that are often used interchangeably. *Phonetics* is the scientific study of speech sounds, including their pronunciation, the action of larynx, tongue, and lips in sound production, and the symbolization of sounds. *Phonics* is the study of the relationship of speech sounds (*phonemes*) to the printed or written symbols that represent them (*graphemes*) and their use in discovering the pronunciation of printed and written words; it is therefore the subdivision of phonetics that is most involved in reading.

those intended for use as a supplement to basal readers. They can also be divided according to the way in which sounds are studied. Most popular at present are the whole-word phonic procedures, in which attention is paid to the sounds within words, without sounding the words part by part. There are also advocates of synthetic phonic procedures, in which words are sounded letter by letter, or in phonic units, and the sounds are blended together. Often a combination of these approaches is used. Information about supplementary phonic programs will be found in pages 260–262. Three of the basal phonic programs are briefly described below.

The *Open Court Basic Reader* program has three foundation workbooks, readers for grades one through six, manuals, storybooks, and supplementary materials. They "serve two main purposes: (1) to teach children to read independently by the end of first grade, and (2) to provide selections of literary quality in the elementary grades." [14] Their foundation program has three stages and is designed for use in the first half of first grade or for remedial use. Stage one consists of teaching listening skills, letter names and writing letters. In stage two, sounds, blending techniques, and dictation skills are introduced and simple stories and poems composed of the sounds taught are read. The remaining sounds are introduced in stage three, so that by midyear, 43 sounds have been introduced. As shown partly in Figure 10, as each new sound is introduced, the child hears and says it, and sees and writes the corresponding grapheme.

The *Basic Reading* [15] program has texts from the preprimer through the eighth-reader level with accompanying manuals, workbooks, supplementary materials, and filmstrips. Although there is a heavy early concentration on phonic instruction (a new element is introduced in each lesson in the four grade-one books), the rate of introduction is not as pronounced as in the *Open Court* program. Like the *Open Court* program, there is little emphasis upon vocabulary control, the only restriction being that, in general, words containing a phonic element are not used in a story until that element has been introduced.

[14] Arther S. Trace and Nellie Thomas, *Teacher's Guide for Reading is Fun* (LaSalle, Ill.: Open Court Publishing Co., 1965), p. ix.
[15] *Lippincott's Basic Reading* (Philadelphia: Lippincott, 1969).

FIGURE 10. Page from a first reader-workbook, Reader 1:1:1. (From Hughes, Ann. *Learning to Read and Write.* Copyright © 1965 by Open Court Publishing Co., LaSalle, Ill.) Reduced in size. The original is in color. Reproduced by permission of the publishers. Children are to darken in the faint letters and words, sounding and blending them as they write.

FIGURE 11. A page from the second book of a phonic-linguistic series. (From McCracken, Glenn and Walcutt, Charles C., *Book B*, p. 24. Lippincott's Basic Reading. Philadelphia: J. B. Lippincott Co., 1969.) The original is in color. Reproduced by permission of the publishers.

Also, the story content tends to differ from that found in many basal readers. A sample page from this program is shown in Figure 11.

The *Phonetic Keys to Reading* [16] program has a manual and three books for first grade, a manual and two readers each for second and third grade, and a manual and reader for each of the intermediate grades. The latter, *Keys to Independence in Reading,* are continuations of the primary grade program. Workbooks and other materials are also available.

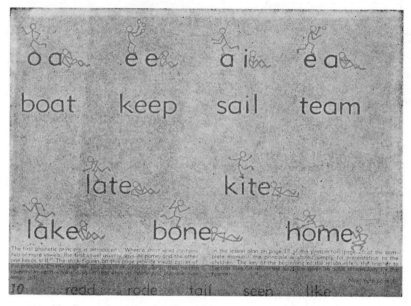

FIGURE 12. Page from an audio-readiness book and pre-primer. (From Harris, Creekmore, and Greenman, *Tag* Annotated Copy. Copyright © 1964 by Economy Co., Oklahoma City. Reduced in size. The original is in color. Reproduced by permission of the publishers.)

A distinctive feature of the programs is the emphasis placed upon phonetic analysis, which is essential to independence in reading and to the understanding of the relationship between language sounds and symbols.

[16] *Phonetic Keys to Reading: A Basic Reading Series* (Oklahoma City: Economy Co., 1964).

This systematic instructional program of the series develops audio-visual readiness for phonetic analysis and provides for the application of generalization in word perception [69 generalizations in the first three books; see Figure 12 for an illustrative page]. Early and sustained attention is also given to reinforcing skills of word perception: structural analysis (including syllabication, identification of compound words, contractions, and prefixes and suffixes), word configuration, and context for the verification of meaning.

From the beginning this program stresses the functions of words, phrases, and sentences in the reading process through activities which parallel those used in building the perceptual skills of reading. This is accomplished, first, through the use of simple experience stories and story charts to acquaint pupils with whole words and phrases and sentence units and, later, through discussion and comprehension exercises related to the reading of stories. Reading for meaning and the basic word-perception skills are developed simultaneously as a dual meaning-discrimination approach to the teaching of reading.[17]

Their recommended program for the first grade is organized as follows: (1) eight weeks of readiness work, emphasizing listening to sounds within words; two weeks with the phonic preprimer material; and two weeks reading the preprimers of regular basal reading series; (2) six weeks of instruction with the phonic primer, followed by six weeks of reading other primers; and (3) five weeks with the phonic first reader, followed by seven weeks of reading other first readers and supplementary materials. The readiness material starts with long vowels, then short vowels, then initial consonants; preprimer reading is started after all single letters have been introduced.

LINGUISTIC APPROACHES

Just as with the phonic approaches, all linguistic reading series place considerable importance on decoding in the initial stages of instruction. Although no two series agree very closely on details (in fact, linguists don't agree as to the contributions they might make to the

[17] Theodore L. Harris, Mildred Creekmore, and Margaret Greenman, *A Teacher's Manual for the First Grade* (Oklahoma City: Economy Co., 1964), p. 6.

teaching of reading), many do have features in common. Usually they: (1) start out with teaching letter names (not sounds); (2) tightly control the symbol-sound association of the letters used with each letter representing only one sound (except that some series introduce words such as "the" early in the program); (3) initially use three-letter (consonant-short vowel-consonant) words; (4) employ the principal of minimal variation (only one letter is different in two or more words being compared. See Figure 13 for an example); and (5) do not teach phonic generalizations (the child is to learn symbol-sound associations by inferring them from the tightly controlled letter-sound correspondence).

Other than the usual differences in content, linguistic series differ on such points as whether or not illustrations are used (some feel it may be distracting and that the child should not learn to rely upon picture clues; some illustrations have little to do with the sentences or "story") and the amount of practice given on particular elements, especially short vowels. It is difficult to classify some series; for example, some could be described as being phonic-linguistic.

SPECIAL ALPHABET APPROACHES

Because English has an imperfect and often arbitrary spelling system with many irregularities in the correspondences between letters and the sounds they represent, there have been, and continue to be, efforts to adopt an alphabet in which each symbol always represents the same sound, and each sound is signaled by only one symbol.

In the past decade, new reading and writing programs have been published that employ an alphabet with consistent sound-symbol relationships. These alphabets are used to develop initial reading skills, with a transition to use of the conventional alphabet (often referred to as "traditional orthography") coming later in the program. The best known of these alphabets is i/t/a (Initial Teaching Alphabet).[18] In i/t/a there is a separate symbol for each of 44 consonant and

---

[18] The Initial Teaching Alphabet is not a teaching approach but rather is an orthography, as shown by its use with both "whole-word" and "alphabet-phonic" methods.

The Nut in the Net

Peg the pig ran to a pit.

It was a big pit.

A nut was in it.

"I can get into the pit," said Peg.

"And I can get the nut."

But a net was in the pit.

"I can get the nut," said Peg.

Peg ran to get the nut.

Peg bit the nut.

14

FIGURE 13. A page from the second book in a linguistic series. (From Rasmussen, Donald, and Goldberg, Lenina. *A Hen in A Fox's Den*, p. 14. Basic Reading Series, Level B. Chicago: Science Research Associates, Inc. 1970. © 1964, 1965 by Donald E. Rasmussen and Lenina Goldberg. The original is in color. Reproduced by permission of the publishers.

vowel sounds, with many of the traditional letters retained, and the new symbols similar in design to the upper half of traditional letters to assist in the transition. Capitals are the same shape as lower-case symbols, only larger. A page from a program which employs i/t/a is shown in Figure 14.

There are other programs with different alphabet systems. One uses characters that can be read by a computer; another makes use of color cues in the initial stages by assigning one hue to all of the letter(s) that may represent a given sound. For example, the *ee* in *meat,* the *ea* in *meat,* and the *e* in *be* all would be printed in the same color.

PROGRAMMED APPROACHES

Programmed materials are constructed so that learning can take place in small steps, and so that the user obtains almost immediate feedback as to the correctness of his responses. Theoretically the child should be able to use the materials almost independently and proceed at as rapid a pace as his abilities will allow.

There are at least two series of programmed readers on the market, and a number of other programmed materials that are designed to be used with teaching machines. The programs that use consumable paper-covered books are primarily phonic/linguistic in method with the programming linear in nature; that is, each step is done in sequence without any deviations. A sample page from one of these series is shown in Figure 15. The left-hand margin which contains the correct answers is supposed to be covered with a marker, and after the child makes his response he slides the marker down to determine whether or not he made the correct response. The series from which this page was taken has 21 books and a set of accompanying "story" books that use the same vocabulary as the programmed reader.

More recently, there have been programs developed for computer-assisted beginning reading instruction. In one such program, the child views visual stimuli on a television-like screen and receives auditory stimuli via a tape recorder. When the ray from a light-pen used by the child touches the screen, the computer determines the correctness of the response. The program used is primarily linguistic and the pro-

"whot ʃhood wee næm mie
nue bruther?" hal askt.
"ie nœ a good næm,"
maggi sed. "mie dog'ꙅ næm
iꙅ spot. næm yoor bæby spot."

FIGURE 14. A page from Book 2, *A Game of Ball* (Spelled in i/t/a), p.
16. (From Tanyzer, Harold and Mazurkiewicz, Albert.
Early-to-Read i/t/a Program, Revised. New York: Initial
Teaching Alphabet Publications, Inc. 1966.) Reduced in size.
The original is in color. Reproduced by permission of the
publishers.

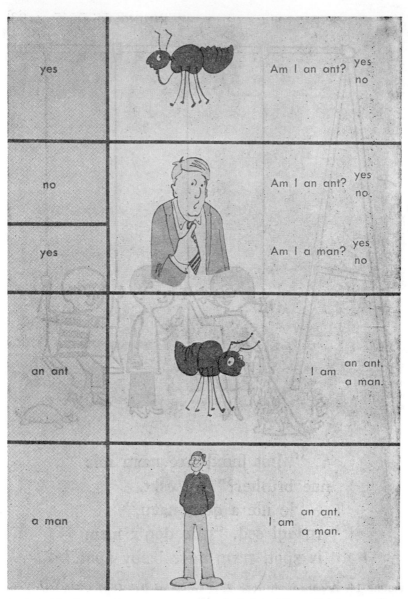

FIGURE 15. A page from a programmed reader. (From Buchanan, Cynthia D., Programmed Reading, Book 1, Revised, p. 3. New York: McGraw-Hill Book Co., 1968.) Reduced in size. The original is in color. Reproduced by permission of the publishers.

gramming is of the branching type (i.e., items can be skipped or repeated, or additional practice to overcome errors can be selected by the computer and presented to the child). There also has been some use made of so-called "talking typewriters" that are tied into a computer.

Rather than program the material, there have been some experiments in programming teaching by giving extremely specific directions on how to tutor a child individually.

Future developments in programmed and computerized programs should be watched carefully because of their potential for individualized instruction. However, it is still too soon to judge their success and feasability.

INDIVIDUALIZED READING IN THE FIRST GRADE

Of all the grades in which a highly individualized method of teaching reading might be tried, the first grade would seem to be the least suitable. The children are young and immature. They are not able to continue with independent work or play for as long periods as when they get older. During much of the year they need help with each new word that they meet, and they are dependent on the teacher for guidance and direction.

Nevertheless, beginning reading has been successfully taught by individualized methods in a few schools. Despite the enthusiasm of some first-grade teachers who have written up their experiences, an individualized program makes more sense after children become capable of doing genuinely independent reading than it does in beginning reading. There is no experimental evidence that individualized reading produces better than average results in the first grade, and it would seem to require an experienced teacher of superior resourcefulness to make it work in that grade. The techniques of individualized reading are described in Chapter 7.

Which Approach Is Best?

The question "Which approach is best?" is frequently asked. There has been much controversy regarding the code emphasis versus the meaning emphasis. In 1964–65 the U.S. Office of Education sponsored 27 coordinated studies in which a variety of programs using differing approaches were compared. The fifteen studies that had overlapping methods and representative populations had their results combined by a coordinating center. Among the more significant findings reported by the coordinating center were:

1. . . . It is likely that Basal programs should develop a more intensive word study skills element, while programs which put major emphasis on word recognition should increase attention paid to other reading skills.
2. Reading programs are not equally effective in all situations. Evidently factors other than method, within a particular learning situation, influence pupil success in reading.
3. . . . The tremendous range among classrooms within any method [Wide differences in achievement were obtained by teachers supposedly employing the same program] points out the importance of elements in the learning situation over and above the methods employed. To improve reading instruction it is necessary to train better teachers of reading rather than to expect a panacea in the form of materials.
4. Children learn to read by a variety of materials and methods . . . Furthermore, pupils experienced difficulty in each of the programs utilized. No one approach is so distinctly better in all situations and respects than the others that it should be considered the best method and the one to be used exclusively.[19]

The last finding was confirmed by five of the six studies in which the children were followed through the third grade.

It therefore would appear that there is no great inherent advantage in favor of any one method. There is evidence, however, that the qualities of the community, of the school, of the teacher, and of the children do influence reading achievement.

Every method of teaching reading that has been developed has worked better with some children than with others, and this is not entirely a matter of differences in general intelligence. Among retarded readers it has been demonstrated that some learn most easily

[19] Guy L. Bond and Robert Dykstra, *Coordinating Center for First-Grade Reading Instruction Programs,* Final Report, Project No. X-001 (Minneapolis: University of Minnesota, February, 1967).

with a visual approach, some with a phonic approach, some with an approach that emphasizes tracing and writing, and some with a combination method. It is not unreasonable to suppose that among children who do learn to read fairly well some can learn more quickly and easily with one approach and others with different approaches. This has yet to be demonstrated by research.

It may be, then, that the ideal method of the future will not be one method used with all pupils, but rather a flexible use of a variety of procedures, each used with the children it fits best. At present many teachers find it challenging enough to use one method with varying rates of progress. To discover the best method for each child and to use several approaches, each at a varying rate, seems to be beyond what many first-grade teachers feel able to do at present. But this kind of individualization, rather than the selection of one method best for everyone, may prove to be the only way to help every child to learn to read as well as his abilities allow. The alternative is to employ a method which gives balanced attention to decoding and to comprehension from the start, and that teaches children to use visual, auditory, and kinesthetic cues in combination with meaningful context in solving new words. Such an alternative may come closest to giving each child kinds of cues that he can employ successfully.

Summary

1. There is no exact point at which prereading readiness ends and systematic reading instruction begins. Some readiness activities may continue after formal reading instruction is begun.
2. The transition from readiness to reading instruction can take place easily and naturally.
   a. During the readiness period the use of labels, signs, name cards, notices, etc., can introduce children to the communicative function of reading.
   b. Experience stories provide a natural bridge between readiness and book reading. Stories composed by the children with the help of the teacher can be used to develop language skills or as material for reading instruction.

    c. As children show readiness by learning and remembering written words, they are usually started in groups on a systematic reading program.

3. The history of the teaching of beginning reading shows a succession of approaches, each aimed at correcting a deficiency of its predecessor and each in turn supplanted as its own defects became evident.

4. Approaches to teaching beginning reading differ mainly in the emphasis placed on decoding as opposed to obtaining meaning, and in the manner in which a child is taught to recognize words.

5. Most schools in the United States depend mainly on a set of basal readers for teaching beginning reading.

    a. Preprimers, primers, first readers, and accessory materials are used with detailed teaching plans given in the teacher's manuals.

    b. There is general agreement that reading lessons with basal readers should include preparation, guided reading and rereading, the teaching of specific skills, and provisions for supplementary enrichment.

    c. Although basal reader series differ on many details, they attempt to provide a reading program with balance: balanced attention to decoding and comprehension, to skills development and the cultivation of interest, to silent and oral reading, etc.

    d. The most recently published basal reader programs introduce phonic skills earlier and more intensively than in past editions, employ richer vocabularies, use more varied and natural language, and contain selections that reflect cultural and ethnic pluralism.

    e. Teachers vary greatly in the closeness with which they follow the lesson plans given in the manuals, with the more experienced, perceptive teacher being selective in attempting to meet individual needs.

    f. The use of one series as basal should be supplemented by extensive reading in library books and in the materials of other series.

g. A good basal reading program in the first grade requires a time allotment of at least 90 minutes a day.

6. The usual way to adapt instruction to meet individual differences is by dividing the class into groups.

   a. In the first grade, most reading activities require direct guidance by the teacher.

   b. Group activities can be combined with whole-class activities and need to be supplemented by special attention to the needs of individual children.

7. There are numerous alternative ways of teaching beginning reading. In addition to basal approaches, there are the language-experience approach, phonic approaches, linguistic approaches, special alphabet approaches, programmed and computer-assisted approaches, and individualized reading.

8. There is no one program or approach that has proven to be distinctly better in all situations and respects.

   a. Teachers supposedly using the same program obtain greatly different results.

   b. There are children who are successful, and others who fail to learn to read, in every approach.

9. Probably the ideal method of the future will not be the same for every child, but will involve helping each child to learn by the particular procedures that are easiest and most successful for him. Meanwhile a balanced, varied approach seems more likely to give every child a chance to learn than an approach that expects all children to learn in the same way.

Recommended Reading

BEERY, ALTHEA, BARRETT, THOMAS C., and POWELL, WILLIAM R. *Elementary Reading Instruction: Selected Materials.* Boston: Allyn and Bacon, Inc., 1969. Ch. 10.

DURKIN, DOLORES. *Teaching Them to Read.* Boston: Allyn and Bacon, Inc., 1970. Ch. 9.

HEILMAN, ARTHUR W. *Principles and Practices of Teaching Reading,* 2nd ed. Columbus: Charles E. Merrill, 1967. Chs. 3–5.

KERFOOT, JAMES E., ED. *First Grade Reading Programs,* Perspectives in Reading No. 5. Newark, Del.: International Reading Association, 1965.

SPACHE, GEORGE D., and SPACHE, EVELYN B. *Reading in the Elementary School*, 2nd ed. Boston: Allyn and Bacon, Inc., 1969. Chs. 3–6.

TINKER, MILES A., and MCCULLOUGH, CONSTANCE M. *Teaching Elementary Reading*, 3rd ed. New York: Appleton-Century-Crofts, 1968. Chs. 20–21.

VILSCEK, ELAINE C., ED. *A Decade of Innovations: Approaches to Beginning Reading*, Conference Proceedings, Vol. 12, Part 3. Newark, Del.: International Reading Association, 1968.

WITTICK, MILDRED L. "Innovations in Reading Instruction: For Beginners," *Innovation and Change in Reading Instruction*, 67th Yearbook of the National Society for the Study of Education, Part II. Chicago: University of Chicago Press, 1968. Ch. 3.

4

Reading in Grades Two and Three

The second and third grades are vitally important in the total reading program because during these years opportunities are provided for continuing rapid progress in all important basic reading skills. So that by the end of the primary grades, most children have developed the word recognition, word analysis, vocabulary, and comprehension skills that allow them to read well orally and silently from their reading books, simple textbooks and reference materials, and a wide variety of library books.

In these grades, developmental reading lessons using basal readers still form the major part of the instructional program in reading, although both functional reading and recreational reading increase in importance. As in the first grade, the class is usually divided into groups progressing at different rates and using materials of different levels of difficulty. Developmental reading tends to occupy a larger part of the school day than any other part of the curriculum, averaging about an hour and a half a day.

It is a great mistake to assume that all the children coming into the second grade are ready for what have come to be considered second-grade reading activities. In some schools children are promoted from first to second grade with little regard to their acquisition of reading skills. In these schools, second-grade teachers may not only find children who are at various levels of first-grade reading, but may even find some who have not yet started to read. With these children the second-grade teacher must be prepared to carry on first-grade reading activities. If the school system has a minimum standard of reading proficiency for promotion, it is usually placed at successful completion of primer reading, so that even the teachers in these systems must expect to have several children who need to begin at first-reader level.

There are some schools in which the first-grade teachers are encouraged to move slowly and gradually in reading, so that at the end of the year only a few children have progressed beyond primer reading. The second-grade teachers in those schools start at various levels of first-grade reading with most children.

At the beginning of the third grade, the range of differences in reading ability is wider than at the beginning of the second grade. Some of the entering third graders can already read successfully at fourth-reader level or even higher. A substantial group is likely to need additional work at second-reader level. Depending on the school's policies about promotion and pupil classification, and possibly other factors, there may or may not be some children whose reading skills are at or below first-reader level.

A successful reading program starts where the children are and gives every child maximum opportunities to develop in reading. When teachers come close to this ideal, the rapid progress made by the fastest learners widens still more the distance between their skills and those of their most limited classmates. Relatively uniform progress tends to signify a program which fails to meet the needs of the most competent learners.

The Developmental Reading Program

BASAL READING MATERIALS

It has become customary for a basal reader series to have two readers for the second grade and two for the third grade. Colorful covers and the colored illustrations on most pages make the books visually attractive, but the role of the illustrations has changed; they now illustrate events in a story that is complete without them, while in much first-grade material the pictures tell a major part of the story. The content is increasingly varied. In some readers the stories are all new material written especially for the book. In others, a major part of the material consists of stories (and poems) by well-known children's authors. Many of the stories are previously published selections that have been shortened and simplified. The characters change from story to story. The stories are usually grouped in a number of units each of which has a central theme. Units that occur in several second-grade readers include life in a city, life in the country, realistic animal stories, fanciful talking animal stories, folk and fairy tales, and humorous tales. Each set of readers is, naturally, somewhat different in content from any of the others.

Basal readers for the third grade tend to get away from the "here and now" emphasis that characterizes first-grade readers and, to a lesser extent, second-grade readers also. Stories tend to have varied settings. Animal stories, humorous stories, and folk and fairy tales remain popular. The length of stories gradually increases and plot complexities tend to get more involved in each successive book.

The reading vocabulary continues to be controlled in the second and third readers, although to a lesser extent than in the first-grade texts. There are wide variations among the basal series as to the number of new words introduced at each level, and in the cumulative total vocabulary. It is difficult to make direct comparison as to vocabulary load between series because some consider derived forms (e.g., adding or dropping -ing, -ed, plural forms) as "new" words; others do not. There is a trend to classify the vocabulary in different ways. For example, one series has Developmental Words—words that are used in the development of words-analysis skills or words that should be taught as wholes because they are unsuited for analysis; Skills Practice Words—words that many pupils will be able to identify with word-analysis skills that they have developed by that time, but for which other pupils will require additional supervised skills practice; and, Assumed Words—words that pupils are expected to identify independently with skills that have become well established. Another series has Basic Words—words that many children will be unable to identify independently; Phonic Sets Words—words derived phonically from a known basic word by substitution or addition of initial or final consonants, consonant blends, or consonant digraphs; and Enrichment Words—words that have limited use, but are interesting and meaningful, and needed at times to improve readability and story comprehension.

The size of the vocabulary is only one of the factors that determine the difficulty of a reader. For one thing, the number of pages varies. If a series has a total of only 349 new words in its second readers and has only 378 pages in the two books, while another series with 544 new words has a total of 502 pages, the two vary only slightly from an average of one new word per page. In addition, there is substantial variation in the amount of print per page; some readers use lines of irregular length, always stopping at the end of a phrase, while others set their material in solid paragraph form. If one series has much more material per page than another series, it may be actually easier when the criterion is the ratio of new words to total running words.

Difficulty involves other factors besides the rate of introducing new words. Words which have unfamiliar meanings are harder to learn than familiar spoken words whose printed forms are new. Difficulty depends in part on the sentence structure, the complexity of the plot, and the sheer length of the story. The familiarity or strangeness of the environment in which the action is set and of the activities in which the characters engage is also significant. It is, therefore, not easy to judge the relative difficulty of two sets of readers. A series may be easier or harder, depending on the backgrounds of the children who use it.

The usual accompanying materials include a manual for the teacher and a workbook for each basal reader. Supplementary materials vary and may include a parallel set of readers, separate paperbound stories, correlated sets of language, spelling, arithmetic, science, or social studies, filmstrips and duplicating masters. Some series have "transition" books which can be used with the children who are not quite ready to learn the skills in the next higher basal reader.

BASAL READER METHODOLOGY

The general plan followed in most manuals that accompany basal readers for the second and third grades is similar to that used with first-grade readers. The four main parts of the plan are, as before: (1) preparation for reading the story; (2) guided reading and re-reading, including discussion and interpretation of meaning; (3) teaching related basic reading skills; and (4) enrichment activities. In recognition of the greater maturity of the children's reading and thinking skills, preparation tends to be briefer than with first-grade materials, and reading and discussing is usually done in units of at least a page at a time, sometimes several pages. The reading skills to be taught and the enrichment activities also change in harmony with the development of the children.

SAMPLE LESSONS FROM TWO SECOND READERS

In *Enchanted Gates*,[1] a 2^1 reader, a story entitled "The Rocket Ride" occupies pages 129–133. In the five pages there are five pictures, each taking about a third of a page. The story tells about using monkeys to test the feasibility of rocket rides through space for man.

The manual devotes approximately eleven pages to the lesson which is summarized as follows:

Preparation. First, the preceding story that supplied background information is reviewed. Next, six words are introduced in a list and in printed sentences and the children are asked to pronounce the new words (using contextual and phonic cues) and tell how they recognized the word. This is optionally followed by a practice exercise (reproduced from the manual or from a duplicating master) with the new vocabulary, and pages in the workbook that prepare the children for the story.

Reading the Story. The title is first read and the illustration discussed. Then a motivating question is presented by the teacher and

[1] Albert J. Harris and Mae Knight Clark. *Enchanted Gates* (New York: Macmillan, 1970). Copyright © 1970 by the Macmillan Company, New York.

after the children read the entire story silently, the motivating question is discussed. Next, there is guided oral rereading for developing specific skills such as recognizing emotional reactions, seeing cause and effect relationships, and making inferences. The suggested questions for page 129 which is shown in Figure 16 are: "What part of the rocket is shown in the picture?" . . . "Did Miss Baker and Able know each other?" . . . "Find and read the sentence that proves that your answer is right." . . . "Read the sentence that tells how the monkeys felt as they waited for the countdown." . . . "How do you think you would feel if you were in the nose cone?" . . . "Read the part that tells about the countdown and blast-off." . . . "Why do you think this signal is called a countdown?" . . . "Do you think the monkeys might have been afraid when they took off?" . . . "Why?"

Follow-Up. The skills taught in the lesson are reinforced with a practice exercise (reproduced from the manual) and workbook pages. Next there are teacher-directed activities that involve recognizing the word part *ad,* seeing the relationship between certain words (e.g., astronaut—rocket, pool—water), reviewing short and long vowel sounds, and recalling the stories in the chapter. This is followed by suggestions on providing for individual differences. Finally, related activities involving a research project, art, role playing, poetry, stories, and music are suggested.

In a 2^1 reader of a different basal series,[2] a story entitled "Jeff's Neighbors" appears on pages 135–140. On these six pages, there are four pictures, each taking about one-third to one-half a page. The story concerns two boys who decide to feed some wild animals during the winter.

The manual devotes approximately six pages to the lesson (it is suggested that the lesson cover two days, with oral reading beginning on the second day), which is summarized as follows:

Preparation for Reading. Old and new concepts are identified through discussion, and old vocabulary is reviewed by presenting the words in sentences. This is followed by an exercise in phrase reading.

[2] William D. Sheldon and Mary C. Austin, *Fields and Fences* (Boston: Allyn and Bacon, Inc., 1968). Copyright © 1968 by Allyn and Bacon, Inc.

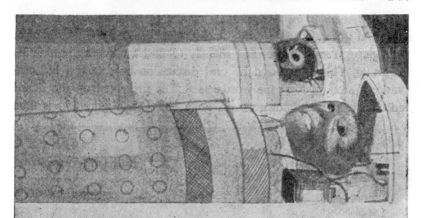

The Rocket Ride

The big day came. The men took
Miss Baker to the rocket. There she saw
the monkey that was to go with her. It was
the first time she had seen this monkey.
Its name was Able.
 Able and Miss Baker were put
into the nose cone of a rocket. They
were not afraid. They did just what
they had learned to do.
 The time for the countdown came. Ten,
nine, eight, seven, six, five, four, three,
two, one, zero! There was a big, big noise and
a very bright light. The blast-off had come!
The rocket was up and away!

FIGURE 16. Page from a second reader (2¹). (From Harris, Albert J. and Clark, Mae Knight, *Enchanted Gates,* Revised Edition. Copyright © 1970 by the Macmillan Company, New York.) Reduced in size. The original is in color. Reproduced by permission of the publishers.

Development of new vocabulary and silent reading. The children are asked to read the story title and to tell who Jeff's neighbors are. Then pages 135–136 are read silently to find out what the animals are doing. This is followed by oral discussion based upon the motivation question. Next the word "seeds" is presented on the board and compared with known words. Page 137 (See Figure 17) is then

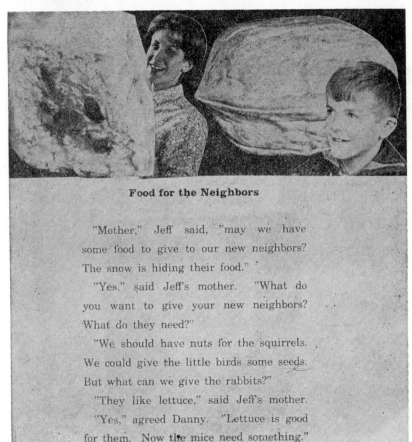

Food for the Neighbors

"Mother," Jeff said, "may we have some food to give to our new neighbors? The snow is hiding their food."

"Yes," said Jeff's mother. "What do you want to give your new neighbors? What do they need?"

"We should have nuts for the squirrels. We could give the little birds some seeds. But what can we give the rabbits?"

"They like lettuce," said Jeff's mother.

"Yes," agreed Danny. "Lettuce is good for them. Now the mice need something."

FIGURE 17. Page from a second reader (2¹). (From Sheldon, William D. and Mary C. Austin, *Fields and Fences*, p. 137. © Copyright 1968 by Allyn and Bacon, Inc., Boston.) Reduced in size. The original is in color. Reproduced by permission of the publishers.

read silently and followed up with a discussion (ten questions are suggested in the manual).

Oral reading. The children are asked to reread the story quickly to find five different sentences that contain certain punctuation marks. These sentences are copied and then read by children with the proper expression.

Developing comprehension and study skills. Eight sentences about the story are placed on the board, and the children are to indicate on paper whether each sentence is true or false.

Developing word recognition and vocabulary skills. The sound represented by "eigh," the generalization concerning doubling the final consonant before adding -*ed* and -*ing,* and contractions are reviewed.

Activity book. Suggestions are given for using the accompanying six pages in the workbook.

Independent activities. An exercise on developing the use of context clues is presented.

Extension of experiences. Suggestions are made for using related basal reader stories, library books, poetry, and audio-visual materials.

COMMENTS ON BASAL READER METHOD

At these grade levels, manuals for teachers are by no means alike. In contrast to the very detailed plans described above, some manuals give a general plan for the story and leave it to the teacher to work out the details. Some give separate plans for fast, average, and slow groups. Some reproduce the pupil's page with directions for instruction below, some are separate paper-bound books, some are bound with the reader in one cover as a teacher's edition.

Usually, however, the manual has a rich variety of activities to suggest for each story. If all of these were to be carried out for each story, progress through the reader would be slow indeed. It is up to the teacher, therefore, to be intelligently selective. Preparation can often be shortened, especially with the better readers. Not all of the comprehension questions have to be asked. Discussion of implications for conduct and of ethical issues arising from the story is desirable but not essential. Enrichment activities can be curtailed.

Of the various kinds of activities, the ones that deserve most faithful adherence at second- and third-reader levels are those concerned with the development of independence in word attack. In typical basal reader systems, training for independence in word recognition is developed in a careful, sequential way, with the major portion to be taught at the first- and second-reader levels or the second- and third-reader levels. If the manual suggestions are carried out, most children steadily improve in their ability to attack new words successfully.

There has been a good deal of criticism of basal reader methodology. Much of this has been stimulated, ironically enough, by teachers who have treated the readers as storybooks and have paid little attention to the plans in the manual. Under the pressure of trying to complete a book within a given period of time, some teachers have used the suggestions about preparation and guided reading, and then have gone on to the next story without teaching the related skills. Such teaching gives some slight basis in fact to the generally unfounded assertion that basal reader systems do not teach phonics.

PROVIDING FOR INDIVIDUAL DIFFERENCES

The most usual way of adapting reading instruction to individual differences in the second and third grades is by grouping. As in the first grade, the most frequent number of groups is three, but some classes can function well with two groups and other classes contain such a wide range of reading abilities that four groups are needed.

The primary basis for grouping is in terms of the reader which the child is ready to use. Thus at the beginning of the second grade a teacher with a bright class may need only two groups, one for those who are ready for a second reader and the other a smaller group at first-reader level. Another teacher, however, may need three groups at first-grade levels (preprimer, primer, first reader) as well as a group at second-reader level. As the year progresses it is usually necessary to do some reorganization of the groups, and it may be advisable to make a separate group for those reading well above grade level.

In addition to the main grouping based on reader level, many teachers set up temporary groups on the basis of need for extra help in a particular skill. Thus a group of children who need practice in reading orally with expression may include children from all the groups. Such a group may need to meet only a few times, and is then replaced by another group with a different need. Still other kinds of grouping are possible in recreational reading and functional reading. The efficient use of groups is discussed in detail in Chapter 7.

INDEPENDENT READING

By the time they are ready for instruction in second readers, children are capable of doing independent reading for pleasure. In addition to primers and first readers of other basal series, there is an ever-growing number of library books that can be successfully read by children with no more than beginning second-reader ability or even lower. As children progress through second and third readers, the reading matter they can cope with continues to expand in variety and interest.

The child who reads extensively is improving his reading skills in the most natural way possible. By doing a large amount of easy reading, he builds speed of word and phrase recognition and becomes a fluent reader. When he tackles a book that is somewhat challenging, he acquires new ideas and concepts, and is stimulated to think and reason.

Independent reading should, therefore, be considered an important part of the total reading program. Suitable materials for it need to be provided. A central library in the school, with a person trained in library work in charge, is a valuable asset. Each classroom should have its own library collection of at least fifty books, varying widely in difficulty, in style, and in content. Time for independent reading should be a definite part of the reading schedule, and many different ways of arousing and stimulating interest in independent reading are available to the teacher. These issues are considered in greater detail in Chapter 13.

Independent reading allows children to read in a highly individualized way. Each child can set his own pace, select his own reading material, and go through it at his own rate. Independent reading helps to correct for the crudities of grouping, in which the best readers in a group may experience little challenge and the poorest in the group may have to exert strenuous effort just to keep up.

PLANNING THE READING PROGRAM

As compared to the first grade, group management is somewhat easier in the second and third grades. The children are more mature and have greater attention spans, so that group sessions can be longer. Children are more self-reliant and need less frequent assistance from the teacher, both in reading and in nonreading activities. While the teacher works with one group, other groups may be able to carry on with their reading activities. It is not necessary that the teacher work with each group every day, and time allotments for independent reading can be increased. Some group activities can be carried on with a pupil leader taking the role of the teacher. Temporary special groups can be set up. On some activities, such as reviewing new words, playing reading games, and checking written work, children can work together in pairs or in small groups of three to six. The program can, therefore, be somewhat more varied and flexible than in the first grade.

A SAMPLE PROGRAM FOR ONE WEEK

A generalized plan for one week is shown in Figure 18. This plan includes the developmental and recreational reading activities, but not the functional reading. Systematic instruction with basal readers on a three-group basis is scheduled three times a week. On the other two days there are provisions for a library visit, independent reading, work with a special group, help to individual children, and individual teacher-pupil conferences.

In the group instruction a systematic sequence is followed. In all groups there is preparation for each new story. In the low group the first reading is under direct teacher guidance as in the first grade, while in the other two groups the first reading is done silently without the teacher. Workbook practice pages are done without the teacher, but are checked by the teacher at the earliest opportunity. Teaching of related skills and oral rereading are provided regularly for each group. While the teacher is working with one group, the other groups have a sequence of assignments so that when they finish the first one there are other jobs to be done. Nonreading activities of various kinds can be used to fill out the group time. Dramatization of a story, shown for only the high group, should be done at times with all groups.

On most days there is some kind of whole-class reading activity. Seven different kinds of whole-class activity are listed in the plan, and these do not exhaust the possibilities.

This kind of plan, combining systematic, sequential instruction by groups with a substantial amount of independent reading, and including whole-class activities and provisions for working individually with children, is recommended as preferable to plans which involve nothing but reading by groups, on the one hand, or plans which rely mainly on independent reading without a planned, sequential program in skills.

Of course, a general plan like that in Figure 18 can be modified in many ways. One way is to combine the middle and upper groups, with the superior readers finishing group assignments quickly and having more time for independent reading. It may seem necessary to work with the slowest group every day. With a generally slow class, a plan more like a first-grade plan (see Fig. 9) may be necessary. With any generalized plan of this kind, it takes careful and conscientious preparation to fit in all of the needed activities and to keep them running smoothly.

It is not necessary to have all group reading sessions exactly equal in length, but most of them will take about 30 minutes. This means that following a plan such as has just been described requires between an hour and a half and two hours a day. Considering the central importance of reading improvement in these grades to provide a foundation for the heavy reading requirements of the later grades, such a time allotment is not excessive. Skimping on time for reading instruction in the primary grades creates trouble later.

Low Group (1^2 Reader)	Middle Group (2^1 Reader)	High Group (2^2 Reader)

Whole class: Directions and assignments for each group, each day (5-10 min.)

MONDAY

Low Group	Middle Group	High Group
T Preparation for new story Guided reading and discussion	Silent reading of new story (preparation on Friday) Related workbook pages	Silent reading of new story (preparation on Friday) Related workbook pages Draw an illustration for the story
Related workbook Draw illustration of story	T Discussion and oral rereading Check workbooks	Independent reading
Make word cards for new words Study and write words	Draw illustration of story Make word cards Independent reading or nonreading activity	T Discussion and oral rereading Check workbooks Preparation for new story

Whole class: Weekly newspaper

TUESDAY

Whole class: Visit to school library
    Preparation: Discussion of behavior, book selections, etc. (10 min.)
    Visit: Librarian tells or reads story. Children select books to take back to class, librarian and teacher helping (45 min.)

Individualized help for absentees and others. Rest of class read library books.

WEDNESDAY

Low Group	Middle Group	High Group
T Related skills Check workbook Oral rereading of selected parts	Independent reading or nonreading activity	Plan dramatization of story with group chairman Rehearse with characters reading their parts orally
Play reading games	T Related skills (phonics, etc.)	

114

Independent read-   Preparation for
ing   new story
Nonreading
activity
                     Silent reading of   T Discuss dramati-
                     new story   zation
                     Related workbook   Related skills
                     pages   Preparation for
                                         new story

Whole class: Phonics review (10-15 min.)

THURSDAY

Teacher works with one group organized according to a special need (phonics, oral expression, etc.). Rest of class
does independent reading. After group lesson teacher has
brief conferences with a few children individually (60
min.).

Whole class: Showing of a filmstrip related to reading program, discussion
Audience reading of favorite parts of library
books
One group presents dramatization of a story

FRIDAY

T Preparation for   Draw illustration   Silent reading
new story   of story   of new story
Guided reading   Make word cards   Related workbook
and discussion   Independent   pages
                     reading or non-   Draw an illus-
                     reading activity   tration for the
                                         story
                                         Independent read-
                                         ing or nonread-
                                         ing activity

Related workbook   T Discussion and
Draw illustra-   oral rereading
tion of story   Check workbooks

Make new word   Make and study   T Discussion and
cards   word cards   oral rereading
Study and write   Independent read-   Check workbooks
words   ing or nonreading   Preparation for
Nonreading   activity   new story
activity

Whole class: choral reading of a poem

FIGURE 18. A three-group plan for the second grade. T indicates the group
with which the teacher is working.

115

Some Special Issues

SILENT READING IN THE PRIMARY GRADES

When children begin to read, many of them find it very difficult to read silently and they mumble or read orally very quietly instead. The printed word is learned through association with the memory traces of the spoken word and its meaning. Actually saying the word helps some children to make this association. It is a mistake to try to get these children to do really silent reading before they have achieved some security in word recognition. The transition from quiet oral reading, to silent reading with observable lip movements, to silent reading without lip movements, does not have to be made by all children at the same time.

By the time children can handle second-reader material they should be able to read without any sound, and lip movements can usually be given up by children at third-reader level, if not before. All that is usually necessary is to suggest to a child that he is now ready to read in a more grown-up fashion, without pronouncing the words or moving his lips. If this does not work, it is wise to wait a few weeks and try again.

The issue of finger-pointing also should not be stressed too early. For some children, pointing to each word with a finger helps them to keep the place; without it, their eyes roam around the page. Pointing is a real aid to these children and if we insist that they stop it we may interfere with their progress. Children who like to point should be allowed to do so through first-grade reading. A transitional technique is the use of a card as a marker, to be placed under each line in turn. First-grade teachers often follow the advice of teacher's manuals and require children to give up pointing and to use a marker instead as early as preprimer reading. That is much too early. The children who persist in pointing usually do so because it helps them to keep the place. As with lip movements, the use of pointing or a marker can usually be stopped safely when children are reading at second- or third-reader level, if the child has not already stopped by himself. The need to do this earlier has been exaggerated by some writers.

Teachers should watch for deviations from good habits when children are reading silently. The book should always be held approximately 12 to 18 inches from the eyes, except for extremely nearsighted children. Children who get very close to the book, or who tend to read with the head tilted to one side, may show a need for an eye examination. Moving the head as well as the eyes should be gently discouraged. Proper reading posture involves sitting with a reasonably straight back, with the book either flat on the desk or table or held in a nearly vertical position.

Eye Movements. While in general primary-grade teachers need not pay much attention to children's eye movements in reading, when a child is found to read extremely slowly, observation of his eye movements may disclose a particular difficulty that can be corrected. To observe a child's eye movements, the simplest procedure is to have him stand facing you and hold the book a little below eye level as he reads silently. The teacher, seated in a chair, is able to observe the child's eyes over the top of the book. If it is impossible to discern separate fixations, the child is not seeing words as wholes, and some training with flash cards to improve ability to recognize words as units may be helpful. Inability to go from the end of one line to the beginning of the next in one quick sweep is another easily observed difficulty for which specific practice can be helpful.

ORAL READING IN THE PRIMARY GRADES

Oral reading is a quite important part of the primary-grade reading program. It contributes to the child's development in many ways. (1) Oral reading performance gives the teacher a quick and accurate way of appraising certain important reading skills, such as word recognition and phrasing, and to note specific words and word recognition techniques on which help is needed. (2) Oral reading helps in the development of good speech practices, and through oral reading one can carry on a good deal of effective speech improvement. (3) Oral reading provides the audience with practice in listening skill. (4) Oral reading gives the reader practice in communicating to a group. (5) Oral reading is an effective vehicle for dramatizing stories.

(6) Oral reading is one of the activities in which personality characteristics such as shyness and embarrassment are clearly evident, and a medium in which a sensitive teacher can help children toward better social adjustment. An insecure child should not be forced to read in front of a group. A shy child with adequate reading ability can be helped to make the transition by having him read parts, behind a screen, for a puppet or shadow play.

In the usual pattern of developmental reading lessons, children read the selection silently before they are asked to reread part of it orally. This gives them the opportunity to concentrate on getting meanings, and when necessary to stop to figure out a word or to correct a mistake without embarrassment. The oral reading after silent reading tends to be more accurate, more fluent, and more expressive than if it were the first reading.

There are some situations, however, in which oral reading first may be desirable. When the teacher wants to get a clear picture of the child's word recognition skills and asks him to read a fairly long selection in private, it is desirable to get all the errors that the child makes in his first reading. Unrehearsed oral reading is useful, therefore, in diagnosis. In helping a child who makes many errors in oral reading, mistakes can be detected and corrected immediately if the first reading is oral, while they often go undetected and uncorrected in silent reading. A group of children who are fluent readers will sometimes enjoy reading ahead at sight as a pleasant variation from the usual procedure. The rule "silent reading before oral" does not always fit the objectives of a particular reading lesson.

Oral reading in the primary grades can be undertaken for a variety of purposes.

1. *Individual reading to the teacher.* It is desirable to have a diagnostic oral reading session with a child from time to time, to check up on progress. While the rest of the class is engaged in some self-directing activity, which may be independent reading, the teacher can call one child at a time to his desk and make a written record of errors, needs, etc., based on the child's performance in reading a fairly long passage orally.

2. *Oral reading in a group.* The traditional reading lesson in which

one child after another was called upon to stand and read a sentence or two was anxiety-provoking for all but the most secure children. Oral reading in turn is more constructive when it is done in a group in which differences in reading proficiency are not great, and when it is done after a previous silent reading of the selection. Group oral reading can sometimes be carried on with a group chairman as leader, freeing the teacher for other activities.

3. *Varied purposes for oral rereading.* The authors of teacher's manuals have thought up quite a variety of purposes to motivate oral rereading and keep it from getting monotonous and boring. Some of these are: to show how the characters feel as they speak, to find the part where a character feels angry or happy or disappointed, to prepare a dramatization of the story, and to make the characters sound real. In the discussion that follows silent reading, asking the children to find and read aloud the particular sentence or paragraph that gives the answer to a question is a natural way to bring oral reading into the total lesson plan.

4. *Audience reading.* When oral reading is a genuine process of communication, the audience does not read along silently while one child reads orally, but rather sits and listens. At least part of the time, a group should close its books and listen attentively while its members read orally.

Another kind of audience reading provides an excellent way of sharing independent reading. Children are given the opportunity to choose a particularly interesting selection to read to the class, from something they have read independently. They are expected to practice until they can present it with fluency and good expression. It is advisable for the teacher to listen to make sure the reading is satisfactory before giving the child a place in the audience reading schedule. An audience reading period once a week helps to motivate independent reading, provides an incentive for improving expression and speech, and affords an enjoyable listening experience.

Still another kind of audience reading occurs when a group presents a favorite story dramatically, as in a T.V. or radio broadcast. There is an announcer, and each character's part is read by a different child. Each group can have a turn at presenting a story in this way to the rest of the class. Stories with a good deal of dialogue, radio scripts, and children's plays can be effectively presented in this way. An imitation microphone on a stand helps to make the broadcast seem real. Still better, the reading can be tape-recorded, and later the group can listen to their own performance and evaluate it.

5. *Choral reading.* Oral reading in unison is particularly well adapted to the reading of poetry and other strongly rhythmical material. When the whole class reads aloud together, the better readers set the pace and the poorer readers join in, being helped with phrasing, rhythm, and interpretation. After the selection has been read in unison, it is possible to assign certain lines as solo parts and other lines to particular groups. With appropriate balance of solo and choral effects, some voices high and others low, some parts read loudly and some softly, some slowly and some at a fast pace, choral reading can provide many of the values of choral singing, and at an age when most children are not yet ready for singing in harmony.

The Eye-Voice Span. The teacher can demonstrate an interesting fact about oral reading in the following way: The teacher starts to read aloud from a book, with one child standing next to him. The child holds a card and is instructed to cover up the page unexpectedly while the teacher is reading. Usually the teacher is able to continue the reading for at least another full line. This demonstrates the *eye-voice span,* the distance between where the eyes are and where the voice is.

A wide eye-voice span allows children to read orally at sight with good comprehension, phrasing, and expression. It also allows children to look up at the audience intermittently without pausing or losing the place.

The eye-voice span can be stretched with specific practice. Children can work in pairs, one reading orally while the other uses the cover card. They can count the number of words in the eye-voice span and keep a progress record. With practice, the eye-voice span gradually increases.

DEVELOPING INDEPENDENCE IN WORD RECOGNITION

In most basal reader programs, the major part of training for independence in word recognition is placed at the first- and second-reader levels or the second- and third-reader levels, and the second-reader level is particularly important. Much of what the intensive phonic programs introduce in the first grade is introduced a year or two later in most basal readers. By the end of the third grade most of the same ground has been covered.

Word analysis involves the combined use of three procedures: use of context, structural (or morphemic) analysis, and phonics. Children are given practice in making intelligent use of the meaningful setting in which a new word appears. Structural analysis (linguists prefer the term "morphemic analysis") means dividing a word visually and mentally into meaningful parts (morphemes) that can be recognized or analyzed as subunits.[3] This includes dividing words into prefixes, roots, and suffixes, and separating compound words (schoolroom) into their components. If long and short vowels have not been introduced earlier, the phonic learnings at the second-reader level may include long and short vowels and most consonant blends and digraphs. Depending on the program, the remaining vowel principles such as *oi* and *ou,* silent consonants (*kn, wr*), and the introduction of syllabication (see page 245) may occur at either the second- or third-reader levels. The use of picture dictionaries is also of value in developing word recognition in the primary grades.

The basal reader approach to word analysis assumes that for most children it is easier to start with whole words and to introduce structural analysis and phonics gradually than to start with letter sounds

---

[3] The manner in which a word is analyzed may vary from child to child, and a given child may use differing methods (some of which may not have been taught by the teacher) in recognizing a word, depending on the word or the situation.

and put them together to make words. In connected reading only those words that cannot be recognized as wholes need to be analyzed. Children are helped to discover phonic principles by comparison of the sound and appearance of known words, rather than by rote learning of sounds and the sounding of sequences of letters.

As has already been pointed out, basal reader systems vary in the thoroughness of their plans for teaching word analysis skills, and teachers vary in the degree to which they carry out the word analysis parts of the lesson plans in the manual. When the basal reader lessons do not seem to be covering word analysis thoroughly enough, the use of supplementary phonics material may be helpful. If supplementary phonics material is used, care should be exercised lest the children become confused by differing approaches, wording of generalizations, etc. Some teachers use phonic material in place of the basal reader phonics program and attempt to correlate the phonics lessons with the other basal reader material.

The content and method of teaching word attack skills are discussed in detail in Chapter 9.

Word Recognition and Word Meaning. During the first grade the vocabulary of basal readers is restricted almost entirely to words that are part of the speaking vocabulary of most children, so as to allow instruction to concentrate on the development of word recognition skills. In the second grade this is still largely true, although some unfamiliar concepts and words are introduced. In the third grade a transition takes place, with a shift of emphasis from word recognition to word meaning.

By the time children are ready for the third reader they usually can recognize over a thousand words at sight (including plurals and other simple derivatives) and have the structural analysis and phonic skills to work out the pronunciation of many more words. Word recognition is no longer a major problem for those who have made normal progress.

The content of third readers is, as we have seen earlier, quite varied. Stories are located in distant places, and some of them are about former times. This expansion of the field of action brings with it an increasing number of new words that are unfamiliar in meaning as well as in pronunciation and recognition. There are also many technical terms needed for textbook reading, the meanings of which have to be carefully taught. The total number of words of unknown meaning is larger than the number that teachers can take the time to introduce properly, so that the selection of the particular words for direct teaching, from those which can be left to the child's own resources, is a problem also.

The special problems of teaching word meanings are considered in detail in Chapter 10.

RECREATIONAL READING IN THE PRIMARY GRADES

As children become more competent readers and more capable of reading independently, the role of independent reading can be enlarged. In the teaching plan which is outlined in Figure 18, a major portion of the reading program is devoted to independent reading on two of the five days, and opportunities for independent reading occur on the other three days also. At second- and third-reader levels much of the independent reading is recreational reading, done "just for fun."

A classroom library with a wide variety of books, ranging in difficulty from first- to fourth- or fifth-reader level, is necessary if the recreational reading program is to be effective. The teacher often gets many of the books from the central school library or the public library. Each child should have a library book handy, which can be read when assignments are finished early as well as in periods designated for independent reading. Much recreational reading can also take place at home. The fostering of recreational reading is discussed in detail in Chapter 13.

FUNCTIONAL READING IN THE PRIMARY GRADES

The use of reading as a functional tool for learning becomes more prominent and more varied as children progress through the primary grades.

Research Reading. In many schools units or projects provide the main approach to learning in specific curricular areas such as social studies and science. A large unit is usually divided into major areas for investigation, and a committee is formed for each area. The committee decides in discussion upon the specific questions to be investigated, and these decisions are usually recorded in lists or in a simple outline form, usually first on the chalkboard and then copied into individual notebooks or on a large chart. The committees are usually chosen by the teacher so that each contains a wide range of reading ability.

Having decided upon the questions, the committee then engages in independent reading in as wide a variety of sources as the teacher can make available. The poorest readers may be able to do little more than inspect pictures carefully. Most of the committee members are able to read for information in easy library books, and the best readers may be able to make some use of the more difficult books and children's encyclopedias. As answers are found, they are copied into notebooks. The committee then gets together to pool information and prepare a joint report. The teacher usually helps them to organize the report, and in that process a number of new experience charts may be developed. Finally the committee presents its report to the rest of the class, in one of a variety of ways.

Some training in the skills of locating information is a helpful preparation for this simple kind of research reading. Even at first-grade level, preliminary practice in the use of the table of contents is started, and this is continued in the second and third grades. Attention to chapter titles, main headings, and subheadings is encouraged. The better readers can be shown how to locate items in an index or glossary.

Simple research reading can also be done individually to satisfy curiosity about a special topic. How to feed and care for pets, rockets and space travel, reptiles and dinosaurs, and many other areas of curiosity motivate the use of independent reading time for informational reading.

Reading in Textbooks. Most schools use specific textbooks for spelling and arithmetic in the second and third grades. In many schools there are also textbooks in English, social studies, science, health education, etc. These textbooks tend to be more difficult than basal readers for the same grade; they are likely to contain more unfamiliar concepts, more unknown words, and more difficult generalizations.

To use textbooks successfully, an adaptation of the method used with basal readers is often advisable. Unfamiliar concepts and words need to be carefully pretaught, and the use of audio-visual aids like filmstrips and movies is helpful when relevant ones are available. Reading purposes can be set up, and discussion and a considerable amount of rereading are usually necessary. Oral rereading to verify answers and conclusions is particularly appropriate.

Relatively little progress has been made in adapting textbook reading to individual differences. Although the situation is steadily improving, often it is not possible to find a simpler book covering the same content for the less proficient readers. Teachers sometimes rely on oral reading by the better readers as a way of "covering" the textbook. This by no means ensures that the children with limited reading skill will either understand or remember what they hear.

Filmstrips, pictures, movies, and recordings that illustrate ideas and concepts can increase the meaningfulness of new material. Simple explanations and interpretations of the textbook by the teacher are often useful. Summaries in simple language, prepared by the teacher and copied from the chalkboard into notebooks, also help to make up for the deficiencies of the textbook. Oral reading and explanation by the parents at home or taping the textbook are other possibilities, but ones that do little to develop either the reading skills or the self-reliance of the children. In various ways, then, teachers can mitigate the inflexibility and difficulty of many of the textbooks that they are required to use.

If a child cannot read the material, efforts must be made to enable him to acquire the concepts being taught so that as he acquires the necessary reading skills, he will have the conceptual background needed to understand the textbooks he is reading. If the child is a poor reader or a non-reader, tests in such subjects as science should be modified or read to him and his answers recorded if he has a spelling or writing problem. A child who understands the concepts being taught but gets a failing grade in the subject because of his inability to read the test is likely to become discouraged.

Summary

1. The reading program in the second and third grades is marked by rapid progress in practically all aspects of reading.

2. A successful program starts from where the children are and gives each child reading experiences according to his needs.

3. Systematic, sequential instruction using basal readers is central in the reading program of most schools.

   a. The basal readers normally used in these grades continue to control the introduction and number of new words, although to a lesser extent than in first-grade materials.

   b. Stories are longer and settings are more varied.

   c. Considerable differences exist among basal readers intended for use at the same grade level.

4. Basal reader methodology continues to employ the same four main divisions as in the first grade: preparation, guided reading and interpretation, related reading skills, and enrichment.

5. Usually the class is divided into groups according to the level of difficulty of the reader used.

6. A judicious combination of instruction in groups with a good deal of independent reading and some whole-class reading activities is recommended, and a sample one-week program has been described.

7. Such habits in silent reading as moving the lips or pointing with the finger need not alarm the primary-grade teacher. While they can usually be given up before the end of the third grade or sooner, early pressure to discontinue them is sometimes harmful.

8. Oral reading has many uses in the primary grades. It usually follows silent reading, and takes a variety of forms, including individual reading to the teacher, audience reading, and choral reading.

9. Teaching for independence in word recognition is an important feature of the primary reading program. Basal readers usually center much of this instruction at the second-reader level and stress the combined use of context cues, structural analysis, and phonics.

10. Recreational reading is given more time in the total reading program as children become more competent to read independently.

Good classroom libraries and school libraries cover both a wide variety of topics and a wide range of difficulty.

11. Functional reading consists mainly of research reading and the reading of textbooks.

a. Research reading is usually done on a committee basis as part of a project or unit, and also includes individual reading for information.

b. Textbook reading in the primary grades presents many problems, and the reading of textbooks should involve the careful preparatory teaching of new concepts and terms, and guided reading and interpretation, much as in the plan used with basal readers.

c. Less success has been achieved in adapting textbook reading to individual differences than in developmental reading with basal readers.

Recommended Reading

DE BOER, JOHN J., and DALLMANN, MARTHA. *The Teaching of Reading,* 3rd ed. New York: Holt, Rinehart and Winston, 1970. Ch. 14.

GRAY, LILLIAN. *Teaching Children to Read.* New York: Ronald Press, 1963. Ch. 9.

HEILMAN, ARTHUR W. *Principles and Practices of Teaching Reading,* 2nd ed. Columbus: Charles E. Merrill, 1967. Chs. 6, 7.

McCULLOUGH, CONSTANCE M. "Balanced Reading Development," *Innovation and Change in Reading Instruction.* 67th Yearbook of the National Society for the Study of Education, Part II. Chicago: University of Chicago Press, 1968. Ch. 9.

SPACHE, GEORGE D., and SPACHE, EVELYN B., *Reading in the Elementary School,* 2nd ed. Boston: Allyn and Bacon, Inc., 1969. Ch. 8.

TINKER, MILES A., and McCULLOUGH, CONSTANCE M. *Teaching Elementary Reading,* 3rd ed. New York: Appleton-Century-Crofts, 1968. Ch. 22.

CHAPTER

5

Reading in the Middle
and Upper Grades

Range and variety should be the outstanding characteristics of reading programs in the middle and upper grades. Learning to read has
been largely accomplished for most children, although by no means
finished. Both recreational reading and functional reading grow in
importance, and reading becomes a tool for learning from textbooks
and reference sources.

Opinions vary greatly as to the importance of developmental reading in grades four through six. Some believe very strongly in the
desirability of continuing to provide for the teaching of basic and advanced reading skills through the use of some systematic program,
most often a basal reader series. Others hold that satisfactory growth
in reading takes place when independent recreational reading is fostered and guidance is provided in the many kinds of functional reading
skills needed for success in the content subjects.

During the 1960's and into the 1970's both trends were in evidence. On one hand, many schools that had previously given little
attention to teaching reading beyond the third grade restored systematic instruction as an important part of their reading programs
in grades four through six. On the other hand, increased attention was
paid to "individualized reading" programs in which increased time

for independent reading replaces the basal reader, and individualized teacher-pupil conferences largely replace systematic instruction with groups.

In this chapter attention is given first to reading instruction in the middle grades. This is followed by a discussion of the problems of teaching reading in the upper elementary or junior high school grades (mainly grades seven and eight).

Basal Reading Instruction in the Middle Grades

BASAL READING MATERIALS

In grades four through six most basal reader series have one thick book for each grade. The readers are in very large part collections of short stories. Each reader tends to have about six to eight centers of interest, or units. Some of the themes used are stories with regional or foreign settings, humorous stories, animal stories, adventure tales, myths and legends, true biographical stories, and stories about science and invention. The amount of non-fiction has tended to increase. At fourth-reader level the typical stories are six to twelve pages long; at sixth-grade level, from ten to sixteen pages. Poems are usually included. Illustrations, usually in color, photographs, maps, and schematic drawings average about one in three pages. The pictures tell less of the story than is customary in primary-grade readers. Some readers contain comprehension questions, most of them have glossaries, and some list the new words page by page.

The vocabulary is considerably more variable than in primary-grade readers. Children are expected to derive variants of known words, so that variants formed by adding such endings as *s, es, 's, ies, d, ed, ied, ing, n, en, y, ly, ily, er, ier, est,* and *iest* are usually not counted as new words. Some readers continue to be very careful about the introduction of new words. In one fifth reader, for example, new words average about two per page, with no more than six new words being introduced in a group of 200 running words. Other series rely on the word-attack skills the children are expected to have learned, and consequently make little effort to control the introduction of "new" words from the fourth reader up.

What is meant by a "new" word is also somewhat ambiguous. The word may not have been used in the preceding readers of the basal series, but it may be quite familiar to many of the children from their independent reading or because it has been introduced in a textbook. Some "new" words are familiar spoken words that need only to be recognized; others are unfamiliar both in appearance and in meaning. Some can be attacked successfully by applying phonic generalizations, while others are unique exceptions. The care with which authors provide context cues to make it easy to infer the meanings and identities of new words is probably as important as limiting the number of presumably "new" words.

The difficulty of reader stories is not entirely a matter of the frequency of new words or unfamiliar ideas. Sentence structure is important. As sentences become longer, complex sentences become more common and there are more inversions of word order, parenthetical phrases and clauses, conditional statements, and unusual expressions. Characters in some stories speak in a way typical of a particular region or of a former era. Plots also become more complicated.

The workbook that accompanies each reader is usually designed as a reinforcing and skill-developing tool which is recommended for use as related reading. Some workbook pages provide a comprehension check on the corresponding story in the reader. In the middle grades it is more typical for the workbook pages to have a correlated vocabulary, but independent content. Comprehension exercises are designed to help to develop specific comprehension skills. Pages devoted to word study may review morphemic analysis and phonics, introduce additional principles of syllabication and morphemic analysis, teach dictionary skills, or emphasize word meanings. When the workbook is designed to be used before the reader as a preparatory aid, comprehension questions for use following the reading of the story may be printed in the reader.

BASAL READER METHODOLOGY IN THE MIDDLE GRADES

The manuals for middle grade basal readers tend to have the same general kind of organization as those for the primary grades. Each starts with an overview and explanation of the general plan, and then provides a teaching plan for each story.

The first step, preparation for the new selection, is likely to be briefer than in the primary grades. The "new" words are listed, and in some manuals the specific phonic or morphemic principles that children can apply to them are indicated. The new words are usually presented on the chalkboard, but instead of the teacher's giving the pronunciation and meaning, as is common in the primary grades, the teacher is usually advised to encourage the children to make use of their word-analysis skills, the context, and the glossary at the back of the reader for the words they do not know. Relation to a preceding story can often be established with one or two sentences. Essential new concepts may require explanation. A guiding question or two is given to motivate the first reading.

Guided reading and interpretation generally call for silent reading first. This may be done one or two pages at a time, but more commonly a short selection, or a several-page unit of a long selection, is read in one setting. In working with groups it is usually necessary to assign a fairly long selection for silent reading while the teacher is working directly with another group. After the first reading there is a check on comprehension. This may involve written answers to written questions, oral discussion, or both. Written questions may be placed on the chalkboard, may be printed in the reader or workbook, or may be on duplicated sheets. Some oral discussion of the selection is usually included. As in the primary grades, most stories are reread at least once. Rereading is sometimes oral, sometimes silent, and varied purposes for motivating rereading are provided.

The teaching of related skills shows some changes of emphasis. In the fourth reader, primary-grade phonic principles are reviewed, and the beginnings of syllabication, which are usually taught in the second or third reader, are reviewed and developed further. Practice is given in locating words in the glossary at the back of the basal reader, and later in the dictionary. The guide to pronunciation is studied and applied. Further refinement of syllabication and dictionary skills is provided in the fifth- and sixth-reader programs. Practice is given in interpreting definitions and in selecting the definition that fits a particular context. Synonyms, antonyms, and homonyms are given special attention, and words are classified in a variety of ways. A sequential program in syllabication, use of the dictionary, and vocabulary development is usually provided in the related workbook. Some attention is also given to other morphemic analysis skills, learning the technique of separating prefixes and suffixes from root words, and studying the meanings of common prefixes and suffixes.

Related practice in comprehension skills tends to be specific. One exercise involves reading for main ideas; another stresses reading for detail; a third, reading to discover cause-effect relationships; a fourth, reading to follow directions; and so on. While most reading in these grades is assimilative in character, some beginnings are made in the development of critical reading skills. Suggestions are given in the manuals for teacher-constructed exercises in comprehension, and at least half the pages in the workbooks are concerned with specific comprehension skills.

There may also be some attention to rate of reading. Directions for conducting simple tests of rate of reading may be given, and suggestions provided for individualized work with the exceptionally slow reader. Timed practice exercises for improving rate may also be recommended for use with the whole class.

There are substantial differences among the various series. Some give separate plans for fast, average, and slow groups. One series has three different texts at a particular grade level for use with children who have poor, average, or above-average reading ability. Another series has two readers for each grade, the regular edition and a "classmate" edition which has the same stories and illustrations, with the language simplified so as to be a grade or more lower in difficulty. The manuals for this series advocate a plan in which whole-class activities are combined with some group activities. Preparation and discussion are carried on with the entire class. In silent reading each group reads its own version, and oral reading is done separately with each group. Manuals vary also in the degree of detail given and in the relative emphasis devoted to various reading skills.

The basal readers for the middle grades are vehicles for the systematic and sequential development of basic reading skills. Teachers who are experienced, capable, and creative can often improve on the lesson plans given in the manuals. This does not absolve them from covering, in their own ways, thc specific skills which are taught by teachers who follow the manuals. Slavish adhering to the manual may result in teaching that is dull and uninspired; ignoring the manual usually means that many important reading skills just are not taught.

PROVIDING FOR INDIVIDUAL DIFFERENCES IN BASAL READING

Nearly all manuals recommend dividing the class into groups for instruction with basal readers. As noted above, some series provide separate sets of plans for groups differing in ability, while most leave it to the teacher to make the necessary adaptations.

In most schools, middle-grade teachers have to deal with a wide range of reading skills. Table II shows the distribution of reading

TABLE II. Distribution of Reading Grade Scores on the Stanford Reading Test (Paragraph Meaning), Intermediate I, at the Beginning of Fourth Grade*

Percentiles	Grade Scores
90–98	5.9–7.2
75–89	5.0–5.8
50–74	4.1–4.9
25–49	3.3–4.0
10–24	2.7–3.2
2–9	2.0–2.6

* Data in this table are taken from the tables on page 18 of the Directions for Administering, *Stanford Achievement Test,* Intermediate I Battery. New York: Harcourt, Brace, and World, Inc., 1964. Copyright 1964–1965 by Harcourt, Brace, and World, Inc. Reproduced by special permission of the publisher.

grade scores on the latest edition of the *Stanford Reading Test* at the beginning of fourth grade. The bottom one percent and the top two percent have been omitted. The range from the 2nd percentile to the 98th percentile is from 2.0 to 7.2, approximately five grades. Most of the bottom quarter scored about as well as second-grade children;

the middle 50 percent scored from the low third grade to the high fourth grade; and the upper quarter scored about as well as fifth, sixth, or seventh graders. In the fifth and sixth grades the range of differences in grade scores is even wider.

Some schools attempt, through administrative arrangements, to reduce the range of reading ability with which a teacher must deal in giving reading instruction. There are many plans in which middle- or upper-grade children, normally in self-contained classrooms, are reclassified for reading instruction (commonly referred to as the Joplin Plan). The children are assigned to reading classes on the basis of test results and teacher judgment. If the school is small, children from two or three different grades may be in the same reading class (cross-grade grouping); if the school is larger, there may be grouping for reading within each grade (cross-class grouping).

In order for these plans to be successful, there must be differentiation of instruction within a reading class and conferences between teachers. There is the danger of considering the class as a "homogeneous" group which may receive only whole-class instruction with little attention being paid to individual needs. If there is little or no communication between the child's reading teacher and his content subject teachers, it will be difficult, if not impossible, to coordinate his learning. For example, teaching word-identification skills could be combined with spelling instruction, the content subject teacher should have information about each child's reading abilities, and the child needs content subject material in order to practice his work-type reading skills.

In setting up a grouping plan for a representative fourth-grade class in which the distribution of reading abilities is similar to that shown in Table II, it is usual to set up three groups. At the beginning of the year the low group would probably start with a second reader, the middle group with a high third or beginning fourth reader, and the high group with a beginning fourth reader. The poorest readers in the low group probably need some individual help in addition to the group activities.

A one-week plan that would be suitable for such a class is shown in Fig. 19. In this plan group instruction is combined with whole-class reading activities and with a substantial amount of independent reading. The teacher does not attempt to have reading every day with every group. This plan indicates three teacher-led periods a week for the low and middle groups and two a week for the high group, but this can be increased by giving more time to the reading program.

All groups are able to carry on some kinds of reading activities when the teacher is working with another group. If the low group is so limited that it cannot do this, nonreading activities can be assigned. The sequence of preparation, guided reading, discussion, rereading, related skills and workbook practice, and enrichment is not always in that order. Using and checking the workbook may come before or after oral discussion and rereading. The high group may use a special workbook that contains challenging comprehension exercises instead of the workbook that accompanies the reader. Related skills and enrichment come in at various times and some are conducted on a whole-class basis. In addition to group periods for independent reading, twice a week the entire class has independent reading at the same time, freeing the teacher to have a series of conferences with individual children.

The duration of periods for each group in such a plan is somewhat flexible but is usually between 20 and 30 minutes, giving a daily total of between 60 and 90 minutes in the fourth grade. In the fifth and sixth grades the daily plan can be quite similar, but with less total weekly time devoted to the teaching of reading.

An alternative plan which some teachers favor is to have only two groups, a smaller low group, using a basal reader one or two grades below the grade level of the class, and a larger group, using a basal reader for the grade. The best readers complete the assignments for the upper group quickly and easily, and fill out the periods with independent reading, or with acting as helpers to classmates. Such a plan is much easier to operate than a three-group plan. It allows the teacher to increase the number of group sessions per week or to devote additional time to independent reading and individual conferences. Of course, it is necessary that the material used be of a suitable level of difficulty for instructional purposes, and that differentiation of instruction take place.

Low Group	Middle Group	High Group

Whole class: Directions and assignments are given to each
group each day (10 min.)

MONDAY

T Preparation, guided silent reading and discussion	Silent reading (Preparation on preceding Friday) Related workbook	Independent reading (entire period)
Related workbook	T Discuss story, check workbooks, oral rereading	

Whole class: Reading and discussing weekly newspapers

TUESDAY

Related skills: practice exercises in word analysis, word games	T Related skills Preparation for new story	Silent reading of new story
Independent reading	Silent reading, new story	T Discussion, oral rereading, related skills

Whole class: Independent reading period, teacher circulates
and has individual conferences or works with a
group that has a special need in common

WEDNESDAY

T Check workbooks, Oral rereading and discussion, preparation for new story	Related workbook If finish early, independent reading	Workbook not correlated with reader, discuss answers with group chairman
Silent reading, new story	T Check workbooks Discussion and Oral rereading of story	Silent reading of new story

Whole class: Word analysis, syllabication, dictionary guide
to pronunciation

THURSDAY		
Related work- book	With group chair- man, plan and rehearse drama- tization of story	T Discussion of story, oral re- reading, related skills
T Check workbooks, discussion and oral rereading	Independent reading	Research reading on special topics

Whole class: Independent reading period, teacher circulates
and has individual conferences or works with a
group that has a special need in common

FRIDAY

Whole class: Independent recreational or research reading,
teacher circulates and has individual conferences
Afternoon: book club meeting, audience reading,
dramatization, oral reports.

FIGURE 19. A three-group plan for the fourth grade.

Special Issues in the Middle Grades

SILENT AND ORAL READING

As indicated in Chapter 4, it is difficult for beginning readers to
read in a truly silent fashion because the original association is one
that links the printed representation of the word with the already
established memory trace of the heard and spoken word. Many children quickly learn to read silently. For others, the reduction of oral
response from quiet mumbling to inaudible lip movements to truly
silent reading takes many years. Although teachers in the primary
grades usually try to get children to give up lip movements, a substantial minority bring the habit into the fourth grade and some of these
continue it through the sixth grade. The habit can be overcome most
easily by efforts at conscious control while reading very easy material.

When good adult readers are confronted with reading material that
is quite difficult for them, they tend to regress to earlier levels of reading performance. They slow down, and many of them who have not

moved their lips for years when reading easy material find their lips moving in this difficult reading. It may be, therefore, that persistent lip movements indicate that the child is struggling with reading material that for him is too hard to allow fluent silent reading. In such cases the lip movements are a symptom indicating the need for using material that is less difficult for the child.

We have already noted that some children come into the fourth grade with reading skills that are still at second- or third-reader level. For these children it is especially important to encourage independent reading in material so easy that even they can read it with little experience of difficulty.

Most children begin to read faster silently than they can read orally when they are at the third-reader level. To reach average reading rates in the middle grades, children must be able to read faster than they can talk. The persistence of lip movements is, then, a deterrent to the development of an average rate of reading. Research seems to show that in the middle grades the encouragement of a large amount of independent reading does as much to speed up reading as does the spending of an equivalent amount of time in practice exercises intended to promote phrase perception and to speed up reading.

For a period of about twenty years, starting in the 1920's, silent reading was emphasized so much that oral reading almost disappeared from middle-grade reading programs. During the past two decades, oral reading has again been recognized as important and useful, although subordinate to silent reading in the time devoted to it.

Oral reading serves the same purposes in the middle grades as in the primary grades: diagnosis, speech improvement, listening practice, communication between the individual and the group, and personality development. The varieties of oral reading that have been recommended for the primary grades (see pages 118–120) are also appropriate for the middle grades. Various types of genuine audience situations, in particular, provide motivation for practicing and polishing oral reading. Sometimes children who are excellent silent readers need considerable help before they are able to read orally with clear diction and suitable phrasing and expression.

VOCABULARY DEVELOPMENT

We have already noted that the emphasis in word study shifts from recognition to meaning as children become proficient in working out the pronunciation of new words. Below the third grade, most new words are already in the child's speaking and listening vocabulary; from the third grade up, an increasing number are words that the child has never heard used in speech, and perhaps never will. In reading stories about the Middle Ages and knighthood, children are likely to encounter words like *forsooth, methinks,* and *eftsoons,* which are archaic, and *cuirass, chain mail,* and *greave,* referring to forms of armor that have not been worn for centuries. The meanings of terms like these can often be guessed successfully without looking them up in the dictionary. If the child expects that he will not have to read the word aloud or use it in his speech, he is likely to be satisfied with an approximate pronunciation. He may know the meaning of a word like *awry* without ever checking to see if the accent belongs on the first or second syllable. Gradually he acquires a reading vocabulary that outgrows his speaking vocabulary.

Vocabulary development in the middle grades is acquired in three main ways. Important new words are discussed and explained by the teacher, particularly those that come up in special curriculum areas. One does not leave to guesswork or to a dictionary definition the meaning of a term like *longitude, oxidation,* or *improper fraction.* Secondly, many new words are absorbed effortlessly while reading, when the context makes their meanings clear. Thirdly, children who become proficient in the use of the dictionary turn to it frequently to get an exact statement of a word's meaning or to check its pronunciation. Training in both the intelligent use of context and the efficient use of dictionaries is, therefore, important for vocabulary development. Provision should be made for recording the new words and reviewing them periodically. Vocabulary development is discussed in greater detail in Chapter 10.

INDIVIDUALIZED READING

In an individualized reading program there is no regular program of instruction in groups with basal readers. The role of independent reading is greatly expanded, with individual teacher-pupil conferences providing the opportunities for guidance in the selection of books, discussion of books read and checking on comprehension, sampling oral reading skills, and noting any special needs or deficiencies. When the teacher finds that several children need the same kind of help, they are brought together in a temporary group. Individual progress records are kept. The class comes together for discussion of what they have read and for audience-type oral reading.

Conditions are more favorable for a successful individualized reading program in the middle grades than they are in the primary grades. Nearly all of the children are able to find some books that they can successfully read by themselves. As they get older, children become able to sustain attention for longer periods of time. They do not need help with unknown words as often as in the primary grades.

The big question about individualized reading programs is: what happens about the reading skills that are specifically taught in a basal reading program? If the teacher is clearly aware of these skills, includes them among his important objectives, tests to see how well they have been mastered, and plans definite individual or group learning activities to develop them, the results can be very good. In practice, however, it often happens in individualized programs that little attention is given to the teaching of specific skills. When this is the case, some children seem to develop many of the skills without direct teaching; others never learn them.

The development of kits or boxes of individualized reading exercises [1] may provide a corrective to this weakness of many individualized reading programs. The possible uses of teaching machines and programmed textbooks in providing individualized practice on reading

[1] Such as: *SRA Reading Laboratory Series* (Chicago: Science Research Associates, 1960); *EDL Study Skills Library* (Huntington, N.Y.: Educational Developmental Laboratories, 1961).

skills are just beginning to be explored. A program in which self-teaching materials would help each child to develop the necessary skills at his own rate of progress, and to concentrate on the skills in which he most needs additional practice, might have advantages over systematic instruction in groups. As of yet, however, their utility has not been thoroughly evaluated.

Individually Prescribed Instruction. One recent attempt at allowing each child to progress in accordance with his capacities is Individually Prescribed Instruction. In such programs, objectives (not always in behavioral terms) are stated and arranged in sequential order. After the child is placed on the continuum by placement tests, he usually works independently on the assignments (prescriptions) given him. He is allowed to progress through each skill area at his own pace, with diagnostic tests being given along the way. Mastery of an objective is judged by "curriculum-embedded" or post-tests on which a certain level of proficiency (e.g., 85 percent correct) is required before the next "step" in the sequence is presented. In some experimental programs the tests are scored and interpreted, and the assignments made, by a specially programmed computer.

One such experimental program lists twelve skill areas (e.g., visual discrimination, literal comprehension, organization skills) with from one to eleven levels for each area. Objectives for a given level range from one to eight. For the most part, Individually Prescribed Instruction is still in the experimental stage.

RECREATIONAL READING

By the fourth grade, sex differences in reading interests are apparent and become more pronounced in the fifth and sixth grades. Many boys give first choice to exciting adventure and mystery tales. Others, perhaps having their "escape" needs satisfied by television, do not want to waste time reading about anything that isn't true. Books about science, invention, mechanics, and hobbies are popular. Astronomy, space flight, rockets, and jets are complex topics in which an intense desire to read is sometimes frustrated by the difficulty of the available books. Stories about horses, dogs, and wild animals are liked by many, and dinosaurs and reptiles have a special fascination. Biography and true accounts of historical events find a large acceptance.

Girls usually like sentimental stories of home and school life. They usually enjoy stories of mystery and adventure, particularly when children are the central characters. Many girls have a particular fondness for stories about horses. In contrast to the boys, few girls are actively interested in science and invention, and they tend to prefer fiction to true historical stories. Books written in series, like the Bobbsey Twins books and Nancy Drew mysteries, retain a perennial popularity.[2] On the whole, girls are more accepting of books written primarily for boys than boys are of books that seem feminine in their appeal. By the sixth grade some girls are already showing an adolescent interest in stories of love and romance.

The marked individual differences among children are greater and more striking than those which are related to sex differences or age differences. Some children have immature reading tastes, while others are precocious. Some have very narrow interests, while others will read almost anything. Some read two or more books a week, sneaking time for reading when they are supposed to be asleep, while others put reading near the bottom of their order of preference for leisure-time activities.

To cater to this great variety of interests and maturity levels requires an extensive library. When we consider that a typical class in the middle grades is likely to have a range of five or more levels in reading ability and needs books on a variety of topics at each of these levels, we get some idea of the inadequacy of many classroom library collections. Convenient access to a central school library and to the public library helps to amplify the classroom resources, and fostering membership in the public library is important.

The home conditions in which many thousands of children grow up are not favorable to reading as a leisure-time activity. Lack of

---

[2] Teachers and librarians often look down on these "series" books. Although they are not good literature, they do appeal to children, get them reading for pleasure, and provide abundant practice in easy materials; for these reasons, they deserve recognition.

privacy, lack of peace and quiet, and the danger of a book's being mutilated by a younger child discourage many children from taking books home. So, although many children do read extensively at home, it is unsafe for the school to rely on this.

The school must, therefore, provide time as well as materials for independent recreational reading. In the plan outlined in Figure 19 the provisions for periods of independent reading reflect this need. Ways of developing and intensifying interest in reading are considered in detail in Chapter 13.

FUNCTIONAL READING

Both research reading and the reading of textbooks grow in importance as children progress through the middle grades. For research reading, children need to learn the location skills; for textbook reading, they need help in adapting their reading habits to the special requirements of each subject. In all kinds of functional reading they need to be selective and to be able to organize and summarize the information they find.

Location skills start with learning to find entries quickly in an alphabetical order. Usually this starts with a glossary or dictionary, and is later extended to the varied requirements of locating items in indexes, in encyclopedias, and in a library card file. Some help in classification, so as to be able to choose alternative possible entries for a particular kind of information, is also needed. Once the relevant pages are located, rapid skimming to find the particular fact needed can be developed with practice.

Textbook reading presents some special reading problems. Many children need to be shown how to make use of headings, subheadings, and marginal notations. Guidance is needed in the interpretation of different kinds of maps, charts, graphs, and tables. The analysis of an arithmetic problem requires a different kind of reading than is employed in reading about a historical sequence of events. In general, these adaptations of reading to the requirements of specific textbooks must be done during subject-matter periods and cannot be assumed to be taken care of by basal reading instruction.

The beginnings of training in the selection and organization of ideas start with the construction of the first experience charts for beginning readers. Every time that plans are formulated and listed, or that the findings of a group or committee are summarized, another step is taken in learning how to condense, classify, and organize ideas and information. In the middle grades this informal training is supplemented by specific training in how to formulate an outline. In a series of graded steps, starting with a complete outline of a selection provided by the teacher and then progressively providing less and less help in subsequent selections, children can be taught how to find the logical skeleton of the author's plan.

The development of specific kinds of comprehension skills and training in the reading and study skills needed in the middle and upper grades are discussed in greater detail in Chapter 12.

Reading Instruction in the Upper Grades

The seventh, eighth, and ninth grades are in a somewhat uncertain position in American school systems. In many places these three grades are administratively and physically separate in a junior high school. In some places the seventh and eighth grades are part of the elementary school and the ninth grade is the first year of high school. In still other places a six-year elementary school is followed by a six-year secondary school, or a five-year elementary school is followed by a three-year middle school.

The provisions made for the teaching of reading are even more varied. For a long time it was assumed that if a child got as far as this in school he knew how to read, and reading was assigned rather than taught. Literature was read and analyzed and textbooks were studied, but reading skills as such were not considered in need of further teaching.

During the 1930's and 1940's the growing awareness that a large number of upper-grade children were not able to do the assigned reading resulted in the development of many remedial reading programs in these grades. Children with normal I.Q.'s and low reading ability were given special instruction in small groups. Little or nothing was done for the good and average readers, or for those poor readers whose I.Q.'s were also low (often on a group test that required reading).

The past two decades have seen the increasing acceptance of the idea that the reading requirements of modern life demand reading skills at a higher level than can be attained in the first six grades. Reading programs have been developed at the senior high, college, and adult levels as well as in the upper grades. Stress is placed on developmental reading, with the central idea that every student can be helped to improve his reading. The refinement of the reading abilities of the able student is now considered an important educational objective.

Departmentalized instruction, which is usual in the upper grades, creates some important differences from the self-contained classroom which is common in the first six grades. Instead of one teacher who is responsible for all reading instruction, several teachers share the responsibility. The teacher of English has the major responsibility for developmental and recreational reading, and the various subject teachers should each be responsible for helping the pupils to read effectively in their subject areas. When English and social studies are combined in a core program, the core teacher is responsible for both developmental reading and some teaching of study skills.

The extremely wide variation in reading skills—in seventh grade, a range from third grade to twelfth grade in reading ability is not unusual—is commonly reduced by sectioning English or core classes according to reading test scores. The class is likely to be scheduled as a unit for other subjects, also. In a small school with just one or two classes at each grade, the problem of individual differences is intensified.

DEVELOPMENTAL READING

Developmental reading ordinarily takes up one or two of the English periods per week. Materials of several types are in use.

Sometimes a basal reader is used which is an extension of the basal readers for the fifth and sixth grades, and strongly resembles them.

The accompanying teacher's manual provides lesson plans for reviewing and extending the reading skills taught in the middle grades. With slow classes, middle-grade basal readers are sometimes used; however, there are now available many texts that contain material of interest to children of this age, and that are designed to develop reading skills usually taught in the middle grades or lower.

A second type of material is a series of readers especially for junior high schools, which in form and content are primarily literary anthologies. In using these books, vocabulary enrichment and literary appreciation are usually stressed.

A third kind of material is a reader designed expressly for reading skill development. One recent book of this type contains sixteen chapters, each designed to develop skills in a particular area. Among the topics covered, each of which is further divided into sections devoted to specific skills, are: understanding the nature of a paragraph, understanding the meanings of words through context, understanding the meanings of unfamiliar words through familiar parts, learning techniques for skimming, making inferences from figurative language, using the dictionary, and practicing good study habits.[3]

There are also several series of paper-covered workbooks which give practice in sharpening reading comprehension skills, developing vocabulary, and improving rate of reading. Some of these are designed so that reading, answering, correcting, and discussing one exercise take about a period. Some of these are planned so that they fit easily into a reading pacing device.

Also available are boxes of individualized practice material including exercises suitable for a wide range of reading abilities. One such set contains fifteen exercises at each of ten different grade levels, from grade three through grade twelve. Each exercise is printed on a separate sheet of heavy, stiff paper and includes an illustration, a reading selection, and several kinds of questions. The set also includes a teacher's manual, a set of answer keys which pupils can use to correct their own answers, pupil notebooks for recording answers and

[3] Joseph C. Gainsburg, *Advanced Skills in Reading, Book 1* (New York: The Macmillan Company, 1967).

charting scores, and a set of short selections for rate practice, also with answer keys.[4] Another type of material, which may be used with slow learners or poor readers, is written so that each unit (published in separate paperback booklets) can be used to develop history lessons and reading skills.[5]

Many schools also use special reading machines to assist in improving rate of reading. The research to date seems to indicate that a well-planned, well-motivated program that does not use any machines can produce as much improvement in rate as can be obtained with machines, so that the value of spending money for reading machines is a hotly debated question.

RECREATIONAL READING

Boys and girls tend to do more independent reading during the seventh and eighth grades than at any other period of their lives. Most of them have attained a level of reading skill that allows them to read with ease materials covering a wide range of maturity and difficulty. The pull of television tends to decline; the combination of heavy homework assignments and much social activity that fills the schedules of many boys and girls in senior high school has not yet arrived. Children have time to read and, with suitable opportunities and encouragement, will use a substantial share of their spare time for reading.

In these grades a sharp distinction is sometimes made between literary appreciation and recreational reading. For literary appreciation, a small number of "classic" selections are read by the entire class and then are analyzed in terms of plot, characterization, description, use of language, imagery, underlying theme, etc. Recreational reading is usually independent reading, to be done outside of

[4] Don H. Parker, *SRA Reading Laboratory, IIIa* (Chicago: Science Research Associates, 1960).

[5] Jack Abramowitz, *American History Study Lessons* and *World History Study Lessons* (Chicago: Follett, 1963).

school. Often children are given a list of approved titles from which to choose. Outside reading is usually checked by some form of written book report. A minimum number of book reports is required; reading beyond that is voluntary.

One of the problems with this approach is that there is often a conflict between the intellectual and the emotional outcome. Too many pupils have discovered that the more a selection is analyzed the less it is enjoyed. By using challenging questions, fostering stimulating discussions, and using dramatization and role playing, some teachers succeed in intensifying the enjoyment of literary selections while building literary insight. The search for clues to character, the interpretation of figurative language, the challenge of attempting to predict the outcome, the identification of words that create vivid images or depict subtle moods and emotions—these activities can be exciting or boring, depending on how they are taught. Similarly, book reporting procedures need to be planned with their probable impact upon the desire to read in mind. A combination of brief written reports with some opportunities for oral discussion of outside reading is usually preferable to long written analyses.

FUNCTIONAL READING

In the upper grades most reading in the content areas is textbook reading, with some independent research reading for individual and group projects and reports.

Textbook reading is usually difficult for the majority of the pupils in the grade, and guidance in how to use the particular textbook is the responsibility of each subject-matter teacher. It is not safe to assume that all that is needed is to tell the class how many pages to read ahead.

The technical vocabulary of the subject requires careful consideration. Which words are essential? Can their meanings be derived from context; is a dictionary definition informative enough; or does the word warrant direct explanation and illustration in class? Can visual aids be used to show and clarify the meanings of technical terminology? If so, where can they be obtained?

Many children find that the time available in school for studying their textbooks is insufficient. If the child is allowed to take the textbook home, he has an opportunity to reread, to look up words, and to write notes or a summary. If the book is entirely too difficult for him, a member of the family can read it to him or with him. The school that does not allow children in the middle or upper grades to take their textbooks home is losing a valuable amount of potential learning. In such schools, whether some children do passing or failing work is often dependent upon whether or not the parents buy their own copies of textbooks for home use. This is not a plea for longer homework assignments, but rather a recognition that some children need more time for textbook reading than the school day provides.

Suggestions for teaching and improving functional reading and study skills will be found in Chapter 12.

Summary

1. Reading in the middle and upper grades is characterized by range and variety. Variety is great not only in the reading done by children but also in the scope and nature of the reading programs.
2. Basal readers are commonly used for instruction in the middle grades.
   a. In the basal readers for these levels, selections get longer, plot and language become increasingly complex, and much less control is maintained over the vocabulary used.
   b. The four main steps of preparation, guided reading and discussion, related skills, and enrichment are still used. Compared to the primary grades, however, preparation is briefer, reading is done in larger units, more of the checking of comprehension is done in writing, acquisition of word meanings becomes more important than word recognition, and oral reading takes a smaller proportion of the total reading time.
   c. Comprehension questions are often aimed at developing ability to read for a specific purpose.
   d. Rate of reading may receive some attention.

3. The range of individual differences in these grades is sometimes reduced by administrative practices, but most teachers find a wide range of reading abilities in their classes. An instructional plan has been presented that involves a combination of basal reader instruction in groups with some whole-class reading activities and with a substantial time allowance for independent reading that incorporates much of the theoretical structure of individualized reading.

4. Oral reading has several useful functions in the middle-grade reading program.

5. Vocabulary development involves a combination of specific teaching of important terms, practice in using context clues, and teaching dictionary skills, as well as learning many new words in independent reading.

6. An individualized reading program is more feasible in the middle and upper grades than in the primary grades.

   a. Care should be exercised lest reading skills not be taught sufficiently.

   b. Many materials and programs that may be useful in individualized reading instruction are now available.

7. Independent reading can include both research reading and recreational reading.

8. Functional reading includes research reading which is usually individualized, and textbook reading which is commonly done on a whole-class basis. It involves training in location skills, guidance in the reading of textbooks, and instruction in the formulation of summaries and outlines.

9. There is no uniformity in the teaching of reading in the upper grades, which are sometimes the top of the elementary schools or in a middle school or junior high school.

   a. Concern about the need to continue systematic reading instruction continues to grow.

   b. Responsibility for developmental reading usually rests with the English or core teacher.

   c. Practice materials include readers and workbooks with a

primary emphasis on skills development, and collections of individualized reading exercises.

d. The value of reading machines in developing rate of comprehension is a debatable issue.

10. Recreational reading is at its peak for many children during these years. Teaching for literary appreciation and methods of checking independent reading can influence the desire to read, and need to be planned so as to foster recreational reading.

11. Functional reading is primarily the responsibility of each subject-matter teacher, since the vocabulary needed and the reading approach best suited to the material differ greatly from one subject to another.

Recommended Reading

GRAY, LILLIAN. *Teaching Children to Read,* 3rd ed. New York: Ronald Press, 1963. Ch. 10.

HEILMAN, ARTHUR W. *Principles and Practices of Teaching Reading,* 2nd ed. Columbus: Charles E. Merrill, 1967. Ch. 10.

McCULLOUGH, CONSTANCE M. "Reading in the Intermediate Grades," *Development in and Through Reading.* 60th Yearbook of the National Society for the Study of Education, Part I. Chicago: University of Chicago Press, 1961.

McKEE, PAUL. *Reading: A Program of Instruction for the Elementary School.* Boston: Houghton Mifflin, 1966. Ch. 7.

SHELDON, WILLIAM D. "Reading Instruction in Junior High School," *Development in and Through Reading.* 60th Yearbook of the National Society for the Study of Education, Part I. Chicago: University of Chicago Press, 1961.

STAHL, STANLEY S. *The Teaching of Reading in the Intermediate Grades.* Dubuque, Iowa: Wm. C. Brown, 1965.

TINKER, MILES A., and McCULLOUGH, CONSTANCE. *Teaching Elementary Reading,* 3rd ed. New York: Appleton-Century-Crofts, 1968. Chs. 23–25.

6

Determining Learning Needs in Reading

The previous three chapters stressed the need to provide for individual differences. In order to do so, decisions must be made about such things as assigning children to groups, selecting appropriate reading material for the group or individual, and determining strengths and weaknesses in specific reading skills.

The first part of this chapter is devoted to ways of determining for each child the levels at which he can profit best from reading instruction and carry on independent reading. In the second section, estimating potential for success in reading is discussed. This is followed by suggestions for appraising specific learning needs. The final section is concerned with keeping appropriate records.

Determining Reading Levels

Teachers who organize their classes into groups for reading instruction have to make an initial decision about the proper group for each child. Assignments to instructional groups is usually made on the basis of general level of reading achievement. For example, teachers using a basal reader program must decide which level reader is most appropriate for reading instruction.

Information that may be helpful in first setting up groups can be obtained from children's cumulative records, if they have been well kept. Such records should indicate which material has been used for reading instruction, the results of standardized reading tests or tests that accompany a reading program, report-card ratings, and teacher comments. This combined information can be used as a first step in grouping children. Although one cannot be perfectly sure that the text employed by the previous teacher was suitable for instructional purposes, or that the child has assimilated all, or even some, of the skills supposedly taught through its use, the next book in the series is a logical one to check for suitability.

A CLASS TEST ON THE BASAL READER [1]

The second step is to try out the entire class on the basal reader intended for the middle group. A quick oral reading survey can be made. The books are distributed and the children are told that the purpose is to find out how well they can read the new book. Preparation is given as if the story were to be used instructionally. Then the teacher calls on each child, one at a time, to read orally two or three sentences from near the beginning of the book. If a child is reluctant to try, he is excused. If he stumbles over words or hesitates, he is immediately prompted. If there are not enough copies for the entire class, those who have the book take their turns and then other children get the books, until all have had an opportunity to read. Two half-hour periods, or at most three, usually provide enough time to cover the entire class in this way.

In rating children on a brief sample like this, which is intended to give only a preliminary rough idea of the child's reading, a three-point rating scheme is sufficient: satisfactory (S) doubtful (D) and unsatisfactory (U). Unsatisfactory ratings should be given to those who: (1) are unwilling to try; (2) need to be helped with more than two or three words; and (3) are excessively slow, hesitant, or repetitious.

---

[1] A similar procedure may be used with materials other than basal readers. Some programs suggest the use of placement tests that accompany their program in deciding at which level to place the child.

A doubtful rating indicates that the teacher is not sure that the book is too hard for the child and that more information is needed. Because comprehension is not checked, the teacher may discover later that although the child was rated as satisfactory, he may have a problem with comprehending the material.

Teachers who have not tried this kind of testing may feel that the standards are hazy or indefinite. The first time one tries a test of this kind it may seem difficult to make immediate judgments; but with repetition, the job of deciding becomes easy.

In grade three and up a silent reading test can be given the next day, using the following selection in the same basal reader. After a typical preparatory session with the whole class, the class reads ahead silently. When they finish the selection, they write answers to a set of comprehension questions, which can be dittoed or written on the chalkboard. As they read, the teacher notes which ones finish early and which are the slowest. Low comprehension scores and very slow reading show up additional children for whom this basal reader is probably too difficult.

The following day or two, the children tentatively chosen for the low group by their records and by performance on the silent and oral textbook tests are given similar oral and silent tests in an easier basal reader, usually one for the preceding grade. If that book also seems too hard for a few children, it is desirable to give each of them a more complete individual textbook test.

INDIVIDUAL TEXTBOOK TESTS

In order to prepare an individual textbook test (sometimes called an "informal reading inventory"), the teacher assembles two copies of each reader in a well-graded series, and chooses a test selection in each.[2] The selection should be typical of the book as to difficulty and style, and should start with the beginning of a story in the early part of the book. The teacher marks one copy with a pencil to show where

---

[2] There is a difference of opinion as to whether the test should be based upon the series that is being used for reading instruction or one that the child has not used before.

the test selection begins and then counts off 50, 100, and 200 words, marking each place with a vertical line and writing the number of words in the margin.

A time is selected when about fifteen minutes will be available without interruption. The teacher should try to put the child at ease. He can be told that they are going to try a number of books to see which one seems to be just right for him. A look at the first illustration and a brief discussion helps to lessen the difference from the usual reading lesson. In the primary grades, proper names should be told. Then the child is asked to read the selection orally at sight from one copy, while the teacher follows in the other copy. Of course it is possible to get along with just one book, but less convenient; unless the teacher has a mimeographed copy on which he records the child's performance. If a child hesitates over a word for five seconds, or asks for help, he is told the word. When he finishes reading, a general question such as "What is the story about?" often brings an answer that is complete enough so that comprehension can be rated without additional questioning. A list of specific questions should be prepared in advance, however, for use if the response to the general question is not very informative.

The amount to be read in the book varies. At preprimer level, 50 words are usually enough. From primer level up, 100-word selections are often long enough, but if the teacher is doubtful about the interpretation, an additional 100 words may settle the question. If a selection is obviously too difficult for a child, it can be discontinued after 50 words or even less.

The teacher starts with a book that is expected to be well below the child's reading ability; this increases the child's confidence and gives him a chance to get over the initial nervousness that is quite common in this kind of testing. The books are tried in order of increasing difficulty until it is evident that the material is much too difficult for the child.

Above the primary grades it is desirable to prepare a comparable set of selections in the same basal readers, for testing silent reading. A watch with a second hand, or a stopwatch, is used to time each reading, oral and silent. Comprehension is checked with questions like those used after oral reading. This makes it possible to see how rate and comprehension compare in oral and silent reading. The rate for silent reading should be faster.

In recording, it is helpful to use a separate sheet of paper for each selection. Some teachers prefer to record the child's performance on a mimeographed copy of the selection being read by the child, as illustrated in Figure 20. The name of the child, name of book, pages used, and number of words read are recorded at the top. Errors in word recognition are written down in a column, what the child said and the correct word, side by side. In another column the teacher records all words on which the child has to be prompted. The headings "Repetitions," "Omissions," and "Insertions" can be written near the bottom, and if the child makes one of these types of errors a tally mark is made next to the proper heading. Remarks can also be noted about voice, posture, nervousness, word-by-word reading, etc. At the bottom the teacher writes the total number of different words not read correctly (repeated errors on the same word are not counted) and divides this by the total number of words read, the result giving the percent of error in word recognition. Errors that the child corrects by himself are not counted, and minor faults, such as adding or omitting a final *s* or substituting *a* for *the,* should be counted only once even if repeated several times.

A convenient published set of reader selections, with comprehension questions, can save teachers the trouble of locating their own test selections and making up their own questions. This material includes selections from preprimer through third-reader level.[3]

Interpretation. In interpreting the results of a set of textbook texts, the teacher's primary purpose is to be able to locate the child's independent, instructional, and frustration reading levels.

The *independent reading level* is the highest level at which the

---

[3] Nila Banton Smith, and others. *Graded Selections for Informal Reading Diagnosis, Grades 1 through 3* (New York: New York University Press, 1959).

Edward R. Sipay, *The Macmillan Reader Placement Test* (New York: Macmillan, 1967).

The *Sheldon Basic Reading Series* (Boston: Allyn and Bacon, Inc., 1968) provides what amounts to an informal reading test in the Teachers' Edition for each reader level.

Name _Rob_ How It Is Nowadays (Level 8) p. 18
Number of words: 96 Word Recognition Errors: 4
Comprehension: Excellent. — answered all 5 questions correctly

THE FARMER'S HUT

Once there was a farmer.

He lived in one room of his small hut

with his wife and her mother

and his three small children.

He worked hard on his farm all day. *long*

When he came home at night,

the noises in his house drove him ~~crazy~~. *P*

His wife talked to him.

His ~~mother-in-law~~ talked to him *P*

His three small children talked to him.

And they all talked at the same time!

The poor farmer put his hands

over his ears and cried,

"Please, please, ~~QUIET~~, please!" *quit*

But they went right

on talking.

FIGURE 20. A child's performance on an individual textbook test as recorded on a mimeographed copy. The symbols indicate that the child (1) omitted the *er* in *farmer*, probably realized his mistake and repeated the whole sentence correcting his error; (2) added the word *long;* (3) had two words, *crazy* and *mother-in-law*, pronounced for him; and (4) mispronounced *quiet* as *quit*.

The page was reproduced, except for the pictures and type, as it is found in *How It Is Nowadays* (Level 8). Copyright © 1969 by Ginn and Co., Boston. The original page is in color. Reproduced by permission of the publisher.

child's reading is fluent, word recognition errors are few, and comprehension is very good. The percentage of error in word recognition should not be more than 2 percent. The child feels that the book is easy for him and that he does not need help in reading it. The independent level is usually about one grade below the instructional level.

The *instructional reading level* is the highest level at which the child can read satisfactorily when the book is used for systematic reading instruction, with the usual activities of preparation, guided reading, discussion, and rereading. The percentage of error in word recognition is usually between 2 and 5. Reading tends to be fairly fluent, but some hesitations and repetitions may occur. Comprehension is mainly correct but some details are likely to be forgotten or recalled incorrectly. If the child is asked how he feels about the book, he is likely to answer that it isn't easy, but he can read it.

The *frustration level* is the lowest level at which reading is too difficult for the child. This is shown not only by the excessive number of errors and poor comprehension, but also by signs of emotional tension or distress. Fluency breaks down and hesitations, repetitions, and word-by-word reading appear. Errors may be made on words which have been read correctly in easier material. Most children begin to show signs of frustration when the percentage of error in word recognition rises above 5 percent.

The standards suggested above should be interpreted with some flexibility. For example, intense interest in the content of a book may motivate a child to continue to read it when, by the usual standards, it would be judged too hard for him to read independently. Another child may be so dependent that he stops and waits to be helped whenever he finds a word he does not recognize, so that in effect he has no independent reading level. The child's feeling about a book is a very important factor in deciding about its suitability for him.

Since one of the most frequent errors made by teachers is giving children books that are too hard for them, the distinction among the frustration, instructional, and independent levels, for which we are indebted to Emmett A. Betts, is an important one that can assist greatly in the proper selection of materials.

The instructional implications of the three levels are quite clear. The instructional level is the one to use in assigning children to groups for basal reading instruction. The independent level helps the teacher to judge which books a child is likely to be able to read by himself with satisfaction. The frustration level warns that reading anything as hard as this is likely to be a painful experience for the child. Also, it is very unlikely that the child will improve his reading skills if he is constantly given material that is frustrating for him.

An example of an individual textbook test record is shown in Figure 21. The test was started at the 2^1 reader level, but the child experienced so little difficulty that there was nothing to record except an occasional repetition and some careless errors which were self-corrected. In the 2^2 reader there were three noncorrected word recognition errors (3 errors out of 200 words equals an error rate of 1.5 percent) and comprehension was excellent, so this was rated as suitable for independent reading.

The 3^1 reader proved to be a little more difficult. The child was prompted on two words and failed to correct three errors, giving 2.5 percent error, with reasonably good comprehension. This was rated as a little too hard for independent reading and within the instructional range.

On the 3^2 reader the child made six mispronunciations, was told six words, and omitted two words, amounting to 14 errors or 7 percent error. Reading was slow and somewhat halting, and comprehension was only fair. This selection was judged to be at the beginning of the child's frustration range.

The general conclusion reached was that the child could read independently in second-reader materials and could probably also read some of the easiest third-reader material independently; that the proper instructional level was 3^1; and that for the present the 3^2 book was a little too difficult. However, since these two ratings were both close to borderline, it was felt that the teacher should watch for signs that he might be ready to move into 3^2 instructional material in the near future.

INDIVIDUAL TEXTBOOK TEST

2^1 Reader   Said   For   Told   Comprehension

2^1 Reader	Said	For	Told	Comprehension
pp. 30-31	a	the (self corrected)		Fluent
100 words	when	then (s-c)		Excellent

Repetitions //

% of errors: 0   Level: Independent

2^2 Reader	Said	For	Told	Comprehension
pp. 22-24	older	old (s-c)	trouble	Excellent
200 words	each	catch (s-c)		
	want	wanted		
	twin	twice		

Repetitions //

% of errors: 1.5   Level: Independent
(words not recognized)

3^1 Reader	Said	For	Told	Comprehension
pp. 47-48	was	wasn't	trembling	Good
200 words	to	into	sylvan	
	a	that		

Repetitions /

% of errors: 2.5   Level: Instructional

3^2 Reader	Said	For	Told	Comprehension
pp. 30-31	ever	never	especially	Fair
200 words	they	then	Granny	
	wall	wall's	dairy	Reading much
	the	a	trudged	slower
	bushes	busy	knitting	
	quite	quiet	company	Word by word
				at times

Repetitions /
Omissions //

% of error: 7   Level: Frustration

FIGURE 21. The record of an individual textbook test.

160

INTERPRETING STANDARDIZED READING TESTS

Decisions about which standardized tests to give and when to administer them are usually made by the principal or some other administrative officer of the school system, rather than by the classroom teacher. The teacher is usually expected to administer the test, strictly according to the directions given in the test manual. Sometimes the tests are sent away to be scored by machine; more often, the teacher scores them with a standard scoring key. When the testing is done in the late spring, the teacher gets the results too late in the year to be of much use in planning the instructional program; the scores are more useful to next year's teacher. When the testing is done in the autumn, as is becoming more common, the teacher can make immediate use of the results.

Most standardized reading tests are silent reading tests of the survey type, intended primarily to give an indication of the general or average reading level. Almost all tests of this kind have two parts, one a test of word meaning and the other a test of paragraph comprehension. Sometimes there is a test of word recognition also, or instead of word meaning. A few tests also sample word-identification skills. Most of these tests are intended to be used in a range of two or three grades, and are planned to start with items easy enough for the poorest readers in the lowest grade, and to present items increasing steadily in difficulty until the hardest items are challenging to the best readers in the highest grade for which the test is intended. The most commonly used tests are of this general type, and include the *Metropolitan, Stanford, California, STEP,* and *Iowa Tests of Basic Skills* reading tests.[4]

A few tests provide a more analytical picture of silent reading skills. They may include tests of rate of reading, accuracy of reading, or some study skills. Included in this group are the Survey Test of the *Diagnostic Reading Tests,* the *Gates-MacGinitie Reading Test,* and the *Iowa Test of Basic Skills:* Work-Study Skills.

[4] Descriptive information about all tests mentioned in this book is given in Appendix A.

THE INTERPRETATION OF TEST SCORES

The scores on standardized reading tests can usually be expressed in more than one way. Most common is the *reading grade* equivalent; a reading grade of 1.8, for example, means that the child's score is equal to that of an average child in the eighth month of the first grade.

Some tests also provide for comparisons with the full range of performance in the child's own grade. This is usually done with percentile scores; these indicate the percentage of children at that grade who make lower or equal scores. A *percentile* score of 75 means that the child's score surpasses or equals the scores made by 75 percent of the children in the same grade. A few tests also provide *stanine* scores, which range from a low of 1 through an average of 5 to a high of 9. Because they are equally spaced steps, stanine scores are particularly useful in comparing a child's performance on different subtests, or the performance of different children at a given grade level. For example, a stanine of 7 is as much better than a score of 5, as a stanine of 4 is better then a stanine score of 2.

Standardized tests of reading are generally quite good at placing the pupils in rank order of reading ability. Since the grade, percentile, and stanine scores are based on comparison with a national sampling of children, they may not show how the child compares with his classmates, who may as a group be above or below the national averages. The grade scores usually come closer to the frustration or instructional reading level than to the independent level. Some tests give grade scores which rather consistently run higher than the instructional level indicated by textbook tests; in these cases, the textbook test is probably the safer guide in deciding what basal reader the child is ready to use.

One must be quite careful in interpreting scores that are near the bottom or the top of the scores obtainable on a particular test. A test once commonly used in the seventh grade, for example, yielded a reading grade of 3.0 even for a paper with no right answers. If a child is near the bottom on a particular test, it is wise to retest him with an easier test; if he is near the top of the scale, he might do considerably better if given a chance at a harder test.

Guessing is a factor in test scores that is hard to evaluate. Normal readers get most of their right answers by reading and thinking, and relatively few points from successful guessing. The poorer the child is in reading, the greater the probability is that his score on a silent reading test is artificially raised by an excessive amount of successful guessing.

By looking over the answers on the test blanks and by careful observation during testing, teachers can usually pick out the children who have received excessive credit from guessing. Most children get almost all of their answers right while the questions are easy for them, then get into more difficult questions in which some of their answers are wrong, and then stop. The excessive guesser starts making errors very early in the test and tends to have a quite high proportion of wrong answers.

Teachers also should realize that standardized reading tests have limitations and are not perfectly reliable measures of reading ability. Any test is only a sample of behavior from which the presence of skills or abilities is inferred. Also, there are errors of measurement in any test. That is, the score a child might obtain on a test may vary within a certain range. For example, if a test which has a standard error of measurement of 0.3 were administered many times to a child whose true grade score was 2.1, two out of three of his scores would fall between 1.8 and 2.4; one of three would fall below 1.8 or above 2.4. Furthermore, there are a number of factors such as extreme anxiety, lack of motivation, or a severe visual problem that may influence a child's test performance. Teachers should, therefore, exercise judgment in interpreting test results.

STANDARDIZED ORAL READING TESTS

A standardized oral reading test contains a series of paragraphs arranged in order of increasing difficulty. As the child reads orally at sight, the examiner makes a record of errors on a duplicate copy or on a special record form. The child starts with a very easy paragraph and continues until the material is too hard for him. Differences among tests exist as to what are considered to be errors, the type and number of scores given, and the number of forms available. For example, the *Gray Oral Reading Tests* have four questions (all factual recall) for each selection; and give but one score, expressed as a grade score, which is based on the number of word recognition errors and the time taken to read each selection. The *Gilmore Oral Reading Test* gives separate ratings for accuracy, comprehension (mainly factual recall), and rate. The *Spache Diagnostic Reading Scales,* which has seven or eight comprehension questions (factual recall, inferences, etc.) for each selection, allows one to estimate the child's independent and instructional levels in a manner similar to that of an informal reading inventory. Oral reading tests are also found in the *Gates-McKillop Reading Diagnosis Tests* and the *Durrell Analysis of Reading Difficulty,* each of which also contains a number of other tests that may be useful in the detailed analysis of the reading performance of children with reading disabilities.

Although there is evidence that some standardized oral reading tests tend to yield higher scores than others, the results generally tend to agree fairly closely with the estimate of the child's instructional level obtained from a well-constructed and administered informal reading inventory. If the staff does not have the knowledge or time to construct a good informal reading inventory, a standardized oral reading test may be employed, provided that the examiner has had adequate training in its administration, scoring, and interpretation. Standardized oral reading tests, however, should not be used with the same child more often than every few months. Each school should experiment to learn which standardized oral reading test gives the most accurate and useful results for their own needs.

Judging Reading Capacity

A generation ago, if a child had great trouble in learning to read it was taken for granted that he was stupid; now we recognize that many children of normal or even well above average intelligence can have special difficulty in learning to read. Most children do about as well on reading tests as on measures of intelligence. About 15 percent score significantly lower on reading tests and a small percent score higher in reading than in mental ability. The child whose reading is well below the level of reasoning and understanding indicated by an intelligence test, as well as below grade level, is said to have a *reading disability*. It is important to distinguish these children from those whose reading is poor because of generally slow or limited mental development.

Suppose, for instance, that a fourth-grade teacher has two children who are reading at second-reader level. They are both just nine years old. One has a recorded I.Q. of 105, indicating that his mental age is a little higher than his chronological age, and is normal for his grade. The other has a recorded I.Q. of 83, and a mental age of seven and a half years, which is average for the second grade. The first youngster has a reading disability; the second child reads just as poorly, but is doing about as well as he can. If the facilities for giving extra help in reading are limited, the first child is a better prospect for improvement than the second, although the dull child also may be able to improve certain reading skills.

For the purposes of the classroom teacher, the simplest way to estimate whether a child's reading is up to his capacity level is to compare his reading age with his mental age.[5] For a difference to be meaningful, the reading age should be at least nine months lower in the primary grades, a year lower in grades four and five, and at least eighteen months lower from sixth grade up.

Children whose reading ages are lower than their mental ages fall into two groups. Those whose reading ability is well below grade level are genuine cases of reading disability who should be given special remedial help. The other group consists of quite bright children whose

---

[5] If the reading test gives a grade score but no age score, an approximate reading age can be obtained by adding 5.2 years to the grade score.

For more accurate ways of determining reading capacity and estimating the degree of reading disability, refer to: Albert J. Harris, *How to Increase Reading Ability*, 5th ed. (New York: McKay, 1970), pp. 208–215.

reading ability is about average for their grade level; they usually need stimulation and motivation rather than extra help with basic reading skills.

If the intelligence test was given more than two or three months ago, the child's mental age has increased during the interval and it is necessary to estimate what his present mental age is. The simplest way to do this is to multiply his present chronological age by his I.Q. For example, a fifth-grade boy whose I.Q. was found to be 93 two years ago and who is now ten years six months old (10½ years = 10.5) has an estimated present mental age of nine years eight months (10.5 × .93 = 9.77). His present reading score on a standardized test is 4.7 and his estimated reading age is nine years nine months (4.7 + 5.2). Although he is reading somewhat below his grade placement, his reading seems to be on a par with his mental ability.

The big question with this procedure is the possibility that the intelligence measure is inaccurate. In the primary grades, children who do not read well are not especially handicapped in taking group mental tests, because the tests use pictures and do not require any reading. From the fourth grade up, many of the group intelligence tests now in use require the child to read the questions, so that a child with very poor reading ability cannot find out what the questions ask and necessarily makes a low score. A low I.Q. on a test that requires reading may show only that the child has a reading problem.

When the intelligence test score is untrustworthy because the nature of the test handicaps a very poor reader, a rough measure of reading capacity can be obtained by using a teacher-made or commercially-produced informal reading inventory. The teacher starts with material at or one level above the child's frustration level, reads a new selection to him, and asks comprehension questions. If he does well (answers at least 70 percent of the questions correctly), the teacher goes to the next higher selection. There also are standardized listening comprehension tests available, such as the ones included in the *Durrell Listening-Reading Series* and the *Sequential Tests of Educational Progress* (*STEP*). If a child's listening comprehension tested in this way is two or more years above his instructional reading level, it is reasonably certain that he has a reading disability. A one-year difference points in the same direction but is more doubtful. When it is possible to arrange for the child to be given an individual intelligence test such as the *Stanford-Binet* or the *Wechsler Intelligence Scale for Children* by a trained psychologist, the results are more trustworthy than either group mental ability tests or teacher-constructed reading capacity tests.

Investigating Specific Reading Needs

To the alert teacher, every reading activity provides opportunities for getting better acquainted with the reading performance of the children. During the preparation for a new story some children are eager and interested, others are not. Some already know the meanings of words that are strange to the others. During silent reading the teacher can notice many relevant characteristics such as lip movements. The discussion that follows silent reading discloses variations in completeness of understanding and recall. In oral reading one can notice difficulties in word recognition, voice, expression, and so on. Day by day, then, the teacher's perception of each child's reading needs can be amplified and clarified.

INTERPRETING PATTERNS IN SILENT READING

Watching the members of a group as they read silently provides opportunities to observe finger pointing, lip movements, head movements, poor reading posture, holding the book too close to or too far from the eyes, and fidgeting. It is easy to see which children finish an assigned selection first and which ones take the longest. Special strengths or weaknesses in comprehension can be observed as children try to answer questions of various kinds, orally or in writing. Some children can only answer questions about details; others grasp main ideas also. Some cannot interpret beyond what is directly stated; others can "read between the lines," respond to what is implied, anticipate developments, and predict outcomes.

The teacher's judgments about silent reading performance can be based in part on the results of a recent standardized reading test. Comparing paragraph meaning scores with word recognition or word meaning scores discloses some children whose paragraph scores are substantially higher. These are usually children whose word identification skills or reading vocabularies are relatively weak and in consequence they usually depend excessively on guessing from the context. They are often called "context readers." When the paragraph reading score is significantly lower than the word recognition or word meaning score, a weakness in comprehension is disclosed that needs further study.

A comparison of rate and comprehension is also likely to be informative, particularly in the middle and upper grades. Those with low rate and substantially higher comprehension probably can benefit from training to read faster. Those with high rate and lower comprehension need training that stresses accurate reading or versatility. When rate and comprehension are both low, the comprehension problem deserves priority in further analysis of the difficulty.

Children who are excellent readers are often both fast and accurate. They do not read everything at the same rate, however, but rather adapt their reading to the requirements of the material. They slow down when the material contains many important details and requires very high accuracy, as is true in much scientific and mathematical reading. They read very quickly in easy narrative material. A flexible rate that varies according to the material and the reader's purpose for reading is more satisfactory than consistently fast or consistently slow reading.

The consistently rapid reader tends to be more successful in grasping the central thought of a selection than in noting and remembering details. He is likely to enjoy narrative material, both fictional and historical, and do well with it. When factual information is presented in highly organized and somewhat condensed form, as is characteristic of many textbooks, the inflexibly rapid reader tends to hit the high spots only and to come out with a rather sketchy and somewhat hazy or inaccurate account.

The consistently slow reader is sometimes slow because he has to decode many words that he should be able to recognize at once; in this case the word recognition problem is primary. There are many slow readers, however, whose word recognition is good. They tend to read as though every word were precious; they are afraid of missing anything. They are sometimes so absorbed with details that they miss the main ideas; they cannot see the forest because of the trees.

INTERPRETING ORAL READING CHARACTERISTICS

The teacher's main resource for analyzing oral reading is a clear understanding of what constitutes an excellent performance, thus providing a set of standards with which each child's reading can be compared. Knowing what is important and what is desirable, the teacher can watch and listen with discerning eyes and ears. The teacher who regards each sample of oral reading as another opportunity to discover specific facts can really use each oral reading situation as an occasion for discovering needs.

When a teacher notes that Billy's voice sounds tense, that he doesn't hold the book securely, that he makes quite a number of repetitions, and that his ears turn pink when the teacher corrects a mispronunciation, these observations can provide a starting point for helping Billy, by stimulating questioning and thinking. Is the book too difficult for him at present? Should he be changed to a group with an easier basal reader? How can he be helped to feel more secure in oral reading? Should he be called on after he has heard others read the same passage? How can he be helped to feel less embarrassed when he makes a mistake? Would it be better to have him read orally alone to the teacher until he becomes more secure? Asking questions like these is the first step to finding solutions.

In good oral reading, the words are grouped in phrases, and thought units are indicated by appropriate pauses. Subtleties of meaning are often conveyed by inflections and the placement of emphasis on one or another word. Thus, the simple question, "Where are you going?" can be spoken so as to express a polite request for information, a sarcastic comment, or an exasperated demand, depending on which word is emphasized, whether the voice rises or falls, and so on. Difficulties in fluency, in phrasing, or in the ability to convey the meaning of the statement are readily observed by teachers.

The child with monotonous, word-by-word reading is easily distinguished from the one who really sounds like the story character speaking. Slow word recognition, hesitations, repetitions, and paying little heed to phrasing or to punctuation are easily recognized. Rapid, jerky reading and inability to keep the place while reading also are easily apparent.

Oral reading is particularly useful in the opportunities it provides for analyzing a child's word recognition skills. Does the child have a sight recognition vocabulary of good size? Does he pick up new words quickly? Does he ignore the context, or does he rely excessively on guessing? When he misreads a word, does the sentence make sense? If not, does he notice that something is wrong and try it over again?

Does the child try to figure out unknown words, or does he wait to be told? Does he try spelling, using the names of the letters? Does he try sounding? Does he know the sounds of the word elements that he should have learned by now? Is he able to use consonant substitution? Can he blend sounds together? If his first attempt is unsuccessful, is he able to shift to an alternative vowel sound or to place the accent on a different syllable? Does he give up easily?

A good reader is able to use several methods of attack on unknown words. He uses morphemic analysis, dividing the word into meaning units. He applies his phonic knowledge in determining a probable sound for each unit and combines the units in left-to-right sequence. He tries the resulting word to see if it makes good sense in the sentence, and if it does not, he tries again.

Aside from fluency and accuracy, the child's voice may be revealing. Is it too loud or too soft, pitched too high or too low? Is it hoarse, or strained, or tremulous? Is there evidence of a speech defect, or a foreign accent, or a regional dialect?

When a teacher listens to a child's oral reading, it is sometimes very difficult to decide how the child is attempting to solve the unknown words and what causes the particular errors that he makes. If the errors are written down as they occur, they can be reviewed later at a time when the teacher is free to ponder over them. Having a written record also makes it easy to compare the frequency of different kinds of faults and to decide what kind of help the child needs most urgently.

If a tape recorder is available, it can help greatly in recording and analyzing oral reading. While the child is reading, the teacher does not have to write anything and so can give undivided attention to listening. The tape can be played back after school and a written analysis made then. Portions that are not easy to record can be played over again. It is also helpful to invite children to listen to their own recorded readings and to encourage them to help evaluate their own performance and to set their own goals for improvement. Tape recordings of the same child's reading made at intervals usually arouse real interest in the children and provide a dramatic but also clear and useful basis for appraising progress.

USING A WORD LIST

Some children are so clever at guessing from context that when they read connected, meaningful material, their weaknesses in word recognition skills do not show up clearly. There are also some children who are overwhelmed or distracted by the other words in context. To get a picture of word recognition as such, it is advisable to test a child on words which are presented one at a time without any meaningful context.

The word lists in Figure 22 have proved to be reliable and useful.[6] If a child has difficulty with four or more words in any list, he is likely to find many unknown words in books of that level, so that material in which he has this much difficulty is probably at his frustration level. If he makes only one error on a list, he should be able to use material at that level for reading instruction. Two or three errors on a list is a doubtful or marginal score.

A teacher can make his own word lists from the vocabularies of the particular basal readers he is using, or thinking of using. In primary

---

[6] An equivalent set of word lists is given in: A. J. Harris, *How to Increase Reading Ability*, 5th ed. (New York: McKay, 1970), p. 178. The lists in Fig. 22 were compiled with the assistance of Myra Skolnick.

QUEENS COLLEGE Form 2
EDUCATIONAL CLINIC
Graded_Word Lists

Preprimer	Primer	1st Reader	Grade 2
and	barn	animal	claw
can	call	dinner	full
down	its	hurry	quickly
we	gave	getting	tent
like	jumped	sled	soup
see	table	nose	neck
my	them	buy	outside
is	water	until	straw
he	please	why	deep
said	morning	say	careful

Grade 3	Grade 4	Grade 5
cheer	adventure	alternate
reindeer	bracket	companion
pleasant	conceal	definite
freight.	enter	estimate
knit	group	majesty
insect	kerosene	glitter
mitten	magnet	particular
press	notion	reverence
shower	poetry	solution
whether	screw	uncomfortable

FIGURE 22. A set of graded word lists for testing word recognition.

grade readers the "new" words are listed page by page at the back of the book. If a book has about 150 pages, a fifteen-word sample can be made by taking one word from every tenth page; a twenty-word sample would involve one word from every 7.5 pages. To make the sample a truly unbiased one, one should decide in advance to choose all words according to the same rules. For example, one fifteen-word sample could be obtained by selecting the first new word on pages 2, 12, 22, etc. An equivalent sample could be made by using pages 3, 13, 23, etc. or by using the second word on the page. Or, if there are 150 "new" words, you simply could use every tenth word that appears in the list. In basal readers for the middle grades, representative samplings of the new words can be compiled from the glossaries at the back of each book.

The results of testing with properly constructed word lists tend to agree closely with the results of the more time-consuming textbook sample tests, particularly at primary-grade levels if the child's main problem is not with comprehension. They can be used to check decisions about the child's instructional and independent reading levels.

In using a word list as a word pronunciation test (a child may be able to pronounce a word but not know its meaning or its particular meaning in a selection), a child may respond at once to some words. Other words may cause him to stop and attempt to decode them. If he misreads a word, the child should be asked to try it again; two corrected errors (corrections made after he is asked to try them again) are counted as one error. If the child misreads a word and corrects it immediately by himself, it is not counted as an error.

It is an excellent idea to ask the child to do his thinking out loud as he struggles with the word, so that the teacher can understand what he is trying to do and can gain insight into exactly what goes wrong. A teacher can often learn a great deal about a child's difficulties in word recognition by listening as he tries to solve unknown words. This discloses the process he is attempting to use, as well as the results.

Every time a child reads orally, the teacher has an opportunity to note errors in word recognition. If these are written down, it does not take long to assemble enough misread words to get an idea of where the child's difficulties in word recognition lie. The problem may include a lack of knowledge about single consonants, short or long vowel sounds, digraphs, blends, or syllabication; there may be inability to blend parts together, carelessness in observing word endings or middles, reversals, excessive guessing, or reluctance to use the word-analysis skills which the child has learned.

The analysis of errors made during connected reading can be confirmed and supplemented by testing on words in list arrangement, as described above, and also by directly testing knowledge of phonics.

TESTING PHONIC KNOWLEDGE

Sometimes it is very useful to a teacher to be able to find out quickly what a child knows and does not know about phonics. Two inexpensive, quick, simple, and yet reasonably comprehensive instruments for testing phonic knowledge are the *Roswell-Chall Diagnostic Reading Test* and the *Botel Reading Inventory.* Group tests that allow the teacher to analyze word-recognition skills include the *Mc-Cullough Word-Analysis Tests,* the *Silent Reading Diagnostic Tests,* and the *Doren Diagnostic Reading Tests.* These are rather time-consuming to administer and to score.

A teacher can construct a simple, fast test of phonic skills that can be given to a child in five minutes or less. What to include would depend on how much phonics instruction the children have received. At third-reader level, this should include single consonants, consonant digraphs (*th, sh, ch, wh*), consonant blends (*bl, cr, str,* etc.), short vowels, long vowels, and vowel digraphs (*ea, oa, ew,* etc.) In the middle and upper grades some common syllables, prefixes, and suffixes might be added.

The phonic elements to be tested can be typed in non-alphabetical order in a sheet of paper or placed on separate cards with a carbon copy used as a record blank; or a number of copies can be made from a stencil. The single letters or letter groups should be well separated, and there should be at least double spacing between lines.

Since children are usually taught phonic elements in whole words, their knowledge of most sounds can be tested by asking them to say a word which has that sound in it. If the child cannot think of a suitable word, ask if he can pronounce the sound by itself. Knowledge of when to use a long or short vowel sound can be tested with pairs of words like *pin-pine, mat-mate,* etc. For letters and combinations that have more than one sound (*c, g, ow,* etc.) any correct answer is acceptable, and the child can be asked if he knows another sound it sometimes represents.

Many children can learn phonic elements but have great difficulty in using them successfully because they have difficulty with blending; after they sound out a word, they cannot put the sounds together. To test a child's ability to blend, one can pronounce a word sound by sound being careful not to distort the sounds, and ask him what word you are saying in this piece-by-piece way. A brief series of words will do, such as *u-s, m-e, a-t, m-e-n, t-a-ck, br-ing, sl-a-te*. If a child has real difficulty with blending, breaking words into larger parts such as syllables is likely to be more helpful to him than a letter-by-letter phonic procedure.

EVALUATING INDEPENDENT READING

Now that independent reading has become a quite important part of the reading program, it is necessary to have ways of evaluating it. The amount of reading that the child claims to have done is easily ascertained. How to keep records of independent reading is discussed in the concluding section of this chapter and in Chapter 13, and from that record the amount done is easily seen. But quantity as such is not the most important consideration.

One of the main goals of the independent reading program is to develop a love for reading as a recreational activity. Some children really enjoy independent reading. Others take it in stride, neither disliking it nor becoming enthusiastic about it. Still others actively dislike reading and manage to waste a good deal of the time assigned to independent reading. The teacher can usually observe indications of feelings about independent reading if he is alert to the importance of doing this.

Since independent reading is usually not checked as frequently or as thoroughly as other types of reading, it is only natural that some children, valuing praise more than the reading itself, should try to receive a maximum of credit for their reading. One honest way is to limit one's reading to thin books with many illustrations and little reading matter. The teacher is well advised, therefore, to keep track of the number of pages read, as well as the number of books. A less straightforward way of padding the record is to skim through a book without really reading it, trying to get just enough of the content to be able to provide the expected kind of report. Taking the trouble to ask fairly searching questions of a child who has finished a book encourages reading with some care.

Many children choose a wisely varied reading diet, some of it easy, some of it challenging, most of it comfortable, with a range of topics. Some good readers restrict their choices to books that are so easy that the child has little to gain from them. Some poor readers consistently pick books that are above their frustration level because they do not want to admit their limited skill. Even though the children are allowed a wide range of freedom of choice, the teacher should be on the alert for children who consistently choose books whose difficulty is inappropriate for them, or who have narrow reading interests.

In independent reading, then, important areas of evaluation include the amount of reading done, the adequacy of comprehension and recall, the honesty of the child's reporting, and the suitability of the books chosen.

EVALUATING FUNCTIONAL READING

There are not many standardized tests that measure functional reading skills. Tests of ability to interpret maps, charts, and tables are included in the Work-Study Skills part of the *Iowa Tests of Basic Skills* and the Social Studies part of the *California Achievement Tests*. The *Comprehensive Tests of Basic Skills,* Levels 1, 2, and 3, include subtests on using reference and graphic materials.

In evaluating functional reading skills, most teachers will have to rely primarily on their own resources. Recent standardized test scores will not often be available and, even when they are, will cover only part of the area. Teachers can learn a great deal by paying careful attention to the signs of difficulties that children may show during directed reading activities in various textbooks. Some reading workbooks contain practice exercises for developing specific study skills which can be used as they are, or which can be employed as sources of ideas for teacher-made exercises.

The teacher in the middle or upper grades may want to test for specific things that have been recently taught. These may include the meanings of technical terms; location skills, involving finding entries in such resources as dictionaries or encyclopedias; and outlining skills. Exercises which are used in the development of these skills also serve to indicate which children have understood and satisfactorily completed the assignment and which ones have not. For the latter group, talking with the child about the difficulties he experienced in doing the exercise may be more revealing than any amount of further testing. A useful procedure is to ask the child to do over again the items he got wrong, giving his reasons and explaining his steps. This kind of simple exploration often discloses the heart of the difficulty and indicates what additional teaching is needed.

Keeping Reading Records

Keeping adequate records is an indispensable necessity if children are to be understood and treated as individuals. Few teachers have such remarkable memories that they can keep track of the details about each child in the class without writing things down. Record-keeping can, however, become a heavy burden unless care is taken to organize it efficiently.

In devising a record-keeping scheme, the teacher will do well to keep in mind the following desirable characteristics: (1) The records should provide a maximum of information with a minimum of writing. (2) Records should be organized so that important points can be easily noticed. (3) Records should emphasize items which have instructional significance. (4) A uniform sequence of items makes it easy to compare records of different children, or to compare summaries made at different times on the same child. (5) A good record-keeping system will call the teacher's attention to kinds of information he should have.

USING A CHECK LIST

One way of simplifying record-keeping is to use a check list. In the preceding sections of this chapter a large number of specific items

READING ANALYSIS CHECK LIST

by

Albert J. Harris

Name _____ Date of birth _____ Date of rating _____
Standardized Reading Test Date given _____ Reading Age _____
  Gd. Scores: Wd. Recog _____ Vocab. _____ Comp. _____ Total _____
Informal Reading Inventory Date given _____
  Levels: Indepd. _____ Inst. _____ Frust. _____
Intelligence Test Date given _____
  I.Q. _____ Estimated present M.A. _____
Reading Capacity Teacher estimate _____ Listening Comp. _____
Rating normal progress _____ achievement up to ability _____
  mild disability _____ severe disability _____
Reading group placement Group name _____ Reader level _____
  Work seems: too hard _____ about right _____ too easy _____

Silent Reading Characteristics
Moves lips _____ Moves head _____ Poor attention _____
Eyes wander _____ Vocalizes _____ Finger points _____
Poor posture _____ Fidgety _____
Holds book: too close _____ too far away _____ at odd angle _____

Comprehension Problems Generally poor _____ Difficulty with:
Main ideas _____ Conclusions _____ Sequence _____ Cause-effect _____
Details _____ Inferences _____ Directions _____ Uncritical _____
Too literal interpretation _____ Other _____

Oral Reading
Fluency. Word by word _____ poor phrasing _____ hesitations _____
ignores punctuation _____ monotone _____ repetitions _____
very slow _____ rapid _____ skips lines _____ loses place _____
poor eye-voice span _____

Word Recognition General. Small sight vocabulary _____
common words misread _____ inserts words _____ omits words _____
reversals _____ confuses these specific pairs: _____
_____

Use of Context. Excessive guessing _____ substitutes words of
similar meaning _____ omits or skips unknown words _____
substitutes whole phrases _____ fails to use context _____
substitutes words which spoil meaning _____ fails to correct
errors when meaning is spoiled _____
Method of Decoding Unknown Words. Does not try _____

Spells ____ Attempts to sound, using: single letters ____
phonograms ____ syllables ____ Uses configuration, size,
shape ____ Attends mainly to: beginnings ____ middles ____
endings ____
Attempts morphemic analysis: words within words ____
roots ____ prefixes ____ suffixes ____ syllables ____
Lacks flexibility in word analysis ____

Specific Word Analysis Difficulties Poor visual
discrimination ____ Poor auditory discrimination: consonants ____ vowels ____ rhymes ____ Blending: letters ____
syllables ____ Reversal tendency ____ letter confusions
(list) ____ Symbol-sound associations: consonants ____ cons.
blends ____ cons. digraphs ____ c and g ____ short vowels ____
long vowels ____ vowel digraphs ____ diphthongs ____
silent letters ____ word families ____ syllabication generalizations ____ phonic generalizations ____ exceptions to
generalizations: phonic ____ syllab. ____

Use of Voice. Nervous, tremulous ____ too loud ____ too
soft ____ too high ____ too low ____ generally poor enunciation ____ slights word endings ____ slurs word together ____
mispronounces particular letters ____ sing-song ____ regional
dialect ____ foreign accent ____

Independent Reading
Enjoys ____ accepts ____ dislikes ____ Comprehension poor ____
recall scanty ____ Reports honestly ____ tends to exaggerate ____
Chooses books that are: too hard ____ too easy ____ poor
quality ____
Special interests:

FIGURE 23. A check list for concise recording of a large amount of information about a child's reading.

have been discussed, on which it would be desirable to have a written
record. A check list makes it possible to record information on many
points with a minimum of writing, since for most items all the teacher
needs to do is to decide which entries to check.

A check list which summarizes the points discussed in this chapter
is shown in Figure 23. The first few lines provide space for recording
identifying data and for listing the most recent scores on reading tests
and measures of reading capacity. The rest of the page provides spe-

cific places to record judgments about over-all performance, silent reading, comprehension, oral reading, word recognition, and independent reading. It is easy to make the most important items stand out by checking them with a red pencil, using an ordinary pencil for the rest of the items.

Teachers may use this check list as it is, or may prefer to use some of the ideas in it in making up check lists of their own. A form like this can be stenciled and duplicated. If the teacher finds that he is unable to fill out certain parts of the check list, he can use his judgment whether or not that information is really necessary for him. The entries that are checked provide leads to particular skills on which group or individual instruction can be centered.

A teacher using a check list will usually fill it out first for those children who have the most trouble in reading. If he takes the trouble to fill it out for the average and superior readers also, he may be surprised to find that even the children who are the best readers in the class have some specific areas in which they can use some help.

Probably the most efficient way to use the check list is to go down the list of underlined headings, checking at the left if satisfactory and using a cross to mean "some improvement needed." Details are then filled in only for the headings with crosses.

OTHER TYPES OF RECORDS

Some teachers like to prepare a file folder for each child in which records of various kinds can be kept, while others prefer to use a loose-leaf notebook. Whichever is used, the reading record of a child should include: (1) the kinds of information that are included in a check list such as that in Figure 23; (2) a cumulative record of the child's independent reading, such as is shown in Figure 45; and (3) in the case of children with special difficulties in reading, a summary of possible causal handicaps and remedial recommendations.

In addition to summaries, there should be provision for filing little notes. For this, it is helpful to have a pad of 3 × 5-inch or 4 × 6-inch paper or cards handy. Whenever the teacher notices something about a child's reading that he does not want to forget, he can quickly jot down the child's name, the date, and one or two comments. These jottings should be sorted once a week or oftener into the children's folders or parts of the notebook. About once a month the teacher should go over the accumulated notes for each child and from them make additions or changes in the child's summary. Information recorded in this way is far more likely to be used than if the teacher relies on his memory.

Summary

This chapter has been concerned with ways in which teachers can determine the reading skills and instructional needs of their pupils. Attention has been given to determining levels of reading achievement, judging capacity for reading, exploring specific reading needs, and keeping records.

1. In determining reading levels, the teacher needs to differentiate between material at the child's instructional level and material at his independent reading level; material at the child's frustration level should not be used for instructional purposes.

2. A quick class survey based upon the material to be used for instruction can be used for preliminary grouping.

3. An informal reading inventory can be used to obtain more detailed information about a child's reading abilities.

4. In grouping children, the teacher should consider information obtained from: standardized tests, informal tests, and records and ratings made by previous teachers.

5. Teachers should distinguish between children who are reading about as well as can be expected and those who have the capacity to read at a higher level.

   a. Reading age should be compared with mental age.

   b. If a dependable measure of mental ability is not available, the child's level of listening comprehension may be used as a rough measure of reading capacity.

6. In everyday reading activities, the teacher should gain informa-

tion about silent reading by observing the children as they read and by analyzing their answers to questions.

7. Helpful interpretations can be made by comparing paragraph meaning with word meaning, and rate with comprehension as determined by standardized tests.

8. Oral reading can provide a wealth of information regarding fluency, accuracy of word recognition, word-analysis skills, use of voice and speech.

9. Word pronuncation abilities can be analyzed by using a set of graded word lists.

10. Phonic knowledge can be surveyed very quickly.

11. In evaluating a child's independent reading, the teacher should pay attention not only to the amount read but also to the child's attitude about independent reading, the honesty of his reporting, his comprehension, and the suitability of his choices.

12. Although some information may be obtained from standardized tests, functional reading skills are appraised mainly by teacher observation and teacher-made tests of the particular skills most recently taught.

13. In a practical record keeping system, a large amount of information is maintained with relatively little writing.

   a. A check list filled out for each child provides information in an organized, accessible, and highly condensed form.

   b. Informal notations, records of independent reading, and special summaries for children with reading disabilities are also recommended.

Recommended Reading

BARRETT, THOMAS C., ED. *The Evaluation of Children's Reading Achievement.* Perspectives in Reading, No. 8. Newark, Del.: International Reading Association, 1967.

BOND, GUY L., and TINKER, MILES A. *Reading Difficulties: Their Diagnosis and Correction,* 2nd ed. New York: Appleton-Century-Crofts, 1967. Chs. 8, 9.

DE BOER, DOROTHY L., ED. *Reading Diagnosis and Evaluation.* Proceedings of the Thirteenth Annual Convention, Vol. 13, Part 4. Newark, Del.: International Reading Association, 1970.

HARRIS, ALBERT J. *How to Increase Reading Ability,* 5th ed. New York: McKay, 1970. Chs. 7, 8.

SCHELL, LEO M., and BURNS, PAUL C. *Remedial Reading: An Anthology of Sources.* Boston: Allyn and Bacon, Inc., 1968. Ch. 3.

STRANG, RUTH. *Diagnostic Teaching of Reading,* 2nd ed. New York: McGraw-Hill, 1969. Chs. 3, 4, 5.

7

Providing for Individual
and Group Needs

Teachers generally accept the reality of large and varying differences in reading ability. Few question the need to meet individual and group needs. Yet, the question most frequently asked by teachers is, "How can we teach reading to all the children in a class and still provide for the special needs of each child?" The answer lies partially in the ways in which the class is organized for reading instruction.

The general idea common to the plans presented in the earlier chapters is that a well-conceived reading program should make use of several ways of organizing the class, using for each kind of reading activity a class organization best suited to it. Each of the plans that have been suggested combines group reading activities, individualized reading activities, and whole-class reading activities. The proportionate emphasis on one or another form of organization varies with the maturity of the pupils, the range of their abilities, and their instructional needs.

In this chapter, the ways in which a class might be organized for teaching reading are discussed in detail. The first section considers grouping; the second, whole-class activities; and the third deals with individualized reading. In each section priority is given to answering the practical questions repeatedly asked by teachers.

Making Group Reading Efficient

VARIED GROUPS FOR SPECIFIC PURPOSES

In a well-organized reading program the teacher uses different kinds of grouping for different parts of the total reading program.

Grouping by Reading Levels. The most commonly used form of grouping within the class, and the one usually given the largest time allowance, is grouping children for instruction with material at a particular level of difficulty. The main basis for assigning children to these groups is their instructional reading level, which can be determined as described in Chapter 6.

Grouping According to Special Needs. Teachers often find that certain specific instructional needs cut across the reading groups and are shared by children whose general reading ability varies widely. Special needs that several children may have in common may be as diverse as confusion about vowels, oral reading with natural expression, skimming to locate specific facts, or arranging events in proper chronological sequence. Confusion between words starting with *wh* and *th* may bother one or two of the above-average readers as well as several of the below-average readers.

It is generally a good idea to have just one or two special need groups at a time, and to meet with them once or twice a week until the weakness they had in common has been overcome. If all but one or two have improved, individual help can be given to them after the group has been disbanded. When one special need group has been discontinued, another group focused on a different special need can be formed.

When administrative steps have been taken to reduce the range of reading abilities in each class by some form of homogeneous grouping or interclass grouping, teachers usually find that, although the children score within a narrow range on reading tests, they may have different needs. Thus a class of average readers at third-reader level may have one group that requires a thorough review of phonics, a group of word-by-word readers, and a group with good word recognition but poor comprehension. In a sixth-grade class special groups might be set up for the very slow readers and the rapid but inaccurate readers.

Interest or Hobby Groups. Sometimes several members of a class are found to share a particular interest. It may be the care and feeding of pets, making model airplanes or rockets, stamp collecting, photography, baking fancy cookies, and so on. A group with a common interest can form a group or club, meet to discuss common problems or questions, exchange information, recommend useful reading to one another, and read independently about the hobby or interest. It is possible for several interest groups to operate in a class at the same time, with membership entirely voluntary. Meetings do not have to be frequent; every two or three weeks is a fairly good interval.

Project Committees. When a class chooses a topic for a major project, some time is spent in preliminary discussion and deciding what the main areas of investigation are to be. Thus a class that wants to learn about Eskimos may decide that the main things they want to learn about are Eskimo clothing; tools and weapons; how an igloo is made; how Eskimos catch and prepare their food; and Eskimo customs. This provides work for five committees, each taking responsibility for one main question. Such committees are usually set up by the teacher, paying attention both to the preferences expressed by the children and to the desirability of having a wide range of reading ability in each committee. Every child in the class is assigned to one of the committees.

Within each committee a list of specific questions is drawn up. Sometimes each member takes certain questions; sometimes the whole committee works on all the questions. The teacher has the responsibility of providing reading material for the project at several levels of reading difficulty. The best readers can use fairly mature books and references. The least capable readers may be able to do little more than study illustrations carefully, but even so they can usually contribute some useful ideas to the group report.

How Many Groups? Grouping is a means for accomplishing the aim of fitting instruction to the needs of children; it is not an end in itself. How many groups one should have varies with the make-up of the class and the skill of the teacher in group management.

Sometimes it is sufficient to divide a class into two groups for basal instruction: those who can use the regular reader for the grade and those who cannot. Children about whom the teacher is doubtful should be started in the lower group. Those in the upper group who finish assignments quickly have extra time for independent reading, and those for whom keeping up with the lower group is a struggle can be given some individual help.

A two-group plan also may be used in the exceptional class where all the children are reading at the same instructional level. In such situations, although the class is using the same level material, groups are formed to facilitate adjustment to differences in rate of work and foster teacher-pupil interaction, which is more likely to take place in smaller groups.

The children who are below grade level in reading are sometimes so varied that the teacher is unable to find a basal reader that is reasonably satisfactory for most of the group. When this is the case, the most obvious solution is to separate them into two groups, using different basal readers. If this still leaves the problem unsolved, individualizing the reading of the low group may be preferable to separating them into three or more subgroups.

The most competent readers in the class may be so far ahead of grade level that they have little or nothing to gain from the basal reader for the grade. Some teachers prefer to keep them in the "at-grade" group to give them social participation in the reading program, and to keep the class organization simple. Other teachers prefer to organize a group for the superior readers, completing the basal assignments quickly and having extra time for a variety of enrichment activities. A third plan is to give them a differentiated program without setting them up as a definite group, giving them almost completely individualized reading programs. They can be excused from many of the group activities, using the time for additional independent reading and for developing higher level reading skills which usually are taught at grade levels beyond the children's actual grade placement. These more competent readers can also enjoy participating in the reading program as helpers or group leaders.

The above paragraphs serve to indicate that the common plan of having three groups (fast, average, and slow) is not the only way to organize a class. Decisions about the number of basal reading groups needed and how to set them up should be made after the reading abilities of the children have been studied. It is better to start with a simple grouping plan, and to expand it later if necessary, than to start with multiple groups and find that the management problems are overwhelming.

FACTORS INFLUENCING GROUP EFFICIENCY

Size of Groups. The size of groups will necessarily vary according to the size of the class and the number of groups used. The decision reached is usually a compromise between two desirable but mutually contradictory principles. On the one hand, it is desirable to keep the organization plan simple and manageable. On the other hand, groups should be small enough so that every child has frequent turns.

In general, the more individual help the children need the smaller the group should be. Children about whose group placement the teacher is doubtful should usually be started in the lower group; if a change is needed, it is better for the child's morale to move from easier to harder material than the opposite. Special need groups and interest or hobby groups can be of any size. Small groups of two to four children each can work well for certain types of practice, such as testing one another on word cards or playing various kinds of reading games.

Group Flexibility. There are two main ways of keeping grouping flexible, both of which are desirable when not carried to extremes.

One is the continuing use of more than one kind of reading group at the same time. For example, the groups organized by instructional reading levels for reading instruction can be balanced by having project committees, each of which contains children with a wide range of reading proficiency. To these two basic forms of grouping it is easy to add one special-need group. Hobby or interest groups meet infrequently, take little class time, and require little planning by the teacher, so that they can be included with little extra effort.

The other kind of flexibility is the willingness to change group placements and assignments whenever there is good evidence that the change will be beneficial for the child. Some children outgrow the group in which they start the year; others find it difficult to keep up. When the teacher is considering such a change, it is desirable to discuss it with the child and find out how he would feel about it. His feelings should be given serious consideration. One child may feel quite relieved at the opportunity to move to a slower-moving group, while another child may plead for the opportunity to demonstrate that he can handle the work of the faster group.

If we call one child a "good" reader and another a "poor" reader, we are referring to differences in competence, not to differences in moral value or worth. One child cannot help being a less competent reader than another any more than a short child can help not being tall. It is generally better to use terms such as higher or lower, faster or slower, more or less competent, in preference to good and poor, because these terms are less likely to convey the impression of a value judgment. Some children are able to work faster than others or at a higher level, but all are equally worthy when they do what they can. When the teacher feels as enthusiastic about a successful effort in the lowest group as about the work of the most capable reader, the children can accept their group placements as natural and helpful. When the teacher makes it clear that only those who perform well can receive his approbation, children begin to regard placement in a lower group as a punishment.

Group Names. The children in a class are usually as clearly aware of the differences in reading performance between one group and another as the teacher is. What a teacher calls the group is less important than how the teacher feels about them. It is desirable to choose group names that do not imply differences in value or importance. It would be quite unwise, for example, to name groups Eagles, Robins, and Hummingbirds, because that would exaggerate and emphasize the differences. One good plan is to allow groups to choose their own names: in a class that is studying about Indians, for example, each group can select the name of a famous Indian tribe. Groups can be named in casual fashion according to the color of the cover of the book they are using, by the name of the text, or by the name of the group chairman. The main point is to avoid using names that are likely to build or strengthen feelings of inferiority.

Physical Arrangement of the Classroom. Movable chairs and desks make it possible to rearrange the classroom according to a variety of instructional purposes. In the primary grades, many teachers like to have a semicircle of small chairs near the chalkboard, to which each group comes for teacher-directed reading activities. For group discussions and oral reading a circular or hollow rectangle arrangement allows each child to see all members of the group. For independent reading it is desirable to minimize interpersonal contact and an arrangement in rows tends to work well. While it is possible to carry on group reading activities in a room that has desks and chairs bolted to the floor in rows, movable furniture makes it much easier.

Every reading classroom should have a library corner. This should contain shelves for books (improvised, if necessary, from grocery cartons or orange crates), a colorful display of books or book jackets, and a table and chairs for browsing and sampling books.

Storage space for sets of readers and other reading materials is of course necessary. Classrooms in which visual aids are used need to have accessory equipment, such as shades that darken the room sufficiently and a convenient screen. If visual aids are used by one group at a time, a projection corner can be set up which can be shielded by folding screens.

READING MATERIALS

It takes time to assemble the materials needed to allow a differentiated reading program to function with real effectiveness. A new teacher usually has to use the materials he finds in the classroom, and this may limit the plans he would prefer to use and require some modification of them. Teachers are most likely to get the materials they want when they know what they want and ask for it several months ahead.

In order to allow foi a rich and varied reading program, the classroom should have available the following types of materials:

1. Appropriate sets of basal readers or other materials for each group, with enough copies to supply one for each child in the group. A sequence of at least two readers should be available for each group. Fifteen copies of each will usually be sufficient.

2. Workbooks that accompany the basal readers. These simplify the assignment of group reading to be done without the teacher, introduce or provide reinforcement of basic vocabulary, and give practice on specific reading skills. Without them, the teacher has a heavy burden of preparing and duplicating seatwork pages and often cannot equal the workbook pages in quality.

3. A collection of reading games and puzzles that can be used independently or in small groups.

4. If the class is working on a project or unit, a collection of books of varying difficulty that provide information useful in the project.

5. A classroom library collection with a few books at each independent reading level in the class and with varied topics, changed, if possible, every few weeks. Children's magazines and picture magazines should also be included.

6. Reference books, including picture dictionaries, elementary and advanced dictionaries, and, above the primary grades, an encyclopedia set, atlases, an almanac, etc.

7. Materials for practice on specific skills, some of which may be devised by the teacher and some collected from a variety of workbooks. It is helpful if these can be organized so as to be self-administering and self-checking.

8. Audio-visual materials including a filmstrip projector, slide projector, movie projector, phonograph, tape recorder, and the filmstrips, slides, films, records, and tapes to go with them. Of course this equipment will usually be school equipment shared by a number of classes.

Reading can be taught, of course, with less quantity and variety of material than is recommended above. In some underprivileged countries, teachers may have little more than a chalkboard and some slates. The richer the materials, the greater chance the teacher has to obtain superior results.

GROUP ASSIGNMENTS

One of the commonest questions about group instruction is, "When I am working with one group, what should the other groups be doing?" When planning assignments for groups, the teacher should keep in mind the following points: (1) The activity assigned must be one that can be carried on by the group without the teacher. (2) Directions must be clear and explicit. (3) Those who finish an assignment before the end of the period should have additional things to do. (4) The use of helpers who can answer questions lessens the number of times the teacher is interrupted.

When a group, such as a first-grade group or a low group in second or third grade, is not able to carry on reading activities unless the teacher is with them, it is necessary to provide nonreading activities which they can carry on by themselves. These should be quiet activities. First-grade children can color, cut, and paste pictures, draw with crayons, paint at an easel, use modeling clay, weave with paper strips or yarn, feed and care for classroom pets, and so on. Of course it generally takes several weeks of patient training before routines for these activities are well learned. Above the first grade the problem is simpler when the children have had experience working in groups in previous grades.

Usually the children who are in the groups not working with the teacher choose their activities during the assignment period. They can learn to get out the needed materials and equipment, work quietly, and clean up and put things away.

In planning the length of reading periods the teacher should take into consideration the length of time that the children engaging in independent activities can maintain attention, as well as the attention span of the group reading with the teacher.

Children who can carry on reading activities without the teacher may finish an assignment before the period is over. Each group can have a list of things to do, which has been worked out in discussion with the teacher. It is helpful to post the list on a chart. One such chart, used in a fourth-grade class, says:

1. Read the assigned pages in the reader.
2. Read and answer the questions.
3. Look up the new words in the glossary.
4. Write the new words in your vocabulary notebook.
5. Read a library book, or
   Draw a picture about the story, or
   Study your spelling words.

When a series of suggestions is in view, interruptions to ask "What shall I do next?" are kept to a minimum.

Pupil Leaders. When a group is reading by itself, some kinds of reading activity require someone to decide whose turn comes next and how long it should last. This authority can be placed in the hands of a group chairman. It is usually better to rotate this privilege among members of the group than to restrict it to the most capable readers. If a child's incompetence as a chairman arouses protests, the complaints can be discussed, and, if necessary, the child's term as chairman can be shortened.

Many teachers use their competent readers as helpers. Some like a buddy system, in which each of the children who read with difficulty has a more capable reader seated next to him, whom he can ask for help.

A helper from a more advanced group can serve as a resource person for a reading group, supplying words, correcting errors, and making it possible for the group to carry on a reading activity that otherwise would require the teacher's involvement. Rotating the privilege of being a group helper among several children instead of restricting it to one or two minimizes the tendency to identify the chosen ones as "teacher's pets" and avoids depriving any child of a major portion of his own reading time.

Sometimes a child appointed as a chairman or a helper becomes officious, bossy, or unnecessarily critical. It is important for the teacher, who of course should be providing a desirable model for the child to imitate, to discuss with the child how he can become a more helpful helper. If he does not improve he will have to be replaced, but he should be given an opportunity to learn.

Teacher aides. Although not employed extensively, in the past few years more frequent use has been made of aides in the classroom. These assistants who, among other titles, may be known as teacher-aides or paraprofessionals have diverse backgrounds and preparation for their roles and responsibilities. Some are paid, others are volunteers. Some are high school graduates, others may have graduate degrees in fields other than Education. When used effectively, these people can be of great assistance to the teacher in individualizing instruction. Such personnel are more likely to be effective if: (1) they are carefully screened; (2) they are given adequate preparation for their job, and receive supervision while on the job; and (3) both the aide and the teacher know not only his role and responsibilities, but those of the other person as well.

Reading Activities for the Whole Class

Some teachers try to fit every reading activity into the pattern of group reading, when this is neither necessary nor desirable. There are quite a few kinds of reading which can be carried on effectively with the whole class. Having some activities in which the whole class reads together is helpful in building a spirit of class unity and in giving every child, the least competent readers included, a feeling of belonging and participating. It also reduces the number of periods for which the teacher has to make multiple plans and so lightens the teacher's work load.

INTRODUCING NEW IDEAS

There are many occasions for introducing new concepts or new reading techniques. These may be specifically needed at the time by one group, but many of them can benefit the rest of the class also. They may include the introduction of new concepts, ideas, and word meanings, the use of visual aids for conceptual background, new phonic and morphemic analysis principles, alphabetizing, locating information, using the dictionary, and so on. Not all children will learn with equal speed and reteaching will probably be necessary for many of the children, but the first presentation is likely to be of some benefit even to the slower children.

TEXTBOOK READING

In many classrooms the teacher is restricted to one prescribed textbook in certain areas of the curriculum. Since these textbooks are often at or above the frustration level of many of the children who have to use them, various expedients are adopted by teachers to cover the needed content. Careful preparation, guided preliminary silent reading, oral rereading, and full discussion form a pattern usable with content textbooks as well as with basal readers. Most of the oral reading can be covered by the more competent readers, and those not able to do much with the book can learn by listening. In such cases it also may be wise to teach listening skills. The use of textbooks on a whole-class basis is, then, usually a matter of necessity rather than one of preference. When the textbook is so difficult that only a few of the children can really read it, the teacher may have to write and duplicate a simpler version, or rely on lecturing and placing summaries on the chalkboard for the children to copy. It also may be possible to obtain, with the help of a librarian, a variety of materials written at easier levels, but that cover the same or similar topics as the text.

READING ABOUT CURRENT EVENTS

The first experience story developed with beginning readers is really the start of reading about current events. In the primary grades and to a lesser extent in the middle grades, the formulation of summaries of current group experiences which are placed on charts for all to read and discuss continues to be a useful kind of reading experience that can be carried on with the whole class.

Many schools have group subscriptions to weekly newspapers which are published for use in specific grades (*My Weekly Reader, Junior Scholastic*, etc.). Sometimes one edition is provided for the entire class, in which case the buddy system is helpful. Preferably, two or more of the graded editions are ordered, and each group reads an edition of appropriate difficulty for them. In the ensuing discussion, each group can contribute information which is given only in their edition, as well as discuss topics that are common to the editions.

In grades six and up, and in bright fourth and fifth grades, it is possible to make some use of daily newspapers. It is particularly helpful for the development of critical reading when the class can read and compare contrasting accounts of the same event as reported in newspapers with opposing points of view.

THE CLASS AS AN AUDIENCE

Most children love to listen when the teacher reads a story to them. Children in any grade can also form an appreciative audience for reading by their classmates. The principles it is wise to observe are: (1) only the performer has a copy of the material and the class listens as a genuine audience; (2) the material should be unfamiliar to most of the class; and (3) the performer (or performers) has rehearsed enough so that his presentation is fluent, expressive, and easy to understand.

One popular kind of audience reading situation is a book club meeting in which several children each read an especially interesting portion of a favorite book. Sometimes one group presents a dramatization of a story they have read. Extensive memorizing can be avoided if children's plays can be presented like radio scripts, with the parts read rather than recited from memory. The child who is to perform before an audience of his classmates has excellent natural motivation for trying to improve the quality of his oral reading.

The audience gains from the experience also. Listening as part of an audience can strengthen a child's listening comprehension and can help to broaden the range of topics about which he may be interested to read.

Other comments about audience reading may be found on page 119.

CHORAL READING

Choral reading, the technique of which has been discussed on page 120, is a kind of whole-class reading that is particularly good for developing appreciation of poetry. It is also quite helpful to shy children, who are likely to be much less inhibited when their voices are merged with those of their classmates than when reading by themselves before their classmates.

Systematic instruction with a basal reader is not included in this list of recommended kinds of whole-class reading. Although there are some classes in which a basal reader can be used effectively with the whole class (see the discussion on page 194), in most classes the range of reading abilities is too great to make this desirable. The use of a uniform reader with the whole class is liable to doom some children continually to read at a frustration level, with the usual accompaniments of emotional distress and lack of progress, or never challenge the more competent readers.

Individualized Reading

Individualized reading is defined in many different ways in the literature. Yet this approach to teaching reading has applicability to various components of a reading program.

INDIVIDUALIZED RECREATIONAL READING

For many years the recreational reading program in the elementary school has centered around the encouragement of a large amount of independent, pleasurable reading. The term *free reading* is often used to emphasize the freedom of choice of reading matter that children are allowed. Extensive independent recreational reading provides the abundance of easy reading practice that helps to build fluency and increase rate of reading. The rapid increase in the number of school libraries and the tremendous growth in the publication of children's books in recent years give evidence to the stress that is placed on wide reading in the elementary school. This aspect of the reading program is discussed in detail in Chapter 13.

INDIVIDUALZED FUNCTIONAL READING

When a major project is undertaken, the class is usually divided into committees, as described earlier in this chapter. Each committee draws up a list of specific questions and then the individual members turn to the available sources of information and hunt for relevant facts and ideas. Since there is usually just one copy of each source book, this reading is necessarily individualized. Then the committee meets and puts together the information they have found relating to each question.

When textbooks are the major sources of information, individual projects and reports are often used as a supplementary enrichment procedure. Each child works independently, selecting a topic, locating sources of information, taking notes, and writing a report. One of the major functions of school librarians is to help children to learn how to use library resources for individual reports. This kind of individualized research reading is naturally more appropriate in the upper grades than in the early school years.

INDIVIDUALIZED PRACTICE ON READING SKILLS

More than thirty years ago Luella Cole [1] envisaged a reading program in which the teacher would make a careful analysis of each child's reading needs and provide a reading skills development program tailored to each child's needs. Materials would be organized so that each pupil could get out the exercise he needed next, do it, correct it with a scoring key, and consult the teacher if he required help. The teacher would be actively involved in giving assistance where needed and evaluating each child's progress.

Very few teachers developed individualized programs of skill development of this type, probably because special materials organized for this kind of program were not available. However, the lack of such materials is no longer a serious drawback due to the fairly recent development of sets of materials for individual practice in reading skills (see page 140) and programmed materials both in the form of books and for use with machines. If the cost is reduced sufficiently, computer-assisted instruction may also become more widely used for this purpose.

[1] Luella Cole, *The Improvement of Reading* (New York: Farrar & Rinehart, 1938).

INDIVIDUALIZED DEVELOPMENTAL READING

Schools have been using individualized procedures in recreational reading and research reading for some time. Beginnings have also been made in developing individualized practice in reading skills. These programs have been, for the most part, supplementary to developmental reading instruction in which the teacher has worked with groups, using basal readers. Recently a number of teachers have been trying plans in which basal readers, or any other preplanned program, are eliminated in favor of individualized instruction.

Seeking, Self-Selection, and Pacing. Those who advocate individualized developmental reading frequently mention these three terms. By *seeking* they mean giving the child an opportunity to explore a wide variety of reading material. *Self-selection* means that the child's preferences in choosing books are respected, even when his choices may seem to the teacher to be unsuitable; suggestions are given when the child requests them, but the child decides what he is to read. *Pacing* means allowing the child to set his own pace in reading, even if this means doing very little reading over a long period of time. Advocates of pacing believe that each child's growth pattern is unique and that when he is given freedom the pace he naturally selects will in the long run be wise. A corollary belief is that if a child does not learn to read the best thing to do is to wait for readiness, even if it takes years; remedial help is considered to be a form of forcing and therefore does violence to the principle of pacing. This interpretation of what pacing means is at complete variance with the beliefs of the present writers. In fairness, it should be pointed out that not all advocates of individualized reading hold these extreme points of view.

Individual Teacher-Pupil Conferences. In an individualized developmental program the pupil is reading silently and independently in a book of his own choosing most of the reading time. Once or twice a week he has a private session with the teacher, which is likely to last between five and ten minutes. During these conferences the teacher is expected: (1) to find out what the child has read since his last conference; (2) to have a discussion of what he has read, which includes questioning to evaluate his comprehension and recall and also gives him opportunity to state his personal opinions about the content; (3) to listen to him read orally a small sample from the material he has been reading silently; (4) to give him an opportunity to talk about what he would like to read next; (5) to make note of any special difficulties or needs that become apparent; (6) to give help with words, teach or reinforce phonic and morphemic analysis skills, ask questions that stimulate thinking, and in general supply assistance as it is needed; and (7) to write a concise summary in the child's cumulative reading record. Of course, not all of these objectives can be met, or should even be attempted, in each conference.

These teacher-pupil conferences are considered to be an essential and uniquely valuable part of the procedure. They provide the main evidence for evaluating the pupil's reading and giving the help a child may need. Although the conferences do not come frequently, the children are said to gain a good deal of satisfaction from having the teacher's exclusive attention, and some writers assert that the number of minutes of personal attention each child receives is as much as, or more than, he would get during daily group reading lessons. It is also claimed that the teacher can get a clearer picture of the child's reading performance when attending to him exclusively than is usual in the more frequent but briefer pupil responses during group sessions.

Group and Whole-Class Activities. Advocates of individualized developmental reading emphasize that the program should not be entirely individualized and that some group activities and some whole-class activities are desirable. The kind of groups that they favor are special-need groups. When the teacher has found several children who need the same kind of help, a temporary group is set up and meets with the teacher regularly until the members have accomplished the purpose for which the group was created. Then the group is disbanded and another group with a different special need may be started.

Whole-class activities are usually of the audience type, providing an opportunity for sharing activities such as reading portions of well-liked books, a panel discussion of a book that several children have read, dramatizations, and so on. Some teachers introduce new reading skills on a whole-class basis, using the chalkboard and teacher-devised practice pages.

Factors Influencing the Efficiency of an Individualized Reading Program. Some classroom situations are more favorable than others for conducting a successful individualized developmental program. The important considerations include teacher competence, materials, class size, maturity of the children, record keeping, and class management.

1. *Teacher competence.* A good individualized reading program requires a higher level of teaching competence than is needed to get good results with any preplanned program such as a basal reader program. The teacher should know the sequence of development of reading skills well, so as to be able to judge whether a child is doing well at his own reading level or is being held back by specific gaps in his skills. The teacher should be perceptive of children as individuals, sensitive to their needs, and able to show a personal interest in each child and to furnish encouragement, reassurance, and support. The teacher should be acquainted with the books in the class library so as to be able to ask pointed questions and understand a child's reaction to each book. The teacher should also be able to discover special needs on the basis of small samplings of the children's reading. All these characteristics are desirable in any reading teacher, but teachers who rely on manuals can get along with lower qualifications.

2. *Materials.* It is often stated that the number of books in the class reading collection for a successful individualized program should be at least three times the number of children, with a wide range in content and in difficulty. Relatively few classrooms can meet this standard at present. Materials for practice on specific reading skills are often not mentioned, but would seem necessary if skills are to be adequately learned.

3. *Class size.* It is obvious that when there is a limited amount of time for teacher-pupil conferences, the more children there are in the class the smaller the share each one gets. In a large class the teacher either has to reduce the duration of the conferences or take longer to

get around the class. This is particularly important in the primary grades, in which a class size of more than 25 children would seem to be unfavorable to the method. In the upper grades, class size may be less significant.

4. *Maturity of the children.* Other things being equal, the older and more mature the children are and the more competent they are in reading the easier it should be to run a successful individualized program. On this basis the primary grades are less suitable for such a program than the middle and upper grades, and the first grade would seem least suitable of all.

5. *Keeping records.* A good record-keeping system is essential. The teacher's record for each child should include a cumulative record of what the child has read, including title, dates started and finished, number of pages, and comments based on observations during conferences. Periodic use of a check list helps to avoid overlooking needs or problems. The child should also keep a record of his own reading, and may also have a vocabulary notebook, a list of specific skills on which he should try to improve, and progress charts for the skills being worked on.

6. *Class management.* It is a common practice to seat the several children who are to have conferences near the teacher's desk. As one conference is finished the child returns to his seat and the next child moves to the chair next to the teacher. While the teacher is having a series of individual conferences, the rest of the class must be provided with activities that do not require the teacher. When the children can read well enough, they can all read independently for the duration of the period. Otherwise it is necessary to provide independent nonreading activities at which they can keep busy.

Conferences with individual pupils should be held on a regular rotating schedule. Allowing some time for some whole-class and some group sessions, and assuming that the reading time will vary between one and two hours, it is likely that the teacher will require three to five days to have conferences with all the children. Some teachers favor the policy of waiting for the child to ask for a conference; this has the grave weakness that the children who most need help and stimulation are likely to be the most reluctant to ask for conferences.

It is, however, consistent with extreme commitment to the policy of pacing.

Evaluating Individualized Developmental Reading. Although the number of careful research studies in which an individualized developmental reading program has been compared with basal reader or other preplanned programs, under carefully controlled conditions, is not large, the results to date seem quite consistent. There are many enthusiastic reports from teachers who are using an individualized procedure, with quite consistent statements that the pupils show a marked gain in reading interest and read much more widely than they did before. The teachers feel that they get to know the children better than they did before and that the extra effort and work that individualized teaching requires is worthwhile. On the other hand, growth in reading skills as measured by standardized tests tends to favor the basal reader programs, especially for the less competent readers, or show no significant difference. The preponderance of evidence does not support the assertion that individualized reading improves the learning of reading skills.

When all the conditions are favorable, there is no question but that excellent results are obtained in some individualized programs.[2] This is also true of other approaches.

Combining Good Procedures

At present the weight of the evidence favors a combined program, in which skills are taught systematically and sequentially to groups functioning at different levels of reading competence, some reading is conducted on a whole-class basis, and individualized reading is used primarily in recreational reading and in reading for individual and group projects. Certain aspects of the individualized reading approach such as individual teacher-pupil conferences can be incorporated into any reading program. Or, it may prove efficient to have an individualized reading program for only one group in the classroom.

[2] For sources of information on individualized reading, refer to Sam Duker, *Individualized Reading: An Annotated Bibliography* (Metuchen, N.J.: Scarecrow Press, 1968).

The proportion of the total reading time that can be used for individualized reading will necessarily vary with the reading abilities of the children and the availability of materials. Unquestionably many teachers do not provide enough time for independent reading activities. It will probably turn out that no one pattern of class organization is best for all classes, and that each class needs to have a program tailored to its particular circumstances.

Many other ways of combining individualized reading with other kinds of reading organization are possible. Stauffer tried out a "Language Arts" program in which third graders were taught conventionally with basal readers every other month.[3] During the months between, the reading program was mainly individualized reading, with some emphasis also on written composition and oral reports. The experimental group was not significantly different from a control (basal reader) group on standardized reading tests, but showed some superiority in word recognition, spelling, and written composition.

Other ways of combining individualized with conventional procedures might include alternating by weeks instead of by months, or even alternating by days. Such plans, which seem reasonable and worth exploring, have not yet been evaluated in the research literature.

In this chapter a number of ways of organizing a class for reading have been discussed separately. Different ways of grouping children, whole-class reading activities, and individualized reading have been described in turn. Each is well adapted to certain kinds of reading activities, less suited to others. A judicious combination which includes group activities, whole-class activities, and individualized reading would seem to have advantages over any one of them used exclusively.

Several plans involving combined programs have been described in preceding chapters. At this point it would be a good idea for the reader to take another look at Figures 9, 18, and 19, and to read again

[3] Russell G. Stauffer and W. Dorsey Hammond, "The Effectiveness of Language Arts and Basic Reader Approaches to First-Grade Reading Instruction—Extended into Third Grade," *Reading Research Quarterly*, IV, No. 4 (Summer, 1969), 468–499.

the discussions and explanations accompanying them. These plans, intended to be suitable for the first grade, the primary grades, and the middle grades, embody the principle of combining different forms of class organization in a total plan and using each for the reading activities for which it seems best suited. These plans are not intended to be copied slavishly, but rather are presented as illustrations showing varying ways of organizing to achieve the objectives of a rich and well-balanced reading program.

Summary

This chapter was basically concerned with organizing reading instruction in the classroom so as to best provide for individual and group needs.

1. Most commonly, reading groups are composed of children reading at the same instructional level, or general level of reading achievement.
2. Other forms of grouping include special-need groups, interest or hobby groups, and project committees.
3. The usual number of groups in a classroom is three, although a two-group plan often can work well. Sometimes three groups are not enough.
4. Flexibility in grouping involves:
   a. Modifying the group structure as required by changing abilities
   b. Using more than one kind of grouping at a time
5. Group names should not imply differences in status or worth.
6. Adequate materials and movable furniture increase the probability of successful teaching by groups.
7. Assignments for groups should be understood by each group member and should provide a sequence of activities.
8. Group chairmen or helpers, and teacher aides, can be used to assist in facilitating the operation of group instruction.
9. Whole-class activities such as the following should be part of the reading program:
   a. Teaching new concepts or skills
   b. Current events

    c. Audience situations

    d. Choral reading

10. Individualized or independent reading is widely used for recreational and research reading.

11. Individualized practice on reading skills has become more popular.

12. Research has not revealed any superiority for individualized reading in the development of reading skills; however, it may have advantages in the development of reading interests.

13. There are many factors that influence the success of an individualized reading program.

14. A combination of systematic instruction in groups with some whole-class reading activities and more individualization of reading instruction will probably produce better results than an exclusive reliance on group reading, whole-class reading, or individualized reading.

Recommended Reading

BEERY, ALTHEA, BARRETT, THOMAS C., and POWELL, WILLIAM R., EDS. *Elementary Reading Instruction: Selected Materials.* Boston: Allyn and Bacon, Inc., 1969. Chs. 4, 12.

GANS, ROMA. *Common Sense in Teaching Reading.* Indianapolis: Bobbs-Merrill, 1963. Ch. 17.

HARRIS, ALBERT J., ED. *Readings on Reading Instruction.* New York: McKay, 1963. Chs. 6, 7.

RAMSEY, WALLACE Z., ED. *Organizing for Individual Differences,* Perspectives in Reading, No. 9. Newark, Del.: International Reading Association, 1967.

SARTAIN, HARRY W. "Organizational Patterns of Schools and Classrooms for Reading Instruction," *Innovation and Change in Reading Instruction,* 67th Yearbook of the National Society for the Study of Education, Part II. Chicago: University of Chicago Press, 1968. Ch. 7.

SMITH, NILA B. *Reading Instruction for Today's Children.* Englewood Cliffs, N.J.: Prentice-Hall, 1963. Chs. 6,7.

VEATCH, JEANNETTE. *Reading in the Elementary School.* New York: Ronald Press, 1966. Chs. 5–7.

8

Learning to Recognize Words

As an adult is reading, he is primarily aware of the meaning he is obtaining and only rarely does he have to be concerned with identifying particular words. Perceiving words is so easy and habitual that it is almost completely automatic for the good adult reader. He can concentrate on understanding the material rather than on attempting to identify words. When necessary, however, word-identification skills are applied almost instantaneously without having to think through the principles and generalizations involved in translating printed symbols into their spoken counterparts or in determining the probable meaning of a word. Because these skills are so easy for adults, they sometimes do not realize that learning to recognize words is difficult for many children. Yet, development of word recognition is vitally important, particularly in the early stages of learning to read. A child who is unable to master word recognition cannot progress to higher levels of reading competence.

Perception of Words

As indicated in Chapter 1, word perception depends both on the patterns of symbols on the page, which are sensed by the eyes, and on the memory traces stored in the reader's brain. Perceiving a printed word means seeing it with an awareness of its sound and meaning. The neural traces representing the appearance of the word become linked through associative learning with the traces of its sound, the motions of saying it, and its meaning or meanings.

Many words have plural meanings, and the setting or context in which the word appears may help the reader to select the one that fits. Consider the following two sentences:

Jimmy wanted to run home.
Willie hit a home run.

The words *home* and *run* have quite different meanings in the two sentences, but anyone who has the slightest knowledge of the game of baseball has no trouble selecting the appropriate meaning for each sentence. Although the *American College Dictionary* states that *run* is a transitive verb, an intransitive verb, a noun, and an adjective, and lists 104 separate meanings for it, most readers of the two sentences above will automatically pick out the intended meaning as they read each of the sentences. With a clear visual impression and an abundance of previous experience involving hearing and saying the word and experiencing it in a variety of meanings, the necessary background is there and the immediate context helps the reader to get set for the particular meaning that fits.

GESTALT CHARACTERISTICS OF PERCEPTION

Our present understanding of perception is based largely on the work of the Gestalt psychologists. Their main contribution was in demonstrating that when we perceive we naturally tend to perceive wholes, and that a whole has a unique, recognizable quality which is more than just the sum of its parts. When a musical melody is transposed to another key every note is changed, and yet the melody seems the same. We often learn to recognize a person's face, or his characteristic way of walking, without being able to describe with any exactness any one of his facial features or any single movement. The term *Gestalt,* which can be translated as "form" or "configuration," refers to this unique total quality.

The wholes perceived by babies tend to be vague, crude, and undifferentiated. As children develop they become increasingly able to make differentiations and to recognize similarities. They become able to discern the parts within the whole, and to detect minor differences that they formerly did not notice. The expert perceiver can recognize the unique Gestalt of a face or a printed word, and at the same time is aware of the distinctive features within it. He shifts his attention from the whole to the parts (analysis) or from the parts to the whole (synthesis). His perceptual approach is flexible and versatile.

Figure and Background. The perceiver is usually aware of a foreground figure that stands out from a more vaguely defined background. The figure tends to have clear boundaries and definite form; its details are easy to notice, and it occupies the center or focus of the perceiver's attention. The background seems more vague, its details are shadowy, and it receives only marginal attention.

In reading, clear perception is made possible when printed material has a marked contrast between black, clear type and an unobtrusive white or almost white, nonshiny paper. The letters within words are printed close together to make it easy to perceive the word as a unit, and spaces between words and between lines allow each word to be seen as a clear figure against a background. When a teacher wants children to pay special attention to a word or part of a word, it can be made to stand out by underlining, by writing it larger or with bolder lines, or by using colored crayon or chalk.

Closure. Closure means the tendency to perceive an incomplete form or Gestalt as if it were complete. Thus we can listen to a few notes of a familiar tune and sing the rest of it, or we can look at a picture in which certain lines have been left out and see it as if the lines were there. In other words, we tend to complete an incomplete Gestalt. A good reader does not have to perceive every part of a word clearly in order to recognize it, nor does he have to be able to recognize every word in a sentence to gain meaning from it.

Good readers can read successfully when the lower half of words is hidden

When the top half is hidden it is harder to read.

Y— c–n –ls– r—d w–th—t th– v–w–ls.

–o—o–a—— a–e –o–e e—e—ia–. (Consonants are more essential)

In reading the above sentences, closure makes meaningful reading possible. The top line generally causes no difficulty for good readers. The second line, with the top halves of the letters erased, tends to require more effort. The line without vowels is usually found to be easy except for "also" and "without." The final line, with the consonants omitted, is almost impossible to decipher without help.

Closure takes place in connected reading whenever the context helps a reader to overcome a difficulty. Consider this sentence:

The jockey climbed on his h---- and put his feet in the stirrups.

A reader who knows anything about horse racing will fill in the word *horse* without hesitation. The other word that might fit into the sentence, *saddle,* is too different in first letter and general shape to create any perplexity.

Now, read the sentence again:

The jockey climbed on his house and put his feet in the stirrups.

Did you notice that instead of *horse* it read *house?* Many good readers are poor at proofreading because they read what they expect to find and often do not notice small errors in typesetting.

Some children depend too much on the closure effect and pay insufficient attention to the details of what is there in print. They rely on context and let their expectations take priority over their perceptions to the point where they become quite inaccurate. Their reading usually makes sense, but sometimes the sense is different from what the author intended.

Other children make insufficient use of closure. They seem to be impelled to look at all details and at every word. In their absorption in details they may fail to integrate successive perceptions into a unified meaning. When they misread words, they often do not seem to notice that the result is nonsense.

Sequence is yet another aspect of perception, which in reading is spatially imposed on the reader. In our culture, the sequence is from left to right, with a return right-to-left diagonal sweep at the end of each line of print going down the page from top to bottom.

Building a Sight Vocabulary

The term "sight vocabulary" refers to all the words a reader can recognize immediately at any level of reading ability. Unless the learner can recognize an increasingly larger number of words at sight and with decreasing cues, he will not become a proficient reader.

Some reading programs first introduce words as wholes. In such programs, the consideration of word parts or word-analysis skills: (1) may come after a certain number of whole words have been introduced; or (2) may be introduced concurrently with the teaching of whole words; or (3) may not be directly taught as in the case with programs that assume children will assimilate phonic skills because only words with tightly controlled symbol-sound associations are used in the reading material. Word parts are taught first in other programs.[1] Yet regardless of the approach used for beginning reading instruction, children must acquire a fund of sight words.[2] Even if the child first learns parts of words through a synthetic phonic method, eventually he must learn to recognize whole words rapidly. If a child stops frequently to analyze words, he cannot be an efficient reader.

The process by which children acquire a sight vocabulary is influenced by the method used for reading instruction, particularly in the initial stages. But due to such factors as intelligence and language

[1] Various beginning reading approaches have been discussed and illustrated in Chapter 3.

[2] The sight words acquired during beginning reading instruction may be referred to as the initial sight vocabulary. In some programs, the term "basic sight vocabulary" means the number of words taught up to a certain point in the program, usually prior to the introduction of word analysis skills. Some authors use the same term to mean the *Dolch Basic Sight Vocabulary* of 220 words that is comprised of high utility words.

facility, even when children are given the same program, they will differ in the rapidity with which they develop a sight vocabulary. Furthermore, cues that may be relied on heavily in the initial stages of acquisition may become less important or useful at a later point of development.

TEACHING SIGHT WORDS

New words [3] are usually introduced in sentences so that the children can use the context as a possible aid in determining word pronunciation and/or meaning. Depending upon the program, the sentence is read first by the teacher and then by the pupils; or, the teacher develops some background and the sentences are first read independently by the children. In either case, the sentences, with perhaps the new words in isolation printed above them, are presented visually on the chalkboard or by arranging printed word cards to make the sentences on a chart holder or flannel board. The other words in the sentence should be in the children's sight vocabulary so they can concentrate on the new words. Children are encouraged to look at the word carefully while saying it in order to learn to associate the printed word with its spoken counterpart. Again depending upon the program, the teacher also may point out how previously learned word-analysis skills can be employed in decoding the new words. The associational tasks required are made less complicated for the children by using words whose common meanings are usually understood by children their age.

Further practice may be given by such activities as calling upon children to "frame" the words with their hands as they pronounce it, to match the word in the chart holder with the same word on the chalkboard, and to select the word spoken by the teacher from a number of word cards or words on the chalkboard.

The new words are included, perhaps in differing contextual set-

[3] "New" means that the word is used for the first time in that particular program. For the exact procedures by which new words are introduced in a particular program, one should read the teacher's manual that accompanies the text.

tings, in the story which accompanies that lesson. Follow-up or preparatory exercises may include reading other sentences containing the new word, and workbook practice in which the word is matched with a picture, used to complete a sentence, or has to be distinguished visually from other words which resemble it. Once introduced, a word usually is repeated a number of times in later stories. Repetition is used as a means of helping the child to "overlearn" the word so that he learns to recognize it rapidly. However, repetition alone will not suffice to establish a sight vocabulary.

Limitations of Repetition. Studies of the learning process have shown that learning takes place when (1) the learner is motivated; (2) the learner is ready in terms of developmental maturation and necessary previous experience; (3) the learner can distinguish the desired response from incorrect responses; (4) the desired response is reinforced and other responses are not; and (5) enough repetition takes place to provide for some permanence of retention. Repetition is helpful when the other conditions are present. But if the learner is not interested in learning, or if he cannot see the difference between the printed symbol and other somewhat similar printed symbols, or if nothing happens to let him know if a response is correct or not, repetition may simply bring about the strengthening of confusion.

It is most important, then, that the learner is motivated, is able to make the necessary discriminations, and finds out immediately if his response is correct or not. Under these conditions, some quick learners can learn a word and remember it with very little repetition. Slow learners may require 30 or more repetitions before they master a new word. The needed repetitions should be provided in ways that keep the child interested and help him to perceive clearly. More practice should be given in reading the word in a meaningful setting than in recognizing it in isolation.

Early Word Recognition Clues. In programs that rely exclusively or heavily on the "whole-word" approach during the initial stages of reading instruction, the child is taught to employ mainly two types of clues as aids in establishing a sight vocabulary: configuration and picture clues. Although these types of clues are used in other reading programs, less emphasis and reliance are placed on them.

1. *Configuration clues.* The configuration or shape of words, their length, and such distinctive visual features as ascending and descending letters are clues which children can and do employ in building a sight vocabulary. Thus a word like grandfather or elephant has a distinctive appearance which makes it easy to discriminate visually from most other words which are introduced. On the other hand, words which are very similar in size and shape, such as went and want, and and said, often cause problems for beginning readers. Many beginners find it difficult to notice a small difference in letters when the two words have the same shape. They sometimes are insensitive to differences in letter sequence (e.g., *was* and *saw*). When the reading vocabulary is small and most words have distinctive shapes, size and shape are often sufficient. The expert reader, using the context and some letter cues also, makes effective use of size and shape but is not dependent on them. He has learned that there are many pairs of words of similar size and shape, and he uses the configuration of the word in conjunction with other aids to word perception. When a beginning reader continues to rely exclusively on configuration, he tends to become increasingly confused as the number of words with similar general appearance grows.

The teacher may aid the child by pointing out how similar words differ; but the child never becomes an independent reader unless he develops skills that enable him to decode words that are not recognized at sight.

2. *Picture clues.* Because the vocabulary in almost all beginning reading programs is restricted according to various criteria, the story line must be told, or supported heavily, through the use of pictures on almost every page. These pictures also provide clues or reminders for word recognition. For example, the names of new characters are usually presented near a picture in which the character can be identified. Nouns are easily illustrated, as are action verbs like *run* and *jump*. Words denoting direction, place, or comparison like *up* and *down, in* and *out, small* and *big,* can be illustrated by contrasting pairs of pictures. Picture clues can supply reminders when a child forgets words; however, the teacher must teach the children to use these clues properly and should not overemphasize their use. Unfor-

tunately, some children tend to neglect the reading matter in favor of the pictures.

PERCEPTION AND IMAGERY

In 1890 William James wrote a most interesting chapter on Imagination in which he assembled convincing evidence of marked individual differences in the vividness of different kinds of imagery. Some adults have very clear visual imagery; they can call up a mental picture that is sharp and lifelike. A person with exceptionally vivid visual imagery may be able to recite what is on a printed page by calling up a mental picture of the page and "reading" what they "see" on it. To most people, who are not gifted with such photographic visual images, such a feat may seem incredible. There are many individuals whose visual images are weak and unclear; they tend to depend mainly on auditory imagery or motor imagery or on a combination of the two. People with strong auditory imagery tend to hear a kind of inner voice as they think or read. They tend to express what they see in words and to remember the verbal descriptions rather than recall the actual visual appearance. Still other people, the so-called "motor type," seem to depend on the imagery of muscular movements. They "think" words by experiencing in greatly reduced form the feelings of the movements of the muscles of the lips, tongue, throat, and larynx that are involved in saying the word. They are helped in remembering a visual form by tracing its outline.[4]

A person can have clear perception and still not have very vivid imagery. William James remarked that his own visual perception was keen and that he was able to draw well, but that his visual imagery was quite weak. On the other hand, imagery cannot possibly be clearer than the original perception. A child who perceives a word in a vague and hazy way cannot call up a memory image of it that is any clearer than the original perception, no matter how many times the experience is repeated. Clear perception is, then, a minimum essential for vivid imagery.

[4] William James, *Principles of Psychology*, Vol. II (New York: Henry Holt & Co., 1890; 1950 Reprint by Dover Publications, Inc.), Ch. XVIII.

IMPROVING CLARITY OF PERCEPTION

Some children are very slow at building a sight vocabulary. They continue to confuse words of somewhat similar shape and repeated practice brings little improvement. When this happens, it is probable that the child does not perceive the word clearly and therefore cannot form a clear memory image. It is necessary, therefore, to help him to improve the clarity and accuracy of his perception. Only after he perceives the word clearly will repetition help him to remember it.

Fairly recently there has been a great deal of interest in visual perception. A number of visual perception tests and visual-motor tests, as well as numerous visual perceptual training materials and programs are available. While such training may benefit certain children in other ways, there is little valid research evidence to indicate that it has any marked effect on reading ability.

Phonics. In the past fifteen years, popular methods of teaching reading have been attacked by zealots who are certain that starting children with an intensive phonics program is the solution to all problems in the teaching of reading.[5] None of these critics appears to have realized that phonics may present difficulties for some young children. For example, some children have extreme difficulty in making symbol-sound associations. Others cannot blend sounds together. The findings of the large-scale Cooperative Reading Studies sponsored by the U.S. Office of Education do not substantiate the extensive claims of the intensive phonics proponents.[6]

As a part of a total word recognition program, phonics is necessary and important. Children who know the sounds of letters and letter combinations and can use these successfully in attacking words that are not within their sight vocabularies have an invaluable tool. For

[5] Rudolph Flesch, *Why Johnny Can't Read* (New York: Harper & Brothers, 1955). Sybil Terman and Charles C. Walcutt, *Reading: Chaos and Cure* (New York McGraw-Hill, 1958). Charles C. Walcutt, ed., *Tomorrow's Illiterates* (Boston: Little, Brown, 1961).

[6] Guy L. Bond, and Robert Dykstra, "The Cooperative Research Program in First-Grade Reading Instruction," *Reading Research Quarterly,* IV (Summer 1967), 115–126.

children whose auditory perception and imagery is good and whose visual perception and imagery is poor, a phonic beginning may be helpful. But an intensive phonic beginning is not a panacea, and adopting such a procedure, or any procedure, for all children is likely to substitute one set of difficulties for another. Children simply do not all learn in the same way.

Tracing. Fernald discovered that some children who were unable to remember words that had been taught visually or phonically could get started in reading when emphasis was placed on tracing words, written in large letters, over and over again with the fingers.[7] This "kinesthetic" method is based on the early psychological observations that some individuals are aided in recalling visual forms by tracing their outlines. It is frequently called the VAKT (visual-auditory-kinesthetic-tactual) method. At present some workbooks used in first-grade reading programs give practice in tracing or printing words as one aspect of the word study program. As a complete program, the tracing procedure is slow and requires a large amount of individual help from the teacher. Its main use has been in remedial reading programs for severely disabled readers. The technique, however, can be modified and used only with certain words (e.g., *what, that*) which give a child problems.

The Visual-Motor Method. Many children who do not need the tracing procedure can be greatly helped by a word study procedure that combines visual study with writing. It is sometimes described as the VAK (visual-auditory-kinesthetic) method. It can be used with a group or with an individual child.

New words are taught as they are needed for connected reading. They are introduced in meaningful context and the meaning is checked or taught as advised in the teacher's manual. After the word has been presented orally and visually, the steps are as follows:

1. The teacher holds up the word card and pronounces the word. The children are encouraged to look at the word carefully in left-to-right

[7] The method is described in detail in Grace M. Fernald, *Remedial Techniques in Basic School Subjects* (New York: McGraw-Hill, 1943). For a brief summary of the method, see A. J. Harris, *How to Increase Reading Ability,* 5th ed. (New York: McKay, 1970), pp. 353–356.

fashion and to try to see it as a whole, while they pronounce it several times.

2. Each child shuts his eyes and tries to "see" the word (form a visual image). He then opens his eyes and compares his image with the word on the card.

3. The card is covered and each child attempts to write (in manuscript or cursive writing) the word from memory.

4. The card is shown again and each child compares his reproduction with the original. If he finds any differences he looks at the card again, paying particular attention to the part of the word he did not remember correctly.

5. If there have been any inaccuracies, the process of looking, saying, trying to form an image, checking, and writing from memory is repeated, until all can write the word correctly from memory.

6. Reading the word in meaningful context and reviewing on subsequent days help to fix the word in memory and provide transfer to genuine reading.

In this procedure, children should be encouraged to pronounce the word as a whole or, if a long word, by syllables. They should not spell it by saying the sequence of letter names, because that leads to rote auditory memory and does not help to form a visual image of the word as a whole. It is better for the letters to be seen as parts within the whole than to be remembered as a chain of separate spoken units.

After some weeks of practice with this method, many children improve in their ability to perceive and remember word forms and can shift to visual study without writing, supplemented by their developing phonic knowledge.

Adapting Word Study Method to the Individual. In view of what we know about the marked individual differences that exist in perception and imagery, it would be surprising if all children learned to recognize words most easily in the same way. No method of studying words has been discovered that works well with all children. Each method seems to work well with many children and poorly with some. If after a reasonable amount of time a child is not doing well with the word study procedure that is successful for most of the class, it is probable that a different method of word study would be better suited to his abilities. Perhaps the old adage, "If at first you don't succeed, try, try again," should be interpreted as meaning, "try another method."

SPEEDING UP WORD PERCEPTION

Once words have been learned, it is obvious that the more nearly instantaneous the process of recognition becomes, the more efficient reading can be. When children still have to struggle with word recognition they cannot devote the major share of their attention to the meaning. Rapid and accurate perception allows the reader to proceed with speed and fluency, and to concentrate on interpretation.

There are four basic approaches that can be used in improving the rate of word perception:

The most natural one is the abundant practice on common words that comes from doing a large amount of easy, pleasurable reading. When children are eager to find out what is going to happen they tend to read at as fast a rate as is comfortable for them, and the words that they see over and over become so familiar that they are recognized unhesitatingly. This is one of the reasons why a good reading program should include a substantial amount of independent recreational reading.

A second form of practice that is widely used in secondary school, college, and adult reading programs is the reading of selections under conditions in which the reader knows that he is being timed and that he will have to answer questions on the content. This provides strong motivation to try to keep the rate going up without loss in comprehension. Practice sessions of this kind can be helpfully used in grades six and up, or with above-average readers in grades four and five.

A third approach is giving practice in which words or phrases are presented for only a short time. Flash card drills in which words that are known are shown for brief intervals are common in the primary grades. In successive sessions the teacher gradually shortens the exposure but tries not to go faster than the children can respond. Of course, timing of the exposure of hand-held flash cards is inexact. Children can also practice speeding up their recognition of individual word cards.[8]

Many schools are now using *tachistoscopes*. A tachistoscope is a device that exposes material for a brief period of time. Projection tachistoscopes are projectors that have a device like a large camera shutter which can be set for a variety of exposure speeds from one second to as little as 1/150 of a second. Some of them use materials printed on lantern slides, others employ special filmstrips. Small spring-powered tachistoscopes that can be held in the hand are available and can be used for individual practice. Research on the value of tachistoscopic practice in the elementary school has produced ambiguous results.

The fourth method is controlled reading. This involves the use of devices that present reading material at a set rate of speed and therefore push the reader to try to keep up. For group-controlled or individual reading practice there are special types of projectors that use material on special filmstrips. Each selection can be presented at any of a wide variety of rates. However, individual differences in speed of comprehension, level of comprehension, and interest make it difficult, if not impossible, to select suitable material and an appropriate speed of presentation for a group. For individual practice there are several kinds of pacing devices on the market, all of which use regular reading material in book or workbook form, and employ a shutter or beam of light that comes down over the page at a pre-set rate. As with the use of tachistoscopes, it is yet to be proved that any form of controlled reading produces better long range results in the elementary school than a well-conceived reading program that includes an abundance of independent reading, without machinery.

With all methods of speeding up perception that employ pressure— by timing the reader, by flashing words or phrases, or by pushing the reader to keep up with material that is exposed at a controlled rate—

---

[8] In presenting flash cards, the card to be shown should be held in one hand and a blank card held in the other hand is used as a shutter, raised and lowered. It is not good practice to raise the card, hold it briefly, and then remove it; this creates a need for interfering pursuit movements of the eyes.

the big problem is transferring the speed acquired in the practice setting to normal reading. Many pupils achieve marked gains in speed of perception in the special practice sessions, but not much of the gain is carried over into their regular reading. The experimental evidence to date indicates that, in the elementary school, a well-conceived reading program that does not use special speed-inducing devices produces as much improvement in rate as is generally attained with special instruments.

Materials for Improving Sight Vocabulary

THE IMPORTANT WORDS FOR PRIMARY READING

Although the total number of words employed may be similar, there may be little overlap between or among vocabularies used in different primary grade reading programs.[9]

A typical basal reading series published during the early 1960's introduced a total of about 1,500 to 2,500 words (plus derived forms) in the preprimer through the third reader level materials. New words were introduced at a controlled rate which varied greatly from series to series. Each new word was usually employed several times after it was first introduced and, depending upon its utility, might be used repeatedly in subsequent materials in the series.

Present-day readers for the primary grades utilize a more restricted vocabulary than those of a generation or so ago. First readers published in the 1920's had an average of 645 different words. In the late 1930's the average had dropped to about 460 different words and in the 1940's and 1950's down to about 350 words. Since the 1950's, however, the trend has been to increase substantially the number of words utilized. To compensate for the limited vocabulary of some basal readers it is necessary for teachers to provide opportunities for extensive supplementary reading.

In deciding which words to use, authors are guided by a variety of considerations. For almost all basal reader programs, the most im-

[9] Arthur V. Olson, "An Analysis of the Vocabulary of Seven Primary Reading Series," *Elementary English,* Vol. 42 (March 1965), 261–64.

portant are: (1) frequency of use as determined by extensive word counts of published materials; and (2) that the meanings of the words be understood by most children. Although somewhat dated, among the lists likely to be consulted are those by Thorndike and Lorge (especially the most frequent 500 and 1000 words), and Stone.[10] Some words are needed for a particular story, such as proper names, or words relating to a particular setting such as the circus. In general, a story is written first, and then the vocabulary is checked against one of the vocabulary lists; if the number of words outside the list seems excessive, parts of the story are rewritten.

Not all the words found in any published list need be learned by the children. Because of their high utility some are more important than others. In teaching developmental reading, the prime concern of the classroom teacher is to teach the words used in the child's reading material because most of that vocabulary is cumulative; that is, they usually reoccur in the material. Less emphasis need be placed on words that occur only once or so in the materials used to develop reading skills.

A number of critics have complained that the vocabulary of elementary school readers has been reduced to the point where children are not being given an opportunity to learn as fast as they can. One such critic stated that Russian children learn about 2,000 words in the first grade and about 10,000 in the first four grades, and questioned whether we are not short-changing American children.[11] His conclusion was that if we should employ a phonic method of teaching from the beginning, as the Russians do, we could almost forget about vocabulary control after the first grade. Characteristically, this critic didn't mention such relevant points as the fact that Russian children begin reading a year later than American children, that the Russian

[10] E. L. Thorndike, and I. Lorge, *A Teacher's Word Book of 30,000 Words* (New York: Teachers College, Columbia University, 1935). Clarence R. Stone, "Measuring Difficulty of Primary Reading Material: A Constructive Criticism of Spache's Measure," *Elementary School Journal,* Vol. 57 (1956), 36–41. This word list is the one now employed in the Spache Readability Formula.

[11] Arther S. Trace, Jr., *What Ivan Knows That Johnny Doesn't* (New York: Random House, 1961).

language has an almost perfect correspondence between the spoken and printed symbols, and that exposing children to a large number of words does not necessarily indicate that they are learned or understood by all the children. Nor did he seem to know that American children read anything besides basal readers.

Advocates of intensive phonic introductions to reading generally ignore the principle of teaching first the words with the highest frequency of use and select their beginning words on the basis of the phonemic elements they contain. Thus a recent phonic program, which starts with short *a* and the consonants *t, m,* and *s,* uses words like *tat* and *mast* because of their phonic units, even though their meanings are unfamiliar to most first graders. The early sentences in such a method are apt to be sentences such as: "Fat Sam sat on a mat," or "Nan can fan Dan." Usually there is no meaningful connection between one sentence and the next. The people who write these sentences are often the same ones who complain that preprimers and primers are stilted and artificial in language and devoid of interest.

In these phonic approaches the words used are generally limited on the basis of four principles: (1) The words must have consistent symbol-sound relationships. (2) Words should not be used until their component letter sounds have been taught. (3) The number of irregular words to be introduced should be kept at a minimum until most of the phonic instruction has been completed. (4) Gradation is from short words of two or three letters toward longer words. One phonic program introduces all of the consonants and all short vowels before using one word that contains a long vowel sound. Another phonic program starts with the long vowel sounds. Still another phonic program teaches the common sounds of each vowel at the same time; the three sounds of *a* as in *at, navy,* and *want* are taught together. The words used vary considerably according to the sequence followed.

A similar emphasis on beginning with words that follow consistent symbol-sound relationships is common to "linguistic" reading programs also. In most linguistic programs, phonic generalizations are not taught, since it is expected that children will develop appropriate generalizations from their experiences with recurring letter patterns.

TEACHER-MADE MATERIALS FOR BUILDING SIGHT VOCABULARY

Materials with which children can reinforce and expand their sight vocabularies are useful to primary teachers and other teachers who have some children still reading at primary-grade levels. Many of these words are, of course, taken directly from the children's current reading material. It is helpful, also, to know the words which are so basic and occur so often that extra practice to make them instantly recognizable is worthwhile.

Picture Word Cards. For supplementary practice, children can make picture-word cards similar to those illustrated in Figure 24.

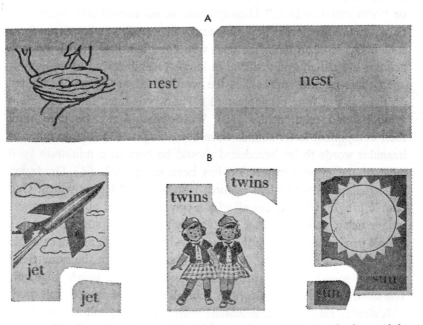

FIGURE 24. Samples of material which may be used for developing a sight vocabulary. The top cards are a pair of picture-word cards (From *Match: A Picture Word Matching Game,* Dolch, E. W., Garrard); the bottom three cards are from the *Picture Word Builder,* Milton Bradley. Reproduced by permission of the publishers.

In A, the word is printed on one side of an opaque card; the child draws a picture illustrating the word on the back of the card. In reviewing the cards, the child tries to name the word, then turns the card over and checks the picture to see if he is correct. In B, the word is printed near the picture and also in a corner. The corner is cut off, using a different irregular shape for each word. When a child is given several "corner" words to match with their cards, he can verify by whether or not the shapes fit.

Flash Cards. Large cards with words printed on them are often used to present new words, to review words, to build phrases and sentences, and to increase speed of recognition. Small cards are often employed for practice by individual children. While flash cards have some uses, many teachers have learned, to their sorrow, that recognition of a word on a card does not guarantee recognition in the book. One reason for this is that some children learn to depend on extraneous and accidental clues, like a bent corner, or a smudge on the card; they become able to recognize the particular card but not the word. Others find the difference between word-on-a-card and word-among-other-words so great that they cannot see that it is the same word.

Flash cards do have some value when properly used. Teachers using them should be careful to observe the following principles: (1) Any flash card that is distinguishable by some visual clue other than the word on it should be replaced. (2) After learning a word on a card, children should have opportunity to find and read the word in connected reading material. (3) Cards should be used to assemble words into phrases and sentences. Probably the safest uses of flash cards are in testing word knowledge and in promoting quick recognition after a word is known.

Games. Many teacher-made games can be constructed which children can use independently or in small groups of two to six, without needing the teacher. The following types of teacher-constructed materials are recommended:

1. *Individual word cards.* The teacher can cut unlined 3 × 5-inch index cards into five strips, 1 × 3 inches. When a child hesitates over a word

that the teacher thinks he should know at sight, the teacher can print the word on a card and give it to him. If the word is one that can be illustrated (usually true of nouns and action verbs), the child can draw on the reverse side a picture that will serve as a reminder. Each child can keep his words in three piles, each kept together by a rubber band or placed in a separate envelope. The child puts a new word in his "Don't Know" pile and tries to move it to his "Know" pile and finally to the "One-look Words" pile. Each time he recognizes a new word without help he gets a check mark on the back; three checks are usually enough to move the card to the "Know" pile. The "Know" pile is reviewed to build instant recognition, and other checks record successful identification without hesitation. Children can work in pairs with their word cards, each testing the other.

2. *Fish Pond.* The teacher selects word cards from those currently being studied by the children in the group. A paper clip is placed on each card and the cards are spread on a table or desk, face down. Each child in turn picks up a card by fishing with a small horseshoe magnet strung from a short stick. If he can recognize the word he keeps the card; if not, he is told the word and has to put it back in the "pond." Several children can play this, preferably with a helper.

3. *Spin the Wheel.* This is an adaptation of the well-known carnival game. A large wheel cut from oak tag is fastened to a backing by means of a two-pronged brass pin. Some teachers prefer to make a new wheel for each group of words; others prefer a more lasting setup, making radial slits near the outside rim, in which word cards can be inserted. An arrow at the right points to a word when the wheel stops spinning. Each child has a turn to spin the wheel and read the word to which the arrow points. Score can be kept in a variety of ways, and well-matched teams can have exciting competitions.

4. *Word-O.* Oak tag is cut into cards about 5 × 8 inches and each card is ruled to make 25 boxes. The center box is "free" and 24 words which are review words for the group are printed on all the cards, but in a different sequence on each card. There should be enough cards in the set to provide a card for each player, and one for the leader. The leader reads the words from his card one at a time, and as each child finds the word he covers it with a small piece of colored paper. The first child to cover five boxes in a straight line calls *Word-O* and wins the game. The cards can then be shuffled, given out again, and the game is repeated. This is, of course, an adaptation of bingo or lotto.

5. *Racing.* There are many commercial games in which a marker is moved along a path, and the first player to get home wins. Usually the number of spaces to move is determined by spinning a wheel or tossing dice. Sometimes there are penalty squares. Any commercial game of this

kind, or a home made equivalent, can be adapted to word review by a simple addition. Word cards are placed in a pack, face down. Before a player can move his marker he has to pick a word card and read it; if he does not know the word, he forfeits his turn.[12]

COMMERCIAL MATERIALS FOR BUILDING
SIGHT VOCABULARY

Many of the commercial materials that are on sale for developing word recognition are designed to teach or reinforce phonic skills, and are therefore listed in Chapter 9. The commercial materials which are usable for building sight vocabulary include the following:

Basic Sight Vocabulary Cards, by E. W. Dolch. The 220 commonest service words, printed on small cards of convenient size. The same words on slightly larger cards in larger print are available as *Popper Words,* Set 1 and Set 2, each containing 110 words (individual and group size cards are available). Garrard.

Picture Word Cards, by E. W. Dolch. The 95 common nouns printed on individual cards, with a picture on the back. The same words plus one other are found in *Match,* 48 words each in Set 1 and Set 2. Garrard.

Schoolhouse Key Lab. Set contains a total of 110 different words on 10 word wheels. Words are on one side with corresponding pictures on the other so that either the word or picture can serve as the stimulus with the reverse side being used to check the response. Also contains notched picture and alphabet cards that can be used as self-checks in word identification and word building. Schoolhouse Industries, Inc.

Language Master (Bell and Howell), *e f i Audio Flashcard System* (Electronics Futures, Inc.), *TTC Magnetic Card Reader* (Teaching Technology Corp.). Commercially prepared or teacher-prepared cards (blank cards are available) are used with these machines. A child can look at the word(s) printed on a card, attempt to identify it, place the card into the machine, and then hear the word pronounced for him. The child also can record his response and play the card back in order to compare it with the response prerecorded on the magnetic tape on the card.

[12] David H. Russell and Etta Karp, *Reading Aids through the Grades,* 2nd ed. (New York: Bureau of Publications, Teachers College, Columbia University, 1959). Many additional ideas for teacher-made reading games can be found in this reference and in Guy Wagner and Max Hosier, *Reading Games: Strengthening Reading Skills with Instructional Games* (Darien, Conn.: Educational Publishing Corp., 1960).

Picture Word Builder. Set contains 36 cards (all nouns) with die cuts that fit together only with the correct picture. See Figure 24. Milton Bradley.

My Puzzle Book. Two crossword-puzzle type paperbacks. Puzzle Book 1 contains the easier half of the Dolch Basic Sight Word List plus 65 other common words. Book 2 consists of the harder Dolch Words, 69 words used in Book 1, and 31 additional words. Garrard.

Grab, a card game involving word matching which can be played with several variations; available in three levels of difficulty. Covina, Calif.: Dorothea Alcock, 324 E. College St.

Simple gadgets with a cardboard frame and shutter can be made from oak tag or some other stiff, heavy paper. The simplest and most flexible type consists of a rectangular screen, about 4×6 inches, behind which individual word cards can be placed so that the words or phrases on them show in an opening when the shutter is raised. With practice, a fairly uniform rate of presentation can be achieved.

Small spring-powered tachistoscopes with an exposure speed of about 1/25 of a second and costing a few dollars apiece are available from several distributors, including Audio Visual Research, Chicago; Educational Developmental Laboratories, Huntington, N.Y.; the Reading Institute of Boston; and Better Reading Program, Inc., Chicago. With most of these, one has to purchase lists of words or phrases printed on rolls of paper or on cardboard circles. Blank materials are available from a few companies.

Lists of words and phrases which have been prepared on lantern slides or filmstrips for use with a projection tachistoscope can be obtained from several commercial organizations, including Educational Developmental Laboratories, Huntington, N.Y.; Keystone View Co., Meadville, Pa.: Learning Through Seeing, Inc., Sunland, Calif.; Stereo Optical Co., Chicago; Perceptual Developmental Laboratories, St. Louis, Mo. Some of these materials are usable only in a special projector distributed by the same company; others are more widely usable.

The limitations of practicing on words and phrases in isolation have been discussed earlier in this chapter. The wise teacher will do well not to devote more than a small proportion of the total reading time to this kind of practice.

Summary

1. Perceiving a word means seeing it with an awareness of its sound and meaning.
   a. What one perceives is dependent on the pattern of sensory excitation and the association made with the memory traces created by hearing the word, saying it, seeing its printed symbol, and learning its meaning or meanings.
   b. When the word has more than one meaning, the immediate context may help the reader to select the correct meaning.
2. The general trend of perceptual development is from vague, crude wholes to highly differentiated perceptions in which both the quality of the total Gestalt and the details are clearly perceived.
3. Closure, figure-ground contrasts, and sequence are important in the perception of words.
4. Most children are introduced to reading in a way that emphasizes developing a sight vocabulary from the start.
   a. The point at which word parts are considered varies among reading programs.
   b. Programs that rely heavily on a "whole-word" approach place an emphasis on picture clues and configuration clues.
   c. Repetition of words strengthens only what has been perceived and reinforced; it does not necessarily build clearer perceptions or clearer imagery.
   d. It seems likely that because of marked individual differences, visual imagery is not sufficient for some individuals.
   e. Stress on phonics is very helpful to some children.
   f. Tracing and writing are helpful to other children.
5. The most natural way to speed up word perception is through abundant practice in reading easy, interesting material.
6. Short exposure practice using flash cards, tachistoscopes, or pacing devices sometimes has disappointingly little transfer to normal reading.
7. Most primary-grade reading materials employ a controlled and gradually introduced vocabulary.

a. Words that the children are most likely to encounter and whose meanings are known to most children are employed in programs that do not use an intensive phonics approach.

b. Words that are consistent in their symbol-sound relationships are used in programs which employ an intensive phonic or linguistic approach.

8. A number of games and devices, teacher-made and commercial, can be used for special practice in developing a sight vocabulary. However, only a small share of the total reading time should be devoted to practice on isolated words.

Recommended Reading

See references listed at end of Chapter 9.

9

Developing Independence
in Word Recognition

As stated in the previous chapter, in order to become an efficient reader a child must develop an adequate sight vocabulary. But before a child can be a truly independent reader he must not only be able to recognize at sight most of the words he meets in print, but also must be able to decode the words that are new or unfamiliar to him.

In teaching methods of decoding unknown words, most teachers follow the procedures given in the manuals that accompany the reading program they are using. Teachers must understand the principles that underlie the word-analysis methods used in their reading program and must recognize that the word-attack part of the program is very important and should be given as much attention as the comprehension skills. They should also know what word-analysis skills each child possesses and should deviate from the program outlined in the manual when necessary to provide for individual needs.

The word-analysis programs found in basal readers are emphasized in this chapter because basal readers are the most widely used instructional materials. Word-analysis instruction in intensive phonics programs differs from these mainly in the earlier and more rapid introduction of phonics. In general, basal reader programs teach four interrelated sets of word attack skills: phonics, morphemic analysis, use of context, and use of the dictionary.

Phonics

Phonics is the study of the speech equivalents of printed symbols and their use in pronouncing printed and written words; it is the part of phonetics most closely involved in reading. Unquestionably it is important for children to learn phonics and to employ their phonic knowledge when they meet words that are not recognized at sight. But there are many differences of opinion as to how this should be done. Intensive phonic programs not only differ with basal reader programs but differ among themselves on many fundamental issues. Yet despite differences among and between programs,[1] there are some basic principles on which word-analysis instruction is planned in most basal reader programs. These principles are as follows:

Phonic principles are developed from sight words.[2] Before a phoneme-grapheme relationship is taught, several words that contain it should have been learned as sight words. Knowing the sound, the meaning, and the appearance of these words, it is easy for the children to note the similarity in sound and the similarity in appearance and to relate the two similarities. When the common phoneme and grapheme have been identified in known words, they can then be found in other words.

[1] Sidney W. Schnayer and Leona A. Robinson, "An Analysis of Phonic Systems for the Primary Grades in Eight Basal Reader Series," *The Journal of the Reading Specialist,* 9 (December 1969), 58–72.

[2] A concise summary of principles of phonics, including syllabication and accent, will be found in Appendix B. At this point, definitions of a few terms that are used in phonic literature may be helpful:

phoneme: the smallest unit of sound that can distinguish one spoken word from another. Phonemes are of three kinds: consonants, vowels, and accent. Sometimes a phoneme is represented by more than one letter (*th, eigh*).

grapheme: an alphabet letter or group of letters that can represent a phoneme.

morpheme: a meaningful unit of language such as a prefix, a suffix, a root word, or an inflectional ending.

digraph: a two-letter combination that represents a single sound. The main consonant digraphs are *ch, sh, th,* and *wh.* Vowel digraphs include *ee, ea, ai, oa,* etc.

Phonic principles should be developed inductively. Instead of memorizing sounds, children should discover for themselves, with the help of the teacher, the significance of letters and letter combinations. Thus they can listen to several words that have a sound in common, look at the printed words to locate the common visual element, and in this way find out that the common grapheme represents the common phoneme. Once a principle has been derived in this way, it should immediately be applied to other words and there should be opportunity to apply it in connected reading. Of course, children who can not learn easily through inductive reasoning should be taught by using deductive reasoning; that is, going from the principle to the examples.

Whole-word phonics. The whole-word phonic procedure was devised to avoid distortion of sounds and difficulty in blending. Emphasis is placed on not sounding phonemes in isolation, but rather using known words in which the phoneme is easily identified. Usually a word that is easily pictured is used as a cue word, and if a child forgets the sound, the picture reminds him of the cue word which in turn suggests the sound. Thus when children have learned *come, can,* and *car* as sight words, they can listen to see if they sound alike at the beginning, look to see if they begin alike, and in this way learn the "hard sound" of *c*. A picture of a car can serve as a cue. If a child forgets the sound represented by *c,* the teacher says something like, "This word begins like *car,*" instead of, "This word begins with *kuh.*" Or, the child can look at a cue card which shows a picture of a car and *c.*

---

blend: a combination of two or more phonemes in which each phoneme can be heard. Consonant blends include *bl, cr, st, spr,* etc. Vowel blends are called *diphthongs* and include the *oi* sound in *boy* and *boil* and the *ou* sound in *out* and *cow*. Blends are called "consonant clusters" by linguists.

prefix: a meaningful beginning which modifies the meaning of the root word to which it is attached (*rewrite, uncommon*).

suffix: a meaningful ending which modifies the meaning of the root word to which it is attached (tender*ly,* consider*ation,* act*or*).

inflectional ending: a suffix which indicates a change of number (box*es*), tense (hop*ed*), possessive (Dan'*s*) comparison (black*er,* black*est*), present participle (rid*ing*), and third person singular (he ride*s*).

affix: a prefix, suffix, or inflectional ending.

A child who has learned the symbol-sound association for *m* and /m/ in the initial position through whole-word phonics and who knows the word *boat* as a sight word can solve the new word *moat* by thinking, "It begins like *man* and ends like *boat; boat, moat.*" This is known as *consonant substitution.* The substitution technique is also used when a new word is similar to a known word except in its ending (ma*n*, ma*d*), or its vowel sound (p*a*t, p*o*t). As vowel sounds are learned, emphasis shifts from consonant substitution to rapid blending of the sounds in one-syllable words.

Sequence. In most basal reader systems the sequence in which letter sounds are taught is based on the combined use of three main principles: (1) sounds should be introduced in order of increasing difficulty, the easiest first; (2) several sight words that have the phonic unit in common are already known; and (3) opportunity to use the principle in attacking a new word or words, and to read these words in context, should follow immediately. Research shows that beginners can discriminate consonant sounds more easily than vowel sounds and that initial consonants are easier than final consonants. Furthermore, consonants are more consistent than vowels in their symbol-sound relationships. Although most programs begin with single initial consonants, the sequence in which they are introduced varies among basal series.

In order to make associations between letters and the sounds they represent, children must have adequate mastery of certain skills. Two important skills related to future success in phonics are auditory discrimination and visual discrimination. If a child has difficulty in noticing the differences between phonemes (auditory discrimination), or has difficulty seeing the differences between letter forms (visual discrimination), he is very likely to have problems in learning to associate phonemes with the graphemes that represent them. Formal instruction in these prerequisite skills begins during the reading readiness period and continues through the program of phonics instruction.

Preprimer words are usually taught as sight words, although phonic instruction is begun very early in the preprimers in some of the more recently published series. At the primer level many initial consonants and some final consonants are introduced, and before the end of the first reader practically all single consonants, some consonant blends, some consonant digraphs (especially *th* and *sh*), and a few inflectional endings (*-s, -ed, -ing*) have been introduced. The pace of the phonic program is increased at the second-reader level and tends to include many consonant blends, the short vowels, the long vowels, vowels followed by *r* and *ll*, and a number of vowel digraphs. During third readers the program is rounded out with the remaining common consonant blends, the diphthongs (*oi, oy, ou, ow*), less common vowel digraphs, and alternative sounds of letter combinations (*meat, head; now, crow*). There has been a recent trend to introduce phonic skills earlier and more intensively in basal-reader programs. For example, short vowels may be taught at the primer level and long vowels at first-reader level.[3]

Phonics Combined with Context. Basal-reader methodology stresses that when a tentative pronunciation of a new word has been worked out, it should be tried in the sentence in which it occurs to see if it makes good sense. In the early stages of phonic knowledge, when the children are depending heavily on configuration and are learning initial consonants, they are encouraged to use the initial consonant in conjunction with the size and shape of the word and the meaning of the sentence.

If in a primer story, the words *birthday, surprise, candles, something,* and *seven* are used, at a point following the teaching of *s* as an initial consonant, the child who uses the *s* will not confuse *surprise* with *birthday* or *candles.* The configuration of *seven* is sufficiently different so that confusion with *surprise* is unlikely. For the child who hesitates between *surprise* and *something,* the sentence "We will s———— Tom" makes sense with *surprise* but not with *something.* Thus children who are attentive to meaning can use partial phonic clues combined with configuration and context to identify words correctly. Adhering to phonic generalizations without attending to meaning or allowing for phonic exceptions creates many difficulties for a

[3] For a more complete sequence of phonic skills, refer to Albert J. Harris, *How to Increase Reading Ability.* 5th ed. (New York: McKay, 1970), pp. 346–347.

young reader. After applying word-analysis skills to a word, the reader should ask himself two questions: (1) Does it sound like a word I know? and (2) Does it make sense in this sentence?

The English language has many pairs of words that sound alike, look alike, or both, while having different meanings. Sometimes the spelling is the same but pronunciation as well as meaning differs (*bow, lead, desert*). Only in a meaningful context can one decide whether *bow* should rhyme with *cow* or *low*, or mean a hair decoration, a weapon, or a bending of the body. These words whose written forms are alike are called *homographs*. When words sound alike they are called *homonyns;* they may be spelled alike also (a country *fair*, a *fair* day), or may be spelled differently (*stake, steak*). According to the generalization about *g* following *e* or *i*, *anger* should be pronounced *anjer;* but if the word is in the child's understanding vocabulary and if he is paying attention to meaning he is not likely to be misled. Whether the *ea* in *thread* should be pronounced as in *mean, head, break, early, beard, bear, real, beauty*, or *heart* is not likely to bother the child who knows that the sentence deals with needles and sewing and who also expects irregularities in the alphabetic representations of English sounds.

AUDITORY DISCRIMINATION

Auditory discrimination is an essential part of instruction in phonics. Children must be able to hear a phoneme in words and to distinguish it from other somewhat similar phonemes as a necessary preliminary to associating the sound with its grapheme. Some of this "ear training" can be given during reading readiness activities. Usually practice on hearing a specific phoneme comes just before the introduction of the grapheme.

In the development of auditory discrimination of phonemes within words, the usual sequence is about as follows:

1. *Likenesses and differences in total words.* The child listens to pairs of words to decide whether or not they are identical, as: *hit, bit; moon, noon.* Depending on the amount of physical energy the teacher

wants to encourage, signaling can be done with such activities as thumbs up or down, raising the arm, or standing up.

2. *Discrimination of initial consonants.* A key word is given, such as *Sally,* and children listen to other words like *some, tall, Sunday, hand,* and signal one way when the word begins like *Sally* and another way when it doesn't. Then they are asked to suggest other words that begin like *Sally.*

3. *Perception of rhymes.* Children listen to simple rhymes and poems and pick out the words at the ends of lines that rhyme. They can also be given rhymes and jingles in which the last word is left out, and they try to supply it. Ability to hear sounds that rhyme is fundamental to the building of one-syllable "word families" like *best, nest, pest, rest, test, west.*

4. *Discrimination of final consonants.* Starting with a word like hot, children can be asked to listen to hear if two words end with the same sound (*hot, ham*), to signal when a word ends like *hot* (*bat, lid, put, ran, coat*); and to supply additional words that end with the same sound as *hot.*

5. *Discrimination of middle vowels.* Practice can be given in hearing vowel differences (*ran, run; pit, pet*); in hearing the same vowel in several words (*man, bag, sack, lad, pat*); in signaling when a word has the same middle sound as *ran* (*pan, tip, band, said, cart*); and in supplying additional words that sound in the middle like *ran.*

6. *Auditory Blending.* Children listen to a word that is pronounced as a whole, and then sound by sound, and imitate. Then they listen as a word is sounded and mentally fuse or blend the sounds to discover what the word is. Some children have no trouble at all with blending; a few have great difficulty with it. Most children improve in auditory blending ability with practice. In providing such practice, the teacher should select words that lend themselves to the pronunciation and understanding of the component elements (e.g., it is difficult to pronounce the component parts of *pant* without distorting the sounds to an extent that makes it difficult for the listener to determine the correct response. The sound of each component (e.g., br/ing, h/a/m) should be given at the rate of one approximately every one-half second. Practice should begin with known words that have only the initial consonant isolated from the rest of the word.

7. *Perception of syllables.* Later, as a preliminary to syllabication, the teacher pronounces words as a whole and then syllable by syllable; the children can beat time to the syllables. Then they listen to new words and try to count the syllables. After the whole word has been pronounced by syllables, practice can be given in listening carefully to each syllable.

The technique of auditory discrimination may be summarized as follows: present several spoken words that contain the element to be heard; get attention focused on the sound which is common to the words; give practice in discriminating words containing the sound from words that do not; encourage the children to think of other words that contain the sound; and provide rhymes, riddles, or incomplete sentences that can be completed with words containing the sound.[4]

Suggestions for Teaching Auditory Discrimination. Some of the activities that a teacher may use in helping children to recognize and discriminate sounds in the initial position of words (/m/ is used as an example) are as follows:

1. Say a sequence of words such as *monkey, man, may, milk, me, morning.* Ask how they are all alike. If necessary, explain that they start alike and repeat.
2. Play a listening game in which children signal one way when the teacher says a word that begins like *monkey* and signal another way if the word starts with another sound.
3. Ask children for additional words that begin like *monkey.* When one child suggests a word, ask another child if the word does begin like *monkey.*
4. Give incomplete sentences or riddles, such as:
   What shines in the sky at night? (moon)

[4] Two very good references for teachers, both of which contain many useful practice exercises for developing auditory discrimination, are:

Lucille D. Schoolfield, *Better Speech and Better Reading,* rev. ed. (Magnolia, Mass.: Expression Co., 1951).

Empress Y. Zedler, *Listening for Speech Sounds* (Garden City, N.Y.: Doubleday, Inc., 1955).

Other auditory discrimination games and exercises, as well as exercises for developing other listening skills, may be found in:

David H. Russell and Elizabeth Russell, *Listening Aids Through the Grades* (New York: Bureau of Publications, Teachers College Columbia University, 1959).

Guy Wagner, *et al., Listening Games* (Darien, Conn.: Teachers Publishing Corp., 1962).

Many helpful suggestions about ear training can also be found in the manuals of some of the phonic systems described on pages 261–262; the procedures in the *Phonovisual, Building Reading Skills,* and *Phonics We Use* manuals fit fairly well into most basal reader programs.

What funny animal can hang by its tail? (monkey)
A house costs a great deal of _____. (money)
We wake up when it is _____. (morning)
5. If children tend to confuse two sounds, such as *m* and *n*, give practice in discriminating between them. For example, if the word starts like *monkey*, the children stand; if it starts like *nest*, they sit.
6. Provide seatwork with pictures that can be named. If the name starts like *monkey*, the children mark the picture. See Fig. 25.

Similar exercises can be used to teach auditory recognition and discrimination of consonant phonemes in the final position, and of vowels.

LEARNING PHONIC UNITS

When a new sound is taught, children have to develop a learned association between the phoneme and the printed symbol or symbols that represent it. While this can be done in a variety of ways, the following steps, still using /m/ as an example, are recommended:

1. *Presenting the cue card.* A large card with a picture representing the cue word (in this case *monkey*) and the letter *M* below it, both capital and small. Sometimes a large chart is used that contains the cue pictures for many letters. The card is discussed and the children are told that the letter represents the sound they hear at the beginning of *monkey*. Usually the card or chart is posted so that the children can refer to it.
2. *Listening for the sound.* As much ear training is provided as the teacher thinks is necessary.
3. *Printing words on the chalkboard.* Teacher asks the children for reading words they know that begin with the same sound as *monkey*. As each word is proposed, teacher writes it on the chalkboard in manuscript and asks, "Does it begin like monkey?" For each word a child is called on to answer; if the answer is "Yes," the child traces over the beginning *m* with colored chalk (or circles it or underlines it).
4. *Presenting letter name and sound.*[5] The teacher says something like,

[5] There is a long-standing argument about the use of letter names and sounds. Basal readers introduce letter sounds and symbols in whole-word settings, and some of them advocate teaching the names of the letters, but advise against ever pronouncing a sound in isolation. Some phonic systems

INITIAL CONSONANT m
PURPOSE. To increase proficiency in recognizing the sound of the initial consonant m.

PROCEDURE. Put X in the box under each picture whose name has the same beginning sound as the name of the key picture, mouse. (The children may respond with m if they know how to form the letter.)

FIGURE 25. Page from a phonics workbook. (Reprinted with permission of the publisher from *Phonics We Use*, Book A, Teacher's Edition, p. 45, Halvorsen, *et al.* Copyright 1966 by Lyons and Carnahan, Educational Division, Meredith Corporation.) Reduced in size. The original is in color.

"The name of this letter is Em and its sound is *mmm*. Do you hear the *mmm* in *monkey?* Listen to the mmm at the beginning of each of the other words."
5. The children suggest other words that start with the letter *m* and the /m/ sound, the teacher prints each word on the board, and a child traces over the *m*.
6. Seatwork is provided in which the child makes an *m* below each picture whose name begins with the sound of /m/.

The procedure outlined above can be generalized and used, with appropriate modifications, for teaching initial consonants, final consonants, vowels, blends, digraphs, and vowel-consonant and consonant-vowel combinations. The phonic unit should first be heard within several words and seen in the printed forms of the words. Its name and sound can be introduced, and further practice can be given in hearing it, saying it, seeing it, writing it, and distinguishing it from other symbols; much of this practice should be on words containing the sound and should involve meaningful reading (see Figure 26).

WHEN SHOULD PHONIC UNITS BE TAUGHT?

Basal reader systems generally introduce phonics gradually, with the vowels and most consonant combinations introduced during the second-reader program. Phonic methods disagree with this. Although they differ among themselves on many important issues, they are in

---

identify letters only by their sounds, introducing letter names much later. It seems psychologically sound and educationally practical to introduce the sound and symbol in whole words; but after the sound has been heard and seen be identified by both name and sound.
within whole-word settings, it is easily abstracted from the settings and can
The main argument against pronouncing sounds separately is that they become distorted, mainly through the addition of an extra "uh" or schwa sound that interferes with blending. But it is primarily the unvoiced consonants *b, c, d, h, k, p,* and *t* with which this problem can cause trouble, and with practice teachers and children can learn to whisper the consonants with little or no extra vowel sound. The child who is taught that "Bee says /b/ as in *baby, big,* and *bird,*" is better off than the child who generalizes for himself, "Bee is in *baby, big,* and *bird,* so Bee says *buh.*" Since the latter reasoning is silent, the teacher may never find out that the child thinks of Bee as *buh* instead of reminding himself of a cue word such as *bird.*

The ir and ur Teams

The **ir** and **ur** teams usually sound like the **er** team in **herd**.

The ir Team

whirl	thirsty	sir	bird
thirty	firmly	stir	birch

1. He pressed the dirt _____ around the plant.

2. The _____ tree has beautiful bark.

The ur Team

spurted	curve	urge	fur
hurled	burns	turned	hurt

1. The water _____ from the old pipe.

2. Did she _____ you to do the work?

At first this test rocket went straight up into the air. Then it turned and curved like a giant bird. After all of its fuel had been burned, it fell into the ocean.

FIGURE 26. Page from a phonics workbook. (From Hargrave and Armstrong, *Building Reading Skills: Rocket Book*, p. 57. Copyright 1965 by McCormick-Mathers Co., Inc., Cincinnati, Ohio. Reduced in size. Reproduced by permission of the Publisher.)

accord on the desirability of teaching phonics early and intensively. In the light of the presently available evidence, it is fair to conclude that while the evidence is not conclusively in favor of very intensive phonics neither does it support a very slow and gradual phonic program. There are still a number of unanswered questions. Dykstra, who reported that the USOE Cooperative Reading Research Studies tended to support the conclusion concerning the superiority of code-emphasis programs in beginning reading, cautioned:

There is no clear evidence that the early emphasis on code *per se* is the *only* or even the *primary* reason for the relative effectiveness of the code-emphasis programs. The major types of programs which were compared differed in a number of respects in addition to the varying emphasis on code and meaning. The possibility exists that some other characteristic of these programs (higher expectation of pupil achievement, for example) may be a more crucial element in determining pupil achievement than the emphasis on code-breaking. It is also possible that some particular combination of factors within the code-emphasis programs accounted for their effectiveness. There is some evidence for this conjecture in that the various code-emphasis programs did not appear to be equally effective. Unfortunately, studies of the nature discussed in this report compare *one complex* of instructional factors with *another complex* of instructional factors, thereby making it impossible to isolate the single characteristic (if indeed there is one) which makes one program more effective than another.[6]

Largely because of the lack of conclusive research evidence, there still remain differences of opinion as to the merits of an early emphasis on phonics in reading instruction.[7]

Basal-reader programs usually state that they introduce a new phonic principle at a point where several words that contain it have been

[6] Robert Dykstra, "The Effectiveness of Code- and Meaning-Emphasis Beginning Reading Programs," *The Reading Teacher,* Vol. 22 (1968), 17–23.

For a discussion of the limitations of the USOE Cooperative Reading Studies see Edward R. Sipay, "Interpreting the USOE Cooperative Reading Studies," *The Reading Teacher,* 22 (1968), 10–16; 35.

[7] For example, see: Jeanne S. Chall, *Learning to Read: The Great Debate* (New York: McGraw-Hill, 1967). Also see the reviews of this book by Ruth Strang in *The Reading Teacher,* 21 (March 1968), 575–576, and by Eldonna Evertts in *Elementary English,* 45 (May 1968), 652–656.

learned as sight words and the children are ready for it. Interpreting several as meaning four or more, and assuming that phonic readiness can be improved in many children by appropriate activities, it seems reasonable to propose that a phonic unit can be introduced when four or more sight words containing it have been taught.

The vocabulary lists of new words at the back of the primary grade readers of a very widely used basal reader series were analyzed to see what would happen if the policy were to be followed of introducing a phonic principle when four sight words containing it have been met. The result showed that it would be possible to introduce phonic principles at a considerably more rapid rate than these basal readers employ. At preprimer level, the criterion of four or more sight words was met by six initial consonants, four final consonants, and three short vowels. At primer level, six more initial consonants, four additional final consonants, the remaining short and long vowel sounds (except long *u*), *th,* and *ay* met the criterion. At first reader level the new consonants included all remaining single consonants except *v, x,* and *z; ch, sh,* and *wh; gr, sl,* and *st.* Vowels included *y,* digraphs *ee, ai, ea, oo,* and *ow* (low), and the *r*-controlled vowels as in *far, her, sir,* and *or.* The remaining common consonant blends, silent consonants, and vowel digraphs and diphthongs met the criterion at second- and third-reader levels.

The specific phonic units have not been listed above in full detail because they would vary somewhat from series to series. An analysis of Stone's Word Lists by Reading Levels [8] suggests a similar rate of introduction, although the sequence is somewhat different.

It would seem probable that many basal reader programs could introduce phonic principles somewhat faster than they do. In particular, the vowel sounds, which most basal readers teach at second-reader level, appear in enough first-grade words so that it should be possible to teach the short vowels during preprimer and primer reading, and the long vowels while a 1^2 reader is being used. Consonants also can be introduced at a somewhat faster rate than is typical in basal reader systems.

[8] Clarence R. Stone, *Progress in Primary Reading* (St. Louis: Webster Publishing Co., 1950), pp. 107–30.

In the above discussion the importance of introducing phonic units in order of increasing difficulty and of waiting for phonic readiness has been minimized. It may be expected that when a phonic unit is first introduced, some children will fail to perceive it clearly enough or to understand, and may either just memorize the words or fail to respond. If the phonic principles are frequently applied and reviewed, most of these children will catch on somewhat later. Meanwhile the ones who can grasp the idea the first or second time can use it profitably. An alternative would be to identify those children who could profit from such instruction, and to teach them phonic skills in separate groups or individually. Teachers, and particularly first-grade teachers, who want to amplify the phonic program given in their reader manuals can without great difficulty develop a sequence that fits the readers they are using employing principles of phonic instruction such as have been discussed above. Some of them may prefer to use commercially published phonic materials, such as will be described a little later in this chapter, in place of the phonic instruction found in the particular reading program being employed.

SYLLABICATION, ACCENT [9], AND VOWEL SOUNDS IN SYLLABLES

By the third-reader level most of the new words that children may have trouble recognizing have more than one syllable. Most basal reader systems therefore introduce the beginnings of syllabication during the second- or third-reader level and reinforce and extend this knowledge in the middle grades. A few simple syllabication generalizations are taught, along with principles that help to determine accent and vowel sounds.

Along with syllables, the problem of where to place accent arises in words of more than one syllable. Children need to have experience in listening to words to distinguish primary accent, secondary accent, and unaccented syllables, and to recognize the marks which are used to represent primary and secondary accent (′,′) in dictionaries. Since

[9] Some authors consider these under the heading of structural or morphemic analysis.

there is a relationship between syllable division, placement of accent, and vowel values, attention is often given to all three together.

At third-reader level (reached by many children in the second grade) one can begin to make children aware of the fact that words are made up of syllables and can provide practice in listening to words that are pronounced by syllables, in counting syllables, and in noting whether the vowel in each syllable is short or long. This can start with many words of two or three syllables that have previously been learned as sight words, and can be extended and applied with new words.

Practice in pronouncing and writing words by syllables is also stressed in spelling, and it is desirable to coordinate instruction in syllabication so that reading practice and spelling practice can be mutually helpful.

The number of phonic generalizations introduced, their rate of introduction, and their wording varies greatly among reading programs, with the highest number and most rapid rate of introduction tending to occur in the intensive phonics systems. As indicated in Figure 27, there is some question as to the utility of some commonly taught generalizations, particularly those involving vowels. In interpreting the data found in Figure 27, it should be noted that in some cases where one generalization was not useful, another one was. For example, the word "singer" is an exception to the syllabication generalization which suggests dividing between two consonants. However, application either of the generalization that states that one should not divide within digraphs and blends (ng), or the generalization that suggests dividing between a root word (sing) and affixes(er), would result in the correct response.

Teachers sometimes forget that the real purpose of teaching phonic and morphemic generalizations is to assist the child in decoding unrecognized words, rather than to assure that the child can parrot back these generalizations, or that he be able to indicate in a workbook which generalization should be applied according to the teacher's manual. Generalizations should be taught so as to give the child useful guidelines or procedures as to how words may be decoded.

When a child encounters a word he does not recognize immediately,

UTILITY OF PHONIC GENERALIZATIONS

A. Vowel Digraphs

	Percent of Utility*		
	Clymer	Bailey	Emans
1. Words having double e usually have the long e sound. (seem) (Been)**	98	100	87
2. In ay the y is silent and gives a its long sound. (spray) (always)	78	100	88
3. The first vowel is usually long and the second silent in the digraphs ai, ea, oa, and ui.	66	58	60
a) oa (roam) (cupboard)	97	96	95
b) ea (bean) (head)	66	62	55
c) ai (nail) (said)	64	83	72
d) ui (suit) (build)	6	0	10
4. The two letters ow make the long o sound. (flow) (down)	59	50	55
5. The letter a has the same sound (ô) when followed by l, w, and u. (all, raw, naught) (canal)	49	24	34
6. When there are two vowels side by side, the long sound of the first one is heard and the second is usually silent. (bead) (chief)	45	18	34
7. W is sometimes part of a digraph and follows the vowel diagraph rule. (arrow) (threw)	40	31	33
8. When e is followed by w, the vowel sound is the same as represented by oo. (blew) (sew)	35	14	40
9. In the phonogram ie, the i is silent and the e has the long sound. (field) (friend)	17	23	31

B. Effect of Position on Vowel Sounds

1. Closed Syllable (ends with a consonant letter)			
a) When there is one e in a word that ends in a consonant, the e usually has a short sound. (leg) (her)	76	83	92

	Percent of Utility*		
	Clymer	Bailey	Emans
b) When a vowel is in the middle of one syllable word, the vowel is short. (hut) (far)	62	73	71
1) when it is the middle letter (dress) (scold)	69	81	78
2) when it is one of the middle two letters in a word of four letters (rest) (told)	59	71	68
3) when one vowel appears within a word of more than four letters (splash) (fight)	46	42	62
c) When a word has only one vowel letter, the vowel sound is likely to be short. (hid) (kind)	57	70	69
d) One vowel letter in an accented syllable has its short sound. (city) (lady)	61	64	65
2. Open Syllable (ends in a vowel letter) If the only vowel letter is at the end of a word, the letter usually stands for a long sound. (go) (to)	74	33	76
3. Vowels followed by r a) When a is followed by r and final e, we expect to hear the sound heard in care. (dare) (are)	90	100	96
b) The r gives the preceding vowel a sound that is neither long nor short. (horn) (wire)	78	82	86
4. Final Silent e a) When there are two vowels, one of which is final e, the first vowel is long and the e is silent. (bone) (done)	63	63	57
b. When words end with silent e, the preceding a or i is long. (cake) (have)	60	48	50
c. In many two and three syllable words, the final e lengthens the vowel in the last syllable. (invite) (gasoline)	46	42	46

Percent of Utility*
Clymer Bailey Emans

C. Variant Sounds Represented by the Letter y

1. When y is the final letter in a word,
it usually has a vowel sound.
(dry) (tray)   84   98   89

2. When y is used as a vowel in words,
it sometimes has the sound of long i.
(fly) (funny)   15   4   11

3. When y or ey is seen in the last syllable that is not accented, the long
sound of e is heard. (baby)***   0   1   0

D. Silent Consonants

1. When ght is seen in a word, gh is
silent. (light)   100   100   100

2. When a word begins with wr, the w
is silent. (wrap)   100   100   100

3. When a word begins with kn, the k
is silent. (knit)   100   100   100

4. When a word ends in ck, it has the
same last sound as in look. (brick)   100   100   100

5. When two of the same consonants are
side by side, only one is heard.
(dollar) (suggest)   99   91   98

6. When the letter i is followed by the
letters gh, the i usually stands for
its long sound and the gh is silent.
(high) (neighbor)   71   100   71

E. Consonant Digraphs

1. When c and h are next to each other,
they make only one sound. (charge)   100   100   100

2. Ch is usually pronounced as it is in
kitchen, catch, and chair, not like
sh. (catch) (machine)   95   67   87

F. Variant Sounds Represented by the
Consonant Letters c and g

1. When the letter c is followed by o
or a, the sound of k is likely to be
heard. (camp)   100   100   100

	Percent of Utility*		
	Clymer	Bailey	Emans
2. When c is followed by e or i, the sound of s is likely to be heard. (cent) (ocean)	96	90	92
3. The letter g often has a sound similar to that of j in jump when it precedes the letter i or e. (genius) (give)	64	80	78

G. Syllabication

1. When the first vowel element in a word is followed by th, ch, or sh, these symbols are not broken when the word is divided into syllables and may go with either the first or second syllable. (dishes)	100	100	100
2. If the last syllable of a word ends in le, the consonant preceding the le usually begins the last syllable. (gable) (buckle)	97	78	93
3. If the first vowel sound in a word is followed by two consonants, the first syllable usually ends with the first of the two consonants. (dinner) (singer)	72	80	78
4. In a word of more than one syllable, the letter v usually goes with the preceding vowel to form a syllable. (river) (clover)	65	40	73
5. If the first vowel sound in a word is followed by a single consonant, that consonant usually begins the second syllable. (china) (robin)	44	47	50

H. Accenting

1. When ture is the final syllable in a word, it is unaccented. (future)	100	100	95
2. When tion is the final syllable in a word, it is unaccented. (notion)	100	100	100
3. In most two syllable words that end in a consonant followed by y, the			

	Percent of Utility*		
	Clymer	Bailey	Emans
first syllable is accented and the last is unaccented. (baby) (supply)	96	100	97
4. When the last syllable is the sound r, it is unaccented. (ever) (butler) (appear)	95	96	79
5. If a, in, re, ex, de, or be, is the first syllable in a word, it usually is unaccented, (reply) (insect)	87	83	84
6. In most two syllable words, the first syllable is accented. (famous) (polite)	85	75	81

*Numbers in each column refer to the percentage of times a generalization, when applied, would result in a "correct answer" according to the following studies:

Clymer, Theodore, "The Utility of Phonic Generalizations in the Primary Grades," The Reading Teacher, 16 (Jan. 1963), 252–258.

Bailey, Mildred H. "The Utility of Phonic Generalizations in Grades One Through Six," The Reading Teacher, 20 (Feb. 1967), 413–418. Used words from eight basal series for grades one through six; 5773 words.

Emans, Robert. "The Usefulness of Phonic Generalizations Above the Primary Grades," The Reading Teacher, 20 (Feb. 1967), 419–425. Used random sample of 10 per cent of the words (1944 words) beyond the primary level in the Teacher's Word Book of 30,000 Words by Thorndike and Lorge.

**The first word in parenthesis is an example of the word that conforms to the generalization, the second is an example of an exception.

***In the dictionary used to determine the pronunciation, the "short i" sound was given (e.g., bā bǐ); however, to many people and in some dictionaries the letter y does represent the "long e" sound.

FIGURE 27. Utility of phonic generalizations as determined by applying commonly taught generalizations to words encountered by children in their reading materials.

he probably goes through three steps, not necessarily in the sequence given here (provided, of course, that he has learned a procedure and *wants* to determine the pronunciation of the word). First, he must analyze the word into some component parts that are small enough for him to handle. He then applies his phonics skills to those parts that he does not immediately recognize. Finally, he must blend the parts into a whole word. The complexity of this task often is not fully realized. It should be remembered that the child really must perform these steps mentally during the reading act. At no time is the word actually seen in parts. Furthermore, the child must retain his responses at each step while performing the next step in the process and assemble them in correct sequence. Which procedures a child uses successfully varies from child to child, and may even vary from word to word with a given child. Yet if a word is in a child's understanding vocabulary and if he uses context clues, a near approximation should allow him to arrive at the correct pronunciation.

In addition to teaching the child to be versatile, phonic generalizations should be taught as involving probability. For instance, the grapheme *ow* represents the "long o" sound very slightly more often than it represents the vowel in *cow;* but, if by using his language skills as a monitor, the child determines that his initial response is incorrect, he should be taught to try the most likely alternative which in this example almost assuredly will be *ou* (cow).[10] Another example is the letters *ea* which are most likely to represent the "long e" sound (bean) or if not, then the "short e" sound (bread). Similarly, if the vowel in an open syllable (one that ends with a vowel) does not represent the "long" sound of that vowel, then the child should try other sounds for that vowel letter.

Two points should be considered in determining which phonic generalizations are worth teaching. First, with what frequency will the application of the generalization result in the correct response? If the percentage of utility is only slightly better than chance and there is no reliable alternative, there is little value in teaching the generalization.

---

[10] This does not mean that the child should be taught all, or even the most probable, phonemes that a grapheme may represent when the grapheme is first introduced.

Second, to how many words which the reader might encounter could the generalization be applied? A generalization might have very few exceptions, but there may be few words to which it can be applied and therefore little opportunity for use.

The following simplified generalizations are suggested as being the ones most worth teaching in the middle grades or sooner for those who can learn and make use of them:

Vowel Phonemes

1. When an accented syllable ends with a vowel letter, the vowel sound usually is long.
2. When an accented syllable ends with a consonant letter, a single vowel letter preceding it usually represents the short sound of that letter, unless the following consonant is an *r*.
3. When an unaccented syllable ends with a vowel letter, that vowel letter sometimes represents a long vowel sound which is reduced in duration.
4. The vowel sounds in many unaccented syllables are diminished to the point where they sound very much alike and can be represented by the schwa (ə).
5. When a vowel letter is followed by *r*, the sound it represents is somewhat changed.

Syllabication

1. Every syllable has one vowel sound.
2. Usually divide between two consonants that are not a digraph or blend.
3. Usually divide a word between the root word and affixes.
4. A single consonant between two vowels may go with either syllable.

Accenting

1. The first syllable of the majority of two-syllable words is usually accented.
2. When the second syllable of a two-syllable word contains a long vowel, that syllable is usually accented.
3. Affixes usually are not accented.

By the time children are introduced to syllabication they can usually recognize and pronounce many syllables at sight, due to their resemblance to known sight words. By this time, also, they have usually developed considerable speed in mentally sounding and blending a sequence of phonic units. As they go through a word from left to right, pronouncing it by syllables, the big uncertainties are where to place accent and whether vowels are long or short. Often the context provides enough of a lead so that configuration and sounding the first syllable or two are sufficient for correct recognition. If the first pronunciation tried does not provide a meaningful word that fits the context, a resourceful reader tries the accent in a different place and experiments with alternative vowel sounds. If the word is within his vocabulary, he should recognize it when he comes to the correct pronunciation.[11]

USING A DICTIONARY GUIDE TO PRONUNCIATION

In the middle and upper grades children frequently encounter words that, after being sounded by syllables in alternative ways, still do not evoke a word whose sound and meaning are familiar. When this happens, the child has three choices: (1) He can rely on the context for a general meaning, and remain unsure of the pronunciation. This is done frequently by superior readers, who may come across a particular word repeatedly and may become quite sure of its meaning without ever becoming sure enough of its pronunciation to use it in speech. (2) He can ask the teacher or another resource person. (3) He can look the word up in a dictionary. For true independence in word attack, skill in using the dictionary guide to pronunciation is essential.

Dictionary use may be started with simple picture dictionaries in the primary grades. These can give practice in alphabetical order and in the interpretation of very simple definitions and illustrations that supplement the pictures. Sample pages are shown in Figures 28 and 29. Good picture dictionaries, some of which are geared to particular basal reading programs, include:

[11] A brief presentation of some of the principles governing accent, as well as syllabication and vowel values, will be found in Appendix B.

FIGURE 28. Page from a first-grade picture dictionary. (From Clark, Mae Knight. *My Self-Help Dictionary.* Copyright © 1970 by The Macmillan Co., New York. Reduced in size. The original is in color. Reproduced by permission of the publishers.)

Courtis, Stuart, and Watters, Garnette. *Illustrated Golden Dictionary.* New York: Golden Press, 1961.

Clark, Mae Knight. *My Self-Help Dictionary.* Revised edition. New York: Macmillan, 1970.

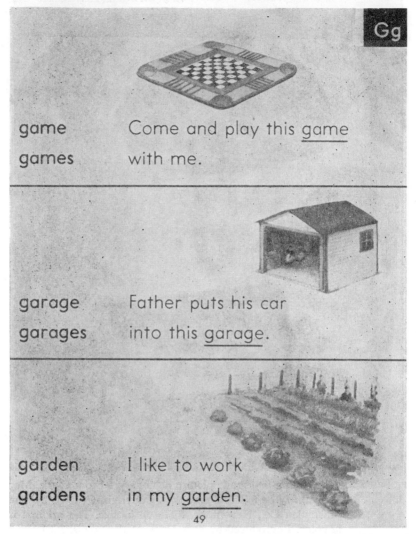

game Come and play this game
games with me.

garage Father puts his car
garages into this garage.

garden I like to work
gardens in my garden.

49

FIGURE 29. Page from a picture dictionary. (From O'Donnell and Townes, *Words I Like to Read and Write.* Copyright © 1963 by Harper & Row, Publishers, Inc., New York. Reduced in size. The original is in color. Reproduced by permission of the publishers.)

Clark, Mae Knight. *My Word Clue Dictionary*. Revised edition. New York: Macmillan, 1970.

Monroe, Marion, and Greet, W. Cabell. *My Little Pictionary*. Chicago: Scott, Foresman, 1962.

Monroe, Marion, and Greet, W. Cabell. *My Second Pictionary*. Chicago: Scott, Foresman, 1964.

O'Donnell, Mabel, and Townes, Willmina. *Words I Like to Read and Write*. Evanston, Ill.: Row Peterson, 1962.

O'Donnell, Mabel, and Townes, Willmina, *Words to Read, Write and Spell*. Evanston, Ill.: Harper & Row, 1966.

Wright, Wendell, and Laird, Helene. *The Rainbow Dictionary*, Revised edition. Cleveland: World, 1959.

At third-reader level and above, many basal readers have glossaries at the back, which are really brief dictionaries that can be used to initiate skills in locating words in alphabetical order, in using a pronunciation guide, and in interpreting definitions.

The major dictionary skills in locating and pronouncing words that can be made the objective of planned lessons in the middle grades or sooner (especially in light of the trend to have glossaries in the third readers of basal reading series) are as follows:

1. Location of words in alphabetical order
   a. Learning the sequence of the alphabet
   b. Practice in determining which letter comes before and which comes after a given letter
   c. Arranging a list of words alphabetically when they all start with different letters
   d. Arranging words that start with the same letter alphabetically according to second and third letters
   e. Learning to use the guide words at the top or bottom of a page
   f. Practice in opening the dictionary at a point near the word
2. Using the guide to pronunciation
   a. Recognizing division between syllables (entry words are not always syllabicated in the same way as their phonetic respellings)
   b. Learning to interpret primary and secondary accents marks
   c. Understanding the pronunciation key and diacritical marks
   d. Pronouncing the phonetic respellings of words

A teacher who is ready to start the use of dictionaries should study carefully the pronunciation guide of the particular dictionary to be used, since there are important differences among dictionaries in the phonetic symbols used. One dictionary uses eight different symbols for sounds of *a;* another gets along with four. Some dictionaries use the schwa (ə) for most unstressed short vowels, while others have a different symbol for each unstressed short vowel. *Furniture* is phonetically spelled in two dictionaries as follows: fėr′ nə chər; fûr′nĭ·tûr. The two phonetic spellings represent exactly the same pronunciation: a situation that may confuse children.

Teachers who are responsible for getting children started on the use of a dictionary can make good use of the *Beginning Dictionary, Webster's New World Dictionary, Elementary Edition,* or the *Harcourt Brace School Dictionary,* which contain a number of lessons on how to use the dictionary.[12]

Just as with other reading skills, children will display differences in their ability to learn and employ dictionary skills. Therefore because not all children will be working at the same level, dictionaries of varying degrees of difficulty should be available in the classroom. The teacher also may find it necessary to provide group and individual instruction and practice in various dictionary skills. Probably the most effective learning will take place when the application of these skills is of practical value to the child.

Morphemic Analysis

Morphemic analysis of words means analyzing them in terms of their morphemes (meaning units), in contrast to phonic analysis by which words are analyzed into syllables and/or into graphemes (printed symbols that represent sounds) and their corresponding phonemes (units of sound). Thus the word "international," when morphemically analyzed, consists of a prefix *inter,* a root word *nation,* and a suffix *al.* The word *nation* can, in turn, be divided into a root of

[12] E. L. Thorndike and Clarence R. Barnhart, *Beginning Dictionary,* 5th ed. (Chicago: Scott, Foresman, 1964).

David B. Guralnik (Editor in chief), *Webster's New World Dictionary, Elementary Edition* (New York: Macmillan, 1966).

Harrison G. Platt (Editor in chief), *The Harcourt Brace School Dictionary* (New York: Harcourt, Brace & World, 1968).

Latin origin and a suffix, but this degree of analysis is not usually expected or necessary at elementary-school level. In a word like *provision* the prefix, root, and suffix all consist of one syllable, so that the syllables are meaning units also. However, many prefixes (*inter, super*), root words, and suffixes (compar*ability,* tragic*ally*) consist of more than one syllable.

The importance of developing competence in morphemic analysis becomes clearly evident when one takes a look at the vocabulary that children meet in textbooks in the intermediate and upper grades. For example, 91 different polysyllabic words appeared on five pages in a particular sixth-grade social studies text. There were 32 words with inflectional endings, 59 words with suffixes, and 21 words with prefixes (some words had all three). These words contained 15 different prefixes and 19 different suffixes, of which nine occurred three or more times. Excluding proper names, only four polysyllabic words were not compounds or did not have a prefix, a suffix, or an inflectional ending.

When a word has been divided mentally into its meaningful parts, the reader can often recognize these at sight because they have become familiar in other words. Many children in the middle grades can see *sternness* as consisting of *stern* and *ness,* each of which they can recognize at sight. If this does not work, the word is then attacked by applying phonic principles.

In basal-reader systems the first step in morphemic analysis is learning to recognize the root words and inflectional endings in such words as *runs, fishes, liked, jumped, traded,* and *looking.* This is usually done in the first grade. Another technique that is usually started by the first-reader level is the division of compound words into the two words that each contains: *something, today, policeman, schoolroom, grandfather.* However, looking for little words inside longer words is not advised as a general technique because often a combination of letters that would be a word by itself is neither a syllable nor a meaning unit when these letters happen to occur in a long word. Finding *in* in *finery,* or finding *at* and *on* in the latter half of *combination,* is misleading.

Sometimes the root word is changed when certain suffixes are added. Among the more commonly taught generalizations in this area (most, if not all, of which are taught in spelling) are the following:

1. When words end with a final silent *e,* the *e* is usually dropped when adding suffixes or inflectional endings that begin with a vowel (e.g., *ed, ing, en, er, est*).

2. When a one syllable word ends with a single consonant (except for *x*), the final consonant is doubled when adding a suffix.

3. When the final *y* in a word is preceded by a consonant, the *y* is usually changed to *i* when adding a suffix (other than *ing*) that begins with a vowel.

During the second- and third-reader levels, but mainly in the third, words with prefixes and suffixes begin to appear with increasing frequency. At this level words are analyzed phonically and the meaning significance of the affixes is usually left for instruction in higher grades, although there is a recent trend to begin such instruction at the third-reader level.

Suffixes help to indicate both grammatical function and specifics of shades of meaning. When *act* changes to *actor* and *action,* the latter two words are both noun forms, one indicating performer and the other indicating function. Because morphemic analysis is not only helpful in recognizing words but, more importantly, can serve to clarify meaning, the study of prefixes, roots, and suffixes will be taken up in greater detail in the next chapter.

Materials for Developing Word Attack Skills

SUPPLEMENTARY PHONIC PROGRAMS

There are several sets of phonic materials that are designed for use parallel to a basal-reader system, or as a supplement to it. These can be used on a whole-class basis, with groups, or with individuals. A supplementary phonic program can be quite helpful in remedial and corrective work, and in teaching children who seem to need a more intensive phonic basis than the basal reader provides. Some teachers who use materials of this type count the time spent as part of the spelling program.

A supplementary or parallel phonic program should have the following characteristics: (1) There should be a good teacher's manual or set of directions. (2) There should be considerable attention to developing auditory discrimination. (3) Phonic units should be introduced at a reasonable rate, in a defensible sequence. (4) The system should avoid extreme reliance on practice with sounds in isolation. (5) There should be a substantial amount of practice in using phonics with sight recognition and context in meaningful reading.

There are many phonic programs available commercially, some of which have none of the features listed above as desirable. Those which are worthy of serious consideration include the following:

Building Reading Skills, 1965 edition, by Leila Armstrong and Rowena Hargrave. Wichita: McCormick-Mathers Publishing Co. Includes a *Teacher's Guidebook,* a series of six workbooks, and a box of large *Phonics Key Cards.* Each workbook is accompanied by a packet of skill builders (key cards and manipulative devices.)

Breaking the Sound Barrier, by Sister Mary Caroline, I.H.M. New York: Macmillan. A teacher's manual, phonic handbook for children, and two supplementary pamphlets. The method emphasizes: "Use the rule. Then use your head." The handbook illustrates and gives phonic rules and generalizations; the teacher has to provide supplementary practice material.

Eye and Ear Fun, by Clarence R. Stone. St. Louis: Webster Publishing Co. A series of four workbooks (1, 2, 3, 4) emphasizing applying phonics in meaningful context. Book 4 reviews primary grade phonics and develops elementary syllabication.

New Phonics Skilltext, 1964 edition, by Rachel G. Brake. Columbus Ohio: Charles E. Merrill Books. A series of four workbooks primarily for teaching readiness and word-analysis skills.

Phonics We Use, 1966 edition, by Mary Meighan, Marjorie Pratt, Lucille Ingalls and Mabel Halvorsen. Chicago: Lyons and Carnahan. Includes a manual for teachers and five workbooks (A,B,C,D,E), the first of which is for auditory discrimination. Exercises emphasize combining phonics and structural analysis with meaning and picture clues.

Phonovisual Method, by Lucile D. Schoolfield and Josephine B. Timberlake. Washington, D.C.: Phonovisual Products, Inc. Includes a

Method Book, large consonant and vowel wall charts, small individual consonant and vowel charts, two workbooks, "flipstrips," several phonic rummy games, a phonograph record, a book of games, and two books helpful in teaching auditory discrimination.

PHONIC ACCESSORIES

In addition to the relatively complete supplementary phonic programs that have been listed above, there are many homemade games and devices that teachers can construct or adapt, to lend variety and interest to the learning of word-attack skills. Many good ideas of this kind can be found in:

Herr, Selma E. *Learning Activities for Reading.* Dubuque, Iowa: Wm. C. Brown Co., 1961.
Kingsley, Bernard. *Reading Skills.* Palo Alto, Calif.: Fearon Press, 1958.
Russell, David H., and Karp, Etta. *Reading Aids through the Grades,* Revised Edition. New York: Bureau of Publications, Teachers College, Columbia University, 1951.
Wagner, Guy, and Hosier, Max. *Reading Games: Strengthening Reading Skills with Instructional Games.* Darien, Conn.: Teachers Publishing Corp., 1960.

There are many published materials that can be quite useful as supplementary aids in teaching phonics. In general, teachers should not expect these aids to teach phonic principles; although some of them can be used to develop phonic understandings and sharpen perception, this calls for well-planned direct instruction by the teacher. Games and practice devices are mainly helpful for reinforcing and reviewing in a way that children find interesting.

Commercial phonic materials include phonic charts, games, and mechanical devices like word wheels. A number of these are listed and described in Appendix B.

Summary

1. Developing independence in word recognition is one of the important goals of reading instruction.

a) Basal reader programs teach four interrelated sets of word-analysis skills: phonics, morphemic analysis, use of context, and use of the dictionary.

b) Most basal-reader programs agree on the following points:

　1) phonic principles should be developed inductively from sight words, with emphasis on hearing the phoneme within spoken words, seeing the grapheme in the words, and associating sight with sound;

　2) basic phonic principles are introduced gradually through the first two or three reader levels, consonants preceding vowels;

　3) Tentative phonic analysis must always be checked to see if the word makes sense in the particular context.

2. Auditory discrimination is an essential part of phonic instruction.

3. Children should be taught the sounds that letters represent as well as letter names.

4. It is recommended that there be a somewhat earlier introduction of phonics than is common in many basal-reader programs.

5. Phonic generalizations differ widely in their degree of utility. Generalizations with many exceptions are of doubtful value.

6. The purpose of teaching phonic generalizations is to assist the child in decoding words that are not recognized at sight.

7. The processes that children use in decoding printed symbols vary from child to child.

8. Children should be taught to check their decoding results by asking themselves two questions:

　a. Does it sound like a word I know?

　b. Does it make sense in this sentence?

9. Independence in decoding polysyllabic words requires skill in syllabication, in accenting (to a lesser extent), in using a dictionary pronunciation guide, and in morphemic analysis that also aids in deriving word meaning.

10. There are a number of supplementary phonic programs available that may be used with basal-reader programs.

Recommended Reading

BOND, GUY L., and WAGNER, EVA BOND. *Teaching the Child to Read*, 4th ed. New York: Macmillan, 1966. Ch. 8.

DE BOER, JOHN J., and DALLMANN, MARTHA. *The Teaching of Reading*, 3rd ed. New York: Holt, Rinehart and Winston Inc., 1970. Ch. 5A, 5B.

DOLCH, EDWARD W. *Teaching Primary Reading*, 3rd ed. Champaign, Ill.: Garrard Press, 1960. Ch. 12.

HARRIS, ALBERT J. *How to Increase Reading Ability*, 5th ed. New York: McKay, 1970. Chs. 13, 14.

HARRIS, ALBERT J., ED. *Readings on Reading Instruction*. New York: McKay, 1963. Ch. 8.

HEILMAN, ARTHUR W. *Phonics in Proper Perspective*. Columbus: Charles E. Merrill, 1964.

HILDRETH, GERTRUDE. *Teaching Reading*. New York: H. Holt, 1958. Chs. 6, 7.

SMITH, NILA B. *Reading Instruction for Today's Children*. Englewood Cliffs, N.J.: Prentice-Hall, 1963. Ch. 8.

STAUFFER, RUSSELL G. *Directing Reading Maturity as a Cognitive Process*. New York: Harper & Row, 1969. Ch. 6.

C H A P T E R

10

Fostering Vocabulary Development

When most children enter school, they use many different words in speaking and understand thousands of other words. Few of these children, however, can recognize any of the printed symbols that represent them.[1] During the primary grades, therefore (as indicated in the preceding two chapters), major attention is given to developing a sight vocabulary and the word-analysis skills that promote independence in reading. The third-reader level generally serves as a transition period in which the teacher's concern switches gradually from an emphasis on decoding "new" words to a greater concern about developing the meanings of words. From then on, one of the major objectives of reading instruction is helping children to build reading vocabularies that are wide ranging, rich, and accurate.

Although in beginning reading materials, efforts are made to employ words that will be familiar to most children, the meanings of even some words found in first-grade materials may not be clearly understood. Careful teachers check to see if supposedly familiar words are really understood.

---

[1] Durkin found that approximately 1 percent of the children she studied could recognize a limited number of words before they entered school. Dolores Durkin, *Children Who Read Early* (New York: Teachers College Press, Columbia University, 1966).

How Concepts and Word Meanings Develop

GETTING A VOCABULARY STARTED

In the latter part of a baby's first year he begins to notice that certain sounds made by his mother or other adults accompany certain experiences. When mother presents the bottle, she may say, "Baby, have some *milk*." With repetition, the baby develops a learned association between the sound of the word and the total experience in which the sound is heard; thereafter, upon hearing the word, he shows an attitude of expecting to be given milk, and this is reinforced every time milk is given. If he mistakes some other sound for milk, no milk follows; through reinforcement and nonreinforcement he learns to distinguish *milk* from other words.

When he experiments with making sounds, he may notice a similarity between a sound he produces and a sound he has learned to respond to, and may attempt to repeat the sound. If mother recognizes a sufficient similarity, she will both offer milk and show delight at the baby's achievement, doubly reinforcing his verbal effort.

Gradually, over a period of many months, baby expands both his hearing vocabulary and his speaking vocabulary. At first he is likely to make one word do the work of a sentence. "Milk!" probably means, "I want some milk." Gradually, baby begins to fit words together. From "Car" to "Daddy car" to "Bye-bye Daddy car" to "Davey bye-bye Daddy car," he becomes increasingly able to express his wishes and ideas. By the time he is two years old he is usually expanding both his hearing and speaking vocabularies at a rapid rate, understands much of what he hears, and employs short sentences that are usually grammatically incomplete.

REFINEMENT AND EXTENSION OF MEANINGS

The concept represented by a word is the generalized meaning that the word comes to have. The concept is refined through many experiences in which correct interpretation is reinforced and incorrect use or interpretation is not reinforced. Thus, any four-footed animal may at first be called *doggie*. Gradually baby learns that doggies can be large or small, with long fur or very short fur, but that cats are not dogs. He cannot verbalize the difference, but he can recognize it. Later he can understand simple explanations, such as, "Dogs bark, but cats meow." However, one look at an elephant is worth more than paragraphs of description. Direct experience is the primary basis for concepts and ideas. Verbal explanation is secondary: it helps to clarify experience but cannot completely replace it.

The concept *dog* is the generalized meaning that develops out of many specific experiences. It has emotional as well as intellectual content. To one young child, dogs make fearsome noises and bite; to another, they lick your face and play with you. The word *dog* (as heard and spoken) becomes firmly associated with this accumulating complex of meaning; it becomes the symbol that represents the concept. Despite the fact that no two children have had identical experiences with dogs and therefore have somewhat different concepts, there are enough basic similarities for the word *dog* to be useful in communication.

If a preschool child sees a pond for the first time and calls it a big puddle, someone is likely to tell him, "This is a pond; it is too big to be a puddle." In this way his concept of *puddle* is refined and his concept of *pond* is started. Generalizations that are too broad become trimmed to correct size through the process of differentiation.

Concepts also grow from specific to general and abstract through the accumulation of experience. To an eight-year-old, *dishonesty* may mean only taking another child's pencil or "swiping" a banana from a fruit stand. Gradually the meaning broadens to include some specific acts and exclude others, until by adolescence dishonesty comes to mean any form of intentional deception or illegal acquisition of property. Even when agreement on a generalized meaning has been reached, problems arise in specific application. In a large city, a front-page article told of the mayor's demanding the dismissal of school building inspectors because they had accepted presents from contractors; the school superintendent, however, demurred because he thought that small Christmas presents should not be considered bribes. The more abstract and general a concept, the more difficulty there is likely to be in getting agreement about its applications.

ESTABLISHMENT OF CATEGORIES

A kindergarten child usually knows what *red* and *blue* mean; he has learned this through many experiences with red balls and blue balls, red books and blue books, etc. He has been able to abstract the color as a quality that can occur in many objects. Redness and blueness are first-level abstractions because they can be abstracted directly from perceptual experience.

The concept of *color* is gained when a child realizes that red, orange, yellow, etc., are all members of a family and are all colors. Color is, then, an abstraction from abstractions, and therefore is a second-level abstraction. If we ask in what way color and other second-level generalizations from perception (like loudness, brightness) are alike, there is no one English word that represents the concept of a third-level abstraction that includes all attributes of perceptual experience. There is little use for such a concept, so a word to represent it has not been devised.

Children tend to learn easily concepts that represent immediate experience and concepts that are first-level abstractions. However, concepts that are abstractions from abstractions are relatively hard to grasp. In trying to teach their meanings, one has to try to create links that connect them to the child's own experience.

When children are asked what words mean, several levels of conceptual development can be distinguished. The most primitive concepts are those which are expressed only in terms of action or function: milk is to drink, a ball is to throw. A step toward maturity is evident when the child combines some description with a statement of function: a ball is a thing you play with. A further step is taken when the child states a category that the concept belongs to and also a distinguishing characteristic: a ball is a round toy. An adult-type definition states the category and one or more truly distinguishing characteristics: a round or roundish body, of different materials and sizes, hollow or solid, for use in various games. Another mature way to define is to give a synonym (honesty means integrity), but then the synonym may need to be defined.

The intelligent, educated adult has many of his concepts organized into categories, and these may be arrayed in a hierarchy of increasing abstraction or generalization. A child is likely to think of a cat as an animal that drinks milk, purrs and meows, and catches mice. A zoologist knows these characteristics; he also knows that the cat is a small domesticated feline, which is a carnivorous, mammalian, vertebrate animal. At each level of generalization he knows both the basic common characteristic of the category and the contrasting characteristics which distinguish one category from another (vertebrate from invertebrate). His knowledge is rooted in experience, but it has been refined, organized, and fitted into a framework of ideas.[2]

VERBALISM

An unfortunately large share of school learning in the past has been the memorization of verbal statements that are misunderstood or only partially understood because they have no real connection with the child's experience. The term *verbalism* has come to mean vagueness, emptiness, or faultiness of understanding concealed by the use of appropriate words. Teachers often can recount humorous experiences occasioned by faulty or incomplete understanding on the part of children.[3] Many of the important concepts of science and the social studies are difficult for children to understand because they are highly abstract and have been learned with insufficient reference to experience.

Voting certainly represents a concept that citizens in a democracy should understand. If a child learns that "voting means casting one's ballot," that may not help much. But if the teacher reminds them about how they have chosen class officers; inquires about their expe-

---

[2] For further information on cognitive development, refer to: Jerome Bruner, *et al., Studies in Cognitive Growth* (New York: Wiley, 1966).

[3] Dr. Coleman Morrison tells the story of the young child who knew that "frugal" had something to do with "saving"; but who, when asked to use "frugal" in a sentence, said, "When I thought I was drowning, I yelled to the lifeguard, 'Frugal me, frugal me!' "

riences in going with parents on election day; explains "casting one's ballot" by telling how the Greeks used to express their choices by dropping a black or a white ball (ballot) into a box, hence the term "blackballed"; and builds from there, a reasonably accurate concept can be developed.

Explaining an isthmus as a narrow strip of land connecting two larger bodies of land may result in some queer conceptions, particularly among children who equate land with dirt and bodies with people. A teacher is well advised to turn to a map of the Western Hemisphere, inquire what the land bridge between North and South America should be called, and then can introduce a verbal definition of an isthmus; after this the children can inspect the map of the world for other examples.

The ability to grasp ideas quickly, to detect the underlying common characteristic that an abstract term represents, and to apply this concept correctly in new situations is very closely related to general intelligence. A teacher has to expect large differences among children in ease of concept formation and in the learning of the meanings of words that represent concepts. In general, bright children do not need as many examples and illustrations as do other children. But all children need an experiential foundation for clear, accurate concepts; without this, one gets verbalism.

SEMANTIC PROBLEMS

Semantics is the scientific study of meanings, and particularly of the relations between words and the concepts they represent. Students of semantics are concerned with the confusions and errors in reasoning that can develop because of ambiguous relationships between words and concepts.

Much of the trouble arises from failure to take adequate account of the fact that the same word can be used in two quite different senses by different people. International discussions often founder because representatives of different countries use fundamental terms, like democracy and liberty, with quite different conceptions of what they mean.

Although unabridged dictionaries list more than a half-million English words, most of the work is done by a relatively small number. A carefully selected list of 850 words, known as Basic English, can express practically any idea that does not call for highly technical terminology.[4] The Dolch list of 220 Basic Sight Words makes up more than 50 percent of the running words in practically any reading material.[5]

The word *run,* for example, is listed in one college dictionary as having 104 separate meanings: 35 meanings as an intransitive verb, 28 as a transitive verb, 41 as a noun, and 2 as an adjective. Even the *Beginning Dictionary* lists 36 regular and 10 special meanings for this word. The child who understands *run* as meaning to move quickly by moving the legs becomes acquainted with running for election, a home run, a run in a stocking, a running brook, and a variety of other meanings. Children should learn how to select the particular meaning of a word that fits the context.

The problem of alternative meanings is complicated by many *homographs,* words that are spelled alike but have different meanings and perhaps different pronunciations. A child who knows *hail* as small pieces of ice may be puzzled by, "He hailed a taxi." Or he may be even more confused by, "An officer can *lead* his troops into a *hail* of *lead."* To further complicate matters there are homonyms, words with the same pronunciation but with different meanings and usually spellings. For example, "He became a *bore* when he began talking again about killing the *boar."*

Errors in reasoning may occur when a speaker or writer starts using a word with one meaning and then shifts to another meaning without noticing that he has switched concepts. Errors in interpreting occur when a reader or listener interprets a word as representing a different concept from the one intended by the writer or speaker.

Good readers know that many words represent a variety of mean-

[4] The list, originated by C. K. Ogden, may be found in I. A. Richards, *Design for Escape: World Education Through Modern Media* (New York: Harvest Books-Harcourt, Brace & World, 1968), pp. 70–71.
[5] Edward W. Dolch, *Teaching Primary Reading,* 3rd ed. (Champaign, Ill.: Garrard Press, 1960), p. 390.

ings, and rely on the context to indicate which concept the word stands for in the particular setting. They may become so expert at doing this that they are not aware of any problem. Special exercises can be constructed for children to help them to compare several meanings of a word and choose the one that fits each of several sentences.

TYPES OF VOCABULARY

As we have seen, babies develop a speaking vocabulary a little more slowly than a hearing vocabulary, and throughout childhood and maturity the latter tends to remain larger. When children begin to read, a major goal is to be able to recognize the printed words that stand for words already in the child's hearing and speaking vocabularies. Writing vocabulary starts to develop a little later than reading vocabulary and usually tends to increase at a slower rate.

As children move up the grades they more frequently meet words in reading that are outside their hearing and speaking vocabularies, and as they develop concepts for these words their total vocabulary grows. Therefore, poor reading ability can hinder the growth of concepts and a child's overall vocabulary. Generally to the end of fourth grade, children's hearing vocabularies are larger than their reading vocabularies. Speaking vocabularies (realizing, of course, that there are differences in formal and informal speech and that children may not have occasion to use all the words they know in speaking) tend to remain somewhat smaller than the two aforementioned types; with writing vocabularies remaining substantially the smallest.[6]

SIZE OF VOCABULARY

The information available at present about the size of children's vocabularies is not very clear. The best available evidence on vocabulary development was summarized by Dale who wrote, "If we

[6] Miles M. Tinker and Constance M. McCullough, *Teaching Elementary Reading*, 3rd ed. (New York: Appleton-Century-Crofts, 1968), p. 132.

assume that children finish the first grade with an average vocabulary of 3,000 words, it is likely that they will add about 1,000 a year from then on. The average high school senior will know about 14,000 to 15,000 words, the college senior 18,000 to 20,000."[7] Of course there will be wide differences among individuals, but using Dale's figures it appears that the average third-grade child will know the meanings of approximately 5,000 words and the average sixth grader approximately 8,000 words.

It is very difficult to obtain accurate data as to the number of "words" a child "knows." In most vocabulary studies a word is considered to be known if the child can select the correct response from a number of possible choices. However, this does not necessarily mean that a child will understand a word if it is used with a different syntactical function, with an inflectional ending, or with an alternative meaning. In American English there are very many words with more than one meaning. Does being able to select a synonym in a multiple-choice question constitute "knowing the meaning" of the word?

The effects of television on the vocabulary growth of children have not yet been adequately measured. It seems evident that young children develop many concepts and learn many words while watching T.V. programs. Some of these concepts and words (derived from animated cartoons and Westerns) may not have much educational value. However, the total effect of T.V. on children's concepts and language development appears to be beneficial.

At every age, differences in size of vocabulary are enormous. Children with a foreign-language background may have meager English vocabularies of just a few hundred words. Educationally disadvantaged children may have a very limited vocabulary of standard English. Bright children who read widely sometimes develop vocabularies comparable to those of their teachers by the time they are in the middle grades, and in special areas of science or hobbies may be far ahead of their teachers. Vocabulary development is influenced by general cultural background, by travel, by reading, by motivation, and

[7] Edgar Dale, "Vocabulary Measurement: Techniques and Major Findings," *Elementary English,* 42 (December, 1965), 895–901, 948.

by direct instruction. Among children with reasonably similar linguistic, cultural, and educational opportunities, vocabulary development is very closely related to general intellectual development.

Helping Children to Improve Their Vocabularies

THE PROBLEM OF VOCABULARY CONTROL

Although the vocabularies of basal readers are carefully graded, especially in the primary grades, the total reading diet of elementary school children includes large numbers of words that are met very infrequently. It has been estimated that books recommended for elementary school children contain a total of about 60,000 different words, of which roughly half occur only about once in three million running words, or about once in 50 children's books.[8] There are about 2,500 words that occur frequently; beyond this, the words a child will meet depend on the subjects about which he reads and on the literary style of the authors.

Adults can often gain meaning from reading material even if 25 percent of the words are missing. It —— probable that children ————— learn words more —————— if writers ————— make better provisions —— help them —— do so. Did that make sense? You probably got the general idea, even if some of the words you filled in were not the original words. Nouns and verbs are most essential for meaning; adjectives, adverbs, prepositions, and conjunctions can often be supplied by the reader. Children also can get ideas from material in which they find some words of unknown meaning. The occasional rare word is usually not a very great hindrance to comprehension.

Learning the meanings of these unknown words, however, does not automatically come when the general gist of the passage has been grasped. If unknown words make up a substantial percentage of the reading material one may be able to attain some meaning, but one is

[8] E. L. Thorndike, "The Vocabulary of Books for Children in Grades 3 to 8," *Teachers College Record*, 38 (1936–37), I, 196–205; II, 316–323; III, 416–429.

unlikely to be able to learn the meanings of the unknown words. If children are to learn the new words they meet, the new words should be less than 5 percent of the total running words; in other words, not more than one new word in twenty, on the average.

DERIVING MEANINGS FROM CONTEXT

If teachers had to teach all the words that children learn, the time required would be exorbitant. Out of the many new words to which children are exposed, teachers have to select the most essential for direct teaching and leave the rest for children to acquire as they read.

Children who read widely learn a great many words by inferring from the context. Coming to an unfamiliar word, the child applies his word-analysis skills to get a tentative pronunciation. If this does not resemble any word in his hearing vocabulary that fits, he infers its meaning as well as he can and usually goes on reading. If the word is one that he will meet again and again, the approximate meaning will be revised and refined to fit the new contexts. If he is dissatisfied with the meaning or the pronunciation that he has worked out, he may use a dictionary.

Authors of books for children can help children to learn meanings from context. They can make the new word conspicuous by using italics or bold type. They can explain or define the term in a sentence, give a synonym or equivalent phrase, show the meaning in an illustration, or write the sentence in such a way that there is only one meaning the word could possibly have. In selecting texts for the content subjects, teachers should consider the care given to making new terms understandable to be one of the main factors affecting ease of comprehension.

Regardless of how well texts are written, most children need systematic instruction in using context clues, other than simply being told to read the whole sentence and to attempt to "guess" the meaning of the unknown word. Context strongly influences word meaning, but it does not necessarily reveal word meaning. In the sentence, "He looked at the bow," neither the pronunciation nor the meaning of the word *bow* is obvious. It is not until one considers the context in which this *sentence* is found that the pronunciation and meaning become clear.

Illustrating, discussing, and providing practice in the following types of context clues should help children to identify and understand unfamiliar words:

1. *Definition.* The unknown word is defined in the descriptive context. For example: A house on a boat is called a *houseboat.*
2. *Synonym.* This type of contextual clue consists of a known synonym for the unfamiliar word. For example: Mother was angry and father was *irate* too.
3. *Familiar expression.* This type of clue requires a background and knowledge of common expressions and acquaintance with familiar language patterns. For example: She was as proud as a *peacock.*
4. *Experience.* Children and adults may depend upon their experience and mental content to supply the meaning of the new word. For example: The color of grass is *green.*
5. *Comparison or contrast.* The unknown word may be compared or contrasted with something known. For example: John is extravagant, but his brother isn't. John's brother is so miserly he could almost be called *penurious.*
6. *Summary.* The new or unknown word may summarize the ideas that precede it. For example: Down the street they came. First there were the girls twirling batons, then the marching band, and then the men in uniform. It was a *parade.*
7. *Reflection of situation or mood.* The general tone of the sentence or paragraph provides a clue to the new or unknown word. For example: The clouds were black and ominous. Occasionally streaks of lightning slashed the sky while low rumblings of thunder could be heard in the distance. Silhouetted against this threatening background was the dark and foreboding house where I hoped to secure refuge against the storm. Without warning, a strong feeling of *apprehension* gripped me.[9]

The ability to use context clues is dependent upon factors other than the direct teaching of these skills. A child with an inadequate sight vocabulary or who is weak in word-analysis skills will find it

[9] Homer L. J. Carter and Dorothy J. McGinnis, *Teaching Individuals to Read* (Lexington, Mass.: D. C. Heath, 1962), pp. 84–85. Used by permission of the publisher.

difficult to use context clues because too many words will be unknown. If a child does not recognize or know the meaning of supposedly familiar synonyms, he cannot gain the meaning of unfamiliar words. Past experiences and the concepts derived from them also influence the ability to use certain types of context clues (e.g., types 3 and 4 above), just as does the ability to understand relationships (e.g., types 5 and 6 above).

PROVIDING EXPERIENTIAL BACKGROUND

Vivid personal experience is the best basis for the development of concepts. A visit to a zoo provides a conceptual basis for reading about wild animals; traveling by car provides a personal basis for understanding geographical concepts. Well-planned excursions and field trips are excellent ways to build conceptual background, provided they are relevant to the subject matter in which the concepts are needed. In providing first-hand experiences, it should be remembered that sensory contact alone is not sufficient to develop concepts. The teacher must know which concept(s) he wants the children to acquire and whether they are ready to acquire such concepts. Then he must guide the children's attention so that the concept and the verbal label for the concept are clearly understood and reinforced.

When first-hand experience is not available, audio-visual materials dealing with the topic can be very useful: movies, flimstrips, slides, pictures, charts, maps, and recordings. A preparatory filmstrip can make the reading level of a booklet seem a grade or more easier.

Teachers can also provide a background by giving a short talk or lecture, by reading to children, and by telling stories. Here the problems are those of verbal explanation in general, as discussed below under Explanation and Discussion.

SELECTING WORDS THAT ARE WORTH TEACHING

In choosing words for direct teaching, two considerations need to be kept in mind. The first is the question of immediate necessity: is this a key word, without which the passage or topic cannot be correctly understood? The second is the question of general utility: is the word common enough so that it is likely to occur many times in future reading matter? Usually a word is worth teaching if it ranks high on either of these criteria.

Because the reading done by children in a particular grade is so varied, it has not been possible to establish a grade-by-grade list of words which should be definitely taught. There are, however, word lists based on laborious counts of millions of running words. These lists are most useful to authors and editors; they are also usable by teachers who want to check particular words.

Although the last three are somewhat outdated, the following vocabulary lists are among the most useful:

Harris, Albert J., and Jacobson, Milton D. *Word List for the 1970's.* New York: Macmillan, *in press.* A graded list based on widely used basal readers, with supplementary lists of technical terms in elementary school English, Social Studies, Mathematics, and Science.

Taylor, Stanford E., Frackenpohl, Helen, and White, Catherine E. *A Revised Core Vocabulary:* A Basic Vocabulary for Grades 1–8; An Advanced Vocabulary for Grades 9–13. Research and Information Bulletin No. 5 (Revised). Huntington, N.Y.: Educational Developmental Laboratories, 1969.

Dale, Edgar. *The Dale List of 3,000 Words.* A list of words known by at least 80 percent of the fourth graders sampled. May be found in Dale, Edgar, and Chall, Jeanne S. "A Formula for Predicting Readability." *Educational Research Bulletin,* Ohio State University, 27 (January 21, 1948, and February 18, 1948), 11–20, 28, and 37–54; and in Hunnicutt, C. W., and Iverson, William J. *Research in the Three R's.* New York: Harper & Row, 1958. Pp. 205–213.

Dale, Edgar, and Eichholz, Gerhard. *Children's Knowledge of Words: an Interim Report.* Columbus: Bureau of Educational Research and Service, Ohio State University, 1960. Lists words, by percentages, known by at least 50 percent of the pupils sampled in grades four, six, eight, ten, and twelve. *Dale List of 3,000 Words* is not included.

Buckingham, B. R., and Dolch, E. W. *A Combined Word List.* Boston: Ginn and Co., 1936. An alphabetical list of over 19,000 words, giving a grade placement for each word as determined by the authors, and also the Thorndike rating and grade placements as indicated by eight other word lists.

Cole, Luella. *Handbook of Technical Vocabulary.* Bloomington, Ill.:

Public School Publishing Co., 1940 (out of print). Includes subject-matter vocabularies for arithmetic, secondary school mathematics, history, geography, English, and general science, based on careful analysis of representative textbooks.

Thorndike, Edward L., and Lorge, Irving. *The Teachers Word Book of 30,000 Words.* New York: Bureau of Publications, Teachers College, Columbia University, 1944. This is an expansion of the Thorndike list, previously issued with the 20,000 most common words. Based on a count of 10,000,000 words, partly from adult material and partly from children's books.

The primary grade lists described on page 222 are also very useful. Words in the primary grade lists are common in harder materials also, and should be understood as well as recognized by children in the middle and upper grades.

There is a common core of words that make up the bulk of any reading that children are likely to do. The various lists agree fairly closely on the words that belong in the most frequent 1,500 words. The first 2,500 of the Thorndike list probably account for more than 90 percent of the running words that elementary school children are likely to meet. The Cole lists are very useful listings of the important technical terms in many major subject-matter fields.

Of course, new words are coming into use, and into the vocabularies of children, all the time. Most primary children today are familiar with such words as *television, astronaut,* and *radar,* all of which have come into use since most of the published word lists were compiled. Important new words should not be neglected just because the word lists have not been revised recently.

WAYS OF TEACHING NEW WORDS

Three of the procedures generally used in helping children to build vocabularies have already been discussed: encouraging use of the context, relating to former experience, and use of audio-visual aids. Among the many other approaches in use, the following are most important: explanation and discussion, individualized word study, using the dictionary, studying prefixes, roots, and suffixes, word origins, figures of speech, and verbal relationships. At present, research findings regarding the effectiveness of different methods of teaching vocabulary are inconclusive.[10] Each teacher will have to determine which procedures are most effective for the individuals in his class.

Explanation and Discussion. Prior to the reading of the material by the children, the teacher selects the words that probably need explanation. These words usually are put on the chalkboard in phrases or sentences (to make use of context clues), and pronounced by the children. Then the teacher explains or checks the children's knowledge of the meaning of each word, shows illustrative material if available, and gives one or two more examples of their use. Finally in order to check their understandings, the children usually are asked to suggest additional sentences in which the words can be used. This is a useful and widely employed procedure.

There are, however, several dangers to be avoided. Verbalism is likely to result if words are explained briefly in terms of other words, with no tie to experience. If the word has other meanings besides the one being taught, this should be pointed out. The number of words introduced at one time should not exceed the absorptive capacity of the children. If the number of words that must be explained seems excessive, the reading material being used is probably too difficult for instructional purposes. Teachers who are aware of these problems are likely to use explanation and discussion wisely.

It is sometimes suggested that teachers wait until after the selection has been read and then ask which words gave the children difficulty. The rationale for such a procedure is: (1) the children probably will ask about fewer words than the teacher would have selected, thus saving time; and (2) the children are more likely to be motivated because learning arises from a felt need. Although this procedure may work well with good readers, poor readers may not be aware of their needs or may be reluctant to admit they do not know.

---

[10] Walter Petty, Curtis P. Herold, and Earline Stoll, *The State of Knowledge about the Teaching of Vocabulary,* Cooperative Research Project No. 3128 (Champaign, Ill.: National Council of Teachers of English, 1968).

Individualized Word Study. Children can be encouraged to be curious about new words, to write them down, look them up, and learn their meanings. The more children engage in independent reading, the more important it is for them to learn the meanings of the words they meet. Some teachers like children to have notebooks, with a page for each letter of the alphabet. Other teachers prefer index cards, a separate card for each word. With cards, each child can have an inexpensive filing box and a set of alphabet guide cards, giving useful practice in alphabetizing. A new word is written on one side of the page or card, and the pronunciation (if needed), definition, and one or two illustrative sentences can be written on the back. Of course, this presupposes that dictionary skills have been learned.

Resourceful teachers can find many ways of motivating individual word study. Children can be "word detectives" on the lookout for strange words. They can keep individual progress charts of the number of new words learned. Discussion periods can be held in which children can report on interesting new words they have found. Sometimes a team competition can be used to revive a lagging interest.

Using the Dictionary. Problems of locating words in the dictionary and using the guide to pronunciation were discussed in Chapter 9 (see page 254). Here we are concerned with the following skills that are needed to gain word meanings:

1. Interpreting typical dictionary definitions
2. Selecting from several listed meanings the one that fits the context
3. When an unfamiliar synonym is given, looking up that word also
4. Relating derived forms to the basic word
5. Distinguishing good current usage from obsolete, archaic, slang, dialect, or colloquial usage
6. Interpreting information about word origins.

A good definition usually has two elements: it states a class or category to which the concept belongs, and it gives one or more descriptive characteristics that distinguish this concept from other members of the category. A dictionary definition of a *fanatic* says: "a person with an extreme and unreasoning enthusiasm or zeal, especially in religious matters." The category is "person"; the rest tells how fanatics differ from other persons. Children can be helped to analyze definitions, to construct their own definitions for familiar words, and to compare theirs with the definitions in the dictionary.

Synonyms are often given as definitions. This is fine when the synonym is already understood or when the synonym is clearly and understandably defined. Learning synonyms is one good way of enlarging one's vocabulary, especially when the dictionary explains fine distinctions, as among *ancient, antique, antiquated,* and *old-fashioned.* Fortunately, circular definitions (fantasy—hallucination; hallucination—a form of fantasy) are very rare in today's dictionaries.

Practice exercises in the use of the dictionary can be found in a number of reading workbooks for the middle and upper grades (see Figure 30), and the *Beginning Dictionary* contains many good pages of teaching material on understanding definitions. Good dictionaries for elementary school use are published by: G. and C. Merriam Co.; Funk and Wagnalls; Scott, Foresman and Co.; Holt, Rinehart and Winston; The Macmillan Co.; and Harcourt Brace Jovanovitch, Inc. From time to time they issue free pamphlets about dictionaries that contain many suggestions helpful to teachers.

LEARNING PREFIXES, ROOTS AND SUFFIXES

Research suggests that vocabulary building by means of studying prefixes, suffixes, and roots is somewhat more beneficial to bright students than to others. It takes some intelligence to see why submission (under-send-act of) should come to mean "surrender of person or power to the control of another." The major part of study of this kind should come after the fourth grade, and much of it belongs in the upper grades and secondary school.

About one quarter of the commonest English words, and a higher proportion of less common words, begin with prefixes that have relatively constant meanings. Some words, like *over*come and *under*stand, are really compounds in which a preposition is used like a prefix. Most of the common prefixes are derived from Latin. A relatively small number of prefixes account for most of the common words con-

▪ CHOOSING THE RIGHT DEFINITION ▪

When you look up a word in the dictionary, you often find that the word has several definitions. You need to read all of these definitions. Then pick out the one that best fits into the sentence you are reading to give it the right meaning.

In each part of the page below, you will find several meanings of a word. Each meaning is numbered. You will also find some sentences. Each contains an italicized word like this: *cane*. Find the right meaning for the italicized word in each sentence. Write the number of this meaning on the line at the end of the sentence. The first one has been done for you.

cane, 1. Any hollow or pithy jointed stem. **2.** A walking stick. **3.** Split rattan used for the seats of chairs.

a. Mr. Steele was lame. He had to use a *cane*. _2_

b. Mrs. Howe took her chairs to a shop to be mended. The *cane* seats had worn out. _3_

c. Most sugar comes from sugar *cane*. _1_

bank, 1. Rising ground bordering a river, lake, or sea. **2.** To cover with fresh fuel to hold the live coals. **3.** A business place where money is held, exchanged, or loaned.

a. Miss Miller put her money in the *bank* for safekeeping. ___

b. Ann enjoyed sitting on the *bank* of the river and watching the ships go by. ___

c. Mr. Stone *banked* his furnace at night so the fire would hold till morning. ___

crop, 1. A pouch in the neck of some birds where food is first digested. **2.** Any farm product grown in the soil, as cotton, corn, fruit, etc. **3.** Hair which has been cut very short.

a. Mr. Robinson, a farmer, had a fine *crop* of wheat this year. ___

b. Usually insects and worms may be found in the *crop* of a robin. ___

c. Soldiers usually have *cropped* hair. ___

mine, 1. A pit from which precious stones, coal, and other minerals are taken by digging. **2.** A rich supply or store of something. **3.** A bomb placed in the water in time of war to destroy ships.

a. Mr. Putnam had a *mine* of rare, old paintings. ___

b. Our battleships watched closely for *mines* during World War II. ___

c. Three men were shut in a coal *mine* without food for several days. ___

plain, 1. A broad stretch of level land. **2.** Without beauty; homely. **3.** Open to the mind; clear.

a. Mrs. Morse was a very *plain* woman. ___

b. The teacher explained the problem until it was quite *plain* to the class. ___

c. Corn grows well in the fertile soil of our great midwestern *plain*. ___

yard, 1. A measure of length. **2.** A small space in front or back of a house or barn. **3.** An enclosed place where work or business is carried on.

a. Judy planted some roses in the *yard* of her home. ___

b. Mr. Sampson works in a railroad *yard*. ___

c. It took five *yards* of cloth to make Rosemary's new dress. ___

FIGURE 30. An exercise to develop the ability to select the correct dictionary definition. (From Smith, Nila B., *Be A Better Reader*, Foundations B., p. 142. Englewood Cliffs, N.J.: Prentice-Hall, Inc., 1968.) Reprinted by permission of the publisher. Reduced in size.

283

taining prefixes and can easily be taught during the middle grades. A recommended list is as follows: [11]

ab (from)	abnormal, abuse
ad, ap, at (to)	admit, appear, attract
be (by)	beside, behind
con, com, col (with)	conductor, commercial, collection
de (from)	deduct, defense
dis (apart, not)	disappear, disarm, disrupt
en, em (in)	engage, enjoy, embrace
ex (out)	exit, export
in, im (in, into)	income, impose
in, im (not)	incorrect, impure
ob, of, op (against, away, from)	obstruct, offend, oppose
pre, pro (before, in front of)	prepare, predict, projectile, promote
re (back)	refer, remodel
post (behind)	postpone
super (over, above)	superior, supervisor
trans (across)	transportation
sub (under)	submarine, subject
un (not)	unarmed, unbroken

Root Words. According to one study, there are 82 Latin roots and 6 Greek roots that occur 10 or more times each in children's vocabulary. The most common Latin roots are the following: [12]

fac, fact, fic (to make or do)	factory, fact, fiction
sta, stat (to stand)	static, station
pos, pon (to place, put)	post, opponent, position
fer (to bear, carry)	transfer, ferry, infer
mis, mit (to send)	submit, admission
tend, tens (to stretch)	tendon, tension, extend
vid, vis (to see)	vision, provide

[11] Russell G. Stauffer, "A Study of Prefixes in the Thorndike List to establish a List of Prefixes That Should Be Taught in the Elementary School," *Journal of Educational Research*, 35 (1942), 453–458.

[12] L. C. Breen, "Vocabulary Development by Teaching Prefixes, Suffixes, and Root Derivations," *The Reading Teacher*, 14 (November, 1960), 93–97.

For a relatively complete list of prefixes, roots, and suffixes, see: Henry A. Bamman, Ursula Hogan, and Charles E., Greene, *Reading Instruction in the Secondary School* (New York: McKay, 1961), pp. 250–257.

mov, mot (to move)	move, motion
spect, spic (to look, see)	inspection, conspicuous
ven, vent (to come)	convention, event
par (to get ready)	prepare, repair
port (to carry)	export, transport

Suffixes. There are many suffixes in English, and the majority of them have more than one meaning, so that teaching only the most common meaning may create some confusion. Those which are both fairly common and have a reasonably constant meaning include:

er, or, ist, ian (performer of)	teacher, sailor, dentist, physician
tion, sion (act of)	temptation, decision
ry, ty, ity (condition of)	finery, safety, purity
al (pertaining to)	formal, musical
ble, able, ible (capable of being)	adaptable, forcible
ment (result of, act of)	judgment, management
ful (full of)	careful, wonderful
man (one who)	policeman
ic (pertaining to)	comic, terrific
ous, ious, eous (like, full of)	joyous, laborious, nauseous
ence, ance (state of)	repentance, persistence
ly, y (in the manner of)	truly, windy

Figures of Speech. The English language is rich in expressions in which a combination of words has an idiomatic meaning that cannot be gained directly from its elements: blue laws, come out with, go in for, highhanded, let on, make out, in short order, palm off, etc. These idioms, when unfamiliar to the children, should be taught like new words. See Figure 31 which shows a practice exercise.

Similes and metaphors abound in poetry, and their interpretation is worth developing. Some children easily catch on to the meanings of figurative expressions; others have trouble getting away from a strictly literal meaning. Not every child understands what is meant by a sky "like a bluebird's wing" or realizes that a ship is meant when a poet says, "The hollow oak our palace is." The central idea of a charming poem by Sargent is the image of wind-wolves hunting cloud-deer. Confused meanings can be clarified in discussion. Children can be

EXERCISE

Read each sentence carefully to find the idiom that it contains. After each sentence three meanings are given. Choose the meaning that best fits the sentence. Write the letter that stands before this meaning.

1. By the end of the summer, *time hangs heavy* with us.
   a. Time passes slowly.
   b. Time weighs too much.
   c. Time seems too short.   1. a

2. We thought the house looked a bit *down at the heel.*
   a. The house did not look tall.
   b. The house looked worn and badly tended.
   c. The house seemed lopsided.   2. b

3. The bus left without us, and there we were *high and dry* in the big city.
   a. We were out of the rain.
   b. We were way up in a tall building.
   c. We were alone and helpless.   3. c

4. When the meeting ended, plans were still *up in the air.*
   a. The plans were not settled.
   b. Everyone still liked the plans.
   c. No one could find the plans.   4. a

5. I'm afraid Jack's job as a cook is a *blind alley* job.
   a. Jack doesn't know what his job is.
   b. Jack's job leads nowhere (it does not lead to a better job).
   c. Jack can't see what he is doing.   5. b

FIGURE 31. A practice exercise on interpreting idiomatic language. (From Lee C. Deighton, *Vocabulary Development,* the Macmillan Reading Spectrum, p. 96. © Macmillan Co., 1964.) Reduced in size.

encouraged to think up metaphors and similes of their own, and the results are sometimes strikingly original.

The distinctions among slang, colloquial speech, and good literary usage can be explained quickly but can be developed only by repeated discussion of specific expressions: "out of hand" is good usage, but "a handout" is slang, and "get the hang of" is colloquial. Since the distinction is not a logical one but rather is based on the historical development of the language, it is important for children to know that new expressions that begin as slang often become accepted as good usage years later.

Studying Verbal Relationships. Words become efficient tools when their relationships are understood and they have been mentally arranged into categories according to similarities, contrasts, and part-whole relationships. It is helpful for children to learn to classify words under headings, to know synonyms and antonyms, and to understand functional relationships. Many kinds of useful classification exercises are suggested in teachers' manuals, and specific practice pages can be found in many workbooks. Teachers can also make up their own vocabulary practice pages. Kinds of questions that can be used include:

Synonyms
1. An *indolent* man is: peaceful, lazy, passive, asleep.
2. Still: patient, lasting, motionless, coiled.
3. List all the words you can think of that mean about the same as *frightening.*
   Use each in a sentence that brings out its particular meaning.
Opposites
1. The opposite of *war* is: battle, peace, treaty, repose.
2. A mouse is tiny; an elephant is _____.
3. A *hostile* person is not: friendly, antagonistic, active, sociable.
Classification
1. Put all the vehicles in one column and all the parts in another column: train, wheel, axle, engine, boat, auto, motor, brake, seat, wagon, bicycle, propeller, cart, airplane, rudder, bumper.
2. List as many as you can under each of these headings: vegetables, fruits, nuts.
3. Put all the causes in one column and all the results in another column: fall, victory, arrival, speeding, injury, battle, collision, trip.

Analogies

1. President is to country as governor is to: city, state, legislature, voters.
2. Glove is to hand as shoe is to _____.
3. Hurry is to go as run is to: away, walk, move, home.

In finding answers to questions such as these a child has to organize his concepts and to seek for the relevant relationships. This is, then, practice in reasoning as well as practice with words.

Another tool for helping children learn to use language clearly and effectively is the thesaurus, a book which contains listings of synonyms whose differences in meaning are clarified (see Figure 32), related words, and antonyms. Two thesauri suitable for use in the elementary school have been recently published by Scott, Foresman: *In Other Words, Beginning Thesaurus* for grades three and four, and *In Other Words, Junior Thesaurus* for grades five and six.

Studying Word Origins. Many English words have interesting histories which enhance their meanings. Some of these words commemorate real or mythical people; boycott, blucher, lynch, gerrymander, tantalize, vulcanize, erotic. *Graft* has a long history, starting with the Greek verb meaning to write, and going through the Latin and French words meaning a sharp-pointed writing instrument, a knife used in grafting, the process of grafting one plant onto another, something added, and finally, the colloquial meaning of using one's position to get something extra (and often illegal). Alphabet comes from the first two letters of the Hebrew alphabet, algebra traces back to Arabic, and check comes from the Persian *shah* (meaning king, through the game of chess). Many words have come practically without change from Latin or Greek: melody, castle, radiant, hypocrite. Some have been borrowed without change from other modern languages: reservoir, kindergarten, piano.

Teachers can select a few words with interesting derivations and use them to arouse curiosity about the origins of other words (see Figure 33). Bright children can enjoy as well as profit by tracing the origins of many words. Since this kind of activity requires ability to use a college-level or unabridged dictionary, it is not very practicable before the upper grades, and then mainly for the brighter students.

ARGUE

Argue means give reasons for or against something. You *argue* with another person in order to convince him you are right and he is wrong. You *argue* in order to persuade him to accept your ideas. He may or may not. Children should not *argue* with their parents. Lawyers *argue* over whether or not someone is guilty of a crime. *The players argued over who should get the ball after it had gone out of bounds.*

disagree
discuss
debate
dispute
quarrel

You *disagree* with someone when you do not share the same opinion. You can *disagree* without having to argue. *I disagreed with the umpire's decision but didn't say anything. The boys agreed to give their father a present but disagreed on the best gift to buy.*

Discuss can mean just talk something over. Persons who disagree may *discuss* their problem calmly and agree on a solution. *The students discussed places to go on their class trip.* The architects *discussed* floor plans.

When you *debate* with another person or group, you consider both sides of a question or problem. You defend your position and attack your opponent's point of view. There are rules to follow when you *debate* in public. You can also *debate* something with yourself. If you are lost, you might *debate* which street to take.

Dispute means argue angrily over something. It can also mean question what another person does or thinks. *The contestants disputed the judge's decision.*

Quarrel means argue noisily. People usually shout when they *quarrel*. You can lose your friends if you *quarrel* with them all the time.

See also OBJECT (v).

ANTONYMS: agree, consent(v)

FIGURE 32. Page from a children's thesaurus. (From Greet, W. Cabell, Jenkins, William A., and Schiller, Andrew, *In Other Words, A Junior Thesaurus*. Glenville, Ill.: Scott, Foresman and Co., 1969.) Reduced in size.

TANTALIZE

to torment with
the punishment of
Tantalus

In Greek mythology, King Tantalus offended the gods and was punished in an extraordinary manner. He was placed in the midst of a lake whose waters reached his chin but receded whenever he attempted to allay his thirst. Over his head hung branches laden with choice fruit, which likewise receded whenever he stretched out his hand to satisfy his hunger. Tantalus became the symbol of such teasing, and his name is the root of our verb *tantalize*.

FIGURE 33. Example of the use of a word's origin to develop a clear and vivid meaning. (By permission. From *Interesting Origins of English Words,* copyright 1961 by G. and C. Merriam Co., Publishers of the Merriam-Webster Dictionaries.)

Materials for Vocabulary Development

In addition to the exercises found in the manuals and workbooks that accompany most reading programs, there are independent materials that may be used to assist in fostering vocabulary development. The following are illustrative of the types available:

Boning, Richard A. *Using Context Clues,* Books D, E, and F. Rockville Centre, N.Y.: Barnell Loft, Ltd., 1962. In each booklet, one for each of grades 4, 5, and 6, there are several hundred short paragraphs with one or two words missing in each paragraph. The child is to select the correct word from a given list of words.

Deighton, Lee C. *Vocabulary Development,* The Macmillan Reading Spectrum. New York: Macmillan, 1964. A series of six programmed workbooks for the intermediate grades. Suitable for individualized practice with children whose reading ability ranges from third- to sixth-reader level.

Farrar, Margaret, and Maleska, Eugene T. Eds. *Series 1, The Junior Crossword Puzzle Book.* New York: Simon and Shuster, 1961. Crossword puzzle suitable for use with children between the ages of 10 to 15.

Hodkinson, Kenneth. *Wordly Wise,* Book 1. and Ornato, Joseph G. *Wordly Wise,* Book 2. Cambridge, Mass.: Educator's Publishing Service, 1967. Each book introduces approximately 375 words (taken from the Thorndike-Lorge List) through a variety of exercises including puzzles and riddles. Suitable for grades 4 and 5 respectively.

Taylor, Sanford E., *et al. Word Clues.* Huntington, N.Y.: Educational Developmental Laboratories, 1962. A series of programmed workbooks emphasizing use of context. Self-administering and self-checking. In each book, one each for grades 7 through 13, 300 words are introduced.

Language Research Staff of New York City, *Building Reading Power.* Columbus, Ohio: Charles E. Merrill, 1968. Programmed nonconsumable booklets (consumable response sheets are used) that are part of a kit. Self-administering, self-correcting, and self-regulating exercises on learning to use context clues. Suitable for children reading at the fifth-reader level or above.

Summary

1. Words acquire meanings by being heard, read, and spoken repeatedly in particular situations.

   a. Concepts are generalized meanings that words come to represent.

   b. With repeated experiences, the concept that a word represents becomes refined and extended when its proper use is reinforced and improper use is not reinforced.

   c. Concepts become both more sharply defined and more generalized as children grow up.

   d. Concepts that are abstractions from abstractions are much harder to understand than concepts based on immediate experience.

2. Two sources of difficulty in developing concepts are verbalism and semantic confusion.

   a. Verbalism means vagueness, emptiness, or inaccuracy of concepts that is likely to occur when concepts are based only on words rather than developed out of relevant experience.

   b. Avoiding verbalism is a major task for teachers.

c. Semantic confusions arise because many words represent varied meanings, and it is possible for a writer to switch meanings or for a reader to select a different meaning from the one intended by the writer, thereby interfering with comprehension (communication).

3. Each child has four types of vocabulary: listening, speaking, reading, and writing.

   a. The listening vocabulary is developed first, followed by the speaking vocabulary, reading vocabulary, and writing vocabulary.

   b. Children's vocabularies are larger, on the average, than the estimates made a generation ago.

   c. Differences in size among children's vocabularies are very great, and where opportunities to learn are similar, vocabulary growth is closely related to intelligence.

4. Helping children to develop large, rich, and accurate vocabularies involves making use of a variety of techniques.

   a. Learning to develop and refine concepts by intelligent inferring from context must be relied on for many thousands of relatively uncommon words.

   b. Real and vicarious experiences are needed if verbalism is to be avoided.

   c. Teachers need skill in selecting words whose meanings are worth teaching.

   d. Perhaps the most common way to teach new word meanings is explanation by the teacher, followed by discussion.

   e. Children can profitably learn individualized word study techniques.

   f. Children need to learn how to interpret dictionary definitions and how to select the particular meaning that fits the context.

   g. Learning to interpret prefixes, roots, and suffixes is useful in the middle and upper grades, particularly for bright children.

   h. Idioms, similes, and metaphors need to be taught like new words and children need help in distinguishing levels of acceptability in usage.

   i. Practice with synonyms, antonyms, part-whole, and cause-effect relationships helps both to organize concepts into useful categories and to give training in reasoning.

j. Some attention to interesting word origins can enliven the study of word meanings.

Recommended Reading

BOND, GUY L., and WAGNER, EVA BOND. *Teaching the Child to Read*, 4th ed. New York: Macmillan, 1966. Ch. 9.

DAWSON, MILDRED, and BAMMAN, HENRY A. *Fundamentals of Basic Reading Instruction*, 2nd ed. New York: McKay, 1963. Ch. 11.

HARRIS, ALBERT J. *How to Increase Reading Ability*, 5th ed. New York: McKay, 1970. Ch. 15.

HARRIS, ALBERT J. *Readings on Reading Instruction*. New York: McKay, 1963. Ch. 9.

STAUFFER, RUSSELL G. *Directing Reading Maturity as a Cognitive Process*. New York: Harper & Row, 1969. Ch. 7.

TINKER, MILES A. and McCULLOUGH, CONSTANCE M. *Teaching Elementary Reading*, 3rd ed. New York: Appleton-Century-Crofts, 1968. Ch. 7.

11

Developing
Comprehension in Reading

The ultimate goal of reading instruction is to develop readers who can, and do, comprehend and react to what they read. Words occur in small groups (phrases), and in larger groups (sentences). These in turn are organized in paragraphs and in series of paragraphs. The ability to comprehend printed or written material, however, involves much more than recognizing words, knowing their appropriate meanings, and reading phrases and sentences. Reading comprehension is a complex process involving many different types of higher level thinking skills. We read for different purposes and in many kinds of materials. Our purpose, as well as the difficulty of the material, helps us to decide whether the material should be read quickly, whether it requires very careful reading, or whether it should be read at all. Efficient reading requires that one adapt his skills to those needed in a given situation.

This chapter considers: (1) the improvement of the interpretation of thought units; (2) the development of comprehension in the primary grades; (3) types of comprehension, with particular attention to their development in the middle and upper grades; (4) the relationship between reading rate and comprehension; and (5) description of materials that may be used to build comprehension and increase reading rate.

Learning to Interpret Thought Units

Most basal-reader programs encourage reading for meaning from the initial stages of reading instruction. Guiding questions before reading, discussion after reading, and rereading to refine understanding are widely used procedures. In addition to general comprehension practice, it is helpful to give some attention to the mastery of the thought units with which reading material is built.

READING IN PHRASES

A phrase is a group of two or more words that form a meaning unit that has the force or significance of a single part of speech. Thus a phrase can be used in the role of a preposition (*in regard to*), an adjective (*of great value*), an adverb (*in a hurry*), a verb (*used to go*), or a noun (*drinking milk* is good for children). Many a phrase can be replaced by a single word without any important change of meaning. Thus the phrases just mentioned are more or less equivalent to *about, valuable, hurriedly, went, and milk.*

Improvement of Phrase Reading. In the primary grades, emphasis should be placed on the phrase as a meaning unit rather than as a perceptual unit. Eye-movement studies show that average readers in the sixth grade make 1.2 fixations per word. Of course, some unfamiliar words that require more than one look influence this average; but even allowing for them, it seems evident that even the average sixth grader does not perceive many phrases as visual units.

Oral reading provides many opportunities for noticing whether or not the children are reading with attention to the natural groupings of words, pausing between phrases rather than within them, and using inflection and accent appropriately to suggest meaning. The child who reads word-by-word in a monotonous voice, ignoring punctuation, stress, and inflection, is very easy to detect.

Teachers should encourage children to read with natural expression. Suggesting that children think of the story setting and say the words just as they would if they were the story character helps to develop fluent oral reading. Two exercises that are well suited to the development of these skills are taking the roles of the story characters (omitting phrases such as "he said" or "she cried") and reading plays. It is helpful, also, for teachers to provide a model by reading a sentence or more to children, and then to ask them to continue the reading in the same way, or read alternate sentences, or read in unison with them.

New words are usually presented in phrases (or sentences) rather than in isolation. Sometimes phrase cards are used for recognition practice. Such cards can be used to assemble sentences on a chart holder or flannel board, to pick out the answers to questions, and as flash cards. When phrase cards are "flashed," the teacher should give a longer exposure than with single words.

Both oral and written questions can be formulated in such a way as to require an answer in phrase form. Written (or duplicated) questions of the following kinds can be used:

1. Where would you go to buy some bread?
   ___ to the store   ___ to the street
   ___ to the school   ___ to the farm
2. A robin usually builds its nest (1) in a tree (2) in the grass (3) in a birdhouse (4) in the water
3. Which of these are places where families often live?

___ in an apartment   ___ in a cellar   ___ in a farmhouse
___ in an attic   ___ in a cottage   ___ in a factory

Many children do not need special practice in reading phrases. Their phrase reading develops naturally in the setting of reading for meaning. Abundant practice in reading provides a situation in which phrases are understood as meaning units, and gradually some common phrases begin to be seen as perceptual units. On the other hand, there are some children who even need to learn what a phrase is.

Materials are available to assist in developing phrase reading.

Some of the workbooks listed on page 325 contain phrase reading exercises such as the one shown in Figure 34. The teacher may construct similar exercises, or he may underline the phrases (e.g., Big cats run quickly. or Big cats run quickly.) or separate them by spaces (e.g., Big cats   run quickly).

Ⓔ **Reading Thought Units**

As your eyes gather up a group of words at one sweep, train them to read the right words together. Read these two paragraphs and follow the groups as they are marked. Which paragraph is easier to read? Why?

> 1. A beginning / reader or / a slow / reader may / see only / one / word or / a part of / a word / at each / pause. A / good reader / reads three / or four / words per / "eyeful." / As your / reading / eye span / grows, / the faster / you can / read.

> 2. A beginning reader / or a slow reader / may see / only one word / or a part / of a word / at each pause. / A good reader / reads three / or four words / per "eyeful." / As your reading / eye span / grows, / the faster / you can read.

FIGURE 34. An exercise intended to develop efficient phrase reading and to diminish frequency of regressions. (From Leavell, Ullin W., and Betty D. Via, *New Journeys in Reading*, Revised, p. 112. The Reading Essentials Series, copyright © 1966. Austin, Texas: Steck-Vaughn Co.) Reduced in size. Reprinted by permission of the publisher.

Phrases also may be flashed by hand or on projection-type tachistoscopes using teacher-made or commercially prepared materials. Yet another type of exercise involves matching phrases presented in two columns in different sequences. Any of the preceding exercises should be followed up with practice in phrasing in daily reading assignments.

READING SENTENCES

Sentences are the natural units of meaning in both spoken and printed language. Beginning readers, who are learning that reading is talk that has been written down, are encouraged to read as if the characters were speaking. When they pronounce the words at about the same rate and with the same stresses and inflections that the character would use, meaning comes as easily in reading as in listening. As long as the book uses words that children understand and can recognize, and employs familiar sentence patterns, the reading of sentences presents no special problems.

Difficulties begin when the complexity of the sentence structure in reading material exceeds the complexity of the sentences to which the children are accustomed in listening and speaking.

Reading interesting stories to children is one way of building listening comprehension of longer and more complex sentences. As their listening comprehension for such sentences grows, their ability to read such sentences with understanding also improves.

Here are two sentences from books used in grades four to six:

By paying a small fee, a farmer can have water pumped to his fields, while he looks on.

Now, jarred loose by a sudden lurch of the crowded float, one end of the log had swung out to the place where Martha would surely hit the water.

In both of these sentences the subject follows a modifying phrase or clause instead of preceding it. Ability to locate the subject and the main predicate of such sentences is essential. One way of helping is to ask questions like, "Who pays the fee?" "What was jarred loose?" Another is to ask the children to divide a long sentence into several sentences, one for each separate idea. The second sentence above could be restated in three sentences: (1) One end of the log was jarred loose. (2) The log had swung out to the place. (3) Martha would surely hit the water where the end of the log was. It is not necessary to wait for the teaching of formal grammatical analysis.

Children who do not have word-recognition or word-meaning problems but who do have difficulty understanding sentences may be helped by asking specific questions (Who? What? Where? When? How? Why?) about separate sentences in a selection. Difficulty with understanding complex or compound sentences may be due to unfamiliarity with the meanings of commonly used connectives. If necessary, children should be taught the use of the following connectives: who, which, what, that, from, whom, to which, how, hardly.

Signal words. There are certain words and phrases that may aid the reader in determining the relationship between and among ideas presented by an author. For example, the reader should be aware that an idea opposed to the one he is now reading is likely to follow the word "but." Signal words include words that in traditional grammar are called conjunctions or prepositions, and phrases which have similar functions. Among the signal words likely to be encountered by children are:

More information to follow: also, and, another, as well as, besides, finally, furthermore, in addition to, in conclusion, moreover.

Opposite idea to follow: although, as a matter of fact, but, either . . . or (implies alternative), even if, however, in spite of, instead of, nevertheless, on the other hand, rather, still, yet.

Cause indicated: as a result of, because, due to, in order to, on account of, since, so that.

Effect indicated: as a consequence, as a result, consequently, so, so as to, therefore.

Exceptions to follow: all but, except.

Conditions to be met: after, as soon as, before, following, if (also may indicate a supposition), provided that, should, while, without, unless, until.

Comparison to be made: as, before . . . after, like, once . . . now, some . . . others, than.

Examples to follow (These words are often followed by *is* or *are*): examples, for example, kinds, ordinal numbers (e.g., (1) . . .; (2) . . .), others, several, some, such as, the following, types, ways.[1]

Teaching the use of signal words may be begun in the fourth grade with good readers, using the examples found in their reading material. Using signal words also aids in determining at what speed material should be read. Words like "and" and "also" indicate that speed can be fairly rapid because something more is being added to the same subject. On the other hand, words like "if" and "because" indicate the possible need to slow down in order to better understand the material.

[1] Many of these examples were taken from James A. Wright, "A Taxonomy of Thinking Skills for Young Readers," *Reading Horizons,* 6 (Fall 1965), 20–25.

READING PARAGRAPHS

In well-written prose, sentences are organized into paragraphs, each of which usually contains one main idea. Children can learn to look for the main idea in each paragraph and to see how the rest of the paragraph explains, illustrates, or elaborates this idea.

Discerning readers are able to identify several common types of paragraph organization. Most common is the pattern in which the main idea is given in the first sentence, and the rest of the paragraph consists of illustrative details, examples, or amplifications. Another fairly common pattern starts with a number of specific examples or details, leading to a general statement in the final sentence. When a chronological sequence of events is described, as in history, a summarizing sentence may occur at either the beginning or the end of the paragraph. Material intended to persuade or to demonstrate a cause-effect relationship usually employs the premises–conclusion or "if–then" kind of paragraph.

Learning to find the topic sentences in paragraphs and to see how the parts of a paragraph fit together is so important both for reading and for writing that it would seem basic in the language arts. At present relatively little is done along these lines in many elementary schools. More attention to the analysis and construction of good paragraphs could easily be given in the middle and upper grades.

FACTORS UNDERLYING COMPREHENSION

Comprehension is an outcome or result which depends on a number of basic reading skills. A minimum essential is ability to recognize the words: possession of an adequate sight vocabulary and ability to use phonics and morphemic analysis in conjunction with context. Closely related is meaningful vocabulary, including skill in selecting the particular one of alternative meanings which a word carries in the sentence. Ability to grasp the meaning of word groups of increasing size—phrases, sentences, and paragraphs—develops along with word recognition and vocabulary.

At all levels of maturity, the child's mastery of the language and, particularly, his listening comprehension put realistic limits to his reading comprehension. Once word recognition is no longer a major problem, a child's reading comprehension is likely to resemble his listening comprehension quite closely because it is unlikely that a child will understand printed material that he could not understand aurally, that is, material read to him. Thus the ability to understand spoken language is an important factor. Listening comprehension, and therefore reading comprehension, is dependent upon experiential, educational, cultural, and linguistic background, and involves the attentive employment of intelligence, which itself strongly influences the ability to comprehend.

LISTENING COMPREHENSION

The research comparing reading and listening comprehension was summarized by Tinker and McCullough.[2]

Although the findings are not uniform, the following trends are evident: (a) At the lower grade levels, *auditory* comprehension tends to be *equal to or better than* reading comprehension. (b) For pupils of lower ability, *auditory* comprehension tends to be *equal to or better than* reading comprehension. (c) For more skilled readers and for those of higher ability, however, *reading* comprehension tends to be *equal to or better than* auditory comprehension. (d) For college students, *auditory* comprehension tends to be superior for easy material, *reading* comprehension for *difficult* material. This indicates the obvious advantage of going slowly and reviewing the difficult parts of what is read. (e) There is a general trend to support the view that *reading comprehension* becomes increasingly effective with increased age among those who read widely and finally comes to surpass listening comprehension in the case of good readers.

There are four main reasons why reading comprehension may be higher than listening comprehension for certain children. First, in reading one has the opportunity to reread if necessary; in listening,

---

[2] Miles A. Tinker and Constance M. McCullough, *Teaching Elementary Reading*, 3rd ed. (New York: Appleton-Century-Crofts, 1968), pp. 187–188. Reprinted by permission of the publisher.

unless the material is recorded, there is only one opportunity to comprehend. Second, the reader sets his own pace; in listening, the pace is set by the speaker. Third, if the listener dwells on a point or lets his mind wander, he may miss other points. Finally, there has been much more instruction and practice in reading comprehension.

Instruction in listening comprehension should be an integral part of a total language arts program if for no other reason than that a great deal of instruction in school is given orally. As for the reading program, it seems likely that improvement in listening comprehension will affect reading comprehension because the same processes are involved in both types of comprehension. As Spache and Spache [3] pointed out,

> The aim of auditory comprehension training is not simply to provide experiences with words, to deepen and broaden the child's knowledge of words or his auditory vocabulary. It provides these stimuli to language development to be sure, but even more significantly the training promotes the child's verbal reasoning, memory, critical thinking, and other intellectual processes. These are the processes he must employ in dealing with ideas encountered later in reading. These are the processes which underlie that rather vague ability, comprehension. Training in auditory comprehension is, in effect, training to think with words.

Those most likely to benefit from auding (listening) instruction and practice are beginning readers, and poor readers whose comprehension problems are highly related to their inability to understand spoken language (in such cases the reasons for this weakness must be determined and considered in planning corrective or remedial work). Children who have decoding problems, particularly older children with severe reading problems, also should benefit from such instruction because it allows them to learn skills and to acquire knowledge that may be applied to reading when the decoding problem is overcome. Moreover, such children often can learn information (e.g., social studies and science concepts) through listening. If disabled

---

[3] George D. Spache and Evelyn B. Spache, *Reading in the Elementary School*, 2nd ed. (Boston: Allyn and Bacon, Inc., 1969), p. 225. Reprinted by permission of the Publisher.

readers do not learn basic and continuing concepts as they progress through school, they are likely to encounter reading comprehension problems in the later grades even after they learn to decode. Disabled readers should be tested orally to determine their knowledge in the various content fields.

Many suggestions for teaching listening comprehension can be found in *Listening Aids Through the Grades* and *Listening Games.*[4] Among the commercially prepared listening programs are the *Listen and Think Program* for grades 3–6 and the *Listen and Read Program* for grades 7–16 (tapes and workbooks) published by Educational Developmental Laboratories, and *Listening Skill Builders* which are found in the SRA Reading Laboratories. In the latter, children are taught to use the TQLR technique which closely parallels the SQ3R technique (see page 342). This technique involves four steps: Tune-in, Question, Listen, and Review.[5]

Building Reading Comprehension in the Primary Grades

Basal reader programs emphasize that reading should be meaningful right from the beginning. From the first grade on, teachers provide a motivating or guiding question before children read ahead, and the first reading is motivated to find the answer. Sometimes the children are encouraged to infer, from the story title and first illustration, what the story is about; then they read ahead and discuss what their inferences were, why they made them, and how they correspond to the story. This is just one of many ways in which purposes can be provided for reading with attention to meaning.

[4] David H. Russell and Elizabeth F. Russell, *Listening Aids Through the Grades* (New York: Teachers College Press, Columbia University, 1959).

Guy Wagner, Max Hosier, and Mildred Blackman, *Listening Games: Building Listening Skills with Instructional Games.* (Darien, Conn.: Teachers Publishing Corp., 1962).

[5] Don H. Parker, *Teacher's Handbook for Reading Laboratory, IIa* (Chicago: Science Research Associates, Inc., 1958), pp. 51–57.

For further information on listening refer to:

Sam Duker, *Listening Bibliography,* 2nd ed. (Metuchen, N.J.: Scarecrow Press, 1968).

Sam Duker, *Listening: Readings* (Metuchen, N.J.: Scarecrow Press, 1966).

304 · EFFECTIVE TEACHING OF READING

Even in the primary grades, many different kinds of comprehension questions can be asked. The manual of a recently published first reader [6] indicates quite a variety of headings relating to comprehension: locating specific information, following detailed directions, summarizing, rereading for specific purposes, reading for details, reading to prove a point, recalling story content, interpreting emotional attitudes, determining sequence of events, making inferences, evaluating motives, predicting outcomes from facts read, finding the main idea, perceiving relationships, and skimming. Some reading selections are good for developing one type of comprehension, but are less suitable for the development of other types.

It is important for teachers to keep in mind what is really significant and what is not worth remembering. David Russell [7] expressed this very well: "Some teachers in second grade are more likely to ask the question, 'What was the color of Mary's dress?' rather than the question, 'Is Mary the kind of a girl you would like to have as a friend?' "

Questions about details usually start with *who, what, where,* and *when.* These have some value, but usually call only for repetition of details that are directly stated in the book; little or no thinking is required. Questions that ask *how* are somewhat more challenging because they require an understanding of process, and the organization of facts or steps into a sequential pattern. Most searching are questions that ask *why,* because they lead into the heart of the matter. They disclose the reasons underlying an answer and show how well the relationships between causes and effects are understood. Questions that call for an opinion or judgment should usually be followed by "Why?" if we are to help children to become individuals whose judgments are based on reason.

Comprehension questioning in the primary grades is usually in the form of oral discussion, with the teacher asking questions and children

[6] Mae Knight Clark, *Teacher's Annotated Edition and Guide to accompany Lands of Pleasure,* Rev. ed. (New York: Macmillan, 1970), pp. 429–430.

[7] David H. Russell, "Reading for Effective Personal Living," p. 13 in *Reading for Effective Living,* International Reading Association Conference Proceedings, Vol. 3 (New York: Scholastic Magazines, 1958).

answering; sometimes volunteering, sometimes called on. It is often a good idea to involve more than one child at a time. Thus, after one child has given an answer, another child can be asked, "Do you agree or disagree? Why?" Expecting this kind of question helps to keep all children in the group attentive. In a spontaneous discussion children can have the freedom to challenge another child's opinion or correct a misstatement. When a group has helped to decide its own purpose for reading, the children may participate in the discussion more eagerly than when the teacher's questions are taken word for word from a manual.

Correlated workbooks also provide varied ways of checking comprehension. After the questions have been answered, the answers can be compared during a group session and questions about which there is some disagreement can be discussed. Often this provides an excellent motive for rereading part of the selection. Absurdities created by misread words, misunderstood concepts, and failure to grasp the true meaning of a sentence are among the most common causes of incorrect responses to comprehension questions.

Learning to Read for Specific Purposes

Research findings do not agree as to whether reading comprehension is a highly unitary skill (i.e., if there are separate skills, they are so interdependent that if a reader is good, or poor, in one skill, he is likely to be almost as good, or poor, in all skills) [8] or whether there are different skills involved. Davis's study,[9] however, does tend to support the desirability of providing instruction and practice in specific kinds of comprehension skills.

There are a number of models of comprehension, with Barrett's perhaps the most extensive.[10] Barrett's taxonomy lists five different

[8] Paul B. Diedrich, "What Does Research in Reading Reveal—About Evaluation in Reading?" *English Journal,* 58 (September, 1969), 853–868.

[9] Frederick B. Davis, "Research in Comprehension in Reading," *Reading Research Quarterly,* 3 (Summer 1968), 499–545.

[10] Developed by Thomas C. Barrett as found in Theodore Clymer, "What is 'Reading'?: Some Current Concepts," *Innovation and Change in Reading In-*

types of comprehension (literal, recall, inferential, evaluation, and appreciation) with subheadings for each (e.g., for inferential: inferring supporting details, inferring main ideas, inferring sequence, inferring comparisons, inferring cause and effect relationships, inferring characteristic traits, predicting outcomes, and interpreting figurative language). Such a taxonomy may be useful for developing reading purposes and questions, and for determining what types of comprehension questions are suggested in teachers' manuals. It also may serve to illustrate the complexity of the ability called reading comprehension.

Specific types of comprehension skills may be classified more simply as indicated by the sections below which correspond to the list of objectives outlined on page 19 under the heading "Reading Comprehension Skills."

Comprehension also may be classified according to three levels: (1) literal comprehension, (2) interpretive comprehension, and (3) evaluative comprehension. The lowest level, literal comprehension, involves understanding ideas that are explicitly stated. Although the first six types of comprehension listed below often operate at this level, obtaining answers to questions about main ideas, sequence, or grasping the author's plan or intent often involves higher-level skills. Interpretive comprehension goes beyond obtaining literal meaning, which is a necessary first step, to understanding ideas that are implied or whose meaning must be inferred. The highest level of comprehension involves evaluating what one has read. In doing so, one attempts to assess such things as the accuracy, worth, or quality of the material.

Even though the types of comprehension are listed separately, they probably do not function in isolation. Rather, they probably are interdependent and overlapping. Furthermore, one cannot assume that if a child is able to perform a skill in one type of material or at a given level of difficulty in a particular type of material, that he will

---

struction, 67th Yearbook of the National Society for the Study of Education, Part II (Chicago: University of Chicago Press, 1968), 19–23.

For summaries of other models of comprehension, refer to Spache and Spache, *op. cit.,* pp. 459–461.

be successful with that skill in all types or levels of reading material. For example, a child may be able to select and recall main ideas from his fourth reader, but have difficulty doing so in the fourth-grade science book. Or, when he reaches the sixth-reader level, he may encounter difficulty because the ideas presented in the particular reader he is using are more complex and further removed from his fund of concepts than those found in lower level materials.

Teachers also should recognize that there are degrees of comprehension. The degree to which a reader comprehends is dependent upon such factors as his competence in the language, his intelligence, his experiental background, and the purpose for which he has read the material. A chemist may read an article to understand thoroughly the processes involved in an experiment; a student may read the same article only to learn the steps in the experiment and its outcome.

FINDING AND UNDERSTANDING MAIN IDEAS

The ability to find out the most important thing an author is trying to say—the central thought or main idea—is perhaps the most important of all specific comprehension skills. Without it, the reader gets lost in a mass of detail, inspecting trees but unable to see the forest. Selecting the main idea from the many other ideas requires comparison, judgment, and discrimination. Because of this, getting the main idea is often easy for bright children but very difficult for children of limited mental ability, who are likely to be more successful with details.

Many kinds of practice can be used to develop the ability to grasp the main idea.

1. *Topic sentences.* Children can be asked to find the one sentence in a paragraph that contains the central thought. In discussing the differences between a topic sentence and other sentences, paragraph structure is analyzed. Children learn that the main idea is usually stated in the first or last sentence, although it may be found anywhere in the paragraph. For some paragraphs, however, the main idea must be inferred from the entire paragraph because not every

paragraph contains a topic sentence. Once skill in selecting main ideas in single paragraphs has been established, similar practice can be given with short selections consisting of a few paragraphs.

What is the main idea in each of these stories? Write its letter in the box.

1. Thousands of years ago, early man learned to use a boat. He may have first noticed a piece of wood floating down a river. He climbed on for a ride. Later, he put three or four of these pieces together and built a raft. Also, he made his raft go by pushing with a pole.

3. Today sea-going ships cross three thousand miles of ocean in five days. These are really floating hotels, fitted with everything for people to enjoy — fine bedrooms, good food, swimming pools, television, and even ship-to-shore telephones! What could ever be better!

2. Time passed and men learned to build better boats than rafts. Boats were rowed and boats had sails. Sometimes these two inventions were used together. Daring men even learned to sail across the ocean. Men kept on studying and experimenting to build better boats.

4. One thing "better" was finally invented — it was better because it was so quick. This was the airplane. Instead of spending days, people now spend hours to cross the ocean. More people cross by plane than by ship. Is something still better yet to be invented?

A. Airships are faster than boats.

B. Men learned to build better boats.

C. Man learns to build a boat.

D. Boats have become floating hotels.

FIGURE 35. An exercise to develop the ability to understand main ideas. (From *A Discovery Book to Accompany Better Than Gold,* 3¹ reader level of The Macmillan Reading Program, page 78. New York: Macmillan Co., 1970.) Reproduced by permission of the publishers and reduced in size.

2. Introductory and concluding paragraphs. In well-written selections there is often an introductory paragraph or section that sets the purpose or explains the scope of the selection, and a concluding paragraph or section that summarizes. Children can be trained to read introductions and conclusions carefully, looking for the main idea or ideas. Reading of introductions and summaries can enable one to obtain an overall impression of the material.

3. *Titles and headings.* An author usually tries to convey his main theme in the title he gives a selection, and in informational material the main ideas of sections are suggested in the headings and sub-headings. The usefulness of this "author's outline" should be discussed with children. Discussion of title and headings sometimes discloses disagreements about interpretation that can be settled by reading the selection to see what the title or heading really means. In more formal exercises, children can be given selections from which titles and headings have been removed. They can be asked to choose among several alternatives in multiple-choice questions, or to write their own headings or titles. News articles for which they are to write headlines are particularly good for this purpose.

4. *One-sentence summaries.* Asking children to state the gist of a passage or selection in one sentence is a challenging way to get them to try to distill the essential idea from the many details. If several summary sentences are proposed, they can be placed on the chalk-board and criteria for choosing the best summary can be developed in discussion. Questions can be worded in various ways. What is it all about? What is the main idea? What would be a good title? What question is the author answering? In interpreting narrative material, understanding of main ideas frequently can be tested by asking how a central character felt at a critical point.

5. *Skimming for general impression.* A very useful procedure is learning to skim through an entire selection rapidly and superficially to get a total impression. This can be helpful in giving an idea of the scope of a chapter that is to be studied carefully; in getting an idea of a writer's main point without bothering about details; in sampling a book to see if it is likely to be interesting, or suitable in difficulty, or likely to contain the information needed. A specific purpose needs to be set that can be satisfied by this kind of skimming.

LOCATING ANSWERS TO SPECIFIC QUESTIONS

In an intellectually alive elementary school, as in the lives of adults, a great many occasions come up in which a question is asked, and the answer is then sought by reading. Adults do reading of this sort when they locate a person's telephone number in a directory; when they scan movie advertisements to find out where a particular picture is being shown; when they consult a timetable; etc. Children think up many specific questions, the answers to which can be found in a dictionary, almanac, atlas, or encyclopedia. When they locate the page or section in which the answer is to be found (by using the index or table of contents) they read rapidly until they come to the specific item. With practice, it is possible to learn to skim through the material very rapidly, without actually reading it, and when one gets to the desired item it seems to "pop out" as if on springs. Children should be taught how to skim to find answers to very specific questions as well as how to skim to obtain a general impression of the material.

There are other times when careful reading and analytical reasoning are required in order to find the answer to a specific question. For example, reading to learn how gasoline is ignited in an internal combustion engine probably would require such reading. The purpose for reading is set by the question that also assists the reader to determine how well he understood the material (Can he answer the question?). Reading of this type requires the ability to distinguish between relevant and irrelevant information.

Much reading to locate answers to questions takes place when children are working on projects, individually or in groups or committees. Many children, even many whose general comprehension is superior, have difficulty distinguishing information that is relevant from that which is interesting but not pertinent; they get lost among many enticing bypaths and find out a great deal, but not the answer to the question.

Teachers can help children to develop skill in reading to find specific answers. Social studies and scientific materials as well as newspapers are well adapted to this. Teachers can formulate a suitable number of questions of the who, which, what, when type, the answers to which can be found in the selection. These questions are given to the children before they read the selection. Answers can be written or spoken, and errors should be analyzed with the children.

Another procedure is to give questions with three alternatives, True, False, and Not Mentioned.

NOTING AND RECALLING DETAILS

Although reading to learn details is usually not as important as getting main ideas, there are many situations in which the details are necessary to give a factual basis for generalizations, and to supply the specifics necessary both in formulating and in applying ideas. This is particularly true of studying in the content subjects where it is necessary to assimilate as much of the information as possible. Children should be helped to learn details in relation to ideas, rather than as separate, isolated bits of information.

Relating of details to main ideas can be improved by proper questioning. First the main idea of a passage is found. Then several kinds of questions can be asked. How is this shown? What evidence is there for it? Where or when does it apply? What are the exceptions? How many kinds are there? What applications are given? Incomplete outlines that call for filling in details under headings can also be used helpfully (see page 351).

Questions about details as such also have their uses. They are the easiest type of question to formulate and answer. Children of limited intelligence often have difficulty with any other type of question. There is, however, the danger that with most children such questions are overemphasized to the point of making reading a dull question-answer period. Even more damaging is the emphasis some teachers place on insignificant details.

GRASPING THE SEQUENCE OF EVENTS

In narrative material, whether fiction, true events, or historical accounts, a series of events is related. In order to understand it is necessary to be able to note and remember the order in which the events took place, and to comprehend, at least partially, the cause-effect chain linking each event with the preceding and following events.

Jeff got dressed for school.	Ted sat down in the chair.
Jeff ran for the school bus.	Ted walked over to the chair.
Jeff jumped out of bed.	Ted went to sleep in the chair.
What did Jeff do last ?	What did Ted do first ?
Billy planted some seeds.	Jud met some boys in the park.
Billy watered the garden.	Jud played with the boys.
Billy dug up the land.	Jud walked to the park.
What did Billy do first ?	What did Jud do last ?

FIGURE 36. Part of an exercise to develop the ability to recognize sequence. (From Early, Margaret, *et al.*, *Reading Skills Four for use with Together We Go*, first reader level of the Bookmark Reading Program, page 80. New York: Harcourt Brace Jovanovich, Inc., 1970. Reproduced by permission of the publishers and reduced in size.)

The most natural way to develop ability to improve grasp of sequence is to ask for a retelling of the story. Children who are not ready to report a sequence from start to finish can be guided step by step. What happened first? What next? Then what? Did Henry hit Bob before or after Bob called him a name?

Another type of practice, often used in workbooks, presents the events of a story in a scrambled sequence. After reading the story, the children number the events in the order in which they occur in the story. When using such exercises or tests, the teacher should be aware that if the child errs on numbering the sequence of one event, particularly if it is the first event, he will also err on at least one other because he has used one of the numbers in the wrong place. Thus the child may appear to be weaker in this skill than he really is.

FOLLOWING DIRECTIONS

In everyday life, ability to follow printed directions accurately is a valuable asset. Cookbooks, handbooks, manuals, and do-it-yourself kits transform people with highly specialized jobs into Jacks-of-all-trades in their so-called leisure time. In school, ability to follow printed directions is important in many kinds of activities: in scientific experiments, in domestic science, in many kinds of shopwork courses, and in general in situations in which children are given printed directions and are asked to follow them.

Practice in learning to read directions carefully and to follow them exactly and in sequence should make use of the kinds of material in which this skill is important. Selections can be chosen from such sources as Boy and Girl Scout handbooks, cookbooks, directions for constructing various kinds of objects such as plane models, projects from *Popular Mechanics,* and explanations of how to perform magic tricks or games. The best test is to let the children carry out the project, with a good result its own reward. When this is not practical, questions can be formulated and provided in duplicated form. Several workbooks contain practice material of this kind. (See Figure 37.)

GRASPING THE AUTHOR'S PLAN AND INTENT

In most books for children, the author's intent is clear and his plan is simple and straightforward. Fictional narratives tend to move ahead in simple chronological sequence, without flashbacks or other time inversions. Expository writing is usually well organized, with an introduction, a body, and a concluding summary. Headings and subheadings help the reader to distinguish between major and minor divisions and disclose the plan of organization.

Sometimes, however, the author's intentions are not so obvious. Children often fail to understand humorous exaggeration and irony, in which the author expects the reader to know that he means the opposite of what he seems to be saying. Adults, too, can miss an

24. Underwater Light

Have you ever wondered how things look at the bottom of a pond at night? Here's a good way to see. Find a large glass jar that will hold your flashlight. Be sure that the top of the jar screws on, so no water will get inside. Switch on your flashlight and lock it, so the light will stay on. Next put the flashlight inside the glass jar and screw the top on tightly. Tie a long, stout cord firmly around the neck of the jar.

Hold fast to the end of the cord while you lower the jar into the dark water of the pond. The light inside the jar will make it possible for you to see many things. The bottom of the pond is a busy place at night. There are sure to be frogs, bugs, and water beetles, and if you are lucky you may see a fish.

Follow these directions:

1. Draw a big circle for the pond. Write the word "pond" on it.

2. Inside the pond make a circle for the jar.

3. Make a very tiny circle to show where the flashlight should be.

4. Write the words that tell where the cord should be tied.

5. Write the names of two things you are sure to see at the bottom of the pond.

author's intent when it is not directly stated. In response to a satire,[11] the writer received a number of requests: (1) to participate in the program, (2) for information as to where the device used in the study might be purchased, and (3) for data on the study. Letters from associates also revealed that when the article was given to students in reading and research courses to evaluate, relatively few realized its satirical nature, despite a final footnote that states, "Don't be too quick to believe everything you read."

When books recommended for children are considered to have genuine literary worth, there are usually deeper meanings below the surface. Is *The Adventures of Huckleberry Finn* just a series of varied episodes or is it also a savage criticism of some aspects of American society? What lesson is exemplified in Beim's *Two Is a Team?* Even when children are reading primarily for fun or thrills, they can be helped to discover some of the ways in which the beliefs of authors are disclosed in their writings.

ANTICIPATING OUTCOMES

The intelligent reader is usually thinking ahead, forming tentative guesses as to what is coming, and testing and revising them as he goes along. We use context not only to infer the pronunciation or meaning of unfamiliar words but also to project the story. If it were not for this habit of anticipation there could be no such thing as a surprise ending.

Children can be given many kinds of guiding questions which encourage them to predict what is going to happen, discuss why they

[11] Edward R. Sipay, "The Effect of Prenatal Instruction on Reading Achievement," *Elementary English*, Vol. 42 (April 1965), 431–432.

FIGURE 37. An exercise to develop the ability to follow printed directions. (From Gates, Arthur E. and Celeste C. Peardon, Reading Exercises, Elementary-FD, *Can You Follow Directions?* New York: Teachers College Press, © 1963, Teachers College, Columbia University.) Reproduced by permission of the publisher.

think so, and then to read ahead and find out if they were right or not. Sometimes this is done before they start to read a story; sometimes it is more effective to let them read part of the story and then predict how it is going to continue. They can think up alternative endings, and then read to see how close they have come to the author's ending. Some workbooks provide brief unfinished stories and ask the child to choose among plausible and unlikely endings (see Figure 38), or to complete the story.

MAKING INFERENCES

Closely related to the skill of anticipating or predicting outcomes is the skill commonly referred to as making inferences. To make an

Animals Help

Grandad went over to see why Nancy and Bill were fighting.

"I was here first," said Nancy. "Now Bill wants the berries I found."

"The berries here are big," said Bill. "I want some of the big ones."

Grandad saw there were many, many berries. He thought for a minute. Then he said, "See how my cows eat breakfast. Each stands alone. Each eats what she finds where she is."

Bill and Nancy looked at the cows. Soon they saw what they would do.

What will Bill and Nancy do?

Eat breakfast with the cows.
Go off alone to get berries.
Put the berries in one bucket.

FIGURE 38. Part of an exercise to develop the ability to predict outcomes. From Stauffer, Russell G. *et al.*, *Studybook for Friends All About*, 2^1 reader level of the Winston Basic Reader Series, page 57. New York: Holt, Rinehart and Winston, Inc., 1960. Reproduced by permission of the publishers and reduced in size.

inference, the child must, through reasoning, use the directly stated information in the reading material and his experiental background to obtain implied meanings. This skill of "reading between the lines" may take many forms, such as: being able to determine the main idea of a paragraph or selection for which the main idea is not explicitly stated, or inferring the emotional climate of a situation, the feelings of a character, or his personality traits. Children who have limited intelligence or experiental backgrounds, or who are weak in understanding relationships, very probably will have difficulty in drawing inferences. Instruction and practice in making inferences from material read to them, even to the point of step-by-step procedures for arriving at the correct inference, will be of value to some children.

EVALUATING WHAT ONE READS

In this modern world, people are bombarded from many sides by reading matter which attempts to influence their behavior and shape their ideas. Vance Packard's *The Hidden Persuaders* opened many eyes to the wiles of advertisers, and particularly to their efforts to make use of unconscious and subconscious motivation. During a political campaign no realistic voter expects to receive unvarnished truth from members of a contending political party. Accounts of the same events in newspapers vary somewhat according to the editorial policy of the paper. The trusting reader who believes everything he finds in print is a potential victim for any writer with a product or an idea to sell.

An enlightened citizen in a democracy must learn to distinguish trustworthy information from slanted or biased accounts. He must be able to evaluate what he reads; that is, he must be able to read critically.

To be able to read critically, one must be able to think critically. In turn, critical thinking requires an open mind, experiential background, knowledge of how and where to find information, a certain level of reasoning ability, and something about which to think critically. A biased or closed-minded individual cannot think critically because he rejects or refuses to "listen to" alternatives to his own fixed beliefs, which often are influenced by emotions. Likewise, it is impossible to judge the accuracy of material if one does not possess knowledge in that area. Such knowledge provides a frame of reference. Since we cannot be experts in all fields (and experts themselves may not agree), it therefore is also necessary to know how and where to find the desired or necessary information. Next the person must be able to understand the relationship between his knowledge and the new information or ideas, as well as be able to reason through or analyze the new material. Yet the preceding skills and attitudes are of little use if children have limited or no opportunity to think or to read critically. The teacher must take advantage of situations that arise and also arrange situations that require children to evaluate what they hear and read. Teachers should develop classroom atmospheres that encourage a questioning attitude, while exercising care not to produce skeptics who challenge everything.

Critical thinking or reading cannot simply be taught in a special course of study alone. It must be learned as a way of reacting in many situations beginning early in life, continuing through the elementary school, and intensifying in high school and college. There are, however, skills related to critical reading that can and should be taught. The following are some suggestions for teaching these skills. Other suggestions may be found in the sources listed below.[12]

Evaluating the Author. Two books on natural history are found to differ on the behavior of rattlesnakes. One is by a professor of zoology with twenty years of post-Ph.D. experience; the other is written by a journalist who has written books for popular consumption in a wide variety of fields. Which is likely to be correct? Is the former leader of a political party or a professional historian more likely to give an unbiased account of a political campaign? While an author's background and reputation are not infallible indicators of his reliability,

[12] Martha King, Bernice D. Ellinger, and Willavene Wolf, Eds., *Readings in Critical Reading* (Philadelphia: Lippincott, 1967).

Dorris Lee, Alma Bingham, and Sue Woelfel, *Critical Reading Develops Early* (Newark, Del.: International Reading Association, 1968).

Russel Stauffer and Ronald Cramer, *Teaching Critical Reading at the Primary Level* (Newark, Del.: International Reading Association, 1968).

they certainly help in judging the probability that his writing is accurate. Children can learn to find out how an author's background may influence his writing, and can look up well-known authors in encyclopedias and current biographical sources such as *Who's Who in America*. Similarly, children should learn to check the copyright date of a publication. Authors have been known to change their minds, and what may have been a scientific fact twenty years ago may no longer be regarded as such.

Comparing Different Versions. Trust in the necessary truth of printed sources of information can be quickly altered when the reader compares two versions in which the same topic is discussed from contrasting points of view. When newspapers of differing political viewpoints are available, their treatments of partisan issues can make enlightening reading that points up the need for critical evaluation and careful comparison. In how many American schools do children compare a British version of the American Revolution with a locally approved history textbook? How much alike are the treatments of the War Between the States as described in history books used in the South and the Civil War as described in history books used in the North? Because this kind of experience sometimes has repercussions in the form of irate parents, many schools have been shy about exposing children to contrasting versions, especially when one of them is known to be locally unpopular. Yet this kind of experience is important if future citizens are to be able to judge what to believe and what not to believe about important issues.

Learning to Detect Propaganda Techniques. There are several well-known propaganda techniques with which teachers should be acquainted, and which they can help older children to learn to recognize. The word *propaganda* simply means promoting a particular doctrine or set of ideas; in itself there is no implication of wrongdoing. It is when the propagandist intentionally distorts and subtly misrepresents that the reader should be alert to detect the signs of falsification. The Institute of Propaganda Analysis called attention to seven types of distortion that careful readers should be able to recognize.

1. *Name-calling.* People or ideas can be made unpopular by identifying them with unpopular labels (e.g., Communist, radical, atheist) whether the label fits or not.
2. *Glittering generalities.* Political victories have been built on slogans such as "a chicken in every pot," so vague as to be almost meaningless.
3. *The plain-folks device.* Here the writer or speaker tries to get his audience to accept him as one of themselves and to regard his opponents as outsiders.
4. *Testimonials.* The endorsement of an idea, a person, or a product by a well-known and respected individual loses its validity when the endorser does it for pay and obviously is not expert on the subject.
5. *Identification with prestige.* Names of prominent people are frequently used to give authority to a particular idea.
6. *The band-wagon effect.* The idea that "everybody's doing it" persuades many people to follow suit, and so majority support is often claimed long before it is attained.
7. *Card-stacking.* This refers to the many ways of distorting facts and misusing statistics to favor a particular conclusion. One of the commonest is the "dangling comparative"—"twice as fast," "three ways better," etc.—without specifying faster than what or better than what. Surveys and opinion polls have at times been planned in advance to favor a particular outcome.

The teacher who recognizes the dangers of ignorance and gullibility about propaganda techniques can easily collect current samples and bring them into class for discussion. Unfortunately, knowing about propaganda techniques does not ensure that a person will recognize them or necessarily prevent him from being influenced; but it at least gives him a chance.

REMEMBERING WHAT ONE READS

While there are inherent differences in natural retentiveness of memory, teachers can help children to improve their efficiency in remembering. Some of the relevant principles have already been discussed. The child who actively looks for main ideas is more likely to remember them than the child who just reads. Details are more easily remembered when they are related to a main idea than when treated as isolated, independent units. Material that is understood is more easily remembered than material which is memorized parrot-fashion. Also important is the intent to remember.

The most important single technique that improves recall is stopping after each section and attempting to recite the content to oneself; if necessary, rereading all or part of the section and again testing one's ability to remember the main idea and significant details. If this one technique were generally practiced, retention of what is read would be far better than it is today.

If material is learned in the first place, it can be kept from fading from memory by reviewing at strategic intervals. Without opportunities to review and use what is learned, forgetting is practically inevitable.

In determining whether a child can remember what he has read, it should be understood that most daily lessons as well as standardized reading achievement tests only sample the child's immediate recall. Just as with reading printed directions, there is little need, and therefore little intent, to remember such information for any length of time. A child may be quite good at answering questions on material that he has just read, but have difficulty remembering the information over a period of time. Such deficiencies are likely to become evident in the content subjects, particularly in the upper grades.

Relating Rate to Comprehension

In the primary grades there is a positive relationship between rate and comprehension. Both are dependent mainly on the speed and accuracy of word recognition. The children who have to puzzle over words and to reread to correct mistakes not only are slow in getting through the material but also have difficulty in getting the ideas, partly because of misread words, but mainly because of the many interruptions in their trains of thought. Speed improves naturally as reading becomes increasingly accurate and fluent.

There are many possible reasons why a child may be a slow reader, such as faulty reading habits, poor comprehension (rate is also influenced to some extent by the rapidity with which one can comprehend the ideas presented), and inflexible rate which may be due to lack of training. Before attempting to improve rate of reading it often is necessary to determine why the child is having difficulty in this area.[13]

COORDINATING RATE WITH COMPREHENSION

In the middle and upper grades one finds all possible combinations of rate and comprehension. The correlations between rate and comprehension vary with the kind of material read, but in general they are low. There is a slight tendency for fast readers to comprehend well and for slow readers to comprehend less well, but there are many exceptions to this generalization. Thus one finds all possible combinations of rate and comprehension: rapid-accurate, rapid-inaccurate, average-accurate, average-inaccurate, slow-accurate, and slow-inaccurate.

When children are both slow and inaccurate, the material being used is probably too difficult for them. They usually need easier material, not above their instructional level, with which they can be helped to improve word recognition, to enlarge their vocabularies, and to read for meaning. Any direct attention to rate should be delayed until there has been substantial improvement in the basic underlying skills. There is some doubt as to the efficacy of direct efforts to improve reading rate before the sixth-reader level, and extreme doubt as to its advisability in the primary grades. Beginning with the sixth grade most children should benefit from direct instruction and practice.

Children who read slowly but very accurately can often learn to read considerably faster without loss in comprehension. Some flashed practice with words and phrases can help to build motivation. A series of timed reading exercises with comprehension checks usually brings a substantial improvement in rate. Each child keeps a chart of his rate and comprehension, and rate usually goes up while comprehension tends, with some fluctuations, to remain fairly constant.

The rapid, inaccurate reader needs experiences in which, by taking

---

[13] For a comprehensive discussion of how to diagnose and improve reading rate see: Albert J. Harris, *How to Increase Reading Ability*, 5th ed. (New York: McKay, 1970), pp. 480–513.

comprehension tests, he becomes aware of his inaccuracy and interested in overcoming it. Often the desire to improve the comprehension scores is sufficient to bring about better attention to meaning. A graph or chart showing the child's scores on successive practice exercises gives the child an incentive to try to keep his scores going up.

A set of workbooks that have been used widely for many years is quite useful in bringing rate and comprehension into balance.[14] Each one-page exercise (see Figure 39) is read with a three-minute time limit, within which the child reads the passage and answers as many questions as he can. The G scores at the bottom of the page are really grade-equivalent scores and provide a powerful motivation for trying to improve. Rapid, inaccurate readers tend to finish but to get low scores because of many wrong answers. Slow, accurate readers tend to get low scores because they do not answer enough questions. With repeated use of the exercises, each child learns to adjust his rate so as to come out with the best possible score. Some slow down, while many find that they can speed up without any loss in accuracy. Nearly all children will show gains, including those whose scores were high to begin with. Intense concentration during the short practice period helps to build the habit of reading with full attention.

ACHIEVING FLEXIBILITY IN RATE

Beyond the primary grades, the relationship between rate and comprehension becomes somewhat specialized. Rapid reading is an advantage when there is a large amount of reading matter to be covered, and mastering details is less important than learning generalizations, getting main ideas, and understanding relationships and implications. Slow reading is advantageous when the reading material is quite difficult or requires an exact and complete comprehension, as in much scientific and mathematical reading.

A really efficient reader varies his rate of reading according to his purpose for reading and according to the nature of the reading material. Four main rates can be distinguished: skimming, rapid reading,

---

[14] William A. McCall and Lelah M. Crabbs, *Standard Test Lessons in Reading*. See page 327 for a description of these workbooks and other materials.

—◇ **45** ◇—

Long before the days of printing, minstrels wandered from castle to castle singing before kings and their retainers. Their songs were usually about the character and brave deeds of a real hero. Often these minstrels, these "gleemen," used their imagination and added mythical deeds. No one at that time attempted to write down these tales, for few knew how to write. The stories were originally handed down by word of mouth, very much in the same way as were the legends of the American Indians. But about A.D. 700 the stories relating to the brave deeds of a hero, Beowulf, were collected by some Anglo-Saxon poet of the time. This poem has since been translated into modern English and today we can enjoy reading the first epic poem in English literature. Beowulf fought two dreadful fights to save a king and one to save his own people.

1. This first epic poem in English literature was written (a) too long ago to remember (b) during the last century (c) when America was discovered (d) after the birth of Christ

2. The selection states that minstrels' songs were usually about the (a) beauties of the country (b) benevolence of a king (c) brave deeds of some hero (d) adventures of a prince

3. Beowulf (a) fought (b) sang (c) collected stories (d) wrote an epic poem

4. Beowulf (a) wandered from castle to castle (b) translated Anglo-Saxon (c) lived before A.D. 700 (d) was a "gleeman"

5. Changes were sometimes made because (a) the king forbade the minstrels to sing (b) the "gleemen" used their imaginations (c) people wrote the songs incorrectly (d) poets sang to please the retainers

6. The best one-word title for the selection is (a) Epic (b) Poem (c) Beowulf (d) Anglo-Saxon

7. The poem Beowulf was originally written in (a) German (b) Anglo-Saxon (c) English (d) French

8. Beowulf was the name of (a) a brave man (b) an Anglo-Saxon (c) a "gleeman" (d) a wandering minstrel

9. Minstrels were (a) translators of English literature (b) servants to the king (c) writers of Anglo-Saxon (d) traveling poets and singers

10. The poem Beowulf was handed down (a) by kings (b) by retainers (c) in English (d) in Old English

No. right	0	1	2	3	4	5	6	7	8	9	10
G score	3.8	4.1	4.5	4.8	5.2	5.6	6.1	6.5	7.0	7.8	8.8

FIGURE 39. An exercise to coordinate rate with comprehension. (From William A. McCall and Lelah M. Crabbs, *Standard Test Lessons in Reading*, Book D. 1961 Edition, p. 45. New York: Bureau of Publications, Teachers College, Columbia University.) Reproduced by permission of the publishers.

normal reading, and careful reading. The kinds of reading situations in which each of these is appropriate are listed in Figure 40. The consistently slow reader who uses a careful rate for everything is like an auto always running in low gear; the consistently rapid reader may have trouble climbing steep reading hills.

Children can be helped to vary their rates of reading according to the situation. They can try reading a page in a story the way they read a page in their arithmetic textbook. They can try reading an arithmetic page as they read a story. The desirability of employing different speeds for different kinds of material is easily demonstrated, and then children can try reading a particular book at different speeds to find the rate that seems to bring the best results. Because the rate at which one reads should be influenced by the purpose for reading that material, children should learn to set their own purposes for reading and to adjust their rates accordingly.

Materials for Practice in Comprehension

In addition to the questioning suggested in the manuals and the comprehension exercises in the workbooks that accompany the materials being used for reading instruction, there is a considerable amount of independent material that can be used to give additional practice in comprehension.

MULTIPLE-PURPOSE EXERCISES

There are a number of workbooks in which each exercise contains several kinds of questions, intended to encourage development of balanced comprehension skills.

Guiler, W. S., and Coleman, J. H. *Reading for Meaning.* Philadelphia: Lippincott. Separate workbooks for grades 6 to 12. Each selection is followed by vocabulary and several types of comprehension questions.

Johnson, Eleanor M., Ed. *Diagnostic Reading Workbooks.* Columbus: Charles E. Merrill. Series of workbooks for grades 1 to 6. Each selection is followed by several types of comprehension questions.

Leavell, U. V., *et al. New Goals in Reading.* Reading Essentials Series.

Skimming		Rapid		Normal		Careful	
Work	Recreatory	Work	Recreatory	Work	Recreatory	Work	Recreatory
To get gist of material To find a reference To locate new material To refresh memory To answer a question	Looking over books, magazines, etc., to get gist of thought To pick out a story to read Reading pictures To review a familiar book or story	To get general idea of content To find specific reference To locate material To review familiar material To get information for temporary use	Reading of familiar narrative for relaxation Informational material for pleasure or relaxation At movies Reading pictures. To reread familiar material	To get details of material To get main thought Reading new material When material is of ordinary difficulty To solve a problem To answer a question To find a new problem To locate a reference To locate new material To commit to memory To supplement thought	For relaxation To keep in touch with current events To know a new story To satisfy sense of humor For devotional purposes To memorize	To master content including details To evaluate material To raise questions To answer questions or problems To get directions for performing an act To outline To summarize To reproduce To analyze thought To remove difficulties of thought or form To supplement thought To solve a problem	When important factual articles are read To search for particular effects To judge literary or other values To supplement thought For spiritual guidance When classical material with unusual words is met To memorize poetry

FIGURE 40. Life uses of reading classified according to rate. (Reproduced by permission of the author from Yoakam, Gerald A., *Reading and Study*, p. 69. New York: The Macmillan Co., 1928.)

Austin: Steck-Vaughn. A workbook of approximately third- or fourth-reader level difficulty intended for remedial use above fourth grade. Exercises involve a variety of word recognition, vocabulary, and comprehension items.

New Reading Skill Builder Series. Pleasantville, N.Y.: Reader's Digest Services, Inc. Two or three booklets for each grade, 1 to 6. Contain adapted *Reader's Digest* stories, each followed by various types of comprehension questions. Attractive to retarded readers because of their mature appearance and content.

New Reading Skilltext Series. Columbus: Charles E. Merrill. Separate workbooks for grades 1 to 6. Each selection followed by various types of questions.

Parker, Don H. *SRA Reading Laboratories.* Chicago: Science Research Associates. Nine different kits, each with a spread of readability levels. Each kit consists of: (1) "Power Builders," short selections followed by questions on word analysis, vocabulary, and comprehension; (2) "Rate Builders," a series of very short selections followed by multiple choice questions (each exercise has a time limit of three minutes); and (3) a series of listening skill exercises and lessons.

Sanford, Adrian B., *et al. Reading Comprehension.* The Macmillan Spectrum. New York: Macmillan. Series of six programmed workbooks covering a variety of comprehension skills. Difficulty ranges from third- to sixth-reader level.

Smith, Nila B. *Be a Better Reader,* Foundations, Books A, B, C (grades 4 to 6) and *Be a Better Reader,* Books 1–6 (grades 7 to 12). Englewood Cliffs, N.J.: Prentice-Hall. Workbooks containing a wide variety of exercises on word recognition, vocabulary, comprehension, and study skills. Particularly suitable for teaching reading and study skills needed in content subjects.

Stone, Clarence R., Grover, Charles C., *et al. New Practice Readers.* St. Louis: Webster Division, McGraw-Hill. Books A–G (grades 2–8). Each booklet contains short selections, each preceded by a vocabulary introduction and followed by vocabulary and six comprehension questions of various types.

SINGLE-PURPOSE EXERCISES

Some workbooks provide concentrated practice on one comprehension skill at a time. In some of these, the whole workbook is devoted to one kind of of exercise. In others, each section of the workbook contains a series of exercises on a different kind of reading skill.

Boning, Richard A. *Specific Skills Series.* Rockville Centre, N.Y.: Barnell Loft Ltd. Workbooks of primary and intermediate grade difficulty. Series of six workbooks each for getting main ideas, getting facts, drawing conclusions, following directions, and locating answers.

Gates, Arthur I., and Peardon, Celeste C. *Gates-Peardon Reading Exercises.* Rev. ed. New York: Teachers College Press, Columbia University. Separate books for four levels of difficulty (grades 2–5). For grades 2 and 3 each selection is followed by three types of questions; main idea, following directions, and details. For grades 4 and 5 there are separate booklets for each type of comprehension.

McCall, W. A., and Crabbs, L. M. *Standard Test Lessons in Reading,* Revised. New York: Teachers College Press, Columbia University. Five booklets ranging from approximately third- to sixth-reader level in difficulty. Each contains 78 one-page exercises. Three minutes are given to read the short selection and answer the multiple-choice questions. Rough grade norms are supplied.

Simpson, Elizabeth A. *SRA Better Reading Books,* Rev. ed. Chicago: Science Research Associates. Series of four workbooks for reading level 5–6, 7–8, 9–10, and 11–13. Each exercise, which is to be timed, contains a selection followed by a comprehension check.

Thurstone, Thelma G. *Reading for Understanding.* Chicago: Science Research Associates. Two kits, one with a readability spread of grades 3–8; the other with a spread of 5–12. Each kit contains 400 lesson cards arranged in 100 steps of difficulty with four cards at each level. Primarily stresses inferential reading.

DEVICES FOR INCREASING READING RATE

A number of devices are available for providing direct practice to increase speed of recognition and reading rate. Although such devices may serve to motivate students, there is some question as to the carryover of such training to actual reading situations, and to the retention of initial gains.

Tachistoscopes are devices that allow brief presentation of visual stimuli, usually numbers, words, or short phrases. These devices range in complexity from simple handmade cardboard ones [15] to hand

---

[15] For directions for making one type, see Albert J. Harris, *How to Increase Reading Ability,* 5th ed. (New York: McKay, 1970), p. 190. Also see pp. 500–503 for descriptions of commercially produced tachistoscopes and pacing devices.

tachistoscopes powered by simple springs or levers, to projectors with variable speeds.

Other mechanical devices are available for controlling or pacing reading rate. There are special projectors that show a line or a part of a line at a time, motion picture films that primarily do the same as the preceding, and pacers that gradually cover a page of printed material through the use of a shutter or beam of light.

Many problems involving poor reading rate can be overcome by placing major emphasis on increased motivation in normal reading situations. Such a program involves three steps: (1) overcoming specific interfering factors and habits; (2) motivating the children to do large amounts of reading in easy materials to develop fluency; and (3) a series of timed silent reading exercises followed by comprehension checks. In the last step, which should be done on a spaced periodic basis, each child charts his own progress. Concurrently, the children should be given practice in setting their own purposes for reading particular material, and in flexibility of reading rate.

ASSEMBLING PRACTICE MATERIALS

Workbooks can become a substantial budgetary item, particularly those in which children write so that they can be used only once, and in some schools quantity orders for workbooks are not allowed. Since some of the best available material for sharpening comprehension skills is in workbook form, assembling a collection of comprehension exercises, varied both in type and in difficulty level, often presents problems.

One solution is to cut workbooks up into separate exercise units. Several workbooks appropriate for the class can be selected, and three copies apiece can be ordered. Two copies are cut down the center so that each sheet is separate. Each exercise is mounted inside a transparent plastic folder or envelope. When each page is a separate exercise, both sides go in one folder, and there are two copies of each exercise. When an exercise is on facing pages, they are placed back to back inside a folder, and two workbooks supply one set of exercises.

Exercises of more than two pages can be mounted in manila folders. If a teacher edition with answers printed in it is available, that is the third copy and serves as a set of answer keys; otherwise, the teacher fills out a third regular copy in red pencil and that becomes the answer key.

A simple classification scheme can be worked out, in which the kind of exercise is represented by a number and the difficulty level by a letter. Exercises from a variety of sources can be combined in one sequence and filed in grocery-carton file boxes.

Sometimes the transparent cover is heavy enough so that children can write their answers directly over the dotted lines with crayon, and this can be wiped off so that the exercise can be used a great many times. Otherwise the children can write their answers on separate paper or in a notebook.

Teachers sometimes feel a need for more exercises of a particular kind or for a kind of exercise that they cannot find in print. Magazine articles can be mounted and supplied with suitable comprehension questions. Teacher-made exercises can be modeled after printed examples or can take quite original forms. An exercise worth preparing is worth mounting in such a way that it can be used over and over.

A collection of practice exercises such as has just been described is obviously intended for individualized practice, since there is usually only one copy of each exercise available. A group or a whole class can be doing comprehension exercises at the same time, but each will be doing a different exercise, preferably to develop a skill in which he needs improvement.

Summary

1. Reading comprehension is a complex process.
   a. Basic to good comprehension are the abilities to recognize words, to know their meanings, and to interpret thought units.
   b. Once the mechanical skills are learned, comprehension becomes increasingly involved with many higher-level thinking skills.

   c. Practice to develop the basic and higher level comprehension skills is given major attention in most basal reader programs.

2. Attention should be given to the mastery of thought units of increasing size and complexity. Suggestions for doing so were made in this chapter.

3. Listening comprehension and reading comprehension are highly related.

   a. Improving children's receptive language skills is likely to result in improved reading comprehension.

   b. Instruction in listening comprehension should be an integral part of a total language arts program.

4. In most basal-reader programs, comprehension is stressed from the first grade on.

   a. Teachers in the primary grades provide questions to guide reading that is followed by discussion.

   b. Teachers need to stress questions that arouse thinking rather than those which simply require a verbatim account of what the book said.

   c. Exercises in basal-reader workbooks provide varied kinds of comprehension checks.

5. There are three levels of comprehension: literal, inferential, and evaluative.

6. Recent research supports the desirability of providing practice in a variety of comprehension skills. Ten different kinds of comprehension skills have been discussed and ways of developing them have been described: understanding main ideas, locating answers to specific questions, reading for details, grasping the sequence of events, following directions, grasping the author's plan and intent, anticipating outcomes, making inferences, critical reading, and remembering what one reads.

7. Reading rate and comprehension are interrelated.

   a. Some children read too slowly for good comprehension; others habitually read too quickly.

   b. Techniques are available to bring rate and comprehension into balance, as well as for developing increased rate and flexibility of rate.

   c. The good reader varies his rate according to his purpose for reading and the nature of the material.

8. There is a wide variety of material that can be used to improve reading comprehension, including many specialized workbooks.

   a. Teachers can assemble a file of practice exercises from various sources, including exercises they construct themselves.

   b. Highly individualized comprehension practice is possible when individualized materials are at hand.

9. There are a number of devices available for increasing reading rate.

   a. Such devices should be used judiciously.

   b. Many problems of poor reading rate probably can be overcome by placing major emphasis on increased motivation in normal reading situations.

Recommended Reading

BEERY, ALTHEA, BARRETT, THOMAS C., and POWELL, WILLIAM R. *Elementary Reading Instruction: Selected Materials*. Boston: Allyn and Bacon, 1969. Ch. 7.

HARRIS, ALBERT J. *How to Increase Reading Ability*, 5th ed. New York: McKay, 1970. Chs. 16, 18.

HARRIS, ALBERT J., ED. *Readings on Reading Instruction*. New York: McKay, 1963. Ch. 10.

HEILMAN, ARTHUR W. *Principles and Practices of Teaching Reading*, 2nd ed. Columbus: Charles E. Merrill, 1967. Ch. 14.

SMITH, NILA B. *Reading Instruction for Today's Children*. Englewood Cliffs, N.J.: Prentice-Hall, 1963. Chs. 9, 11, 24.

STAUFFER, RUSSELL G. *Directing Reading Maturity as a Cognitive Process*. New York: Harper & Row, 1969. Ch. 10.

12

Developing
Efficiency in Functional Reading

Each of the three major parts of a total reading program—developmental, functional, and recreational—plays an important role. Developmental reading is not an end in itself, but lays the foundation for success in utilizing reading. The skills learned in the developmental strand are utilized for two main purposes—reading to learn (functional reading) and reading for pleasure (recreational reading). Many children pass successfully through school without ever developing a deep and abiding love of reading as a recreational activity. This situation is unfortunate; however, it does not prevent children from succeeding in school. Children cannot succeed in school without learning to read for information, an ability that requires more than simply applying the reading skills learned in the developmental strand. Functional reading skills become increasingly more important as children progress through school; a third grader may get along without such skills, but a seventh grader would find it extremely difficult to do so. Reading has been, and will continue to be for some time to come, the most necessary tool of intellectual inquiry and learning.

As defined in this book, functional reading includes those activities in which reading functions as a tool in the learning process. Others have preferred to use such terms as *work-type reading, study-type reading,* or the *work-study skills.* These terms can generally be used interchangeably.

The first of the five sections of this chapter deals with the development of skills needed in locating information. Considered in the second section are the application of general comprehension skills to studying and various kinds of informational reading, and the development of specific reading techniques needed in specific subjects. The third section discusses the techniques of organizing and summarizing, while the fourth section is concerned with study habits, which determine whether the child's reading skills will be effectively used. Materials that may be used for teaching and practicing the skills discussed in this chapter are described in the final section.

Learning to Locate Information

The ability to locate needed information is a vitally important tool. A well-educated person does not have to memorize the thousands of facts he may need at one time or another. For most purposes, it is quite satisfactory to know what sources of information to consult, where to find them, and how to discover the needed information in them.

MASTERING ALPHABETICAL ORDER

Many sources of information use an alphabetical arrangement of items, so that the ability to locate items quickly in an alphabetical sequence is a very useful skill. Alphabetical sequences are employed in dictionaries, glossaries, directories, encyclopedias, and in indexes of many kinds. Beginning work on alphabetizing often starts in the first grade, with the arrangement of word cards according to first letter; sometimes by second letter also.

Systematic instruction in alphabetization usually is given as an introduction to use of the dictionary, which may begin with picture dictionaries in the first grade. The first step is to determine the extent to which each child knows the complete alphabet in correct sequence. This can be done by asking the class to write the alphabet. Each child who is unable to do so may then be asked individually (apart from the rest of the class) to recite the alphabet. Some children, particularly first graders, are unable to write or print the letters, but do know the correct sequence.

As with most skills, wide variations occur. Some children will have complete knowledge, while others may not even know the names of the letters, let alone their alphabetical sequence. Therefore, instruction may need to be varied. With some children, the teacher may need to start by presenting a letter (probably "a" and following along in alphabetical order) and teaching them to associate the letter name with the printed symbol. For those who know letter names, but not alphabetical order, instruction may involve placing three to five letters in correct sequence until the complete alphabetical order is learned. Charts showing the alphabet may be helpful; and, although it simply involves rote memory, singing the alphabet jingle in unison aids some children.

Once the alphabet is known in sequence, it is desirable for children to learn where letters belong without having to recite the sequence from the start. The teacher can go around the room, asking such questions as: What letter follows *p?* What letter comes before *h?* What letter comes between *b* and *d?* Exercises with many questions of this type can be duplicated and used for individual, group, or class practice.

Next, children can learn to arrange words in sequence according to first letter, if they have not already mastered that skill. It is advisable to try a pretest of about ten words, each starting with a different letter, before doing any systematic teaching and practice. Help can be given on a whole-class, group, or individual basis, depending on the number of children who need it. From arranging according to first letter they go on to words which have the same first letter and differ in the second letter. They can start with pairs of words like: *apple, axe; bread, book,* etc., deciding which should come first in each pair. Then they can be given a series of words differing in second letter, such as: *copper, candle, cute, center, cradle,* etc. When they can do this well, the same general procedure can be used with the third letter: first, pairs of words like *bring, brake; strung, string;* then a series

starting with the same two letters, like *read, rewrite, reduce, remind.*
After the basic knowledge of alphabetical sequence has been
learned, some practice in applying it in specific situations can be
developed. The dictionary is the natural place to start. To find words
quickly, the child should be able to open the dictionary somewhere
near the entry; decide whether he has to turn forward or backward;
use the guide words at the top of the page to locate the page the
word is on; and then skim down the columns to find the word.

To make practice of this kind interesting, it can be done under
timed conditions, with each child recording his own time and trying
to make it grow less in successive practice sessions. A simple way to
do this is to write a list of ten or twenty assorted words on the board.
At a signal, all start looking in their dictionaries, and as they locate
each word, write the page and the immediately preceding word. As
each child finishes he looks up and copies a number, which the teacher
has been changing every half minute.

Once skill in locating words in the dictionary has been achieved, it
is usually not necessary to have similar practice sessions in other
kinds of alphabetized references except as noted below. Usually it
suffices to point out to most children that they can apply the same
skills in using any reference set up in alphabetical order.

The Index. In using the card index of a library, children need
specific information about the ways in which books are indexed. In
many card indexes, books are entered by author's name, by title, and
by topic. Some of the questions that may puzzle children are illustrated by the following: Can one find a book about Abraham Lincoln
without knowing either the author's name or the exact title? If so,
should one look in the A's or in the L's? What do you do when the
author has a last name that is shared by many other authors? Why
do you have to copy down the number on the index card? Can you
tell from the index card where to look for the book in the library?

The indexes of books can present problems also. Some indexes are
carefully made, so that if you want to locate information about the
legibility of letters (of the alphabet), you can find the relevant pages
listed under both *legibility* and *letters.* In other indexes, there would
be a brief notation: *letters, see legibility.* Sometimes checking both

words is the only way to be sure to get the necessary information. If a child needs to find out the value of the annual tobacco crop in Virginia, should he look first under *value, annual, tobacco, crop,* or *Virginia?* Why? Practice in discussing and solving problems of this kind can greatly improve efficiency in using an index.

Certain specific kinds of information about indexing should be explained to children. For example, *a* and *the* are disregarded in alphabetizing items. With items like *Kingdom of Portugal* and *Isle of Wight,* the proper name takes priority: *Portugal, Kingdom of,* and *Wight, Isle of.* Not all children discover these details for themselves. Children need opportunities to practice locating information in indexes and to seek help from the teacher when they are puzzled.

Reference Works. An encyclopedia of many volumes is an invaluable source of information, but learning how to locate an answer to a specific question in one is helped by some guidance. The index usually occupies all or most of the last volume and may be so complex that children accustomed to simpler indexes will need assistance. Sometimes the list of subheadings under a topic is almost a little index in itself. The continuity of paging from one volume to the next may be confusing. The alphabet guide on the spine of each volume requires a new application of alphabetizing: is *Mississippi River* to be found in LEUX-MEND or in MEND-NEGR? If you want information about what civil engineers do, should you look up *civil* or *engineering* or *professions?* The teaching sequence of skills needed in locating entries in encyclopedias and other similar works should include: (1) learning what types of information can be found in various reference works; (2) deciding under which heading or entries the information is likely to be found; (3) locating the correct volume in works of more than one volume; and (4) interpreting commonly used abbreviations.

Each of the skills mentioned above can be organized into a sequence of relatively brief, sequential lessons. At each higher grade these skills should be tested, reviewed if necessary, and brought to a higher level of efficiency.

There are many kinds of reference works with which children should become acquainted before they get into senior high school.

These include atlases, almanacs, yearbooks, *Reader's Guide to Periodical Literature,* a biographical dictionary, a thesaurus, etc. An introduction to each of these by a teacher or librarian can open up a new avenue for independent learning.

The technique of skimming for information was discussed in Chapter 11. This specialized kind of reading skill finds its greatest use in the search for information in special reference works and can be developed by using for practice the kinds of books in which the skill is usually employed.

Developing Functional Comprehension Skills

Word recognition, vocabulary, and comprehension skills that are the outcomes of developmental reading activities provide a necessary foundation upon which functional reading skills can be built. It is necessary to build upon these skills because even if one could expect the developmental skills to transfer directly to reading in the content areas, they would not be sufficient for functional reading. Most of the material in some basal readers, which can well serve as a vehicle for developing basic skills, is of a narrative type. As such, it does not lend itself to the development of all the skills necessary for success in the content subjects. Content subject materials require that the reader be able to interpret expository material. Aside from the fact that other skills, such as study skills, are important, the possible difficulty a child may meet is shown by studies that have indicated that content subject texts may be more difficult than the grade-level designations assigned to them by the publishers.[1]

Even these approximations may be misleading because they were based on the application of readability formulas, none of which considers concept load as a factor. Most content subject material is compact with a high concept density. Many concepts, which are often interrelated and perhaps cumulative, are presented, and at a much

---

[1] For a review of the literature in this area see Samuel Weintraub, "Research," *Reading Teacher,* 21 (December, 1967), 283–285; and Betty Daniel Roe, "Readability of Elementary School Textbooks," *Journal of the Reading Specialist,* 9 (May 1970), 163–167.

more rapid pace than encountered in narrative material. It is indeed difficult, if not impossible, to write about complex ideas without using complex terms, sentences, and paragraphs. To understand and make use of the information requires the application of known skills and the acquisition of special reading-study skills.

Functional reading involves learning specialized vocabularies, learning to use basic comprehension skills in content areas, developing specialized reading skills required in certain content subjects, and learning the skills of organizing and recording.

LEARNING SPECIALIZED VOCABULARIES

Each important content area makes use of many technical terms. As Smith has pointed out, specialized vocabulary is of four types.[2] First are the "readily identifiable words"—those that have significance only in a particular field: *adverb, divisor,* and *electrode.* Children often lack an understanding of the concepts for which these words are labels. The second type, which usually causes less of a problem, are the "overlap words" whose fundamental meanings do not vary greatly from one field to the next. For example, *group* has basically the same meaning in social studies and mathematics. Another type may be classed as "polysemantic words" that have acquired specialized meanings in different subjects: the *product* obtained in multiplication is different from the *product* of a factory. These differences may need to be pointed out to children. Lastly, are the "little words" whose meanings may change from one subject to another. In a sentence in English, *are* indicates existence; in an arithmetic text it means *equals.* Teaching the meanings of such words is often overlooked.

The Teacher's Handbook of Technical Vocabulary [3] is still a very useful reference for teachers, although it is now more than thirty years old. It includes lists of essential elementary terms and concepts

---

[2] Nila B. Smith, *Reading Instruction for Today's Children* (Englewood Cliffs, N.J.: Prentice Hall, 1963), pp. 342–344.

[3] Luella Cole, *The Teacher's Handbook of Technical Vocabulary* (Bloomington, Ill.: Public School Publishing Co., 1940). Out of print.

in thirteen school subjects: arithmetic, algebra, plane geometry, English composition, foreign language, American literature, geography, American history, hygiene, general science, chemistry, physics, and biology. The words are classified under subheadings: for example, in arithmetic the headings are nomenclature of fundamental processes with integers, fractions, units of measure, practical measurement, words used in problems concerning retail buying, abbreviations, signs and symbols, and words used in banking, investment, and business. For each word the Thorndike rating is given, indicating the comparative frequency of use.

It was stressed in Chapter 10 that clear, accurate concepts call for a linking to children's experience and require careful illustration and development. Knowing which concepts are essential is a great help in deciding which concepts require careful teaching; the teacher can concentrate on them and make sure that the basic concepts of the subject, and the terms representing them, are mastered. Teachers can often decide how important a concept is from their own knowledge; when in doubt, a reference list is useful.

APPLYING COMPREHENSION SKILLS IN CONTENT AREAS

The comprehension skills that are begun in the developmental reading program can be utilized in functional reading of many kinds, and teachers can do much to make this effective.

Trying the Textbook on for Size. Practical techniques for determining the instructional and independent reading levels of children in basal readers were described in Chapter 6. The same kind of procedure can be used to determine the suitability of content textbooks.

Ability to comprehend the text can be tested by selecting a typical section of the textbook, preparing a set of comprehension questions for it, and giving it as a class silent reading test. After the answers have been marked, they can be discussed. The children who make comprehension scores lower than 70 percent may need a great deal of help with the book, or it may be utterly beyond them. They can be asked to read part of the test selection orally to the teacher, to check further on how difficult the book is for them. If it is unquestionably above their frustration levels, as is often true, special measures will be necessary if they are to have a fair chance to learn the subject. The other children whose comprehension scores are less than 100 percent will have less serious difficulty, but they also will need some guidance.

Even when content subject texts are of a suitable level of difficulty, instruction needs to be given on how to use the material.

TEACHING READING WITH CONTENT TEXTBOOKS

Some teachers who find that a textbook is quite hard for some of the pupils resort to oral reading as a way of "covering" the book. They go around the class, calling on one child after another to read a portion. Better readers are given longer and harder passages to read; poor readers are either given short, easy selections or are not called on. This procedure does give every child an opportunity to hear what is in the book; but otherwise it has little to recommend it. It becomes as boring, monotonous, and threatening to the poor reader as the read-around-the-room kind of oral reading using basal readers. So much time is spent in oral reading that little time remains for developing concepts and for discussion.

A better plan is to use a methodology with content textbooks very much like that ordinarily followed with basal readers. The usual four-step procedure has been described in detail, as applied in primary, middle, and upper grades, in Chapters 3 and 4. With some adaptation, the same steps provide an effective instructional plan for subject-matter textbooks also.

Preparation involves tying in with previous experience, teaching new concepts and words, and providing motivation for reading ahead. When children are lacking in related experience, visual aids such as movies, filmstrips, and slides can often be used effectively. New words and concepts can be introduced, and a challenging question or two provides a purpose for reading ahead.

The second step—guided reading—usually starts with silent reading. In addition to the purpose-setting questions, additional questions can be asked after reading. This silent reading may be done in class, or it may be assigned as homework. The specific skills one is trying to improve and the nature of the material both help to determine the kinds of questions to use. The nine main varieties of comprehension skills described in Chapter 11 can all be included from time to time.

Depending on the maturity of the children, one can use oral or written questions and call for oral or written answers. When children write out their answers, they should be corrected quickly and any errors in understanding should be discussed and clarified. Children can be asked to reread orally to defend their answers or to locate a reason for their misunderstanding.

Related practice is not always necessary. It can include review and word analysis of new vocabulary. Guided practice in outlining, note-taking, and summarizing, as described later in this chapter, can also occur at this point.

Enrichment activities are optional. Supplementary reading can be suggested or assigned. Many kinds of self-expressive activity can be employed from time to time. Illustrations can be drawn or painted, models can be constructed, experiments can be carried out, and historical events can be dramatized.

Herber suggested the use of a three-step procedure, Instructional Framework, which differs primarily from the typical directed reading activity plan in its use of the "structure within" the lesson.[4] In this "structure within," use is made of reading and study guides that have three elements: (1) reaction to pattern—how to perform a task; (2) attention to transfer—how to transfer the skill to a new but similar situation; and (3) modification of pattern—students are allowed to adapt the skill to suit their personal styles and needs.

Systematic Study Procedure. A systematic study procedure, commonly referred to as SQ3R, was developed by Robinson.[5] The plan, which appears theoretically sound but upon which little research has been done, has five steps: Survey, Question, Read, Recite, and Review. During the survey, the reader attempts to obtain a quick over-

---

[4] Harold L. Herber, *Teaching Reading in Content Areas* (Englewood Cliffs, N.J.: Prentice-Hall, 1970), pp. 28–50.

[5] Francis P. Robinson, *Effective Reading* (New York: Harper & Row, 1962).

view of the material. This preview, which may help to determine how fast the material should be read, may involve reading the table of contents; skimming the introductory and summary paragraphs, as well as the headings; and studying pictorial aids. In order to make reading an active process, the second step requires turning headings, subheadings, or topic sentences into questions. Hopefully, this helps to establish a purpose for reading. The next step involves reading to answer the questions, while taking care not to ignore other important information. Reading is then followed by recitation, which may assume different forms depending upon individual preferences. What one has read may be summarized by underlining, taking notes, outlining, or reciting aloud. This fourth step helps to determine if the material was understood and also provides an immediate review. The final step involves immediate and spaced review in order to aid in remembering the material.

HELPING THOSE WHO CANNOT READ THE TEXTBOOK

When a textbook is so far above the instructional level of certain children that they can do little or no reading in it, teachers have to look for alternatives. Sometimes an easier textbook on the same subject can be found, which can serve in place of the text for those children. Easy trade books dealing with one or another part of the subject matter can be employed. When it is considered essential for the child to learn what is in the particular textbook, the problem can be discussed with parents and it may be practicable for some member of the family to read the book to the child, and discuss and review the information with him. Lessons and materials also may be tape recorded and used by the children, particularly when they have severe reading problems or when it is impossible or unlikely that assistance can be obtained at home. When information is to be acquired through listening, it becomes important to teach children how to listen (see page 301).

Occasionally a teacher finds that a textbook is so difficult that it is above the frustration level for the majority of the class. Under these conditions it is advisable to use the text only as a reference and collection of illustrations, centering the main instructional program around other materials. A project approach to the subject makes it possible to use a wide variety of materials as references on particular issues, rather than follow sequentially through a textbook. Sometimes teachers are reduced to presenting the main factual material themselves, giving lectures and providing dittoed material or putting notes on the board for children to copy. These procedures should be accompanied by discussion and clarification of the concepts involved in the material.

When it is necessary to make adjustments so that children can acquire concepts in ways other than by reading, adjustments also should be made in determining the child's knowledge of the concepts. If tests are used, either the teacher must construct a test that the child can read or administer the test orally. Children are likely to become discouraged if they are learning, but fail the subject simply because they cannot read the tests.

Many children find that the time available in school for studying their textbooks is insufficient. If the child is allowed to take the textbook home, he has an opportunity to reread, to look up words, and to write notes or summarize. If the book is entirely too difficult for him, a member of the family can read it to him or with him. The school that does not allow the child in the middle or upper grades to take his textbooks home is losing a valuable amount of potential learning. This is not a plea for long homework assignments, but rather a recognition that many children need more time for reading and studying their textbooks than the school day provides.

GUIDING INDEPENDENT READING IN CONTENT AREAS

When a project or unit approach is being followed in a particular subject, the main topic is usually divided into several major headings, and each heading becomes the responsibility of a committee. Ordinarily the committees are deliberately set up so as to have a wide range of reading ability in each. In discussion (usually with the help of the teacher) the heading is analyzed into specific issues and questions, and these are organized into an outline of what the committee wants to find out. Then the members of the committee turn to the available printed sources of information.

Of course, the teacher has tried to find and bring into the classroom a large number of books containing information on the project, and these books cover a rather wide range of difficulty. The possibility of children with limited reading ability finding sources that they can really read is usually better this way than it is with the use of a uniform textbook.

The time when children are turning to the references is an excellent time for the teacher to bring in direct instruction and guided practice in locating information and applying their comprehension skills. While the children are perusing books and pamphlets individually, the teacher should arrange to be free to provide help and guidance. Circulating around the room, the teacher can spot the children who are having some difficulty and can confer briefly with them, one at a time. Individual problems in using an index, skimming, determining what is relevant, understanding a book's language, and so on, can be taken up and help can be given that is just what the child needs. Ordinarily these skills will have been previously taught on a whole-class or group basis, but individual help in applying and using these skills can make them functionally effective. Even when a curriculum is centered around covering a textbook, carrying out a project from time to time can be very helpful in providing rich and varied opportunities for putting reading skills to use. Research-type reading skills develop when there is a real need to do research-type reading.

DEVELOPING SPECIALIZED READING SKLLS

Some subjects make use of reading materials that require rather specialized reading procedures. Here it is possible to indicate only a few of these special issues. When a departmentalized form of school organization is in effect, it is each subject teacher's responsibility to help the children to learn how to adapt their basic reading skills to the special requirements of the reading material.

Arithmetic and Mathematics. It will come as a surprise to nobody to learn that the reading of mathematical material has to be done very carefully and exactly. Success in mathematics is dependent upon a number of specialized reading skills. In solving number problems such as $2 + 2 = \square$, one must understand what the symbols mean. To solve written problems necessitates understanding the technical vocabulary and abbreviations used. In addition, because facts are presented in arithmetic problems, the reader must be able to determine which details are significant and to understand their relationship. Furthermore, he must learn to focus on the question asked in the problem because it is this question which determines the significance of the facts given in the problem.

The following is an example of a two-step problem that many children find difficult to solve. "Mrs. Jones had fifteen apples. She sold nine of them and divided the rest equally between Alice and Joan. How many apples did each girl get?" In order to find the answer the child has to understand the following: (1) "the rest" means what was left, or the remainder; (2) therefore one has to subtract what was sold from what he had; (3) "divided . . . equally between" means that each received half of "the rest"; (4) "the rest" is, therefore, to be divided by two. The key operations are suggested by the two expressions indicated by quotation marks above.

There are several ways of reading arithmetical and mathematical problems. One helpful sequence is: (1) read carefully to discover what is wanted as an answer; (2) read again to find what is given; (3) interpret clues to operations that are given by such expressions as *all together, each one, was left,* etc.; (4) decide what operation comes first, and in problems requiring more than one step, what the sequence ought to be; (5) get a trial answer; and (6) check or verify the answer. If the answer is wrong, start over again.

A more general pattern in problem solving is suggested by Spache and Spache.[6] The problem is first read rapidly to obtain a general understanding. This is followed by a second, slower reading to identify the details and their relationships. After the first or second reading, the child should restate the problem in his own words before

[6] George D. Spache and Evelyn B. Spache, *Reading in the Elementary School,* 2nd ed. (Boston: Allyn and Bacon, Inc., 1969), pp. 305–306.

beginning computation. When the problem involves more than one step, the child should, after the second reading, visualize or express the computational steps he intends to take.

When children come out with erroneous or absurd answers to problems, it is often due to incomplete comprehension when reading the problems. Answers are often given in feet instead of yards; the wrong operation is chosen because the problem was misunderstood; and in a large variety of ways, reading errors induce erroneous solutions. When arithmetic reasoning is worse than computation, it can often be helped by treating the difficulty as a specialized form of reading difficulty. Leading the child through the problem sentence by sentence, asking questions that reveal his interpretations and inferences, helps to locate the specific mistakes and to correct the misunderstandings.

When children get into the beginnings of algebra and geometry they really have to learn a new kind of language. The concepts of mathematics are both abstract and very sharply defined. The concepts represented by the equals sign, the meaning of zero, the use of alphabet letters to represent both constants and unknowns, concepts like *congruent* and *parallel* and *perpendicular* are specialized ideas that are fundamental to any understanding of what the operations mean. Concept development is, therefore, extremely important if children are to do more than memorize formulas.

Social Studies. Social studies provide many opportunities for applying basic comprehension skills, particularly the location of information about specific questions, relating details to main ideas, grasping a historical sequence of events, reading to draw cause-effect conclusion, and critical reading. Glib verbalism has at times been allowed to mask emptiness of understanding. A classic example is the high school girl who defined the Civil War as "the war fought with knives." Questioning disclosed that this idea came from a picture in the history text, showing soldiers of that war marching with fixed bayonets. Not having any concept of the meaning of *civil,* she had drawn an incorrect inference. When teachers take care to check on and refine important social studies concepts, such errors do not often arise. The vocabulary found in social science materials, however, may present particular problems because some words have rather abstract or indefinite meanings (e.g., *democracy*).

Social studies books provide a great deal of information by using pictures, maps, graphs, charts, and tables, which are not always explored and interpreted correctly. Pie charts, bar graphs, line graphs, and other kinds of data representation may occur in social studies textbooks well before the interpretation of these ways of presenting data is taken up in mathematics.

In a widely used test of study skills, map-reading ability is tested by asking searching questions about the interpretation of many different kinds of maps: political, topographical, rainfall, population, elevation, etc. The map practice exercises that occur in many workbooks that accompany social studies textbooks often call only for the filling in of blank spaces on outline maps. This can often be done by just copying from a map in the text, without understanding very much of what the map has to tell. If a map is considered to be a form of reading matter, one can approach it in the usual fashion: preparation, including reference to experience, concept development, and motivation; study (silent reading), followed by comprehension questions and discussion. Filling in outlines merely enforces attention to details, without ensuring that understandings are developed.

Similarly, each chart or graph or table can be treated as a reading selection, whose structure needs to be understood, whose concepts need to be mastered, and whose meanings and details are worth exploring. If some maps and charts and graphs are given detailed attention as reading material, the chances are good that other illustrations of the same kind will be read and understood.

Science. Scientific reading, like mathematical reading, usually requires a very careful approach, with considerable time given to thinking about the content. Rereading is sometimes needed because the ideas are too complex to be grasped in one reading. Sometimes rereading is necessary because a sequence needs to be more fully grasped or because the relationship between a generalization and certain details needs clarification.

Diagrams and schematic drawings are often used to depict scientific processes. These are not self-explanatory, and time spent in discussing illustrations and diagrams is as important as time spent in discussing verbal information.

Accounts of experiments and directions for performing experiments provide excellent practice in reading to follow directions. If this is found to be weak, extra practice on following directions can be given, using relatively simple sets of directions to start. The Gates, Peardon *Practice Exercises in Reading,* Book C (see page 328), contains nothing but exercises in reading to follow directions and can be quite useful when extra practice is needed.

Many scientific concepts are very abstract and therefore are hard for children to understand. Children who memorize definitions that they do not comprehend often miss the essential meanings of sentences or paragraphs in which these concepts are important. Careful attention to concept development and careful checking on what children think scientific terms mean is, therefore, at least as important in science as in any other curricular area.

Developing Skills in Organizing and Recording

Learning how to summarize what one reads is a basic skill for students. Whenever reading involves going to sources other than a single textbook, a good written summary makes it unnecessary to reread each source of information. Whether the purpose is reviewing for a test or bringing together information from various sources in a report, a condensed summary saves time.

Aside from its value as a written record, the very act of summarizing requires that one read carefully, thoughtfully, and with the intent of discovering the structure of the author's plan. One must try to select the main ideas, decide what is worth writing down, see how supporting details are related to the main ideas, and restate the author's ideas into one's own words. Summarizing enforces the employment of comprehension skills.

ORGANIZING AND RECORDING IN THE PRIMARY GRADES

Children are introduced to the beginnings of summarizing in a natural way in the first grade. In planning a little trip, the important things to look for are discussed, and then the teacher lists them. Each experience story is a summary, developed in group discussion and recorded by the teacher. Children get practice in deciding what is important, in stating ideas clearly, and in arranging them in proper sequence.

Whenever a project or activity is planned, additional practice in organizing and recording is gained. Of course, guidance by the teacher is essential. Children need help in separating the essential from the nonessential, the important from the inconsequential. The teacher can guide discussion skillfully so that the children have opportunities to evaluate ideas and to decide which of alternative ways of stating an idea is the best. Main questions are listed, and specific questions are listed under each. As answers are found, they are entered under the questions. An organized summary gradually takes shape. At the same time, reading in which practice is gained in locating answers to questions, in selecting main ideas, and in relating details to them helps to lay a groundwork for outlining and note-taking.

THE FORMAL OUTLINE

Specific training in the technique of outlining is often started in the seventh grade. It can well be started a year or two earlier. The material best suited is factual material in which the thought structure is easy to identify.

The outlining of single paragraphs should come first. The main idea is identified by Roman numeral I, and the details are indented and identified by capital letters. Each idea is expressed in a condensed form. The first paragraphs are done by the teacher, explaining the process and asking children to suggest ways of wording the items. The second step is to provide a complete skeleton with a few items (either headings or details) filled in. During the next stage, the structure of the outline is given and the children are to fill in the headings and details. In stage four, only the number of main headings is indicated. Finally, the children are to complete an outline without any assistance.

When some competence in outlining single paragraphs has been attained, one can move on to the outlining of a short selection of a few paragraphs. As with single paragraphs, it is desirable to do this in three stages. For the first selection or two, the teacher does most of the work, getting suggestions from the children. The second step is providing a skeleton outline of the selection, with a few of the headings filled in, the rest to be filled in by the children. Figure 41 illustrates an exercise of this kind, in which a model outline is given for the first paragraph, the second and third paragraphs show the number and arrangement of items, and the fourth paragraph is to be done without help.

I. *The camel is a queer-looking animal.* _____

   A. *Body like a horse, except has a hump.* _____

   B. *Neck and legs too long for body.* _____

   C. *Rough hair hangs from neck.* _____

   D. *Eyes small, mouth wide and homely.* _____

II. _____

   A. _____

   B. _____

   C. _____

   D. _____

III. _____

   A. _____

   B. _____

   C. _____

FIGURE 41. Part of a workbook exercise on outlining. A four-paragraph selection about the camel is used. The first paragraph's outline is given; the number of subtopics is given for the second and third paragraphs; the outline for the fourth paragraph, which is to be done on a separate sheet, is left to the student entirely. (From Nila B. Smith, *Be a Better Reader,* Book II, page 58. Englewood Cliffs, N.J.: Prentice-Hall, Inc., 1963. Reproduced by permission of the publisher.)

Next, one can go on to material in which there is a more complex pattern, with headings, subheadings, and subsubheadings. The children can be taught the usual sequence of subordination: Roman numeral, capital letter, Arabic numeral, lower-case letter, Arabic numeral in parentheses, lower-case letter in parentheses. In actual practice, children will rarely have occasion to go beyond the fourth, or lower-case letter, level of subordination. A formal outline of this chapter, for example, does not need to be carried beyond the fourth level. In such an outline, the present paragraph would be represented as follows (preceding parts of the outline being omitted):

Developing Efficiency in Functional Reading

III. Developing Skills in Organizing and Recording
   C. The formal outline
      4. Introducing finer subdivisions
         a. subheadings can be further subdivided
         b. the customary system of symbols: I, A, 1, a, (1), (a)
         c. usually four levels of subordination are enough
         d. the present paragraph as an illustration

The instructional procedure should be like that used with single paragraphs. The first step is to analyze a complete selection with the children and develop a complete outline, which they can use as a model. In the second step, they are given the skeleton of an outline with a few of the main headings, and fill in the rest. Finally, they are asked to do a complete outline without assistance.

The amount of practice needed at each step varies from class to class, and will usually involve a series of learning sessions and later practice in applying outlining in many reading situations.

LEARNING TO SUMMARIZE

The ability to express the essential thought content clearly and succinctly is a precious asset. We do not usually want to carry it as far as Calvin Coolidge did, when he summarized a preacher's two-hour sermon by saying, "He was against sin." But so much verbal expression, oral and in print, is filled with elaborate and unnecessary detail, and sometimes with digressions and irrelevancies, that the talent of cutting to the heart of the meaning and stating it economically is a timesaver of genuine value.

Learning to summarize has two main features. One is developing skill in finding main ideas and in deciding whether the main idea is enough to record, or some amplifying detail is also needed. Learning how to read for main ideas and relate details to them has been discussed in Chapter 11. The other main feature is learning how to state the essential thought of a sentence in one's own words as briefly as possible.

Learning to restate an author's thoughts in one's own words is worth the expenditure of considerable time and effort. It is probably true that one does not really understand an idea until one can get away from the particular verbal formulation in which one finds the idea stated and can clothe it in one's own language. Analyzing and writing headlines for newspaper articles is one very useful kind of practice in stating ideas briefly. Another is taking well-written prose and paraphrasing it, sentence by sentence, always striving for a sentence briefer than the original but having the same essential meaning. One learns to delete adjectives, adverbs, and nonessential phrases and clauses, cutting sentences down to the minimum essentials of subject and predicate. The preceding sentence, for example, could be summarized as follows: Sentences should be stripped to minimum essentials. Such a brief representation of the idea obviously is less explicit than the original sentence and cannot convey the full meaning to a person who has not read the original sentence, but it is sufficient to serve as a reminder of the full thought if one has read the original.

LEARNING NOTE-TAKING

Note-taking demands selective, thoughtful reading. One cannot read passively because in order to take good notes, one must select what is worth recording, separate main from subordinate points, consider the relationships between ideas, and put the author's ideas into his own words. The outlining and summarizing skills needed for note-taking are most often put to use in making records of what we read; somewhat less often, in recording lectures. In writing a summary, to be used only by oneself in later reviewing, the full use of a formal outline is unnecessary, and brevity can be fostered not only by shortening sentences but also by using grammatically incomplete sentences and by employing abbreviations. It is advisable to indent subordinate ideas as in a formal outline, without bothering to label them with numbers or letters. Important concepts or ideas can be underlined to make them catch the eye when going over the notes.

In underlining in a book or other material (a form of outlining), the reader should set up some key whereby main ideas are differentiated from minor or supporting points. For example, main ideas might be double underscored or starred; and, subpoints underscored, numbered, or lettered. Some readers prefer to underscore entire sentences; other to underline only key phrases or words. Often the reader is inclined to underline too much. One way of preventing this is to underline only after a section with a center or sideheading has been read. This prevents underlining as one reads along, only to find the material summarized at the end of the selection. Furthermore, if the material is clearly understood, the reader should have little difficulty in deciding what to underline. If he does have difficulty, rereading is indicated.

Efficient reading notes on the immediately preceding subsection might look something like the following:

Learning to summarize
  Valuable—saves time
  Two features
    Finding main ideas and related details: cf. Ch. 11
    Restating ideas briefly in one's own words
      headlines
      paraphrasing sentences
      serves as a reminder of full meaning

In addition to taking notes on relatively long selections, such as textbook chapters, students often need to assemble information from a variety of sources in order to write a report. For this, some training in the use of index cards is helpful, both to summarize sections and to copy quotations that may be desirable to quote exactly. It is also necessary for the student to learn how to record the origin of the information on the card so that a footnote citing the reference can be written later, if needed.

Improving Study Habits

Study habits, as distinguished from study skills, refer to the habitual trends that individuals develop in regard to the amount of time they spend in studying and the conditions of time, place, and circumstances that determine to a considerable degree how well they can use the reading and study skills they have learned.

Teachers are almost always very much concerned about helping students to learn the contents of their subjects. It is perhaps just as important to help the students to become efficient users of time, who can apply sound reading and study skills under self-selected conditions that make for efficient learning.

FINDING THE FACTS ABOUT STUDY HABITS

Finding the facts about study habits is important in two different senses. One of them is finding out just what does happen when the students study. The second is bringing out, through appropriate reading perhaps, but more importantly through group discussion and consideration of individual difficulties, the conditions that make it easy or hard to study efficiently.

Charting the Use of Time. Of all the varied causes of poor academic work, one of the most frequent is devoting insufficient time to it. Many boys and girls do not realize how much of their time is frittered away, being used neither for study nor for worthwhile recreation or socialization. The first step in helping them with this problem is to help them to discover the facts.

In junior or senior high school a teacher or guidance counselor can recommend keeping a chart of the use of time for some typical week. A page is ruled into seven vertical columns, headed with the names of the days of the week. Then the page is ruled horizontally into appropriate time intervals. Time spent outside of school can be ruled in half-hour intervals, and time in school according to the length of school periods. For one week, the boy (or girl) records what he does each day, from getting up to going to bed.

One of the problems about recording study time is the large amount of it that some boys and girls manage to waste. They dawdle before they actually start working; they take time out for getting a drink, looking out the window, or just daydreaming. The easiest way to take account of this is to fill in the time chart immediately after each period of study, and to rate in percent the proportion of the time that was acually spent in studying; these ratings can range from 100 percent down to less than 50 percent.

The value of any procedure such as this depends on the interest and cooperation of the group and their motivation for carrying it through honestly. If they are convinced that the purpose is entirely to help them to become better students and that honest self-ratings will not be used against them in any way, reasonably honest record-keeping can be expected from most boys and girls.

After a time chart has been kept for a typical week, each student can count up the number of hours spent in each of such activities as living routines (dressing, eating, etc.), attending classes, travel, study, chores or work, and recreational and social activities. Many students are genuinely surprised to find that they actually spent in studying considerably less time than they thought they did. At this point the teacher can help clarify the question of how much time is usually needed to study a subject conscientiously. Each student can then formulate a time plan for the next week, which he will try to carry out. An example of such plans is shown in Figure 42; of course, no two students will ordinarily set exactly the same goals for themselves and come out with identical plans.

Teacher Observations. In the higher grades there are usually some supervised study periods, or subject periods in which part of the time is spent in reading for information. During such periods, useful observations can be made. All the teacher needs is a seating chart and the willingness to carry out a simple observational plan. Usually two

One Kind of Activity Plan

	Mon.	Tues.	Wed.	Thurs.	Fri.	Sat.	Sun.
7 — 7 30 a. m.	Study						
7 30 — 8	Breakfast						
8 — 8 45	On way to school				Breakfast	
8 45 — 9	Study					Study	
9 — 1 p. m.	Classes						Breakfast Church
1 — 2	Lunch					Free	Free
2 — 3 30	Classes						Study
3 30 — 5	Track and shower						
5 — 5 30	On way home						Free
5 30 — 6 15	Free						
6 15 — 7	Dinner						
7 — 8 30	Study						
8 30 — 9	Free						
9 — 10	Study						

Another Kind of Activity Plan

	Mon.	Tues.	Wed.	Thurs.	Fri.	Sat.	Sun.
Before Breakfast	✕	✕	✕	✕	✕	Study	Study
Breakfast to lunch	Classes	Classes	Classes	Classes	Classes		
Lunch to end of classes	Classes	Classes	Classes	Classes	Classes		
Between last class and dinner	✕	Study	✕	✕	✕		
After dinner	Study	✕	Study	Study	Study		Study

Crosses show periods set aside for a part-time job and free time.

FIGURE 42. Two one-week time plans. (From Ralph C. Preston and Botel, Morton, *How to Study*, p. 89. © 1956, 1967, Science Research Associates, Inc. Reduced in size. Reproduced by permission of the publisher.)

different symbols are enough. One is used when a child interrupts his own work in a way that does not disturb others (gazing out the window, etc.). The other symbol is used when a child does interrupt or disturb others (whispering, passing notes, making noises, etc.). Each time a child stops studying, the appropriate symbol is entered in his box on the seating chart. At the end of the study period it is usual for some boxes to be empty, while others are quite well filled.

When there is a pattern of poor concentration and frequent interruptions, the results of study-period observations are best taken up with individuals in privacy. Those with least ability to sustain attention during study periods often present other problems as well, and the inability to concentrate is often a part of a larger problem of general adjustment. When teachers find some children who have serious difficulty in attending to studying, it is often wise to take this up with the guidance counselor rather than attempt to do something about it oneself.

Physical Conditions for Studying. It is relatively easy to list the desirable conditions for studying; it is much harder to provide them. They would include: privacy, freedom from distracting sights and sounds, freedom from interruptions, good nonglare lighting, a comfortable straight-backed chair and a desk of appropriate height with room enough to allow the spreading out of books and papers.

It is possible for students to get work done under highly unfavorable conditions. Some manage to concentrate while working at a kitchen or living-room table, with perhaps a telephone conversation going on in one corner of the room and a television set providing light and sound effects. Some children get so accustomed to studying with the radio playing popular music that they have trouble in concentrating when it is quiet. The concentration some students are able to maintain while reading textbooks in a crowded, noisy, swaying subway train is really amazing. These facts are testaments to human adaptability; they do not contradict the general desirability of freedom from distractions and a physical setting that provides for a comfortable study posture and freedom from eyestrain.

A teacher can learn quite a bit about home conditions for study by asking the students to fill out a simple questionnaire. Sometimes children from underprivileged homes live under such crowded and unsatisfactory conditions that study at home is almost impossible. It would be a mistake to assume, however, that children from well-to-do homes necessarily have satisfactory conditions for study at home. Sometimes their parents are either indifferent to their study needs or do not realize what is needed.

CREATING MOTIVATION FOR IMPROVEMENT

Today the pressure on children to do well in school and to qualify for admission to a well-regarded college is greater than ever before. Some parents begin to worry about school success before a child is even in kindergarten. Many children take their schoolwork quite seriously by the time they reach the middle grades. When parents and children are interested, motivation for improvement is self-generated and the teacher's role is one of helping to analyze difficulties and to make suggestions about ways in which study habit problems can be overcome. In these cases, motivation is not a real problem.

Some children react against parental stress on schoolwork by becoming resentful or rebellious, using sloppy or insufficient study and the resulting unsatisfactory marks as a weapon in a battle against their parents. The classroom teacher who becomes aware that this kind of problem exists is usually not professionally trained to deal effectively with parent-child problems, and if there is a counselor, psychologist, or social worker to whom the problem can be referred, that is the best thing to do.

Even when socioeconomic conditions create a general lack of interest in school success, much can be done to increase motivation for study. The College Discovery and Development project in New York City has shown that the school marks, and the percentage graduating from high school and going on to college, of youngsters from underprivileged backgrounds go up when appropriate steps are taken in junior and senior high school.[7] It is most important to convince

[7] Lawrence Brody, Beatrice Harris, and Genaro Lachica, "Discovering and Developing the College Potential of Disadvantaged High School Youth: a Report for the Third Year," Research Report 69–1, Division of Teacher Education, The City University of New York, 1969.

underprivileged children of two things: (1) that they personally have the ability to do well in school, despite their previous records, and (2) that opportunities for higher education and for prestige-type occupations are open to them. They need to feel that it is worthwhile to try to succeed in school. When they have that feeling, they are as responsive to instruction and guidance as other groups of children are.

Materials for Practicing Functional Reading Skills

As previously indicated, functional reading skills are best taught and applied in practical situations. There are, however, times when other materials can be useful in teaching and practicing certain skills. Whenever such materials are employed, the teacher must determine if the children can and do apply the skills in the actual content subject material.

Among the growing number of materials becoming available are the following. Some are designed for use across content areas; others are more specifically oriented.

General-Purpose Material

O'Donnell, Mabel, et al. *Harper Row Basic,* Strand II. Evanston, Ill.: Harper & Row.

A graded series of books (grades 1–6) for teaching reading and study skills needed in the content areas.

Naslund, Robert A. *Graph and Picture Study Skills Kit,* Grades 4–6. Chicago: Science Research Associates, Inc.

Kit contains material for learning to interpret photographs, cartoons, charts, diagrams, etc.

Naslund, Robert A. *Organizing and Reporting Skills Kit,* Grades 4–6. Chicago: Science Research Associates, Inc.

Kit contains six skill units: Form of the report, Sticking to the point, Order in the paragraph, Quality in the paragraph, Note-taking and outlining, and Making an outline.

Robinson, H. Alan; Taylor, Stanford E.; and Frackenpohl, Helen. *The EDL Study Skills Library: Reference Skills.* Huntington, N.Y.: Educational Developmental Laboratories.

Separate kits for seven grade levels (3–9), each containing a sequence of self-directed activities for developing reference skills.

Smith, Nila B. *Be a Better Reader,* Books A–C (grades 4–6) and Books 1–6 (grades 9–12). Englewood Cliffs, N.J.: Prentice-Hall.

Each workbook contains a variety of exercises on specialized vocabulary, basic study skills, and special reading and study skills in four content areas.

Science

Branley, Franklyn M., Ed. *Reader's Digest Science Reader.* Pleasantville, N.Y.: Reader's Digest.

Four separate books ranging in readability from third- to sixth-reader level. Each, using the typical *Digest* format, is organized around four areas: the earth, living things, matter and energy, and astronomy and space.

New Science Reading Adventures. Columbus, Ohio: American Education Publications.

Separate workbooks for grades 1 to 6, each containing short selections for developing science concepts.

Parker, Don H., and Stotler, Donald W. *Earth's Atmosphere Laboratory; Weather and Climate Laboratory; Solar System Laboratory; Biogeography Laboratory.* Chicago: Science Research, Inc.

Each of these four separate kits presents a series of "Big Ideas." Each "Big Idea" is introduced in booklets which are written at five different readability levels (3.5 to 7.5).

Robinson, H. Alan; Taylor, Stanford E.; and Frackenpohl, Helen. *The EDL Study Skills Library: Science.* Huntington, N.Y.: Educational Developmental Laboratories.

Separate kits for seven grade levels (3–9), each containing a sequence of self-directed reading activities using science materials to develop study skills.

Social Science

Map Skills for Today. Columbus, Ohio: American Education Publications.

A sequence of six workbooks (separate books for grades 2 to 7) for developing map reading skills.

Map Skills Project. Englewood Cliffs, N.J.: Scholastic Book Services.

Three separate paperback books for developing map skills. Book I for the primary grades, Book II for the middle elementary, and Book III for the upper elementary grades.

Naslund, Robert A. *Map and Globe Skills Kit.* Grades 4–8. Chicago: Science Research Associates, Inc.

Kit contains separate cards, of progressive levels of difficulty, concerned with the skills needed in making effective use of maps and globes.

Robinson, H. Alan; Taylor, Stanford E.; and Frackenpohl, Helen. *The EDL Study Skills Library: Social Science.* Huntington, N.Y.: Educational Developmental Laboratories.

Separate kits for seven grade levels (3–9), each containing a sequence of self-directed reading activities using social science materials to develop study skills.

Summary

1. Functional reading skills, which involve the use of reading as a tool for learning, become more essential as children progress through school.

2. Learning to locate information requires that alphabetical order first be mastered, followed by practice in locating items in alphabetically arranged references.

3. Certain special understandings are needed to use indexes, encyclopedias, and other kinds of reference materials.

4. The application of basic reading skills in content areas requires careful teaching of the important concepts and technical terms, as well as unusual or specialized meaning of common words, in each subject.

   a. Textbooks are often too difficult for some children; therefore, brief informal tests of textbook suitability should be given.

   b. Instructional procedures similar to those used with basal readers can be employed for guided reading lessons in content subject textbooks. The SQ3R method also provides a guide. A number of things can be done to help poor readers acquire concepts.

   c. For those who cannot read the textbook, several alternatives, or combinations of them, are possible: easier books on the same topic, varied reference reading, help at home, use of tape recordings, and use of oral rather than written tests.

   d. Special projects provide opportunities for the learning and application of location skills and research-type reading activities.

5. Specialized reading skills are needed for certain kinds of instructional materials.

   a. Suggestions were made about how to teach the reading of arithmetical problems, social studies, maps, graphs, charts, and scientific experiments.

   b. Special problems of concept development in these curricular areas also were discussed.

6. Organizing and recording enforces careful reading and often makes rereading unnecessary.

   a. Preliminary experiences in organizing ideas may start as early as the first grade.

   b. Direct training in outlining and summarizing is usually not begun before the intermediate grades.

7. Formal outlining can be taught in a five-step process.

8. Paragraph outlining comes first, followed by short selections, and finally by longer selections with several levels of subordination of ideas.

9. Learning to summarize requires practice in restating an author's ideas in one's own words, as briefly as possible.

10. In note-taking, one should use an indentation pattern similar to that of a formal outline, and reduce the amount of writing by employing incomplete sentences and using abbreviations.

11. Study habits deserve more attention from teachers than they usually receive.

    a. The use of a one-week time chart can show whether or not enough time is being devoted to studying, and how much time is being wasted.

    b. Students can be helped to plan their use of time in advance.

    c. Teachers can easily identify students who have poor ability to concentrate by observing them during study periods.

    d. Despite human adaptability, both students and parents used to be informed about the conditions which make it easy to study efficiently: privacy, freedom from distraction and interruption, and suitable furniture and lighting.

    e. Where there is a genuine desire for school success, finding motivation for improving the effectiveness of study habits is easy.

12. There is an increasing number of materials available to aid in teaching functional reading skills.

Recommended Reading

GANS, ROMA. *Common Sense in Teaching Reading.* Indianapolis: Bobbs-Merrill, 1963. Chs. 10, 11.

HARRIS, ALBERT J., ED. *Readings on Reading Instruction.* New York: McKay, 1963. Ch. 11.

HERBER, HAROLD L. *Teaching Reading in Content Areas.* Englewood Cliffs, N.J.: Prentice-Hall, 1970.

MAZURKIEWICZ, ALBERT J., ED. *New Perspectives in Reading Instruction: A Book of Readings.* New York: Pitman, 1964. Chs. 10, 11.

SMITH, NILA B. *Reading Instruction for Today's Children.* Englewood Cliffs, N.J.: Prentice-Hall, 1963. Chs. 10, 23.

SPACHE, GEORGE D., and SPACHE, EVELYN B. *Reading in the Elementary School,* 2nd ed. Boston: Allyn and Bacon, Inc., 1969. Ch. 9.

TINKER, MILES A., and McCULLOUGH, CONSTANCE M. *Teaching Elementary Reading,* 3rd ed. New York: Appleton-Century-Crofts, 1968. Ch. 13.

13

Improving Reading Interests

We have been conspicuously more successful in teaching the American public to read than in instilling a lasting interest in reading. Surveys continually show that we are not a nation of book readers. While the American public consumes millions of newspapers every day and millions of magazines every month, relatively few adults are serious readers of books or readers of serious books.

What we can do to improve this situation is the theme of this chapter. Reading interests can be improved in many ways, among which helping children to learn to enjoy reading is the most important. We also can improve reading interests by expanding the range of topics and variety of reading material that they become interested to read. And we can improve reading interests by helping children to move from less to more mature preferences and to recognize and prefer material that has literary merit.

This chapter first takes up the nature of interest and the background necessary for understanding and studying the reading interests of children. What might be done to develop a liking for reading is considered in the second section, followed by a section on improving the range and maturity of reading interests. The final section discusses resources for locating interest-fostering materials.

365

Learning About Children's Interests

A psychology dictionary tells us that interest has a variety of meanings, including "the tendency to give selective attention to something" and "a tendency to engage in an activity solely for the gratification of engaging therein." We use the word both for the feeling of liking something, as when we say, "I am interested in music," and for the object or activity we like, as in, "Music is an interest of mine." A particular activity or topic is a person's interest when it is one of the activities or topics to which he devotes some of his time when he has a free choice.

HOW INTERESTS ARE BORN AND DEVELOP

An interest is born in a pleasurable experience, which leads the child to hope that if he repeats the activity the experience will again be pleasurable. When several additional experiences of the same sort continue to be pleasurable, a relatively lasting disposition to expect pleasure from the activity, and to turn to it voluntarily, is developed. When most of the experiences are satisfying, an occasional disappointing one can be taken in stride. But when an interest is in the beginning stages, one experience that results in fear, anger, embarrassment, shame, or disappointment can nip the interest in the bud. An interest is, therefore, a learned preference.

Interests develop and become deep and lasting when the conditions necessary for their nourishment are present. This nourishment can be provided in several ways.

1. *Pleasure in the activity itself.* Some activities are inherently pleasant. The enjoyment of tasty food and liquids, the pleasure of moving rhythmically and easily, the delight in the gentle touch of a caress, are built into our natures. As children develop, this quality of intrinsic pleasantness extends to many kinds of actions.

2. *The feeling of ease and security.* Young children in particular tend to enjoy activities that are easy for them and in which they feel safe and secure. They sometimes want to carry repetition far beyond

adult limits of tolerance. The familiar is reassuring and comforting to many children.

3. *The feeling of accomplishment.* In the dynamic process of child growth the need for security and safety would lead to stagnation if it were not for an exploratory tendency that causes children to venture into new activities and topics. Repetition eventually produces satiation, unless it also involves a challenge, an opportunity to use one's abilities and to test them. Ideally an interest should involve an inherently pleasurable type of activity, in which the child feels reasonably secure, yet which provides an opportunity to do better and better in repeated efforts. The feeling of satisfaction that results from knowing that one has successfully accomplished something that is not too easy is a very powerful interest strengthener. The desire to improve is itself a powerful motivation, when there is reason to expect it to be fulfilled.

The knowledge that one is doing well tends to increase interest; the realization that one is doing poorly tends to decrease it. The talented tend to use their abilities and develop them, while the untalented do less and fall further behind. Interest and ability generally go together and reinforce each other.

4. *Social approval.* From babyhood on, children are very responsive to adult approval and disapproval; not only the words used but the facial expressions, gestures, and tones of voice. For the young child in the primary grades, the teacher's reactions to his efforts often become more important than the reactions of his parents. As children get older, the approval of their peers becomes increasingly important. By the fifth grade, boys tend to form clubs or gangs. Whether the group is an antisocial gang, a "secret society" with initiation, passwords, etc., or a Boy Scout troop, the group's standards and code of conduct become a paramount influence on behavior, often outweighing the combined influence of parents and teacher.

READING'S COMPETITORS FOR CHILDREN'S TIME

During the past fifty years, reading has always faced strong competition for children's time and attention from the mass entertainment media. During the 1920's the big competition was from the movies; some children were going to the neighborhood theater as many as five times a week. Radio blossomed out as a prime attraction during the 1930's and 1940's. During the late 1940's and the 1950's television spread gradually over more and more of the country, and wherever it arrived it immediately took over much of the time previously devoted by children to movies, radio, and reading.

Television. The results of years of studies of children's television watching have been summarized by Witty.[1] By 1965 nearly all children in the United States had television in their homes, and in suburban areas many had two or more sets. The average elementary school child spent an average of 20 hours a week watching television; with the average time being slightly less for primary-grade children, and slightly higher for intermediate graders. This had remained quite constant for several years. Parents spent almost as much time with T.V. as their children (averaging 20 hours a week), while high school students (13 hours) and teachers (12 hours) spent much less time. For all groups, much more time was spent in watching T.V. than in reading, although there was a reported increase in voluntary reading for both elementary and secondary pupils.

Research has failed to show an inevitably damaging effect of heavy T.V. watching, although undesirable effects do occur in individual cases. Problems of fatigue, impoverishment of play, lack of interest in school, increased nervousness, reduction in reading, eyestrain, and mealtime disturbance have been reported by a relatively small percentage of parents and teachers. Several studies have shown a relationship between heavy T.V. watching and low achievement in school, although whether this is a direct cause-effect relationship or both are related to other underlying causes remains to be investigated. A child who is a poor reader or who does not like to read is likely to spend his free time in ways other than in reading. The cumulative effect of watching programs filled with violence worries many adults, and in

[1] Paul A. Witty, "Studies of the Mass Media—1949–65," *Science Education,* 50 (1966), 119–126.

Paul A. Witty and Lloyd Melis, "A 1964 Study of TV: Comparisons and Comments," *Elementary English,* 42 (1965), 134–141.

individual cases T.V. has taught criminal techniques to youngsters already predisposed toward delinquency. There is a good case for parental regulation and supervision of T.V. watching.

On the other hand, T.V. may have positive effects on the intellectual and educational development of children. Many children bring to school large vocabularies and extensive knowledge about current events, science, and foreign lands, which they have learned from T.V. A popular T.V. program can send children to books. The Walt Disney programs on Davy Crockett, the dramatizations of E. B. White's *Stuart Little,* Butterworth's *The Enormous Egg,* or Seuss's *How the Grinch Stole Christmas* and *Horton Hears a Who* have sent millions of children to the library for books. There are great possibilities in using T.V. programs as motivation for related reading, and these have not been fully exploited. However, some T.V. programs designed especially for a young audience now close the program with a recommended reading list for those children who wish more information, and some programs broadcast over educational television are based on children's books.

Comic Books. Since the advent of television, adults tend to worry less about comic books than they did before, but these little books are still read in the hundreds of millions. Young children prefer comics with humanized animal characters like those in movie cartoons. Older childern prefer the adventure and science-fiction types. The difficulty level of the reading material in comic books tends to be at intermediate grade levels, and many children pay attention only to the pictures. Forbidding comic books just makes them seem more desirable. While so-called comic books that emphasize sadism and crime should probably be kept out of the hands of children, the main problem is not how to stop children from reading comic books but rather how to get them to enjoy more worthwhile reading matter. Children can be helped to compare comic books with one another and discriminate the better from the poorer ones. The interests shown in comic book preferences can be used in book selection, by directing children to books on the same or similar topics.

Radio. Aside from weekend storytelling programs, radio is mainly used by children as a source of music and news. Many of them like to have the radio on while they read or study. A background of unobtrusive music does not seem to interfere with concentration; it may help, actually, by masking other sounds that would be distracting. The more attention-compelling the program the more it is likely to disrupt attention to reading or study.

THE READING INTERESTS OF CHILDREN

The many diverse fields in which children like to read are hard to summarize briefly. To get the picture of how reading interests broaden out as children grow up, one way is to analyze the table of contents of a comprehensive listing of children's books.[2]

For the primary grades, 25 headings are used. First come fiction categories, with Mother Goose, folk and fairy tales, and bedtime stories. Social studies areas include home and family, country and seasons, regions of America, other countries, and jobs and ways of life. Other headings include humor and nonsense, adventure, toys and dolls, cowboys, Indians, autos and boats, history, nature and science, easy reading and other languages.

In the categories for grades four to six, fiction has many headings: family reading, tales oft retold, old favorites, fairy tales, legends and tall tales, classic tales and legends, historical fiction, mystery, adventure, fantasy, and science fiction. Animals remain, modern stories appear, and biography grows in importance. Social studies topics include world history, the world we live in, transportation, communication, citizenship, geography, and neighbors around the world. Science increases greatly in importance: anthropology, archaeology, geology, weather, nature, human body, energy and power, engineering, experiments, mathematics, weapons, astronomy and space, and transportation.

The headings for grade seven and up show further maturing, and many of the subdivisions would also be used in classifications of adult reading. Fiction includes: old favorites, myths and folklore, adventure stories, sports stories, mystery and suspense, animal stories, girls'

[2] *Best Books For Children,* 1969 edition, compiled by Doris Solomon (New York: R. R. Bowker).

stories, career fiction, historical fiction, and science fiction. Social studies headings include world history, American history, Indians, America today, government, natural resources, language and communication, and people and places. Science is now classified as mathematics, astronomy, physics, chemistry, archaeology and paleontology, anthropology, nature, physiology and medicine, inventions, technology, electronics, experiments, aeronautics, space frontier, and weapons and warfare (the classification of "warfare" under "science" is a wry commentary on our times). Other headings include true adventure, war stories, humor, travel, philosophy, and biography.

There is also a section on Special Subjects which are not arranged by age groupings. These include: art, dance, theater, music, poetry, religion, holidays, sports (how-to), party games, crafts and hobbies, pets, careers, homemaking, guidance for growing up, and sex education.

What a range of topics is now available to the young! No matter in what direction a child's curiosity leads him, there is likely to be at least one book on the subject that is written clearly and simply for children. Books for children continue to appear at a great rate; approximately 2,500 new "juvenile" books were printed in the United States in 1969 alone.

During the primary grades there are few differences between the reading interests of boys and girls, both preferring short fanciful tales. In the middle grades, girls tend to like mystery and adventure, sentimental stories of home and school life, animal stories (particularly about horses), and begin to get interested in romantic fiction. Boys tend to enjoy adventure, war, and mystery, animal stories, science, invention, hobbies, biography, and historical fiction. Girls will often read books intended for boys, but boys will rarely touch a book that is identified as meant for girls. In the upper grades, girls tend to like mild adventure, humor, animals, romance, home and family life; they tend to avoid science and grim adventure. Boys tend to enjoy adventure, sport stories, school life, mystery and detective stories, humor, animals, patriotic themes, and male characters; they tend to avoid romance, domestic settings, and female characters.

Reading interests, like reading ability, are related to intelligence.

Bright children are often (but by no means always) avid readers; their range of interests is usually wide, and they tend to like books written for somewhat older children. Mentally slow children are restricted by their limited reading skills to relatively simple books, they tend to read much less, and their preferences tend to be a little immature for their ages.

There are often marked differences between what adults think children ought to like and what children actually do like. Many of the books which have won the Newbery Medal (for the most distinguished work of children's literature for the year) have failed to achieve popularity with children. On the other hand, the "series" books (Tom Swift, Jr., the Bobbsey Twins, etc.), which librarians frequently refuse to purchase because they do not rate highly as literature, are devoured one after the other by a great many children.

The most important fact about the reading interests of children, however, is the tremendous individual differences. These far outweigh group tendencies that are related to age, sex, or intelligence. To understand the reading interests of children it is necessary to consider each child separately.

STUDYING THE INTERESTS OF CHILDREN

The classroom teacher can discover many indications of children's interests in their everyday behavior. During a show-and-tell period they have an opportunity to bring in objects that interest them and to talk about their experiences. The drawings and paintings of some children repeat the same theme again and again. When children are encouraged to talk about their hobbies and to bring them to school to show to classmates, all kinds of things are likely to appear. There are almost certainly going to be some collections, ranging from insects and stamps to matchbox covers. Some will bring in airplane or ship or train models that they have built. Many children are devoted to pets and have a vital interest in all kinds of animals. Each of these interests, discernible in the behavior and conversation of children, can suggest kinds of reading matter that will have a special appeal.

With children old enough to write compositions, topics can sometimes be assigned specifically to encourage writing about special interests. Such topics as "What I like to do after school," "My hobby," etc., will give some children incentives to write about interests that have not become evident in previous classroom activities. Sometimes very helpful leads can be gained from compositions on a topic such as "I would read more if . . ."

Interest questionnaires can be used. A very simple questionnaire that is practical for elementary school teachers is shown in Figure 43. With young children these questions can be asked during an informal conference or interview, and the teacher can write down the child's answers. The questionnaire can also be used as an interviewing form with older children. In the fourth grade and above, a questionnaire like this can be duplicated and answered by the class in writing.[3] Children usually do not hesitate to tell about their interests when given this kind of opportunity; they like it when the teacher shows a desire to know more about them and what they enjoy.

Increasing Children's Liking for Reading

There are many procedures that teachers can use to help children to learn to enjoy reading. Basic to all of them, of course, is teaching the children to read well enough so that the act of reading can be reasonably fluent and accurate and the content understood.

DEVELOPING A LOVE FOR STORIES

From the simplest bedtime story to the finest play, motion picture, or television play, a good story well presented enthralls its audience. Children in the elementary school love to listen when the teacher reads books to them or tells them stories. This is true not only in the primary

---

[3] More elaborate questionnaires can be found in:
Albert J. Harris, *How To Increase Reading Ability,* Fifth Edition (New York: McKay, 1970), pp. 464–465.
Paul Witty, *et al., The Teaching Of Reading: A Developmental Process,* pp. 406–410 (Englewood, N.J.: D. C. Heath and Co., 1966).

Name................THINGS I LIKE TO DO
Devised by
Albert J. Harris

1. What do you like to do after school?

....
....
....

2. What do you like to do when it rains?

....
....

3. What do you like to do in the evening?

....
....

4. What do you like to do on weekends?

....
....
....

5. What kinds of movies do you like?

....
....

6. What are your favorite television programs?

....
....
....

7. What books that you have read do you like best?

....
....

8. What kinds of things would you like to read about?

....
....

FIGURE 43. A simple interest questionnaire for children.

grades, where a story period is often part of the daily routine, but in the middle and upper grades as well.

With little children, it is helpful if they can be seated on the floor or on mats close together, so that all can hear well, can see the illustrations when the teacher turns the book around to show them, and can have a feeling of intimacy. Above the second grade a special seating arrangement is not important.

Stories to be read or told should be selected with the maturity and special interests of the group in mind. The language used can be considerably more mature than what most of the children can read for themselves, and listening to fine stories and poems is one of the best ways in which children can painlessly build their understanding of language and extend their concepts and grasp of sentence structure. Students can be given additional practice, perhaps as part of a book club, by reading their favorite stories to the class in an audience situation, or by taping these stories and sharing them with the class in groups or individually. The teacher also may use material that he pre-records or commercially prepared recordings to stimulate interest.

A good story deserves to be rehearsed. The teacher should go through it in advance, deciding how to differentiate the characters, when to show illustrations, and when to speed up or slow down, raise or lower the voice, or read with emotion.[4]

BRINGING CHILDREN AND BOOKS TOGETHER

The more accessible books are, the greater the likelihood that they will be read. In addition to public and school library resources, each classroom should have its own book collection. The classroom library should contain at least fifty different titles ranging from very easy to quite challenging, and including a wide variety of topics, fiction and factual. When there is a central library in the school, the classroom libraries are usually borrowed from it. Public library books can also be borrowed by teachers. If a project is going on, there should be a special collection of references related to it. The classroom library should, if possible, be changed at least several times a year. A school librarian or children's librarian can give invaluable help to teachers in selecting books for classroom collections or for individual children.

[4] Excellent suggestions on storytelling and story reading can be found in: Ruth Sawyer, *The Ways of the Storyteller*, rev. ed. (New York: Viking Press, 1962); Ruth Tooze, *Storytelling* (Englewood Cliffs, N.J.: Prentice-Hall, 1959); and Eileen Colwell, *A Storyteller's Choice* (New York: H. Z. Walch, 1964).

Although the principles of seeking and self-selection can largely be followed for independent recreational reading, teachers can help children to avoid a good deal of time-wasting browsing in books that they are very unlikely to read. Books can be arranged under a few broad headings, such as "make believe," "true stories," "animals," etc. By sticking little tabs of colored paper on the book spines, their difficulty can be indicated in broad categories: white, easy; yellow, average; red, hard.

It is helpful to have one corner of the classroom set up as a reading corner. The furnishings should include shelves for the books (if necessary, improvised from grocery cartons), a table or two, and chairs. Decorations can include posters, book jackets, and pictures illustrating some of the books. Children who have helped to furnish and decorate the reading corner are likely to feel a personal interest in it. In many classes a simple system of checking books in and out can be set up, which can be operated by child librarians, and being appointed librarian for the week can be a cherished privilege.

Time for independent reading should be provided during the school day. In the discussions of class organization for reading in Chapters 3, 4, and 7, considerable time was allocated to independent reading. In addition to time that is definitely scheduled, children should have books handy in their desks, to which they can turn when they finish an assignment early. Allotting class time for independent or recreational reading offers evidence to children that the teacher places importance on such activities.

TEACHER ENTHUSIASM

Interest in books can be infectious and contagious. A teacher who is an enthusiast about reading, and who reads and enjoys many children's books as well as adult books, cannot help but convey some of this enthusiasm to children. Such a teacher will read many good stories to the class; will call their attention to new books when they arrive, perhaps reading to them just enough of the story to whet their interest; will help children to find books that they will enjoy reading; and will see that favorable conditions for independent reading are maintained.

ENSURING ENJOYMENT

As indicated near the beginning of this chapter, interests are nourished by pleasure in the act itself, by ease and security, by the feeling of accomplishment, and by social approbation. Pleasure in the act of reading is a by-product when the difficulty is suitable for independent reading and the content is absorbing. The best readers do not always read books which are at their reading level; they often shift back and forth between very easy books that are far below their reading level and other books which are close to their frustration levels. The reluctant reader becomes less reluctant when he can be guided into selecting books that are very easy, as well as being in line with his interests. For the confirmed readers this factor of ease is much less important. They at times enjoy the challenge of material which contains exciting new ideas even if it is quite taxing. From reading "at their growing points" they both grow in skill and gain the feeling of accomplishment.

ESTIMATING THE READABILITY OF MATERIALS

A number of formulas are available for estimating the difficulty of reading materials.[5] Probably the most widely used are the Spache Formula [6] for primary-grade materials and the Dale-Chall Formula [7] for intermediate and upper-grade materials.

[5] Refer to the following for comprehensive treatments of readability:
Jeanne S. Chall, *Readability: An Appraisal of Research and Application,* Bureau of Educational Research Monographs No. 34 (Columbus: Ohio State University, 1957).
George R. Klare, *The Measurement of Readability* (Ames: Iowa State University Press, 1963).
John R. Bormuth, Ed., *Readability in 1968* (Champaign, Ill.: National Council of Teachers of English, 1968).
[6] George D. Spache, "A New Readability Formula for Primary Grade Reading Materials," *Elementary School Journal,* 53 (1953), 410–413. Also found in Spache's *Good Reading for Poor Readers,* rev. ed. (Champaign, Ill.: Garrard, 1968), pp. 166–176.
[7] Edgar Dale and Jeanne S. Chall, "A Formula for Predicting Readability," *Educational Research Bulletin,* 27 (1948), 11–20, 37–54. Reprinted in C. W. Hunnicutt and William J. Iverson, Eds., *Research in the Three R's* (New York: Harper & Row, 1958), pp. 194–212.

Application of readability formulas is time consuming. Therefore whenever possible teachers should consult sources that list the reading difficulty of books (see page 390). When such information is not readily available, an experienced teacher can obtain a rough estimate by studying a few pages of the material to determine: (1) the vocabulary employed; (2) the load and complexity of the concepts presented; and (3) the length and complexity of the sentences. The techniques for individual textbook tests presented on pages 154–160 can be used in selecting recreational reading material for individuals. For independent reading, the child generally should be able to recognize at least 98 percent of the words and should have good to excellent comprehension.

PROGRESS CHARTS

An individual progress record of independent reading can serve both as a report of reading done and as an incentive to read more. The bookcase chart that is shown in Figure 44 has been widely and successfully used for more than thirty years. Some teachers duplicate the outline; others prefer to have each child draw his own. Many variants have been employed. Children can add leaves to a tree, windows to a house, fish to a pond, or rockets to a space station. Usually there is not room enough on a decorative chart of this type to enter the details such as author's name, title, number of pages read, and when started and finished, so it is a good idea to have a more complete record kept on a form like that shown in Figure 45. Every child likes to see his bookcase fill up and his reading record get longer. The purpose of recording the number of pages is to make it easy for both teacher and pupil to distinguish between picture books of 50 pages or less and full-length books. This also takes care of books that are started but not finished.

However, these motivational devices need to be used cautiously by teachers. By stressing individual completion of a particular form, the teacher often inadvertently places an emphasis on quantity rather than quality. To ensure a head start on the chart, highly competitive youngsters will select five or six "thin" books to read. Slow readers tend to feel defeated before they start. Thus, what started as a motivational device results in meaningless competition rather than meaningful reading.

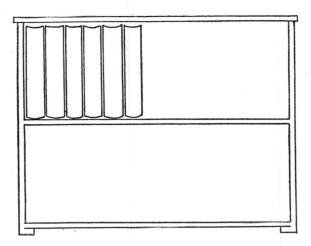

FIGURE 44. A bookcase chart for recording independent reading. When the child finishes a book, he draws another book into his bookcase. Coloring the books adds to the attractiveness of the chart. (Reproduced from Albert J. Harris, *How to Increase Reading Ability*, 5th ed., p. 468. New York: McKay, 1970.) Reproduced by permission of the publisher.

However, progress charts have proved useful especially for group participation. In groups children can make an article of clothing, representative of a favorite character they have read about, to hang on a clothesline stretched across the classroom; also they can add sections, representing the book recently read, to a large reading "book worm" that stretches around the room. A time line can be used to have children place a picture about their book in its proper place. A large outline map of the United States or the world could be used for children to place drawings showing the settings for their stories. Each of these suggestions is not limiting in any way, but instead offers each

MY READING RECORD

Name........................

Author	Title	No. of Pages	Date Started	Date Finished

FIGURE 45. A form for recording independent reading.

child an opportunity to contribute creatively to a group project. No matter which device is selected, a frequent change of presentation would be recommended to encourage student participation.

BOOK REPORTS

The problem of book reports is always with us. The more satisfactory a required form of report is as a review of the book the more likely it is to be regarded as a distasteful chore and the more liable it is to dampen enthusiasm for reading.

A desirable form of book report should have the following characteristics: (1) it discloses enough about the book to demonstrate that it was read and understood; (2) it does not lessen interest in reading or tend to reduce the number of books read; (3) it gives an opportunity for creative expression, verbally or otherwise.

Since most written book reports that are detailed enough to satisfy the first criterion fail on the second and third, teachers have explored a variety of other ways of reporting on books. The following kinds are usually successful:

1. *Oral book reports.* Many teachers have a period for oral book reports once a week or so. Children can report by telling briefly what the book is about and why they would or would not recommend it. Or, they can prepare a very funny or very exciting passage for audience reading. When several children have read the same book, they can have a panel discussion about it, or can prepare an informal dramatization of a scene from the book, reading dialogue from the book, or invent their own dialogue, or sometimes can prepare a puppet show. Individuals who volunteer to report on books can become members of a "reviewers' club" or some similar honorary organization.

2. *Artistic book reports.* Children who like to draw and paint can often prepare a visual book report. Several kinds are possible: designing a colorful and descriptive book jacket, illustrating an incident of central importance, making clay models of characters, building a diorama of the setting, etc.

3. *Shared written reports.* Writing reports can seem worthwhile

when the child knows that they are to be read and used by his classmates. A teacher can file evaluative book reports in a loose-leaf-notebook, in which children can look up what classmates have said about a book, either before reading it to see if they want to, or after reading it to compare impressions.

4. *Individual oral reports.* It is a central part of individualized reading procedure to have private discussions or conferences with children, during which the reading they have done is discussed; when this is done, other types of book reports are not really necessary.

5. *Cumulative book reports.* The teacher provides a manila folder for each book shown to be of particular interest to students in the grade. Each student who reads the book is asked to record his personal comments for the folder. These folders are available in a central place for all students to consult. This kind of reporting allows the child to read what other members of the class have said about the book and at the same time does not force the child to respond to a book in a particular pattern typical of printed book report forms. Most children are inclined to provide information for other readers not covered by previous reviews.

6. *Individual reaction reports.* For certain book report assignments a child is given a 4 by 6 index card. On this card he is asked to make his personal critical comment on a book. Teachers can direct these comments to have a child respond about the funniest, happiest, saddest, etc., event of the book; the specialness of the details of the setting of the book; the funniest, etc., character of the book. The possibilities of this type of reaction report are limitless and again encourage creativity on the part of the child reviewer.

HOW PARENTS CAN HELP

Long before children begin to read, parents who read stories to them regularly are paving the way for success in reading. Once children have started to read, many parents stop reading to them and telling them stories. These parents do not realize that even the easiest library book requires at least high first- or second-reader ability and that many children do not become able to do much independent reading until they are nine or ten years old. Even for children who read well, the sharing of books with parents through family reading helps to enhance the pleasure of reading. How parents can foster a love of reading through reading to children is illustrated by this quotation from a preface written by an author and editor of children's books: "To my mother and father, who read to me constantly as a child and introduced me to reading and books as a source of continual pleasure."[8]

In addition to sharing reading with children, parents can help their children to become independent readers in several other ways.

1. *Providing a model.* The child who grows up in a home in which the parents enjoy reading and spend much of their own free time in reading is likely to adopt the family attitude toward reading.

2. *Providing books.* Relatively few homes have satisfactory collections of children's books, and many communities have no store in which a good selection of children's books can be purchased. Parents need to be reminded that a fine book makes a fine present, and they need guidance in what kinds of books to buy. As shown in Appendix A, there are book clubs available for children of all ages. The school can help parents by supplying lists of recommended books, by celebrating Book Week with appropriate displays, and by holding a Book Fair from time to time.[9] The school can also work through the local parent organization to convey to parents the importance of children's becoming regular visitors to the public library.

3. *Understanding the reading program.* Many parents have dim and distorted recollections of how they learned to read, and do not understand what the schools are trying to do in the reading program. In addition to teacher-parent discussions of reading instruction, the parents can gain helpful information both about what the schools are

[8] Nancy Larrick, *A Teacher's Guide to Children's Books* (Columbus, Ohio: Charles E. Merrill, 1963), p. x.

[9] Specific, practical suggestions about how to organize and run a Book Fair can be obtained from the Children's Book Council, 175 Fifth Ave., New York, N.Y. 10010.

doing in reading and about what they as parents can do to help, from the following books:

Arbuthnot, May H. *Children's Reading in the Home.* New York: Scott, Foresman, 1968.
Larrick, Nancy. *A Parent's Guide to Children's Reading.* 3rd ed., revised and enlarged. New York: Pocket Books, 1969. (Paper, 95¢)

These references also contain many good suggestions about books that parents can read to children or get for them.

STIMULATING SUMMERTIME READING

Summer vacation is a time when recreational reading should flourish. When no special effort is made to encourage and guide summer reading, scores of reading tests given just before and after the vacation tend to show no change on the average or may actually get worse. When a real campaign to stimulate summer reading is planned and carried out, good gains have been reported. Although some children read a great deal during the summer, it seems evident that the majority do not do so unless special efforts are made to promote reading during the summer vacation.

Ingenious teachers can find a variety of ways to encourage summer reading. One is to take the class on a visit to the public library late in the spring, with the librarian giving a sales talk and encouraging those children who do not have library cards to apply for them. Another is to distribute a recommended reading list, with provision for the children to check the books they read and return the list in September. Many public libraries run special summer reading recreational programs including story hours, book discussions, and movies. Various forms of recognition are provided for those students who achieve at a particular level. Supplying a summer reading record form, and asking for it to be turned in after school reopens, is another generally useful incentive. Improving the reading skills of poor readers by reading while school is closed is more likely to be successful if the children are given material that they find easy to read and interesting, and if direct efforts are made to improve their reading skills.

Improving the Range and Maturity of Reading Interests

OPENING UP NEW INTEREST AREAS

It is the teacher's responsibility to set the stage for the development of new reading interests, in addition to using interests that children have already acquired. It is not difficult to provide conditions in which children become eager to read in previously untouched areas.

Let us suppose that a third-grade class has done little or no reading about pets and other animals, and the teacher wants to get them interested in this area. She can bring to class a pet such as a hamster, rabbit, or turtle, or can invite one or two children to bring in their pets. In a skillfully led discussion about the pets of all kinds of questions are likely to arise. How big do they grow? How long do they live? What do they eat? Do they bite? At the strategic moment the teacher discovers that she has some books about pets, and the hunt for answers can get started. While reading about one kind of pet, children are likely to peruse information about other kinds of pets. It is easy to lead the children on to fiction and factual books about dogs, cats, ponies, horses, farm animals, and on to wild animals. Another approach that can be used successfully is to start things off with a visit to a zoo, or with a filmstrip or movie. Sometimes a television program about animals can be used as a starter.

This interest-building technique, which can be applied in many areas, involves the following steps: (1) open up a new, interesting area of real or vicarious experience; (2) stimulate the asking of questions; (3) make available reading material in which answers can be found; (4) provide books on closely related topics.

Often a wide-awake and curious child will bring in a lead to a new interest area. Current news reports keep children excited about a great many topics in the area of science and invention: space satellites, atomic submarines, rockets, jets, manned space travel—the science fiction of a generation ago is daily coming into reality. For today's teacher, keeping personally in touch with what is going on in the world requires more and more effort; keeping curious children supplied with the information they want is often more than the teacher can manage.

Questions that children raise can be handled in a variety of ways. One is to write on a card each question that comes up, and periodically to distribute one card apiece to a number of children, as a project for individual research. Another is to turn a group of related questions over to a committee. Such techniques help children to become active seekers for information and relieve the teacher of the compulsion to try to know all the answers.

When the language patterns used by authors are strange to children and hard to grasp, oral reading by the teacher is often necessary. Poetry, for example, uses unfamiliar words (e.g., *ne'er*), and the arrangements of lines often makes it difficult for the children to get the continuity of thought. When they listen to the teacher read poetry, the children can experience the rhythm and cadence of the language and can develop appropriate meanings and feelings, without having to struggle with the printed representation. Once children have some familiarity with a poem they are likely to enjoy reading it for themselves, and choral reading also can be effective and enjoyable. The usefulness of a teacher presentation is just as great with upper grade children as in the first grade. Once a taste for poetry and some familiarity with poetic forms has been acquired, children can proceed to some independent reading of poetry and often try to write poems themselves. An excellent source to encourage independent reading of poetry is the series *Poetry and Verse for Urban Children,* Book 1— *Poems and Verses to Begin on;* Book 2—*Poems and Verses About Animals;* Book 3—*Poems and Verses About the City,* Donald J. Bissett, Ed. (San Francisco: Chandler Publishing Co., 1968).

PROVIDING READING LADDERS

Maturity in taste is never achieved in a giant step; it comes about gradually, through reading many books, mediocre and excellent, babyish and mature, and coming gradually to prefer the finer and the more mature. Taste is achieved through discrimination, and to be able to compare and choose one must read both literature and trash. Teachers and librarians who want to restrict children's reading to what teachers and librarians consider worthwhile are ignoring the psychological principle that personal standards are built from direct experience in comparing and contrasting works of varying degrees of merit.

To help boys and girls raise their levels of taste and broaden their range of reading interests, it is necessary to start from where they are and to recommend and provide a ladder of books of increasing merit and maturity which they can be encouraged to climb, one rung at a time.

Let us suppose that we have a third grader who loves animal cartoons and comic books but does not seem to care for reading. One could start with *Harry the Dirty Dog,* an easy book. Next one might try *Curious George,* about a mischievous monkey, and if this is enjoyed, it has several sequels. From there one could lead into other easy books in which animals get into ridiculous situations: perhaps the Dr. Seuss books like *The Cat in the Hat* and *Horton Hatches the Egg.*

If a fifth-grade girl wants to read nothing but *Black Stallion* books, be patient. There are only about a dozen of them, and when she has read them all, one can suggest other stories about horses, such as *Black Beauty, Misty of Chincoteague,* and *Justin Morgan Had a Horse.* If *The Wild Heart* is enjoyed, how about an animal story with a somewhat similar theme, like L. M. Boston's *A Stranger at Greene Knowe* or DeJong's *Hurry Home, Candy.* This could lead into other animal tales or books like Burnford's *The Incredible Journey,* or Street's *Goodbye, My Lady.* Then one could go into other stories with human-animal relations as the theme, which also deal with the problem of growing up and accepting reality. For such purposes, *The Yearling, The Red Pony,* or *Dorp Dead* could be used.

READING AND PERSONAL DEVELOPMENT

Reading has a powerful effect on the development of personality and character as well as on intellect. Children identify strongly with the heroes and heroines they admire, and hate the villains. In their imaginative play and daydreams they often put themselves in the hero's role. Whether the characters are real or fictional, they try to emulate them. The reading they do has a powerful influence on the formation of their ideals, beliefs, and aspirations. Career choices are often motivated in large part by reading; the senior author has no hesitation in crediting much of his early interest in the biological sciences to *The Microbe Hunters* and *Arrowsmith*.

Stories that last and become classics are stories that appeal to deep and widespread human emotions. The most popular character of all time is the person handicapped by deformity, ugliness, lowly station, or social rejection, who meets adversity bravely and triumphs in the end. We meet him in many guises: *Cinderella*, *The Ugly Duckling*, *The Frog Prince*, *Mike Mulligan's Steam Shovel*, *Lentil*, and *Chester the Worldly Pig*.

The term *bibliotherapy* has been used for the deliberate selection of reading material to try to fit the known needs and problems of the reader. Thus De Angeli's *A Door in the Wall* is often mentioned as a fine book for children with physical handicaps because it is a moving tale about a lame child and how he learned to live with his handicap. There are good books which may fit a particular child's needs because they are about a child who faces problems of loneliness or of unpopularity because of shabby clothing or being different from the majority in appearance, speech, race, or religion.

Bibliotherapy can be helpful, within limits, but the idea can produce a misleading oversimplification of the situation. It is perhaps more important for the multitude of noncrippled children to understand and to be sensitized to the problems of the crippled, so that they will not mock or tease, than it is to give courage to the crippled—who often have plenty of courage already. If *Call Me Charley* can help a black child to face the problems of going to a school in which the other children are white, it can be even more helpful in improving the attitudes of the white children among whom he has to live. Other books helpful in this area include *Whistle for Willy*, *What Mary-Jo Shared*, *Sam*, *The Snowy Day*, and *Two Is a Team*. To help to improve attitudes toward and between groups, authors like Lois Lenski and Joseph Krumgold could be used effectively.

By all means let us try to place in children's hands books which can help them to understand life and to develop fine traits of character and personality. In doing this, let us not be bound by a narrow problem-recipe formula, but let us strive to bring children together with books that help them to see life whole.

Learning About Books for Children

If we accept the idea that a teacher should be well versed in content as well as in methods of instruction, the teacher of reading needs more than a nodding acquaintance with children's books. This acquaintance should include library or so-called trade books, as well as readers and textbooks. If one has not had a course on children's literature, books like the ones by Arbuthnot and Larrick listed on page 384, can help one to get oriented in this field.

To be an enthusiastic and convincing salesman for children's books one must know one's goods. To bring children and books together effectively one should both understand the children and have a broad acquaintance with the books that might suit them. If teachers are to discuss children's reading with them in individual or group discussions (and this is vital to a program of independent reading), the teacher should know the book well enough to ask intelligent questions about it and to be able to judge the adequacy and accuracy of the answers. It is impossible to know all the books in this way, but the teacher should be personally acquainted with a sampling of reasonable size. Reading children's books need not be a disagreeable chore for teachers; a book that is good for children should also be an enjoyable experience for an adult who has not completely buried his childhood interests and enthusiasms. Many of the recent science books for children are just the right speed for many teachers.

With about twenty-five hundred new juvenile books coming out each year, in addition to the older books, teachers have to be highly selective and must rely largely on the recommendations made by specialists in books for children. Being able to consult with a librarian who has made a special study of children's books is very helpful. The librarian, in turn, frequently depends on special book lists and reviews which can also be used as references by teachers. Among the manv good listings of children's books, the following are especially recommended:

A Basic Book Collection for Elementary Grades, compiled by Miriam Snow, *et al.* Chicago: American Library Association. A selected list of 1,000 books, arranged according to the Dewey Decimal System, with brief annotations and approximate difficulty ratings; author and title indexes. There are similar A.L.A. book lists for junior and senior high school.

Best Books for Children, 1969 edition, compiled by Doris Solomon. New York: R. R. Bowker. Lists 4,000 books recommended by *The Booklist, School Library Journal, Book Review, ABA Basic Book List,* or H. H. Wilson Company lists. Arranged in groups for primary, middle, and upper grades under many headings; has author index and title index. Revised annually.

Bibliography of Books for Children. Washington, D.C.: Association for Childhood Education International. About 1,700 books recommended for children from age 4 to 12; particularly good at the preschool and primary levels. Arranged informally by subject. Revised every two years.

Books for Children, 1967–68. Selected and reviewed by *The Booklist* and *Subscription Books Bulletin.* Chicago: American Library Association, 1968. Compiled annually, this is a graded, annotated list combining reading or interest age with comparisons of other books on the same topic or by the same author.

Eakin, Mary K. *Good Books for Children: A Selection of Outstanding Children's Books Published 1950–1965.* Chicago: University of Chicago Press, 1966. Lists 1,400 books previously given favorable reviews in the *Bulletin of the Center for Children's Books.* Indicates reading level, interest level, and relation to school curriculum.

Junior Plots: A Manual for Teachers and Librarians. Compiled by John Gillespie and Diana Lembo. New York: R. R. Bowker, 1967. Arranged by goals; for example, earning a living, achieving self-reliance, evaluating life, etc. Contains plot summaries, theme statements, highlights for oral reading, and recommendations for books on related themes.

Introducing Books: A Guide for the Middle Grades. Compiled by John Gillespie and Diana Lembo. New York: R. R. Bowker, 1970. Each discussion of the 88 titles, which are treated under one of eleven thematic headings, includes a plot summary, information on thematic material, suggestions for presenting the book and suggested related readings.

Perkins, Ralph. *Book Selection Media.* Champaign, Ill.: NCTE, 1966. Descriptive guide of many book selection aids.

Two highly selective lists, which are revised annually, are so inexpensive that they can be purchased by a parent organization to be given to all members. These are:

Growing Up with Books, compiled by the staff of *Junior Libraries*. New York: R. R. Bowker. Booklet containing a number of briefly annotated books.

Growing Up with Science Books, compiled by the staff of *Junior Libraries*. New York: R. R. Bowker. Similar to *Growing Up with Books* except that it gives a more comprehensive listing of science books.

Special lists of books dealing with human relationships include the following:

Behavior Patterns in Children's Books, compiled by Clara Kircher. Washington, D.C.: Catholic University of America Press, 1966.
Rtading Ladders for Human Relations, 4th ed., edited by Muriel Crosby. Washington, D.C.: American Council on Education, 1963.

Comprehensive lists of magazines and newspapers for children, series books, children's book clubs, and children's book lists, as well as reading materials recommended for poor readers, can be found in the following:

Spache, George D. *Good Reading for Poor Readers.* Rev. ed. Champaign, Ill.: Garrard Press, 1968.
Strang, Ruth; Phelps, Ethlyne; and Withrow, Dorothy. *Gateways to Readable Books,* 4th ed. New York: W. H. Wilson Co., 1966.

Teachers who want to keep abreast of the latest good books for children can find reviews of high quality in periodicals such as *Junior Libraries, Elementary English,* and the *Horn Book,* as well as in the children's book sections of *The New York Times.*

Summary

1. Interests are learned tendencies to prefer specific activities or objects.
2. Interests develop when activities are inherently pleasurable or are accompanied by a feeling of ease, a feeling of accomplishment, or social approval.

3. The mass entertainment media compete with reading for children's free time.

   a. Most of the competition comes from television which elementary school children watch an average of three hours a day; however, there is little evidence to indicate that watching T.V. is the reason why there is not more voluntary reading done by children.

   b. The possibilities of using T.V. to promote reading need further exploration.

   c. The strategic way of meeting the competition of the mass media is by making reading more enjoyable.

4. Reading interests are related to age, sex, and intelligence.

   a. Although there are some similarities, there is a wide range of individual differences as to reading interests.

   b. Interests can be ascertained by observing children's behavior, activities, and conversations, through interviews and compositions, and through questionnaires.

5. Children's liking for reading can be increased by reading and telling stories to them, by making books easily accessible, by a display of teacher enthusiasm, by helping children to select books they can enjoy, and by using appropriate reading records and book reports.

6. Parents can help to stimulate interest in reading by reading to their children (particularly during the preschool and early school years), by providing a model, by providing books and other reading materials, and by understanding the children's school reading programs.

7. Efforts to stimulate summer reading can be rewarding.

8. Teachers can stimulate children to read in previously untouched areas by providing experiences that arouse curiosity.

9. Reading poetry to children or having them listen to recordings helps them to become interested in reading poetry themselves.

10. The improvement of reading taste should start where the child is and provide a succession of books through which the child can gradually move to more worthwhile books.

11. Reading has character-building potentialities and can help sensitize children to the problems others encounter in life.
12. Teachers need to know children's books as well as how to teach reading.
   a. There is no adequate substitute for personal reading of books for children.
   b. There are many reference sources, including the librarian and book lists, that can help teachers to find "the right book for the right child."

Recommended Reading

ARBUTHNOT, MAY HILL. *Children and Books,* 3rd ed. Chicago: Scott, Foresman, 1964.

BEERY, ALTHEA, BARRETT, THOMAS C., and POWELL, WILLIAM R. *Elementary Reading Instruction: Selected Materials.* Boston: Allyn and Bacon, Inc., 1969. Ch. 8.

CATTERSON, JANE H., ED. *Children and Literature.* Newark, Del.: International Reading Association, 1970.

GRAY, LILLIAN. *Teaching Children to Read,* 3rd ed. New York: Ronald Press, 1963. Ch. 13.

HARRIS, ALBERT J. *How to Increase Reading Ability,* 5th ed. New York: McKay, 1970. Ch. 17.

ODLAND, NORINE. *Teaching Literature in the Elementary School.* NCTE/ERIC Studies in the Teaching of English. Champaign, Ill.: National Council of Teachers of English, 1969.

ROBINSON, EVELYN R., ED. *Readings About Children's Literature.* New York: McKay, 1966.

SMITH, JAMES A. *Creative Teaching of Reading and Literature in the Elementary School.* Boston: Allyn and Bacon, Inc., 1967.

SMITH, NILA B. *Reading Instruction for Today's Children.* Englewood Cliffs, N.J.: Prentice-Hall, 1963. Chs. 12–14.

14

Achieving Maximum Reading Goals for Every Child

$\mathbf{M}$ost people would be dismayed if they were told that 50 percent of all children were reading below average. Yet, by definition the term "average" means that 50 percent are above and 50 percent below a certain level. A grade-equivalent score on a standardized reading achievement test, which indicates the median performance of a large number of children, necessarily has as many children below it as above it. Very few score exactly at the median. Efforts to get all children to achieve "at the norm" not only deny this fact but also overlook the wide variations in achievement that are characteristic at every grade level. Norms should not be considered to be standards.

Some children will inevitably be better readers than the others in their class. Other children are doing as well as can be expected at that point in time, even though they are not reading "up to grade level," when one considers the factors that influence reading achievement. Still other children, who are reading "at grade level," should be performing at higher levels. Educators should aim at helping each child to make the most of his opportunities and abilities. The closer we come to this ideal, the wider the differences in performance will become.

The children whose achievement in reading is significantly below the norms for their ages and grades are generally referred to as being "retarded in reading." Within this group, at least half are children whose general mental development is slow and whose reading is about on a par with the rest of their educational and intellectual growth; they show varying degrees of general retardation. The remainder are significantly below expectancy for their intelligence and age, as well as being disparate with their cultural, linguistic, and educational experiences. These children, who represent approximately 10 to 15 percent of the school children in the United States (excluding the culturally and educationally disadvantaged), have a *reading disability*, or a special difficulty in learning to read.[1] Among the retarded readers, whether the retardation is general or special, we find a high percentage of children with behavior and conduct problems, personality disturbances of many kinds, and delinquent behavior. Help in reading is by no means all that these children need, but it is a highly significant item.

Children who are well above average in mental ability deserve special attention in the reading program. They include bright underachievers and children whose reading ability is already superior and needs continued nourishment.

The first section of this chapter takes up the reading problems of the generally slow learner. This is followed by a consideration of the child with a mild to severe reading disability: identifying him, discovering handicaps that can be corrected, motivating him to exert more effort, analyzing his particular difficulties and strengths in reading, and teaching what he specifically needs. The next section considers the reading needs of mentally superior children; and the final section deals with the educationally disadvantaged.

Reading Needs of Generally Slow Learning Children

The generally slow make up approximately the bottom 25 percent of children in general intelligence. The total intellectual distribution

---

[1] Some writers have been using *reading retardation* in the sense in which we use *reading disability*. This ambiguity in terminology is confusing and regrettable.

is as follows: top 10 percent, superior, I.Q.'s of 120 and above; next 15 percent, bright, 110 to 120; middle 50 percent, average, 90 to 110; next 15 percent, dull normal or mildly retarded, 80 to 90; the borderline group, 70 to 80, about 7 percent; and the seriously retarded, below 70, about 3 percent. Sometimes a dividing line is drawn at I.Q. 75, for the purpose of establishing special classes. The seriously retarded are usually subdivided as educable (I.Q.'s of 50 and above) and trainable (I.Q.'s 35 to 50).

It is generally agreed that the seriously mentally retarded fall so far below most children in learning ability that they are in need of special education programs. Usually the upper limit for such special programs is placed at an I.Q. of 70 or 75.

Although school group intelligence tests can identify children as possibly or probably retarded, no child should be considered to be definitely retarded except on the recommendation of a psychologist after an individual examination. Teachers have at times misjudged children to be retarded when the real trouble was a severe emotional difficulty, a sensory defect such as a severe hearing loss, a speech defect, a receptive or expressive language handicap, or a severe reading disability. In most communities, special classes for the mentally retarded are provided. When a child who belongs in such a class remains in a regular classroom, many problems may arise. It is important for teachers who have such children to understand the limits of their learning ability, so as not to expect the impossible of them. Excessive pressure for achievement levels far beyond their capacity has made the lives of many retarded children miserable. On the other hand, they should not be treated as though it is impossible for them to learn. As in any situation, the teacher's attitude toward the child and his capabilities influences not only the child's desire to learn but his self-concept as well.

The dull, however, include about 15 percent of all children (20 percent if we include the 75 to 80 I.Q. group). Knowing what can reasonably be expected scholastically of such children helps teachers to understand their limitations. In this way the teacher is relieved of guilt feelings when the child cannot come up to the norm, and the child is relieved of pressure to try to do what for him is impossible.

Reasonable achievement levels for slow children are shown in the lower part of Table III. The table shows the mental maturity reached

TABLE III. Approximate Mental Grade for Children of Different I.Q.'s at Chronological Ages Eight to Thirteen

I.Q.	Mental Grade at Chronological Age of					
	8–0	9–0	10–0	11–0	12–0	13–0
130	5.4	6.7	8.0	9.3	10.7	11.9
120	4.6	5.9	7.0	8.2	9.4	10.6
110	3.9	4.9	6.0	7.1	8.3	9.3
100	3.0	4.0	5.0	6.0	7.0	8.0
90	2.2	3.1	4.0	4.9	5.9	6.7
85	1.9	2.7	3.5	4.4	5.3	6.0
80	1.5	2.2	3.0	3.9	4.6	5.5
75	Kgn.	1.7	2.5	3.3	4.0	4.8
70	Kgn.	1.3	2.0	2.9	3.5	4.1

by children with various I.Q.'s in one-year intervals; mental maturity is expressed in terms of corresponding grade level. According to the table, an eight-year-old with an I.Q. of 80 is doing normal work for his ability if he is achieving at middle first-grade level. An eleven-year-old with an I.Q. of 85 would be functioning normally if achieving at middle fourth-grade level. Grade expectancies for many other combinations of age and I.Q. can be found in the table. The slow child who is achieving at or above the grade level indicated in Table III as appropriate for his age and I.Q. is working well for his limited ability and should be relieved of pressure to try to catch up to the mythical average.

Slow children need reading programs that are adapted to their limited learning ability and that take into consideration their special needs. They generally benefit from a prolonged readiness period, during which specific readiness skills are developed. Some of them do comparatively well in learning to recognize words, while many of them are slow in building a sight vocabulary and learning to use phonics. Nearly all of them have limitations in comprehension. These limitations are likely to show up especially strongly when the task is to infer a conclusion that is not specifically stated, to anticipate an outcome, or to find the main idea. Their concepts are usually quite specific and narrow and they have trouble with abstract ideas and generalizations.

The reading interests of slow children tend to be a little less mature than the average, but closer to the interests of average children of their age than to their own mental level. For independent reading they do best with books in which the language is simple and clear and the ideas are easy to understand, while the topic is interesting to children of their own age.

In some school systems, slow learning children are required to spend an extra year in the primary grades; this is usually based more on slow progress in reading than on their I.Q. scores. This is usually done at the end of the first grade (preferable) or at the end of the third grade. This tends to lessen the gap between their performance and the grade norm. For the children with I.Q.'s near 90, this gives an opportunity to work at an average level. For the many with I.Q.'s well below 90, an extra year reduces the discrepancy but does not bring them up to average mental maturity for their grade placements; in the middle and upper grades, they are still likely to be functioning in reading and other academic work a year or more below their grade placements. Repeating a year more than once in the elementary school may induce or aggravate conduct and personality disturbances that are more undesirable than the academic difficulties of keeping a child with an age group in which he is always below average. Even if we help each child to read as well as his mentality allows, the generally slow child will remain with us in large numbers and will require the continuation and improvement of efforts to help him to learn at his own pace.

There are some practical suggestions that are generally applicable in the teaching of mentally slow children: [2]

---

[2] Other suggestions for teaching these and other types of exceptional children may be found in *Exceptional Children,* a journal published by the Council for Exceptional Children, NEA.

1. It is important, even more than with average or bright children, to make sure that the material used in their developmental reading lessons is not above their instructional reading levels.
2. Slow children usually require extra repetition and planned, spaced review.
3. In view of their difficulties with abstract ideas, important concepts need to be carefully developed from ample experiences and illustrations, and the meanings that these children arrive at need to be checked; they often resort to memorizing verbal formulations that they do not understand. Whenever possible, concepts should be related to practical concrete examples that fall within the children's experiences.
4. Considerable use of audio-visual aids is helpful in making up for their deficiencies in real and vicarious experience.
5. It is desirable to watch for signs of special talent or interest in such nonverbal areas as art, music, athletics, and handwork, and to look for ways to use these interests in their recreational reading.
6. Slow children do not have any uniquely different ways of learning; the teaching procedures that work with other children are effective with them also, provided that due care is taken regarding their readiness for new steps, and their generally slower pace in learning.
7. In content areas, their limitations in grasping ideas and in being able to read textbooks make it highly desirable to try to provide simpler reading material and to keep the curriculum to minimum essentials; often projects can be used to provide simpler tasks for the slower children.[3]

If interest in reading seems low, responsiveness can often be increased by giving some attention to the common words that serve as important signals in their environment. Sign words like *stop, go, wait, danger, keep out, poison, entrance, exit, men,* and *women,* if recognized and understood, can sometimes save them from embarrassment or even from serious danger.[4] Names of local streets and bus routes can be used for word recognition practice and phonic analysis. So

---

[3] Some materials are available for teaching content subjects and reading skills to slow learners. For example, see: Jack Abramowitz, *Study Lessons in Our Nation's History; World History Study Lessons; American History Study Lessons* (Chicago: Follett).

[4] For a comprehensive list of such words and phrases refer to: Corlett T. Wilson, "An Essential Vocabulary," *The Reading Teacher,* 17 (November 1963), 94–96.

can the names of products often purchased in the local supermarket. The more reading can be made to relate to their own lives, the more they are likely to recognize it as worth the effort to learn. With older boys and girls, reading matter that relates to trades and occupations they might be able to enter is often welcome.[5]

Identifying the Child with a Reading Disability

In a typical elementary school, about 10 percent of the children (a half to a third of the poorest readers) read at levels lower than their mental ability should make possible. Some of these are bright children who are under-achievers; the rest are children with genuine reading disabilities.

GENUINE READING DISABILITY

A genuine reading disability exists when a child's reading is significantly below what is normal for both his grade placement and his mental development. The measure of mental development can be the mental age on a satisfactory intelligence test that does not involve reading (see page 166); when such a test score is not available, a teacher-made listening comprehension test can be used to obtain a rough estimate.[6] Oral reading as well as silent reading should be taken into consideration, since the weaknesses in word recognition and fluency that show up in oral reading frequently underlie inadequate comprehension.

[5] Among the materials that might be used are: *Vocational Reading Series; Turner-Livingston Reading Series; Turner Communications Series* (Chicago: Follett); and the *New Rochester Occupational Reading Series* (Chicago: Science Research Associates).

[6] When a satisfactory intelligence score is available but is more than a couple of months old, the mental age has to be corrected for growth since the date of the test. Present mental age can be estimated with the following formula: $MA_{est} = CA \times IQ$. For a child 11 years 0 months old with an IQ of 84, this would be $MA_{est} = 11.0 \times .84 = 9.24$ years. By subtracting five years, this gives a reading expectancy of 4.24, or low fourth grade. With a listening comprehension test, listening grade level can be compared directly with reading grade level or the child's instructional level.

No test, whether of achievement or intelligence, furnishes results that are completely accurate. Most good intelligence and reading tests have probable errors of measurement ranging between two and six months. Unless the difference between two scores is fairly large, it may be due to errors of measurement. A safe rule to follow is to select cases for remedial teaching in which reading is at least a year below the grade norm, and the difference between reading age and mental age is at least nine months for children in the first three grades, twelve months in grades four and five, or a year and a half for children above the fifth grade.[7]

Corrective Reading Cases. Corrective reading is the term usually employed in referring to giving help to children with relatively mild reading disabilities within the structure of class room instruction. In general, children for whom corrective reading is appropriate have instructional reading levels that fall within the limits of the low reading group in the class. Like those with more severe disabilities, they often have persisting handicapping conditions which should be identified and corrected when possible. If the teacher is able to recognize their needs, teach the skills they require during group lessons or in some supplementary individual help, and arouse their motivation and interest, many of these children make quite satisfactory progress and grow out of their disabilities.

Remedial Reading Cases. The relatively severe cases of reading disability are called *remedial reading* cases; this implies that they need help that should be given, if possible, by a teacher who has had special professional training for such work, and is outside the regular classroom program. Remedial reading is usually done with from one to six children at a time. Some schools have special remedial reading teachers who work with these children. A few large school systems have reading clinics in which expert diagnosis and remedial teaching are available. Some school systems have reading consultants who study the child's needs, work with him long enough to get him started, and then work closely with the classroom teacher who keeps the remedial program going. Sometimes the school makes use of a reading

[7] For a more accurate procedure, refer to Albert J. Harris, *How to Increase Reading Ability,* 5th ed. (New York: McKay, 1970), pp. 211–215.

clinic in the community or refers parents to qualified remedial teachers who work privately.

In severe remedial cases reading skills are far below grade placement and are often two to five years below mental maturity level. The child is usually such a poor reader that the work of the lowest reading group in the class is still well above his frustration level, so that he makes little or no progress in the group lessons. He needs so much highly individualized help that many competent teachers are unable to meet his needs in a classroom situation. Often the picture is complicated by the presence of interfering handicaps and by emotional problems that require special attention. When there are no special facilities in the school system or the community, it is up to the classroom teacher to do the best he can; but if the child does not improve, the teacher should not feel guilty or incompetent.

For the remedial case, and to a lesser extent for the child with a corrective reading problem, the program of help should include discovering and correcting interfering handicaps, diagnosing specific learning needs, effective motivation, and teaching that concentrates on the child's special reading needs.

Discovering and Correcting Handicaps to Reading Progress

Finding the original causes of a reading disability is often impossible. Usually several years have passed since the child entered school, records are incomplete, and memories are faulty. Even if one could discover all the facts that are relevant, there are usually several potential causes present, and the relative significance of each in the particular case is likely to arouse disagreement even among experts.

For the classroom teacher, and the remedial teacher also, it usually is preferable not to worry about the original causation and to concentrate on trying to find out what is preventing improvement now. There are many factors, other than intellectual, that can interfere with progress in learning to read, and it is possible to give only a brief summary of them here.

PHYSICAL FACTORS

Uncorrected visual defects are the most common physical handicaps among children with reading disabilities. The *Snellen Chart*, used in most schools to test vision, is quite unsatisfactory except as a test of nearsightedness. The kinds of visual defects that are most liable to interfere with reading are farsightedness and various kinds of eye muscle difficulties, resulting in quick ocular fatigue, difficulty in forming a clear retinal image, and difficulty in obtaining good fusion of the separate pictures seen by the two eyes. These defects often allow a child to make a perfect score on the Snellen Chart; they can be detected on more elaborate visual screening tests used in many schools. However, a thorough visual examination by an optometrist or ophthalmologist is desirable for every child who has a reading disability.

Hearing defects, endocrine problems, and neurological defects are sometimes very important. Lack of energy may be present because of a chronic debilitating condition like asthma, malnutrition, or heart disease. Lack of sufficient sleep because of a late bedtime is sometimes the very simple basis of drowsiness in school.

A constitutional predisposition to reading disability tends to run in some families. These children, usually boys, tend to have quite severe disabilities, and they usually also show marked directional confusion, poor visual and auditory perception, and some delay in speech development; yet their general intelligence is normal or above.

When reversals are prominent in a child's reading and spelling, there is likely to be a basic directional confusion. This is more common among the ambidextrous than among either the thoroughly right- or left-handed, and least common among the consistently right-sided.

Dyslexia. In the past few years a great deal of interest and attention has been focused on children who have extreme difficulty in learning to read. These are the children, who long after their peers of similar age and mental ability have learned to read (most have at least average intelligence), have not yet learned to decode words or have not yet learned to decode words or have not yet developed a sight vocabulary. They not only find it exceedingly difficult to acquire the basic mechanical reading skills, but also have a problem in retaining the skills they have apparently "learned." Their problem seems to be one of making associations. Different labels have been attached to these children (e.g. strephosymbolia, word-blindness, minimal brain damage, primary reading disability) with probably the most common being "dyslexia." There is little agreement as to what causes dyslexia (i.e., Is it an inherited characteristic? Is it due to cerebral immaturity? Brain damage? Maturational lag?) and even less agreement as to its definition.[8] As for its possible symptoms, Clements listed almost 100 signs and symptoms under 15 categories for "minimal brain dysfunction."[9] In practice, some of these symptoms, but certainly far from all or even most, are present in each case, with the only one common to all being the learning difficulty. Therefore, the term preferred in this book is "severe reading disability."

Educators too often seem to be satisfied with pinning a label on a child. What needs to be done is to determine each child's specific strengths and weaknesses and to devise highly individualized programs for them so that learning in general, not just reading ability, can take place effectively. Such programs are often beyond what can be expected of classroom teachers. However, they can play a very important role in helping the child by working cooperatively with outside experts (hopefully in an interdisciplinary team) in conducting and evaluating the child's program. When such assistance is not available, the classroom teacher must do the best he can. Following the principles of remedial instruction offered by Bryant may assist the teacher in working with severe reading disability cases.[10] At our pres-

[8] Richard B. Adams, "Dyslexia: A Discussion of Its Definition," *Journal of Learning Disabilities,* 2 (December 1969), 6–23.

[9] Sam D. Clements, *Minimal Brain Dysfunction in Children: Terminology and Identification,* National Institute of Neurological Diseases, Monograph No. 3, Public Health Service Publication No. 1415 (Washington, D.C.: Government Printing Office, 1966).

[10] N. Dale Bryant, "Some Principles of Remedial Instruction for Dyslexia," *Reading Teacher,* 18 (April 1965), 567–572.

ent state of knowledge, no one can prescribe a panacea for severe reading disability. It may be that a number of different types of disability exist within this general category. We still have a great deal to learn about the reading act and reading disability.

EDUCATIONAL FACTORS

Among the school-related problems that can interfere with progress in reading are frequent or prolonged absence and frequent moving from one school to another; these the school cannot prevent. Schools are responsible for the following, all of which are present in some cases of reading disability: starting reading instruction before the child is ready, failing to give systematic instruction in word analysis skills, using reading material that is above the frustration level of the child, frightening children or habitually using sarcasm and disparagement, failing to arouse the child's interest in reading, and failing to detect and correct difficulties while they are still new and minor. One of the factors often unrecognized in reading disability is poor teaching.

SOCIAL FACTORS

The attitudes toward reading displayed in the neighborhood and particularly in the home are very important. It is difficult to help a child if his parents are uninterested and uncooperative, or if gang influence sets anti-intellectual standards. Aside from interest, the presence or absence of positive educational and cultural stimulation in the home has a pervasive influence on the schoolwork of children. Disturbed and maladjusted parents sometimes create very distressing conditions for children. Parents often aggravate a reading disability by scolding, punishing the child for his poor reading, disparaging, comparing him unfavorably with a scholastically successful brother or sister, or trying to teach him in inappropriate ways. Other parents, often due to social pressures, overpressure their children to achieve in school.

EMOTIONAL FACTORS

Failure in school is in many cases intimately connected with the child's total personal and emotional adjustment. In some cases an emotional problem present before the child entered the first grade has persistently interfered with concentration, attention, and motivation. In other cases, failure in the attempt to learn to read produces gradually increasing discouragement, the child tends after a while to try to avoid or evade reading, and is likely to become upset and confused when he cannot escape from reading. Whichever comes first, the emotional problem or the learning difficulty, eventually is of little importance. A vicious cycle becomes established in which each bad experience with reading produces unpleasant feelings, and the strong emotion of fear, anger, shame, or embarrassment interferes with clear thinking and makes it ever more difficult for the child to learn in a reading situation.

CORRECTING READING HANDICAPS

There are very realistic limits to what teachers can do about many of the conditions that handicap the disabled reader. The teacher cannot change the child's constitutional make-up. The teacher (and school nurse) can recommend a visual examination or some other kind of medical examination, but can do nothing except try to persuade the parents to follow advice. Sometimes it is a major victory just to get a pair of broken eyeglasses replaced. The teacher as an individual can do very little about the neighborhood conditions and has no jurisdiction over the child's playmates or out-of-school activities. The parents often resent inquisitiveness about their own personal problems, and sometimes the suggestion that a child may need help for an emotional difficulty meets with the reply, "Teach him to read and he'll stop being nervous."

The teacher should try to make use of specialized school personnel when they are available. Parents are likely to discuss the child's health problems more freely with a school nurse or physician, and to discuss problems of their own adjustment and their child's problems more freely with a school psychologist, school social worker, visiting teacher, or guidance counselor. The parents are also more likely to accept recommendations from people whom they regard as specialists. Both in discovering causal handicaps and in getting action for their correction, specialized personnel can be a great help.

Nevertheless, there are times when nobody but the classroom teacher can take the initiative, and the conscientious teacher will do what he can to help a child. In taking on a responsibility that would be carried in other schools by special personnel, the teacher should proceed cautiously and with all the tact he can muster. If the teacher can get across the idea that he knows that the parents want to do the best they can to help the child, and that his own interest in helping the child is genuine, a situation in which parents and teacher pool their information and try to think problems through together can at times be successfully established. The parents need to feel that the things they know about the child and the opinions they have are important and are respected. Instead of telling parents bluntly, "Johnny should have had a thorough eye examination by now," a teacher is much more likely to succeed if he leads gently into the subject. "Mrs. Jones, I notice that Billy blinks a lot and his eyes fill with tears and turn pink when he tries to read. The school eye tests don't show anything, but maybe there is something wrong with his eyes that the school tests cannot detect. Has he ever been examined by an eye specialist?"

Tact and patience often bring results in the long run, even if action does not take place quickly. Whether or not action to eliminate causal handicaps can be taken or stimulated, it is up to the teacher to do what he can to teach the child to read.

Motivating the Disabled Reader

BUILDING RAPPORT

The teacher's first objective, in a corrective or remedial reading situation, is to lay the groundwork for a good working relationship with each child. *Rapport* is a term used by psychotherapists to describe the kind of relationship they try to establish with their clients: a comfortable and unconstrained relationship of mutual confidence. Getting this kind of relationship established is just as important in remedial work as in psychotherapy.

The teacher must in one way or another get across to the child the feeling that he is liked, appreciated, and understood. When the teacher's feelings are genuine, the child will gradually warm up; if they are faked, the child will know the difference. Gushing and making a sentimental fuss over the child are to be avoided. A pleasant but businesslike attitude is desirable, in which the teacher provides learnable tasks, encourages, accepts poor performance without criticism or discouragement, explains or repeats with inexhaustible patience, never scolds or disparages, and conveys the impression that he confidently expects improvement. The teacher is not disheartened when the child has an off day, and celebrates every sign of real progress.

ENSURING SUCCESS

The remedial or corrective teacher must be prepared to find that, after years of chronic failure, the disabled reader often has the feeling that he is hopeless and stupid. Replacing this discouragement with hope is most important. For this reason, it is usually desirable to start with learning activities that are well below the child's instructional level, to make sure that he will succeed in them. An informal textbook test can indicate the child's independent reading level, and reading at this easy level for a while may not provide much new learning, but it can produce a major change in attitude. In the early lessons, the amount of material covered in a lesson, the number of new words introduced, etc., must be far less than the teacher has become accustomed to in regular classroom instruction. After the child has become convinced that he is making progress, the pace and difficulty can be gradually increased; but the reading activities should always stay below the child's frustration level and within the amount that he can absorb at one time. Learning how little to try to cover is one of the hardest tasks for the teacher who is new at remedial teaching.

CELEBRATING PROGRESS

Children with reading disabilities have had such a scarcity of praise and experience of success that when they do something worth noting it should be celebrated. Many of these children have such deep-seated feelings of inadequacy and inferiority that visible, dramatic evidence of their improvement needs to be kept before them. Having built up a self-image of chronic failure, the child finds it hard to believe that he is finally succeeding unless he sees incontrovertible evidence that he is actually learning.

It is desirable to set up three or four major goals for the remedial program and to set up a visually effective progress chart for each. Thus, a child who is still struggling at first-reader level might have a progress chart that records each new word learned, one for the total number of pages read, and one for new phonic principles mastered (see Figure 46). For a sixth-grade child reading at third-reader level, it would probably be better to chart stories read or books finished than pages read, and to keep a separate account of independent reading done between lessons.

MAKING READING INTERESTING

For children who have come to hate books, a modified experience story approach often works well as a starter. The teacher gets the child to talk about one of his interests or experiences, and together they formulate a brief story which the teacher prints in manuscript, and later types. The words that the child cannot recognize are taught, one by one, by whatever word study method seems to work best with this child, and the selection is reread (with different purposes) until it can be read fairly well by the child. It can then be taken and read to the classroom teacher, and sent home to be read to the parents. This continues with new selections; gradually the child takes over the writing and typing. Usually it does not take very long until the child indicates that he would like to try reading in a real book.

Getting children to accept books that are easy enough for them is

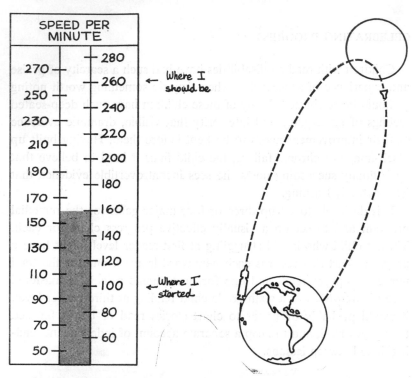

FIGURE 46. Individual progress charts. Left, rocket speedometer chart for recording improvement in rate of reading. Right, moon-flight chart for recording the completion of units of work; as a unit is finished the pupil draws or moves his rocket ship toward the moon, then upon reaching the moon draws his space capsule back toward earth.

often a problem, and sometimes a sales campaign is needed. The *Begin-Over Approach* is one in which the teacher explains to the child that most words in books that he would like to read are the short, easy words, and it is necessary to learn them before tackling the longer and harder words. Therefore it is desirable to start back near the beginning, with a book in which these words are almost the only ones that have to be learned. Low-difficulty material can be made more palatable when the child is given a genuine and valid reason for using it, which he can understand and accept.

The recent appearance of many very easy books that are interesting to older children has made the selection of remedial materials much easier than it used to be. There are several series of supplementary readers that start at about primer level. See Appendix A for a list and Figure 47 for a sample page. There are also a number of very easy series of independent trade books (see Appendix A). It is now easy to avoid the re-use of any of the basal readers with which the child has already had painful experiences.

Word recognition practice and phonic practice can be made to seem like fun. Original teaching and learning of new items are best done with straightforward teaching techniques. Reviewing can, however, be dressed up in many ways, in the form of a game or contest. Many reading games are available commercially (see pages 458–460), and there are many suggestions that teachers can follow in making their own reading games and devices.[11]

Giving older children the feeling of being active participants both in studying their learning needs and in selecting reading activities often works very well. Reading test scores can be shown and analyzed. The child can be told that he is a reading detective, helping to discover clues. He assists in identifying the faults in his reading and in listing specific skills in which he needs improvement. Sometimes he knows quite well what his trouble is; all you have to do is ask him. Teacher and pupil select reading activities in relation to these problem areas, and as each problem is cleared up it is crossed off the list. When the first problems have been solved, new ones at higher reading levels are discovered.

CONSIDERING THE FAMILY

Since reading problems are often related to home conditions, it is highly desirable to get the parents to work cooperatively with the

[11] Albert J. Harris, *How to Increase Reading Ability*, 5th ed., 1970.

David H., Russell and Etta E. Karp, *Reading Aids through the Grades*, rev. ed. (New York: Bureau of Publications, Teachers College, Columbia University, 1961).

Selma E. Herr, *Learning Activities for Reading* (Dubuque, Iowa: Wm. C. Brown Co., 1961).

Chapter Four

DIVING FOR TREASURE

"The treasure ship!" said Salty. "The treasure ship!"

"Yes," said Carlos. "We have found it. Good work, Dan!"

The crew of the *Sea Watch* asked Dan many things about the ship he had found.

"Is it a big ship?" asked Bill.

"It looked big," answered Dan.

"Did you see the gold?" asked Andy. "Was there a treasure chest with gold in it?"

"Andy!" laughed Dan. "We have found the ship, but our work is far from over."

"That is one thing Andy does not know," said Carlos. "He does not know that it will take time to find the treasure in the ship."

teacher, not only in eliminating handicaps but also in carrying forward a positive remedial program. There are two aspects of this: the positive one of getting them to do things that are helpful and the negative one of trying to get them to stop doing things that are harmful.

Most parents are eager to have a part in helping their children. If they are not given something to do, they are likely to follow their own ideas, and these often do more harm than good. They are particularly likely to continue home teaching, and to keep this a secret from the teacher if they think he disapproves.

There are several ways in which the parents can be helpful, and these should be emphasized. They include: (1) attending to any health problems, getting any special examinations that may be recommended (vision, etc.), and following through with treatment when indicated; (2) showing more appreciation of the child's talents and positive qualities, helping to build his morale; (3) helping to build his experiential background, by taking him on trips and visits to museums and other places of interest, by including him in family conversations about interesting topics, and by encouraging him to watch some television programs that have educational merit; (4) taking him regularly to the public library, and enlisting the librarian's help in finding books that he is likely to be able to read and enjoy reading; (5) showing real pleasure at any indications from the teacher, or from their own observations, that his reading is really improving.

Whether it is wise to encourage parents to help in teaching reading is a debatable issue. Some remedial teachers spend considerable time with parents, showing them exactly what to do and how to do it. Others try to keep the parents out of the teaching role as much as possible. Still others make up short review exercises that parents

---

FIGURE 47. Page from a high interest–low vocabulary load book. (From The Deep-Sea Adventure Series, *Treasure Under the Sea*, 1959, p. 21. Readability level of this book is second reader; interest level is fourth grade and up. San Francisco: Field Educational Publications, Inc., 1959. Copyright © 1959 by Field Educational Publications, Incorporated. Reproduced by permission of the publisher; reduced in size.)

can go over with the child at home and on which a successful performance is almost guaranteed by the child's previous mastery of what the exercise involves. If the parents are involved at all in the teaching, it is important for the teacher to guide and supervise what they do. Whether or not parents can help with teaching depends on the patience of the parents and on the emotional relationship between parents and child.

On the negative side there are a number of common parental practices that parents should be requested, as tactfully as possible, to stop. Before doing this, it is wise to indicate that you know they have been trying to help the child, and these practices have been done with the best of intentions; with their child these practices just haven't worked, so it is time to try something else. The common list of don'ts includes: calling the child dumb, dopey, or stupid; comparing him unfavorably with a brother or sister, or holding up some child outside the family as a model; punishing the child severely for his poor grades in school (beatings and deprivation of play are quite common); and going over the child's reading with him in long sessions that usually end with the parent angry and the child in tears.

Analyzing Specific Learning Needs

Efficiency in corrective and remedial teaching requires that little or no time should be wasted. The disabled child needs to learn at a rate that is not only much faster than before but is also more rapid than the rate of progress of normal learners, so that he can gradually make up for lost ground. It is not efficient to go through all the steps and teach all the skills that are included in a good developmental reading program. As far as possible, one should try to find out what the child has already mastered, where the gaps or difficulties are in his reading skills, and how he can best learn.

PRELIMINARY TESTING

With children who are reading below third-reader level, one can start with an individual textbook test, followed by a word recognition test and a test covering the essentials of phonics (see Chapter 6, especially Figures 20, 21, and 22). For children who can read at or above third-reader level, a silent reading test also is desirable, either a standardized one or a textbook test. Careful analysis and comparison of these tests should make it possible to fill out all or most of the check list shown in Figure 23 or to record the important facts and conclusions about the child's reading in some other suitable form.

One should then be able to draw tentative conclusions in answer to the following questions:

1. Is the child able to read independently at any level? If so, what would be the most suitable level for starting independent reading?
2. What is the child's instructional reading level? Considering the child's feelings about reading, should he be started at this level or below it?
3. What are the outstanding characteristics of the child's sight vocabulary? Does he make certain kinds of errors with special frequency? Is there a particular method of word study that seems to work best for him?
4. What does he know about phonics? Can he blend sounds together? Does he need to start with phonic readiness, or simply need some polishing and filling in of gaps?
5. Are there comprehension difficulties that do not seem to be secondary to word recognition difficulties? If so, are there as yet any clues that help to explain why comprehension is poor?
6. What interests has the child shown that might be useful in the selection of reading materials?

On the basis of the answers to these questions, a teaching plan is formulated and the remedial program begins.

DIAGNOSIS AS A CONTINUOUS PROCESS

Diagnosis, the development of a thorough knowledge about a problem condition, is something that the remedial teacher is doing all the time. The teacher watches the suitability of the material, both for difficulty and for interest appeal. Each lesson clarifies the picture of what the child does and does not know, about the identification of printed symbols, about word meanings, about informational background, about how to read understandingly. Each word misread is a signal of something that needs to be taught.

The faster the child improves, the oftener it is necessary to reappraise his performance and change the instructional program. A nine-year-old may begin at high first-reader level, with a small sight vocabulary and knowledge of the sounds represented by only a few initial consonants. In a few months he may be reading well at second-reader level and may have mastered the major part of first- and second-reader phonics. A more complete picture of his personality and interests gradually emerges. As he completes each instructional objective, the teacher looks ahead to see what he should tackle next. Should he do some more reading at second-reader level or is he ready for instruction at third-reader level? What remaining phonic learnings does he still need? Is it time to lessen the emphasis on oral reading and word recognition and put more emphasis on silent reading? Is his speed improving satisfactorily or does it need some special attention? Each lesson brings out new evidence on the basis of which the remedial teacher is continually evaluating and, when necessary, changing the program.

Teaching the Disabled Reader

FITTING CORRECTIVE READING INTO THE CLASSROOM

Most of the help that classroom teachers can give to children with reading disabilities will be planned for the relatively less serious cases, who generally fit fairly well within the lowest reading group, or lowest third of the class. When the reading program is highly individualized, these children can be seen somewhat more frequently and for longer conferences than most of their classmates. When developmental reading is taught with groups, as is most typical, special attention can also be given to them.

The lowest reading group is usually a mixture of mentally slow children who are doing about as well as they can, and brighter children with varying degrees of reading disability. Although the group members are all more or less at the same instructional reading level, there are often marked differences in the particular areas of reading skill in which the group members are strong or weak. More often than not, the dull children are fairly good in word recognition and in reading for directly stated details, but tend to be slow and somewhat monotonous in oral reading and to have trouble in getting main ideas, seeing implications, anticipating outcomes, or understanding cause-effect relationships. The disabled readers, on the other hand, are very likely to have their main reading problems in word recognition and word analysis, and to do relatively well in reading for meaning in material that is at or below their instructional levels.

The teacher who is alert to individual needs can do much during a group lesson to meet these needs. In preparatory activities, the teacher will check one child's recognition of the word and another child's grasp of its meaning. In discussion after reading a selection, the brighter children can be asked the more searching questions and the slower children can be asked questions that can be answered directly from the book. Related practice in word recognition and phonics can stress the needs of the ones with special problems in this area.

Additional help can be given the disabled readers through setting up a special need group, which other members of the class can be invited to join. Such a group can meet one or more times a week as long as their particular weakness has not been mastered.

The independent reading program can be used helpfully also. It is worth a special effort to locate books that are mature enough to interest the disabled reader and yet easy enough so that he can read them by himself. If he can be successfully launched on a program of independent reading, the benefits to his reading may be as great as those from direct instruction. When he reports about a book during a book review session or reads an excerpt during an audience reading period, the rest of the class can recognize his improvement and they are usually generous in their comments. The resulting strengthening of his feelings of being accepted and acceptable gives a boost to his morale and is likely to encourage him to make further efforts.

Rivalry. Most retarded readers are hungry for social approval. Sometimes they attempt to shine by disparaging the work of their group mates. Such a tendency must be checked, not by reproving or punishing, but by holding up to the group a set of more appropriate standards. The teacher can emphasize in various ways that a child's reading should be judged in comparison with his past performance, not by comparison with other groups or with the other members of the group. One child's mistake does not make another child any better. Each child is competing with his previous reading performance, and trying to exceed it; when he succeeds, he deserves praise. Patient reiteration of these ideas usually is successful in reducing the tendency of retarded readers to pick on one another.

It is also vital to avoid the appearance of playing favorites. Within the low group the teacher may be more hopeful of producing marked improvement in some children than in others; but this should not be at all evident during group activities. Each member of the group is deserving of teacher attention and needs recognition and approval, whether he has the potential for improving greatly or not. Special interest in certain individuals can be shown in individual contacts with them.

REMEDIAL WORK WITH AN INDIVIDUAL CHILD

Sometimes a classroom teacher undertakes to give help to a child whose disability is such that he cannot learn much during group lessons. Privacy and exclusive attention to the one child sometimes are more essential for progress than what is taught. The presence of other children when he tries to read gives an occasional youngster such stage fright that he becomes mentally paralyzed. Others need individual help because they are too far below the lowest reading group or because they are highly distractible and tend to disrupt a group session. Although such children should be taught by a remedial teacher who has had special training, when such a teacher is not available, the classroom teacher can try to help. If the child is receiving special help, the remedial specialist and the classroom teacher must work together to coordinate their efforts. Without such cooperation, the child may become confused by the use of differing methods, materials, and goals.

Surprisingly good progress has been made by some seriously disabled readers when given individual help for just a few minutes a day.

Teachers can often find time for this before or after school, or during part of a free period. Ten- or fifteen-minute sessions can often accomplish a great deal. If help is given privately after school hours, a 45-minute period two or three times a week is usually desirable. Periods may be shorter for young children and longer for older children.

The special magic of individual remedial help is that the child receives the total, undivided attention and appreciation of an adult. For many children this is a unique experience; there have always been brothers, sisters, playmates, or classmates. Usually the child values this relationship very much. The rapport that can develop is very much like that in successful psychotherapy, and the personal relationship with a remedial teacher sometimes helps a child to overcome emotional problems as well as educational difficulties.

Individualized remedial teaching gives a teacher the opportunity to try to use to their maximum effect the basic psychological principles that underlie all good teaching. There is no need to compromise between what one child needs and what another child requires. There is no set curriculum to cover nor any predetermined timetable to set the pace. The teacher can give exclusive attention to discovering the child's needs, establishing readiness for each new step, finding and using established interests, motivating the child to try new directions, presenting facts and principles in the clearest and most understandable way possible, using gamelike reviews, and reteaching as often as necessary to produce permanent learning. There is nothing unique in the learning activities or in the teaching techniques; the special value lies in the personal relationship and in the opportunity to fit the instruction more precisely to the child than is usually achieved in the classroom.

REMEDIAL READING WITH A SMALL GROUP

Classroom teachers are sometimes asked to give remedial help to a small group of from two to six children. For example, first-grade and kindergarten teachers whose children come to school for only a half day are sometimes assigned to remedial work with children from higher grades, whether or not the teacher has had any special training for remedial teaching.

Quite often the children in such a group are so diverse in reading skills that little group instruction is possible. When this is the case, most of the period must be spent working individually with one child after another, while the rest of the group carries on with assigned reading activities. The entire group is brought together for some activity in which they can share with reasonable equality. With children at primary-grade reading levels this can be a word recognition game, an audience reading session, or the teacher reading an installment of an exciting story. With a more advanced group a short rate-and-comprehension exercise, which group members can take at varying degrees of difficulty, sometimes fits. During the brief individual sessions the teacher can discuss outside reading with the child, listen to some oral reading, review sight words, teach a new phonic principle, do some further testing, etc.

Managing such a group requires careful planning and efficient use of time. The group is like a miniature classroom, with each child a group in himself. Rivalry and group spirit can be handled constructively. With efficient planning of reading that the group members can do by themselves, each child's learning goes on when the teacher is with other children as well as when he is receiving personal attention.

The remedial teacher whose heart is in his work usually comes to regard each child's problems as a battleground on which he is fighting for the child's chances for future success and happiness. There are few experiences which can equal the warm glow of satisfaction that such a teacher feels when a child is transformed from a frustrated and defeated individual into a person who has mastered a severe handicap and can look forward to the meeting of other difficulties with confidence and expectation of success. After once tasting the sweetness of such a victory, the teacher should be committed for the rest of his career to the principle of teaching children as individuals, respecting their individuality, studying their differences in aptitude and learning ability, and adapting instructional practices to their needs. Into the hands of such teachers, parents can safely entrust the education of their children.

Fostering the Continuing Growth of the Superior Reader

READING EXPECTANCY FOR THE BRIGHT CHILD

In a large group of school children, about a quarter have I.Q.'s of 110 and above. About 15 percent have I.Q.'s between 110 and 120, about 7 percent between 120 and 130, and about 3 percent 130 and above, ranging in very rare cases to as high as 200 or more. The two-and-a-half-year-old child who was recently granted a personal library card because she read prolifically in books of middle grade level is a rare but genuine instance of extreme precocity.

These children are the future leaders of the country. From their ranks will come the scholars, the scientists, the professional men and women, the political and military leaders, the business executives, and the creators of the arts and literature. Educators have always felt responsible for helping these children to achieve well.

In the upper part of Table III (see page 397) the mental grade levels of bright and intellectually superior children are shown, for I.Q.'s of 110, 120, and 130. The top 3 percent (I.Q.'s of 130 and above) tend to have mental maturities at least two years above the grade which is normal for their age. A child with an I.Q. of 130 is capable of understanding and learning fifth-grade (provided of course that he has the necessary conceptual background and prerequisite skills) when he is eight, eighth-grade work when he is ten, and tenth-grade work when he is twelve; about 3 percent are more accelerated than this. The large group with I.Q.'s between 110 and 130 will supply the bulk of the future college population; they tend to be one to three years ahead of the average child in achievement, intelligence, and general adjustment.

Teachers often do not recognize the superior possibilities in some of the children whose work is average. A few years ago, teachers in several schools were asked to select the one child in each grade who was most nearly average.[12] Almost all of the pupils selected by the

[12] Albert J. Harris, "What Is a Normal Child?" *Journal of Teacher Education* (March 1952).

teachers turned out to be average in reading, but several of them had I.Q.'s well above average when tested individually by a psychologist, ranging as high as 132. Some of these children who tested as bright or superior on careful individual intelligence tests had scored similarly on group I.Q. tests, but the teachers hadn't believed the results. A small number of them had made only average scores on group I.Q. tests. Recognizing superior potentiality involves more than just looking at test scores.

Teachers who are doubtful about the meaning of a child's test scores have other kinds of evidence they can consider. Superior potentiality may be shown in one of the academic areas like science or mathematics, in an unusual gift for writing, or in highly developed hobbies. The child's sentence structure, vocabulary usage, and quickness in understanding new concepts can be quite revealing of latent mental ability. A listening comprehension test is probably the most dependable way of finding out if a child has the ability to comprehend at a level well above his reading level (see page 166).

Under-achieving in very bright children varies greatly in its significance. If a ten-year-old has a mental age of fourteen and is reading at seventh-reader level (corresponding to a mental age of twelve) he is not reading up to his own potentiality, but the problem is not a really serious one. But if he is reading only at fifth-reader level (average for his age), there is a serious failure to read up to ability. The child may have persisting difficulties in word recognition, may be an usually slow reader, or may just never have become interested in reading. The reading problem may be related to an emotional disturbance. When reading ability is above average but below mental level, the problem is sometimes one of lack of motivation or of lack of teacher guidance in attaining high-level reading proficiency.

When lack of motivation is the real problem, an extra effort to apply the interest-arousing principles described in Chapter 13 is in order. In addition, it is advisable to help these children to set higher goals for themselves. A ten-year-old like the one described in the preceding paragraph should know that, although he is a "satisfactory" reader, the teacher thinks that he could raise his reading level substantially.

A program to upgrade the reading level of a bright child who is an under-achiever, when there are no persisting gaps in basic skills, does not have to be elaborate. An effective program might have only two major parts: (1) use of the McCall, Crabbs exercises or similar rate and comprehension exercises with which reading efficiency can be sharpened, with a progress chart kept of all scores; and (2) effective motivation to increase the amount and quality of independent reading, including the use of appropriate progress charts. In addition, there should be continuing expression of genuine interest and encouragement by the teacher; this is probably the most important requirement.

When reading progress of the bright child is held to a mediocre level by the persistence of interfering handicaps or by incompletely mastered basic reading skills, the principles described above for disabled readers also apply.

FOSTERING SUPERIOR READING

As we have already noted, many very bright children in today's schools are achieving in reading at levels which correspond with their intelligence, or close to it. The school has a very real obligation to do what it can to help these children to continue their accelerated rate of growth in reading abilities and interests. In the past, concern with the average child and especially with the retarded reader has at times blinded teachers to the needs of their best readers.

Some educational practices actually tend to prevent superior children from improving in reading as much as they could. One of them is exclusive reliance on whole-class instruction or on a rigid instructional pattern in which all reading is done in two or three groups; even the rate of progress of the fast group may seem slow to a very bright child. Another is failing to provide the diet of rich and varied reading materials that bright children can eat up at a great rate, one after the other; a meager library collection is costly in wasted opportunities for growth. A third is in failing to free the very bright child from much of the review and repetition that average and slow children need. A fourth is failing to excite their curiosity about many things that there is not time for the class to explore, but which the very bright child can look into on his own. A final one is using the bright child so much as a helper, a class librarian, or a leader of a slower group that his own time for reading is seriously curtailed.

Some suggestions about how the reading needs of the very bright child can be met are implied in the above list of negative practice. A few positive suggestions now follow.

Freeing the Bright Child from Lockstep Boredom. If an eight-year-old is already able to read and understand fifth-reader material, little is gained by requiring him to spend a year on two third readers and their related workbooks. If school regulations permit, such a child can be given a reading program better adapted to his needs. It might include: (1) a variety of vocabulary and comprehension exercises difficult enough to challenge him and selected to help develop higher-level reading skills; (2) large blocks of time for independent or individualized reading, including some time usually spent in group developmental reading lessons; and (3) both individual and group projects which entice him into extensive research reading.

If school policy requires that every child complete the basal reader program for the grade, this can be done without requiring the whole year to be spent at it. If there are just one or two such children in a class, they can be allowed to use the basal reader for independent reading, reading ahead at their own rates, with the teacher checking periodically in individual conferences.

If there are enough such children to form a group, the group can cover the basal reading program at a rapid rate. They do not need much preparation for stories; they read the stories quickly; discussion does not have to be lengthy; and rereading can often be eliminated. Some workbook exercises can be assigned, especially those introducing new skills, but many pages can be skipped. In this way the basal program can often be covered in half the usual time, or even less, freeing the remainder for the three kinds of reading activities listed above.

Teachers often ask if superior readers should be allowed to use above-grade-level material for instructional purposes (e.g., a third grader using a fourth reader in a basal series). If they can profit from such instruction, particularly when it involves advanced skills, and if adjustments are made accordingly in their future instruction, they should be encouraged to do so. If serious objections are raised by the teachers who might normally use these materials at their grade levels, other procedures might be employed. One plan allows the child to progress above grade level in a reading program other than the one normally used for instructional purposes. The main objection to this plan is that it requires the superior reader to "go through" the guarded on-grade text even though he already possesses the skills it teaches. Another plan allows the child to pursue what amounts to an individualized reading program using library books that are above his age level in maturity and difficulty. Even when the child is allowed to use above-grade-level reader material, the latter plan should be incorporated into his program.

Mentally superior children are our nation's most precious natural resource. They are usually curious and interested in learning, if the school does not blunt this interest by stressing conformity and repetitive drill. The best policy with such children is to make the finest books available and accessible to them, and to assist them in making as rapid and as much progress as possible.

Teaching Educationally Disadvantaged Children

Another area of recent, and long overdue, concern is the educationally disadvantaged child. Such children have been with us for many years. Among the labels attached to them are "culturally disadvantaged" and "culturally different"; however, the term preferred in this book is "educationally disadvantaged." The attitude of disparaging their culture, particularly their language, often has created problems in school.

Educationally disadvantaged children do not represent any single race or nationality. Children of varying shades of skin color are found in our urban centers and in rural areas. The languages they speak include various dialects of American English; or perhaps their only or first language is Spanish or that of some American Indian tribe. In order to help culturally different children, teachers should at least attempt to understand them. It is not absolutely necessary to accept their behavior, language, mores, etc.; nor to "love" them. It is important, however, to try to understand who these children are and why they are as they are. An excellent summary of the "who" and "why" was presented by Whipple who referred to them very appropriately as "children without":

The families lack sufficient resources to provide the basic needs of food, clothing and shelter. They live in crowded substandard housing without enough space for play, reading, and study. The children do not have stable family ties. Many come from one-parent homes. Others have frustrated parents who move about looking for work they can't find. The children receive little personal attention.

Physical handicaps are much more common among children without than among children with. Children without more often suffer from eye defects, hearing loss, and neurological problems. They are more subject to malnutrition and disease. Many have never had the services of a doctor, and fewer have had dental care.

These children are seriously retarded in language development. The language they hear at home is often a special dialect different from standard English. The children from Mexican or Puerto Rican homes are bilingual but their Spanish is just as inadequate as their English.

Children without do not have sufficient vocabularies to express their ideas. They are unable to carry on connected discourse when they enter first grade because they have mainly heard imperative and partial sentences at home. They use incorrect word forms and immature sentence structure and cannot elaborate their ideas. Their language deficiency, in turn, dwarfs their power to think, reflect and imagine.

The constricted lives of these children have prevented them from acquiring the concepts needed in school. Most of their parents are indifferent to the ultimate values of education, and have not instilled in them a desire to learn. Because of the noisy, crowded homes, the children have developed the habit of ignoring sounds, and by school age they are markedly deficient in listening skills. They have short attention spans. Their aspirations are low and they seek immediate satisfactions rather than distant goals.[13]

Educationally disadvantaged children frequently are weak in reading readiness skills, particularly in auditory discrimination. Efforts

[13] Gertrude Whipple, "The Special Needs of Children Without," *Reading for Children Without—Our Disadvantaged Youth* (Newark, Del.: International Reading Association, 1966), pp. 1–2.

to overcome these problems have not met with great success. Perhaps if auditory discrimination training were combined with systematic instruction in Standard American English as a second dialect or language, more success could be obtained. Many of these children do not possess simple concepts that we often take for granted in first graders. Furthermore, not only do they have difficulty in understanding the teacher, but also in expressing what they want to say.[14]

Children whose only or first language is not English have particular problems in these areas.[15] When they begin formal reading instruction, the written structure of the language may cause problems because it differs greatly from the structure of their own speech. In learning to make symbol-sound associations (phonics), they may encounter difficulty because the phonemes in their speech, particularly vowels and final consonant sounds, differ from those of Standard American English. Teachers often spend a great deal of time and energy trying to get these children to "pronounce the sounds properly." The purpose of phonics is to assist the reader in decoding words that are not recognized at sight. If he can decode them, he probably will pronounce the words using his own dialect (speakers of what might be considered "Standard American Dialects" do the same).[16] The key

[14] For information on teaching reading to educationally disadvantaged children see:

Joan C. Baratz and Roger W. Shuy, Eds., *Teaching Black Children to Read* (Washington, D.C.: Center for Applied Linguistics, 1969).

S. Alan Cohen, *Teach Them All to Read: Theory, Methods, and Materials for Teaching the Disadvantaged* (New York: Random House, 1969).

Thomas D. Horn, Ed., *Reading for the Disadvantaged: Problems of Linguistically Different Learners* (New York: Harcourt Brace Jovanovich, Inc., 1970).

J. Allen Figurel, Ed., *Reading Goals for the Disadvantaged* (Newark, Del.: International Reading Association, 1970).

[15] For suggestions in working with these children see: Miles V. Zintz, *Corrective Reading* (Dubuque, Iowa: Wm. C. Brown Co., 1966), pp. 115–155. For other possible readings, refer to: Carl L. Rosen and Philip D. Ortego, *Issues in Language and Reading Instruction of Spanish Speaking Children*, Annotated bibliography (Newark, Del.: International Reading Association, 1969).

[16] For excellent discussions of dialects see: Henry Lee Smith, Jr., "Dialects of English," in *The American Heritage Dictionary of the English Language* (Boston: American Heritage Publishing Corp. and Houghton Mifflin Co., 1969), pp. xxv–xxx.

question is whether or not he understands what the words mean. This is not to say that children should not be helped in acquiring standard American speech, but rather that perhaps this should not be attempted through teaching phonics in the reading program.

Once the mechanical skills have been mastered, the need becomes one of increasing the ability to obtain meaning. Instruction should then focus on concept formation, vocabulary improvement, mastery of the linguistic structure of Standard American speech and writing; all with an aim toward improving reading comprehension. In response to good teaching, culturally different children can achieve at higher levels.[17]

Reading materials using multi-cultural characters have become more available in the past few years. Although there is little research evidence that the use of such characters or the structure of the accompanying programs facilitate learning to read, there may be some accrued benefits (e.g., easier identification with book characters, awareness of other cultures and their contributions to society) that cannot be readily measured by tests. There also are materials that use the oral language patterns in written form for teaching reading. For example, one program has parallel stories. One contains "everyday talk" (e.g. "I Be Scared When It Be Dark"); the other, "school talk" (e.g. "I Am Scared When It Is Dark").[18] As yet, the effectiveness of such materials has not been adequately evaluated.

As emphasized in this book, each child is an individual. It is when his particular strengths and weaknesses are considered that learning is most likely to take place. This is no less true of the educationally disadvantaged. They are not all the same. Their success in school will

Raven I. McDavid, Jr., "Variations in Standard American English," *Elementary English,* 45 (May 1968), 561–564; 608.

[17] Albert J. Harris, *et al., A Continuation of the CRAFT Project: Comparing Reading Approaches with Disadvantaged Urban Negro Children in Primary Grades,* Final Report, U.S.O.E. Project No. 5-0570-2-12-1 (New York: Selected Academic Readings, 1968).

[18] Olga Davis, Mildred Gladney, and Lloyd Leaverton, *The Psycholinguistic Reading Series: A Bi-dialectal Approach,* experimental ed. (Chicago: Board of Education of the City of Chicago, 1969).

vary greatly, and will be dependent not only on the factors (conceptual development, motivation, etc.) that they bring to school, but also on the school's attitude toward them and what is done to assist them in the learning process.

Summary

1. Children whose reading achievement is significantly below the age and grade norms are referred to as retarded readers.
    a. This group includes those whose general mental development is slow; and,
    b. Those who have the capability for achieving at a higher level. These are cases of reading disability.
2. Intellectual slowness in children varies from low average to severe deficiency.
    a. Children who are mentally dull need reading programs that are adapted to their limited learning ability and take their psychological characteristics into consideration.
    b. The seriously mentally retarded need special education programs.
3. Children with genuine reading disabilities include a majority with relatively mild disabilities (corrective cases), who can be helped within the structure of classroom instruction, and more severe cases (remedial cases), who often require special individual help.
4. Handicaps that interfere with progress in reading can be intellectual, physical, educational, social, or emotional:
    a. Often there is a combination of several handicaps.
    b. Teachers get best results in their efforts to find and correct these handicaps when they make use of specialized personnel and proceed cautiously and tactfully when talking with parents.
5. There are some children who have extreme difficulty in learning to read.
    a. They are often referred to as being dyslexic, a term whose definition lacks agreement.
    b. The exact causes of severe reading disability are still unknown.

6. Motivation is centrally important in any corrective or remedial program.
   a. The teacher tries to build rapport, to ensure success, to celebrate progress, and to make reading interesting.
   b. Parents should be given positive suggestions about things they can do to help.
7. Corrective reading involves providing for the special needs of the disabled reader in regular group and individual reading activities in the classroom.
   a. Unhealthy rivalry must be avoided.
   b. Emphasis should be placed on each child striving to exceed his previous best.
8. Small remedial groups resemble classrooms in miniature and require careful planning and preparation, with a large amount of individualized reading and instruction.
9. Remedial reading with an individual child allows the development of a special kind of rapport and the fitting of instruction to the individual child.
10. Mentally superior children deserve not to be overlooked in the reading program.
    a. Bright under-achievers are often children whose interest has never been aroused.
    b. Sometimes their achievement is due to persisting handicaps or to continuing gaps in basic skills, and requires corrective or remedial attention.
11. Capable readers of superior intelligence are often hampered in their reading progress by being required to go through a reading program geared to much slower learners.
    a. These children need to be freed to read at their own levels and on topics of real interest to them.
    b. A large amount of independent reading should be encouraged, and basal readers should be covered quite rapidly.
12. Educationally disadvantaged children have particular problems in learning to read, primarily because they often lack motivation, concept development, and language skills.

Recommended Reading

BEERY, ALTHEA, BARRETT, THOMAS C., and POWELL, WILLIAM R., EDS. *Elementary Reading Instruction: Selected Materials.* Boston: Allyn and Bacon, Inc., 1969. Ch. 13.

DURR, WILLIAM K., ED. *Reading Instruction: Dimensions and Issues.* Boston: Houghton Mifflin, 1967. Chs. 7, 8.

DURR, WILLIAM K., ED. *Reading Difficulties: Diagnosis, Correction, and Remediation.* Newark, Del.: International Reading Association, 1970.

GANS, ROMA. *Common Sense in Teaching Reading.* Indianapolis: Bobbs-Merrill, 1963. Chs. 19, 20, 21.

HARRIS, ALBERT J., ED. *Readings on Reading Instruction.* New York: McKay, 1963. Chs. 15, 16.

HARRIS, ALBERT J. *How to Increase Reading Ability,* 5th ed. New York: McKay, 1970. Chs. 9, 10, 11.

STRANG, RUTH. *Reading Diagnosis and Remediation.* ERIC/CRIER Reading Review Series. Newark, Del.: International Reading Association, 1968.

ZINTZ, MILES. *The Reading Process: The Teacher and the Learner.* Dubuque, Iowa: Wm. C. Brown Co., 1970. Chs. 19, 20.

APPENDIX

Resources for Teachers of Reading

This Appendix brings together several kinds of information that are often requested by teachers of reading. The first section lists and describes tests of reading and mental ability. The second section gives information about several kinds of materials in which reading teachers are interested, including magazines, films, filmstrips, and recordings.

A Selected List of Tests

A number of published tests of reading skills and mental ability have been mentioned in various places in this book, and especially in Chapter 6. The alphabetical listing below gives a brief description of each of these tests, indicating the type of content, the grades for which it is intended, forms, and publisher. The data in this listing are taken from the more comprehensive listing in Appendix A of the Fifth Edition of the senior author's *How to Increase Reading Ability*.

To obtain detailed descriptions and critical evaluations of these and other reading tests refer to: O. K. Buros, Ed., *Reading Tests and Reviews* (Highland Park, N.J.: Gryphon Press, 1968). Detailed descriptions and evaluations of psychological tests may be found in the six *Mental Measurement Yearbooks,* also published by the Gryphon Press and edited by Buros.

433

Complete names and addresses of the publishers mentioned are given in Appendix C.

READING READINESS TESTS

Gates-MacGinitie Readiness Skills Test. Samples listening comprehension, auditory discrimination, visual discrimination, following directions, letter recognition, visual-motor coordination, and auditory blending. A word recognition test is available to help detect early readers. Teachers
Harrison-Stroud Reading Readiness Profiles. Contains five subtests: using symbols, visual discrimination, using context, auditory discrimination, using context and auditory clues; and an individually administered letter names test. Houghton
Kindergarten Evaluation of Learning Potential: KELP. Attempts to determine readiness, particularly of culturally different children, through teaching lessons. California
Lee-Clark Reading Readiness Test, 1962 Revision. Contains tests of visual discrimination and concept development. California
Let's Look at Children. Can be used for both teaching and assessing readiness. Particularly useful with culturally different children. ETS
Macmillan Reading Readiness Test, Rev. ed. Subtests include quantified rating scale, visual discrimination, auditory discrimination, vocabulary and concepts, letter names, and visual-motor skills (optional). Macmillan
Metropolitan Readiness Tests, 1965 Revision. Two forms, each containing subtests of word meaning, listening, matching, alphabet, numbers and copying. Harcourt
Monroe Reading Aptitude Tests. Includes measures of visual and auditory discrimination and memory, motor control, speed and articulation in speech, and language development. Some subtests must be administered individually. Houghton
Murphy-Durrell Reading Readiness Analysis. Samples visual and auditory discrimination, letter names, and learning rate. Harcourt

READING ACHIEVEMENT TESTS

American School Achievement Tests
   Primary I Battery, grade 1, word recognition, word meanings, numbers
   Primary II Reading, grades 2–3, sentence, word, and paragraph meaning
   Intermediate Reading, grades 4–6; Advanced Reading, grades 7–9, vocabulary and paragraph meaning. Bobbs

California Reading Tests, 1963 Norms. Each test has two main parts (vocabulary and comprehension) with subtests. Also included in California Achievement Test batteries. Lower Primary, grades 1–2; Primary, grades 3–4; Elementary, grades 5–6; Junior High, grades 7–9; Advanced, grades 9–12. California

Gates-MacGinitie Reading Tests. Separate tests for grades 1–3, each measuring vocabulary and comprehension. Separate tests of speed and accuracy available for grades 2 and 3. Tests for grades 4–6 and for grades 7–9 sample vocabulary, comprehension, and speed and accuracy. Teachers

Iowa Every-Pupil Test of Basic Skills. Part of a battery. Elementary, grades 3–5; Advanced, grades 5–9. Includes subtests on vocabulary, comprehension, and work-study skills. Houghton

Iowa Silent Reading Tests: New Edition. Elementary, grades 4–8; Advanced, high school and college. Includes measures of rate, comprehension, vocabulary, sentence and paragraph meaning, and locating information. Harcourt

Iowa Test of Basic Skills. Tests for grades 3–8. Tests overlap grade levels: vocabulary, comprehension, and work-study skills. Houghton

Metropolitan Reading Tests, Revised. Also included in batteries.

Primary I, grade 1, word knowledge, word discrimination, comprehension.

Primary II, grades 2.0–3.5, word knowledge, word discrimination, comprehension.

Elementary, grades 3–4; Intermediate, grades 5–6; Advanced, grades 7–8, vocabulary and comprehension. Harcourt

Nelson Silent Reading Test, Revised. Vocabulary and comprehension tests for grades 3–9. Houghton

Sequential Tests of Educational Progress—STEP. Part of a battery. Includes subtests of reading and listening comprehension. Separate tests for grades 4–6, 7–9, 10–12, and college. ETS

SRA Achievement Series: Reading. Test for grades 1 and 2 includes verbal-picture association, language perception, comprehension, and vocabulary. Tests for grades 2–4, 4–6, and 6–9 include vocabulary and comprehension. Word-study skills in test for grades 4–6. SRA

Stanford Reading Tests, 1964 Revision.

Primary I, grades 1.5–2.4. Word reading, comprehension, oral vocabulary, word-study skills.

Primary II, grades 2.5–3.9. Vocabulary, comprehension, word-study skills.

Intermediate I, grades 4.0–5.4; Intermediate II, grades 5.5–6.9; Advanced, grades 7.0–9.9. Vocabulary and comprehension. Harcourt

Traxler Silent Reading Test. Grades 7–10. Samples rate, comprehension, word meaning, and paragraph meaning. Bobbs

SPECIALIZED READING TESTS

Botel Reading Inventory. Grades 1–12. Includes mainly group administered tests of phonics, word recognition, word opposites reading, and word opposites listening. Follett

Dolch Basic Sight Word Test. List arranged on one sheet to test basic 220 words. Garrard

Doren Diagnostic Reading Test. Grades 2–8. Group test with eleven subtests for measuring word-attack skills. American Guidance

Durrell Analysis of Reading Difficulty: New Edition. Battery of diagnostic tests for individual administration to determine reading difficulties. Harcourt

EDL Reading Versatility Tests. Basic, grades 5–8; Intermediate, grades 7–12. Skimming and scanning of fiction and nonfiction. EDL

Gates-McKillop Reading Diagnostic Tests. Battery of individually administered diagnostic tests for retarded readers. Teachers

Gilmore Oral Reading Test, New Edition. Grades 1–8. Individually administered oral reading test. Separate scores for accuracy, comprehension, and rate. Harcourt

Gray Oral Reading Tests. Grades 1–12. Individually administered oral reading test. Accuracy and rate combined in a composite score; comprehension not included in score. Bobbs

McCullough Word Analysis Tests. Grades 4–8. Group test sampling seven word-analysis skills. Ginn

Roswell-Chall Diagnostic Reading Test. Short individually administered test of phonic skills. Essay

Silent Reading Diagnostic Tests. Grade 3 and up. Group test with 11 subtests of word recognition and phonic skills. Lyons & Carnahan

Spache Diagnostic Reading Scales. Grades 1–8. Individually administered tests of word pronunciation, oral reading, and phonics. California

Stanford Diagnostic Reading Test. Level I, grades 2.5–4.5; Level II, grades 4.5–8.5. Group tests of vocabulary, comprehension, rate, and word analysis. Harcourt

MENTAL ABILITY

Ammons Full-Range Picture Vocabulary Test. Preschool to adult. Individually administered test of verbal intelligence. Reading or expressive language ability not required. Psychological Test

California Short-Form Test of Mental Maturity, 1963 Revision. Eight

levels, kindergarten to college. Group test which yields separate language, nonlanguage, and total M.A.'s and I.Q.'s California
California Test of Mental Maturity Long Form, 1963 Revision. Longer form of previous test. California
Detroit Beginning First Grade Intelligence Test. Group test that does not require reading ability. Harcourt
Henmom-Nelson Tests of Mental Ability. Group tests for grades 3–6, 6–9, and 9–12. Require reading ability. Houghton
Kuhlmann-Anderson Measure of Academic Potential, 6th and 7th Editions. Nine levels, one each for kindergarten to grade 6; 7–8; 9–12. Group tests of general intelligence. Little reading ability required below test for fourth grade. Psychological
Kuhlman-Finch Intelligence Tests. Separate tests for grades 1–6; junior high, and senior high. Group test that is completely nonverbal at lowest two levels, and mostly nonverbal at other levels. American Guidance
Lorge-Thorndike Intelligence Tests, Multi-Level Edition. Grades 3–13, with eight levels of difficulty, or separate levels edition. Group test that yields verbal, nonverbal, and total scores. Houghton
Otis-Lennon Mental Ability Test. Six levels, kindergarten to grade 12. Group verbal intelligence test requiring reading at most levels. Harcourt
Peabody Picture Vocabulary Test. Ages 2–18. Individually administered verbal intelligence test. American Guidance
Pintner General Ability Tests: Verbal Series. All group tests.
    Pintner-Cunningham Primary Test, revised 1965. K-2, group test that does not require reading ability.
    Pintner-Durost Elementary Test, grades 2–4. Group test that requires reading.
    Pintner Intermediate Test, grades 4–9. Group test that requires reading. Harcourt
Revised Stanford-Binet Intelligence Scale, Third Edition. Ages 2 to adult. Trained psychologist should administer this individual test. Houghton
SRA Primary Mental Abilities Test. Levels for K-1; 2–4; 4–6; 6–9; and 9–12. Group administered test which provides separate M.A.'s and I.Q.'s for 5 areas. SRA
Wechsler Adult Intelligence Scale. (WAIS) Age 16 to adult. Only trained psychologist should administer this individual test that yields verbal, performance, and full-scale I.Q.'s. Psychological
Wechsler Intelligence Scale for Children (WISC). Ages 5–15. Similar to *WAIS.*
Wechsler Preschool and Primary Scale of Intelligence (WPPSI). Ages 4–6.5. Similar to *WAIS.*

Leading Series of Supplementary Reading Books

In recent years a number of publishers have brought out books that form a series in that they are biographies, or deal with historical events, or have some other common theme, but do not form a graded sequence. These are generally used as individual library books. Many of these series are useful with retarded readers. The approximate range of reading difficulty and interest level is given for each series.

	Reading Grade Level	Interest Grade Level	Publisher
The First Reading Books	1	1–4	Garrard
Beginner Books	1–2	1–4	Random
Basic Vocabulary Series	1–3	2–4	Garrard
The Button Books	1–3	1–4	Benefic
Cowboy Sam Books	1–3	1–4	Benefic
Sailor Jack Books	1–3	2–7	Benefic
Curriculum Motivation Series	1–3	2–7	Lyons
Dan Frontier Books	1–3	1–7	Benefic
Checkered Flag Series	2	6–11	Field
Jim Forest Readers	1–3	3–6	Field
Gateway Books	2–3	3–9	Random
The Interesting Reading Series	2–3	4–11	Follett
Space Age Books	2–3	2–6	Benefic
Step-Up Books	2–3	3–9	Random
The True Books	2–3	1–6	Childrens
All About Books Series	2–4	2–8	Childrens
The Deep Sea Adventure Series	2–4	3–9	Field
Discovery Books	2–4	3–6	Garrard
Junior Everyreaders	2–4	2–7	Webster
The Morgan Bay Series	2–4	4–9	Field
What Is It Series	2–4	4–8	Benefic
The Wildlife Adventure Series	2–4	3–8	Field
American Adventure Series	2–6	4–9	Harper
World of Adventure Series	2–6	4–9	Harper
Folklore of the World Books	3	2–8	Garrard
Frontiers of America Series	3	3--8	Childrens
Pleasure Reading Series	3–4	3–5	Garrard

	Reading Grade Level	Interest Grade Level	Publisher
Interesting Reading Series	3–4	3–6	Follett
Junior Science Books	3–4	3–6	Garrard
The First Books	3–5	3–8	Watts
Americans All Series	4	4–7	Field
Signal Books	4	5–9	Doubleday
Exploring and Understanding Series	4	4–9	Benefic
Pioneer Series	4	4–7	Benefic
Middle-Grade Books Series	4	3–7	Childrens
Pleasure Reading Books	4	3–6	Garrard
Every Reader Library	4–5	4–10	Webster
Childhood of Famous Americans Series	4–5	4–9	Bobbs
Teen-Age Tales	4–6	6–11	Heath
Getting to Know Books	4–5	5–9	Hale
The Reading Motivated Series	4–5	4–10	Field
Simplified Classics	4–5	4–10	Scott F.
Simplified Classics	4–6	4–10	Globe
We Were There Books	4–5	5–9	Hale
All About Books	4–6	5–11	Random
Modern Adventure Series	4–6	4–11	Harper
American Heritage Series	5–6	5–9	Aladdin
Strange Teen-Age Tales Books	5–6	5–11	Heath
World Landmark Books	5–6	5–11	Random
Landmark Books	5–7	5–11	Random

Magazines for Children

Magazines and periodicals form a very important category of reading materials for children as well as for adults, and good magazines can fill a valuable place in the recreational and reference reading of children. Three kinds of magazines used by children are listed below. The first group are those published for direct sale to parents or children. The second group are sold in group subscriptions to schools. The third group lists some adult magazines that are interesting to children.

CHILDREN'S MAGAZINES

American Girl. Middle and upper grades. Girl Scouts of America, 830 Third Avenue, New York, New York 10022.

Boy's Life. Middle and upper grades. Boy Scouts of America, 2 Park Avenue, New York, New York.

Calling All Girls. Girls ages 7 to 14. Better Reading Foundation, Inc., 52 Vanderbilt Avenue, New York, New York 10017.

Child Life. Preschool and primary grades. 3516 College Avenue, Indianapolis 5, Indiana 46205.

Children's Digest. Primary and middle grades. Parents' Magazine Enterprises, Inc., Bergenfield, New Jersey 07621.

Children's Playmate. Primary and middle grades. 6529 Union Avenue, Cleveland, Ohio 44105.

Highlights for Children. Ages 2 to 12. Highlights for Children, Inc., 2300 W. Fifth Avenue, Columbus, Ohio 43212.

Humpty Dumpty's Magazine. Preschool and primary grades. Parents' Magazine Enterprises, Inc., Bergenfield, New Jersey 07621.

Jack and Jill. Kindergarten to middle grades. Curtis Publishing Co., Independence Square, Philadelphia, Pennsylvania 19105.

Nature and Science. Middle and upper grades. Natural History Press, Garden City, New York 11530.

Junior Natural History. Junior high. American Museum of Natural History, Central Park West at 79th Street, New York, New York 10024.

Model Airplane News. Middle to upper grades. Air Age Inc., 551 Fifth Avenue, New York, New York 10036.

PERIODICALS PUBLISHED FOR MASS DISTRIBUTION IN SCHOOLS

Co-Ed. For home economics classes, grades 7–12. Scholastic.

Current Events. Grades 6–8. Weekly. American Ed.

Current Science and Aviation. Grades 7–12. Weekly. American Ed.

My Weekly Reader. Editions for each grade, 1–6. Weekly. American Ed.

Read. Grades 6–9. Twice a month. American Ed.

Scholastic News Pilot, News Ranger, News Trails, News Explorer, News Times, and *Junior Scholastic.* Edition for grades 1 through 9. Weekly. Scholastic.

The Urban School News. Intermediate grades. Urban Educational Publications, Box 7191, North End Station, Detroit, Michigan 48220.

ADULT MAGAZINES OF SPECIAL INTEREST TO CHILDREN

Field and Stream	Mechanix Illustrated	Popular Science
Life	National Geographic[1]	Sports Illustrated
Look	Popular Mechanics	

Book Clubs for Children

Book clubs have become an increasingly important factor in the promotion of recreational reading and in getting parents and children to purchase books and build home libraries. The leading children's book clubs are listed below.

American Heritage Junior Library. One book received bimonthly by subscriber. 336 West Center Street, Marion, Ohio.

Arrow Book Club. Several paperback books offered each month; minimum club order, 15 books, bonus books. Scholastic.

Beginning Reader's Program. Subscriber receives one book (first–second-reader level) each month. 575 Lexington Avenue, New York, New York 10022.

Junior Deluxe Editions Club. A children's classic offered each month; minimum order, 6 books per year. Garden City, New York.

Junior Challenges. Paperbacks offered monthly for grades 7–9; bonus books. American Ed.

Junior Literary Guild. Five books offered each month, preschool to upper grades. 575 Madison Avenue, New York, New York 10022.

Lucky Book Club. Monthly paperback selections for grades 2–3; minimum club order, 15 books; bonus books. Scholastic.

Parents' Magazine Book Club for Children. Offers one book a month for junior-senior high level. 52 Vanderbilt Avenue, New York, New York 10017.

Science World Book Club. Paperbacks offered bimonthly for junior-senior high level. Scholastic.

Young Folks Book Club. Kindergarten to sixth grade. Books sent to school for previewing. 1376 Coney Island Avenue, Brooklyn, New York 11230.

[1] The publishers of *National Geographic* also publish monthly *World Traveler,* which uses the same photographs as the parent magazine but is written at the third-reader level.

Weekly Reader Children's Book Club. For ages 5–8 and 8–12. Members choose 6 books a year. American Ed.

Special Booklists and Indexes

In addition to the booklists that were mentioned in Chapter 13, there are some bibliographic aids that are quite specialized. Those that are listed below suggest the wide range of references that are available. For a comprehensive listing, see Spache's *Good Reading for Poor Readers,* Rev. (Champaign, Illinois: Garrard Publishing Co., 1970).

Baker, Augusta, *Books About Negro Life for Children.* New York: New York Public Library, 1963.

Children's Books for $1.25 or Less. Washington, D.C.: Association for Childhood Education International, 1962; revised periodically.

Colwell, Eileen, *A Storyteller's Choice.* New York: Walck, 1964. Stories to be read to children; chapter on story-telling techniques.

Eakin, Mary K., and Merritt, Eleanor. *Subject Index to Books for Primary Grades.* Chicago: American Library Association, 1967. Gives specific page references in a large number of books on a wide variety of topics.

Horn, Thomas D., and Ebert, Dorothy W. "Suggested Reading for the Partially-Sighted Child," *Elementary English,* 41 (December 1964; January, February, and March, 1965).

Huus, Helen. *Children's Books to Enrich the Social Studies.* Washington, D.C.: National Council for the Social Studies, 1961.

Interracial Books for Children. Council on Interracial Books for Children, 9 East 40th Street, New York, New York 10016.

Sell, Violet. *Subject Index to Poetry for Children and Young People.* Chicago: American Library Association, 1957.

The AAAS Science Booklist for Children. Washington, D.C.; AAAS Publications, 1515 Massachusetts Avenue, N.W., 20005.

Professional Journals for the Teacher of Reading

Articles about the teaching of reading in the elementary school appear in a wide variety of periodicals. The following journals are of especial interest because they not only print original contributions, but also have departments that keep the reader informed about what is being published about reading instruction in books and in other periodicals.

Elementary English. Eight issues a year. Covers the language arts. NCTE

Elementary School Journal. Eight issues a year. Covers the elementary school curriculum. University of Chicago Press

Journal of Reading. Eight issues a year. Covers reading in the junior-senior high school. IRA

Reading Research Quarterly. Presents scholarly research reports including an annual summary of recent research. IRA

The Reading Teacher. Eight issues a year. Entire journal devoted to reading, primarily for the elementary school and remedial teacher. IRA

APPENDIX

B

A Concise Summary of Phonics

This Appendix is intended to provide a concise summary of the facts and principles of phonics that should be part of the background knowledge of elementary school teachers. Many teachers seem hesitant and uncertain about the teaching of phonics because they do not feel secure in their own knowledge of the subject. It is generally agreed that teachers should be well prepared both in their knowledge of subject-matter and in how to teach it. Methods of teaching phonic and other word analysis skills have been described in Chapter 9, and it would be repetitious to repeat here what has already been covered there. The material below is intended as reference material for teachers.

Because this is reference material, the information below has been organized for convenience in locating specific facts and principles. The sequence is not intended as a teaching sequence. More technical vocabulary is used than would be needed by children or helpful to them, and children do not need to know all of the information given here; it is assumed that teachers should know more than they are expected to teach. It is also not intended that this material should be read in sequence and studied like a chapter; after the first section, it is probably better to take only one section at a time, and to refer to specific facts and principles as needed.

444

The principles that govern the introduction of phonic principles in most basal reader systems are: Phonic principles should be developed inductively from sight words; sounds should be introduced in order of increasing difficulty; several sight words that have the phonic unit in common should be already known; and the opportunity to use the principle in attacking a new word or words, and to read these words in context, should follow immediately (see pages 232–236). Although the teacher should know that the letter t occasionally represents sounds like /ch/ (na*t*ure) or /sh/ (na*t*ion) and is occasionally silent (pi*t*cher), it is advisable not to mention these when introducing the usual sound represented by t, but rather to wait, with each of these exceptions, until one or more of the words in which it occurs are met in reading. The same principle, of waiting until there is an occasion to use the knowledge, should govern the introduction of other relatively uncommon sounds.

The first section defines phonemes and graphemes and discusses the problems created by the relatively poor correspondence between the phonemes and graphemes of the English language. The second section gives the facts about consonants. The third section is about vowels. The fourth section is about syllabication and accent. The final section lists and describes some supplementary phonic materials.

Phonemes and Graphemes

A *phoneme* is a unit of sound in spoken words.[1] Phonemes are of three main kinds: consonants, vowels, and accent. A *grapheme* is a graphic unit (a letter or group of letters or accent mark) that represents a phoneme. *Phonics* is knowledge about phonemes and graphemes; it involves the development of associations between phonemes and the graphemes that represent them, and an understanding of the principles governing the relationships of spoken words to written or

[1] According to Smith, a phoneme is really a family of closely similar speech sounds which are accepted by speakers of varying dialects as being equivalent. *See* Henry Lee Smith, Jr., *English Morphophonics* (State University College, Oneonta, N.Y.: New York State English Council, 1968).

printed words, which allows accurate translation of printed or written language into spoken language, and of spoken language into written or printed language.

The number of phonemes in American English is a question on which linguists and phonetic experts have not reached agreement. The *American College Dictionary* uses a set of 44 alphabetic symbols, plus two accent marks, to represent all of the sounds in English words, while *Webster's Third New International Dictionary of the English Language* (Unabridged) employs 62 alphabetic symbols. It is possible to get along with eighteen symbols for the vowel sounds, while one well-regarded linguist distinguishes 36 vowels when regional variations are included.[2] It seems necessary to choose between a very complete but cumbersome set of symbols and a shorter set, more practical, and yet not too different from actual speech. Many educated adults cannot perceive a number of the fine distinctions that Smith makes. On debatable issues this Appendix will follow the *American College Dictionary,* whose pronunciation guide is almost identical with those in the widely used Thorndike-Barnhart series of school dictionaries. Of the 44 graphemes used in this system, 19 represent vowel sounds and 25 represent consonant sounds.

The alphabet that we use, however, does not have enough symbols to represent this number of phonemes, so practically every letter has to represent more than one sound, singly and in combinations. Our alphabet contains 26 letters, of which five are vowels (**a, e, i, o,** and **u**), three are called semivowels (**h, y,** and **w**), and 18 are consonants. Of the 18 consonants, three are superfluous because they duplicate sounds already represented by other letters or letter combinations (**c** = /k/ or /s/, **x** = /ks/ or /gs/, **qu** = /kw/). In addition to single-letter graphemes there are *digraphs,* two-letter combinations that represent a single sound. There are vowel digraphs (**ay, ea, oa,** etc.), and consonant digraphs (**sh, th,** etc.). There are also clusters or *blends,* in which sounds partially merge but are distinguishable. Consonant blends may be of two or three letters (**cl, str**). Vowel blends are called *diphthongs,* the main ones being the /**oi**/ sound in *toy* and *boil,*

[2] Henry Lee Smith, *Jr. Linguistic Science and the Teaching of English,* The Inglis Lecture (Cambridge: Harvard University Press, 1956), p. 34.

and the /ou/ sound in loud and cow. There are also many words in which one or more letters are silent.

Many graphemes represent different phonemes in different words. Although the letter t usually represents the sound as in *tot*, it can also represent the /ch/ sound in *nature* and the /sh/ sound in *mention;* and it can be silent as in *pitcher*. Each vowel represents several different phonemes. The letter v is the only letter that does not represent more than one sound, by itself or in digraphs. The digraph ea is usually thought of as representing the long e sound as in *meat;* but it also represents the vowel sounds in *rear, head, steak, pear, pearl,* and *heart;* and it is not a digraph in *creation*. All letters except j, q, v, and x are silent in some words.

Regional variations in pronunciation also can create some phonic confusion. More than a third of the words in *A Pronouncing Dictionary of American English* have more than one accepted pronunciation. In most of the United States, *path* and *laugh* have the same vowel sound as *sat;* but in much of New England and the British Commonwealth these and many other "short a" words are pronounced with an a that sounds like the ä in *father*. In several localities it is impossible to hear a difference between short a and short e. In other localities short i and short e are almost undistinguishable. In the South, long i tends to sound like ah. The r's in *Harvard* are not audible in the speech of residents of Boston. Difficulties arise when the teacher does not take account of differences between his pronunciation and that of the children, or when they do not hear any differentiation between two sounds that to his ears are distinct.

Many vowels that occur in unstressed syllables are not as clearly sounded as the same vowels in stressed syllables. Long vowels are shortened in duration but not changed much in quality. Short vowels tend to lose their distinctive sounds so that it is difficult to hear any difference between the a in *ago,* the e in *agent,* the i in *sanity,* the o in *comply,* or the u in focus. These diminished vowel sounds are represented in some dictionaries by separate symbols, and in others by the common symbol that linguists call the *schwa* (ə). Good usage permits considerable variation in the clarity with which these unstressed vowels are pronounced, but tends toward diminishing them enough so that a listener cannot usually be sure, from the sound alone, which vowel letter is used in spelling the word.

To complicate matters still further, nearly every phoneme is represented by more than one grapheme. The long **e** sound has eleven spellings, as in *Caesar, quay, team, see, deceive, people, key, machine, field,* and *amoeba.* The short **e** sound is also represented in eleven different ways, eight of which sometimes represent long **e,** and nine of which represent other vowel sounds as well. The /**sh**/ sound can be represented in thirteen ways, as in *she, ocean, machine, official, pshaw, sugar, schist, conscience, nauseous, tension, issue, mission,* and *action.* The only phonemes that do not have two or more spellings are the voiced and unvoiced /**th**/ sounds. The name of a vowel represents one of its several sounds, and the name of a consonant usually combines the consonant phoneme with a preceding vowel (Em) or following vowel (Bee). Altogether, the 44 phonemes recognized in the *American College Dictionary* are represented by 251 spellings.

There are, then, many irregularities in the relationship between phoneme and grapheme in English. Almost every phonic generalization that children can be taught, or can be led to discover, has exceptions. This makes the teaching and learning of English phonics considerably more difficult than it would be if each grapheme represented just one phoneme and each phoneme were represented by only one grapheme, as is true, or nearly true, of several European languages.

Because there are so many irregularities, alternatives, and exceptions, it is important that children should learn and regularly apply two basic principles in analyzing words: (1) try every tentative pronunciation in the context of the sentence to see if it makes sense; and (2) when the use of the grapheme's most unusual phonemes does not produce a meaningful word that fits the context, try alternative phonemes and alternative accent patterns.

Consonants

A consonant is a phoneme produced with more or less obstruction of the breath by tongue, teeth, and lips; also a grapheme that represents a consonant phoneme. The consonant facts are listed below under the following headings: single consonants, double consonants, consonant digraphs, consonant blends, and silent consonants.

SINGLE CONSONANTS

There are 18 consonant letters, and three semivowels (**h, w,** and **y**) which serve as consonants part of the time. They are often classified as *voiced* (**g, j, l, m, n, r, v, w, y, z**) or unvoiced (**b, h, p, d, k, s, t**). They can also be classed as *sonorants,* with little obstruction of the breath (**f, h, l, m, n, r, v, w, y**); *fricatives,* with substantial obstruction (**ch, j, sh, s, z, zh, th**); and *stops,* with complete obstruction (**b, d, g, k, p, t**). Sometimes they are classified according to the part of the mouth where obstruction takes place: *labial* (the lips), *dental* (the teeth), or *glottal* (the tongue). Thus **k** is an unvoiced glottal stop, while **g** is a voiced glottal stop, and **j** is a voiced glottal fricative.

Several single consonant letters at times represent phonemes other than their most common phoneme:

c usually like **k** before **a, o,** and **u** (*c*at, *c*ome, *c*up)
c usually like **s** before **e, i,** and **y** (*c*ent, *c*ity, i*c*y)

d usually as in *did*
d followed by **u** is sometimes like **j** (indivi*d*ual)
d followed by **ge** is usually silent (e*d*ge)

f usually unvoiced as in *f*all, of*f*
f occasionally voiced like **v** as in o*f*

g usually hard when followed by **a, o,** or **u** or at the end of words, as in *g*o, ra*g*, ton*g*ue
g usually soft like **j** when followed by **e, i,** or **y** (*g*entle, *g*iant, biolo*g*y) (exceptions include *g*eese, *g*et, *g*irl, *g*ive)

h at the beginning of a word or syllable has an aspirate sound as in *h*ave and *h*ungry
h following a vowel letter usually forms a vowel diagraph as in O*h*!
h following **s, t,** or **p,** forms part of a consonant digraph
h occasionally silent at the beginning of a word, as in *h*onor

s usually unvoiced as in *see*, cap*s*

s Usually voiced like **z** after a vowel or a voiced consonant (goe*s*, her*s*) (exceptions include bu*s*, pur*s*e, wor*s*e)

s usually like **zh** or **sh** when followed by **u** (*s*ugar, *s*ure, trea*s*ure) (exceptions include *s*uck, *s*ue)

t usually an unvoiced dental stop as in *t*en*t*

t usually like **sh** when followed by **ion, ial, ious** or **ient** (por*t*ion, par*t*ial, cau*t*ious, pa*t*ient)

t followed by **u** often like **ch** (vir*t*ue, ac*t*ual, pic*t*ure)

t followed by **ch** is usually silent (ca*t*ch)

w is a consonant at the beginning of a word or syllable (*w*ar, path*w*ay)

w following a vowel is usually part of a grapheme for a vowel (ra*w*) or diphthong (cro*w*d)

x usually like **ks** (a*x*e, bo*x*, e*x*pect)

x usually like **gs** when preceded by **e** and followed by a vowel (e*x*act, e*x*ertion)

x at the beginning of a word, like **z** (*x*ylophone)

y at the beginning of a word is a consonant (*y*es, *y*ourself)

y at the end of a syllable acts like long **e** or short **i** depending on regional dialect (bab*y*, tin*y*)

z usually voiced as in *z*ebra, crazy

z occasionally like **zh** as in azure

DOUBLE CONSONANTS

When a consonant is doubled, the first of the pair is usually sounded and the second is usually silent (*sitting, stirred*). There are only three exceptions to this generalization.

cc when **cc** is followed by **e** or **i**, the first **c** is hard and the second is soft, like **ks** (ac*c*ent, ac*c*ident)

gg as in su*gg*est

ss when **ss** is followed by **ion** it represents the sound of **sh** (mi*ss*ion, pa*ss*ion)

CONSONANT DIGRAPHS

The consonant digraphs are two-consonant combinations that represent one sound. The common consonant digraphs are **ch, ck, sh, th,** and **wh.** The combinations **ng** and **nk** are considered here to be blends rather than digraphs.

ch usually as in *ch*in, tou*ch*, *ch*ur*ch*
ch usually like **k** in words of Greek origin (*ch*ord, *ch*orus, *ch*aracter)
ch occasionally like **sh** (ma*ch*ine)
ch may represent a gutteral sound as in Scottish lo*ch*

ck like **k;** generally used at the end of syllables with short vowels (ba*ck*, lu*ck*).

gh usually silent (hi*gh*, ti*gh*t, nei*gh*bor, thou*gh*, tau*gh*t)
gh like **g** at the beginning of words (*gh*ost, *gh*astly)
gh occasionally like **f** (rou*gh*, cou*gh*)

ph like **f** (*ph*one, *ph*otogra*ph*)

qu although usually a blend, **qu** sometimes has the sound of **k** (uni*qu*e)

sc like **s** or **sh** when followed by **e** or **i** (*sc*ience, a*sc*end, con*sc*ience)

sh as in *sh*e, wi*sh*, fa*sh*ion

th sometimes unvoiced (*th*in, mo*th*)
th sometimes voiced, soft (*th*en, wi*th*, mo*th*er)

wh usually like **hw** (*wh*en, *wh*ich); or like **w** in some regional dialects
wh like **h** when followed by **o** (*wh*o, *wh*ole)

CONSONANT BLENDS

A consonant cluster or blend is a combination of two or more consonant letters representing separate phonemes which are slightly merged but are still distinguishable.

ng nasal, with the **g** barely perceptible (sa*ng*, ri*ng*, hu*ng*)
nk sounds like **ngk** (ba*nk*, thi*nk*, su*nk*)
bl, cl, fl, gl, pl, sl (*bl*ack, *cl*ean, *fl*ag, *gl*ow, *pl*ay, *sl*eep)

br, cr, dr, fr, gr, pr, tr (*br*ing, *cr*y, *dr*ess, *fr*og, *gr*een, *pr*ince, *tr*ip)
sc, sk, sn, sp, st, sw (*sc*amper, *sk*in, *sn*ow, *sp*in, *st*op, be*st*, *sw*ing)
spl, spr, str (*spl*ash, *spr*ing, *str*ike)
thr (*thr*ee, *thr*own)
tw (*tw*in, *tw*inkle)
qu like **kw** (*qu*een, liq*u*id)
squ like **skw** (*squ*are, *squ*ash)
sch like **sk** at the beginning of words (*sch*ool, *sch*olar); like **sh** in some
words of foreign origin

SILENT CONSONANTS

When two or more consonants occur together, sometimes one of
them is silent.

gn   g is silent before **n** at the beginning of a word (*gn*aw, *gn*ome)
kn   k is silent before **n** at the beginning of a word (*kn*ife, *kn*ow)
wr   w is silent before **r** (*wr*ite, *wr*ong)
ps, pn   p is silent before **s** or **n** (*p*sychology, *p*neumonia)
gh   is usually silent (cau*gh*t, si*gh*t, wei*gh*t, *th*ough)
lm, lk   l is usually silent before **m** or **k** (ca*l*m, wa*l*k)
mb   at the end of a syllable, **b** preceded by **m** is silent (co*mb*, thu*mb*)
mn   n is sometimes silent after **m** (sole*mn*)
sl   s is sometimes silent before **l** (ai*s*le, i*s*land)
tch   t is usually silent when followed by **ch** (pit*ch*er, wat*ch*)

As noted above, in doubled consonants the second consonant letter
is usually silent.

Vowels

A vowel is a sound produced without obstructing the breath. The
regular vowel letters are **a, e, i, o,** and **u,** and **h, y,** and **w,** are semivowels. Each vowel letter occurs in combinations with other vowel
letters and can represent alternative phonemes.

SINGLE VOWELS

Each of the regular vowel letters stands for two main sounds, the
long sound and the short sound. The long sounds are the same as

their alphabet names: ā as in ape, bake; ē as in even, athlete; ī as in as in ivy, ripe; ō as in over, bone; ū as in usual, cute. **Y** following a consonant at the end of one-syllable words stands for the sound of ī (cry, by).

The short vowels are: ă as in apple, cat; ĕ as in egg, bed; ĭ as in igloo, fish; ŏ as in octopus, top; ŭ as in umbrella, duck. At the end of words of more than one syllable, **y** represents ē or ĭ depending on regional dialect (happy, family).

w never occurs as a single vowel letter, but only in the combinations **aw, ew,** and **ow.**

a sometimes represents the sound of ä (car, father)

a sometimes represents the sound of ŏ or ô (ball, talk)

o is sometimes pronounced like ŭ (son, money)

o is sometimes pronounced like **oo** (do, to)

o may represent a sound, ô, between short **o** and long **o** as in or, and as a regional alternative to short **o** in many words.

u is sometimes pronounced like o͞o (flute)

u is sometimes pronounced like o͞o (put)

The sounds of single vowels are also modified when followed by **r** and when they occur in unstressed syllables; these effects are discussed below.

SILENT VOWELS

There are two situations in which vowels are normally silent.

1. In vowel digraphs, usually one of the two vowels is sounded and the other is silent. Usually the first vowel is sounded and the second is silent (feat, boat) but sometimes the first vowel is the silent one (pear, friend). The phoneme represented is usually long but may also be short (beard, bread).
2. When **e** comes at the end of a syllable containing another vowel, the **e** is silent and the other vowel is usually long (robe, blue, became).
3. **u** is often silent when it follows **g** (tongue), and is sometimes silent following **q** (unique).

VOWEL DIGRAPHS

A vowel digraph is a two-letter combination that represents one sound. Usually the first letter represents its long sound, less often its short sound, and the second letter is silent. Less commonly the first letter is silent and the second letter represents its long sound. Alternative sounds are listed below only when they occur in a number of words.

ay (ā) d*ay*, rep*ay*
ai (ā) s*ai*l, w*ai*t (exception: s*ai*d)
au and **aw** (ŏ or ô) *au*to, s*aw*
ee (ē) sh*ee*p, s*ee*m
ea (ē) l*ea*p, dr*ea*m
ea (ĕ) br*ea*d, h*ea*d
ea (ā) st*ea*k, br*ea*k
ei (ē) c*ei*ling, dec*ei*ve
ei (ā) when followed by gh (n*ei*ghbor, w*ei*gh)
ei (ī) an alternative pronunciation in *ei*ther and n*ei*ther
eu, ew, (ōō, ū) n*ew*s, f*ew*, n*eu*tral
ey (ē) k*ey*, donk*ey*
ey (ā) th*ey*, pr*ey*
ie (ī) in one-syllable words (p*ie*, cr*ie*s)
ie (ē) p*ie*ce, gr*ie*ve, cook*ie*s
oa (ō) b*oa*t, c*oa*st
oo (ōō) b*oo*t, sh*oo*t
oo (ŏŏ) f*oo*t, st*oo*d
ou (ŏŏ) c*ou*ld, sh*ou*ld
ow (ō) bl*ow*, sl*ow*

VOWEL BLENDS OR DIPHTHONGS

There are two diphthongs which are generally recognized.

oi, oy (oi) b*oi*l, t*oy*
ou, ow (ou) l*ou*d, c*ow*

Some linguists state that the long vowel sounds are really diphthongs. The long ā sound is said to consist of a short ĕ sound, followed by short ĭ (or, by the consonant sound of y); long ī consists of ä and ĭ or ä and y. In teaching phonics to children this refinement is usually ignored.

VOWELS FOLLOWED BY R AND L

The sounds of vowels are somewhat modified when they are followed by **r**. The short vowels are considerably altered. The sounds of **er, ir,** and **ur** are indistinguishable. Long vowels are only slightly affected by a following **r** and while some dictionaries use special symbols to represent these sounds (especially â and ê), other dictionaries do not.

ar (ä) *ar*m, f*ar*
or (ô) *or*der, f*or*ceful
er, ir, ur (ů) or **(ur)** h*er*, f*er*n; th*ir*sty, g*ir*l, s*ir*; f*ur*, c*ur*tsey, h*ur*t. In unstressed syllables a vowel followed by **r** is often represented by the schwa: sist*er*, sail*or*.

Long ī, ō, and ōō are relatively unchanged by a following **r**. Long ā, ē, and ū are modified in that the vowel is shortened a little, coming out somewhere between the long sound and the short sound. In the primary grades the difference between the long sound and its modification when followed by **r** is often ignored, but some dictionaries recognize this difference.

are, air (â or **ā)** c*are*, p*air*
eer, ere (ê or **ĭ** or **ē)** ch*eer*, h*ere*
ure (yōōr, ər) p*ure*, end*ure*, treas*ure*

There is a recent trend in some dictionaries to simplify the representation of vowels by using a macron to represent a long vowel whether or not it is followed by an **r** (peer, **pēr**).

When **a** is followed by **l, ll,** or **lk,** its value may be deepened to an **o** sound or a broad **a** sound.

al, all (ô or **ŏ)** *al*ways, t*all* (exceptions: sh*ă*ll, *ă*l′ly)
alk (ô or **ŏ)** ch*al*k, t*al*k

VOWEL SOUNDS IN ONE-SYLLABLE WORDS

The sounds of vowels in monosyllables can, with some exceptions, be determined by the application of three generalizations.

1. When a monosyllable ends with one or more consonants, a single vowel is usually short (sat, west, think, rob, cup) unless modified by r.
2. When a monosyllable ends with a vowel, the vowel is usually long (he, me, go, by. Exceptions: do, to, too, two).
3. When a monosyllable ending with e has a preceding single vowel, the e is silent and the preceding vowel is usually long. This is sometimes called "the rule of silent e" or "magic e." (ate, bathe, range, here, line, tie, hoe, store, cute, blue. Exceptions: shoe, done, gone, edge, badge).

Syllabication

A syllable is an uninterrupted unit of speech containing one vowel sound, forming either a whole word or part of a word; also, the letter or letters representing the spoken syllable. A syllable may consist of a vowel only (vi-o-lin), it may have one or more consonants preceding the vowel (pre-view, stray), one or more consonants following the vowel (ac-knowl-edge), or consonants before and after the vowel (un-friend-li-ness).

PRINCIPLES OF SYLLABLE DIVISION

While many rules or principles governing the division of words can be stated, numerous exceptions to these rules can be found, and in many words one rule can be observed only by breaking another rule. It is desirable, therefore, to teach only those rules which have wide application and relatively few exceptions. When in doubt about how to divide a word, it is advisable to consult a dictionary.

1. When the word has a prefix, usually divide between the prefix and the root word (pre-fix, re-capture).
2. When the word has a suffix, usually divide between the root word and the suffix (sing-ing, love-ly, invit-ed).
3. When two consonants that are not a digraph or blend come between vowels, usually divide between them (dic-tate, fan-cy; rack-et, de-scribe).
4. A single consonant between two vowels may go with either syllable (se-cure, prom-ise).

ACCENT

Accent is the prominence given to a syllable in a word (or to a word in a sentence) that makes it stand out in comparison to adjacent syllables (or words). Here we are concerned only with accent within words. *Stress* is generally used as a synonym for accent. In words of two syllables, one syllable is usually accented. In words of three or more syllables, one syllable has a primary accent (′); there often is a secondary accent (′) on another syllable. In some compound words of two syllables, both syllables may have primary accents (school′room′).

Some words can be accented in either of two ways, with differences of meaning. For example, *absolutely* conveys more emphasis when the third syllable is stressed than when the first syllable is accented. Sometimes only a difference in accent determines which of two spoken words a homograph represents (des′ert, de-sert′). Because of this interdependence of meaning and accent, many English words have no fixed accent.

1. In the majority of two-syllable words, the accent usually is on the first syllable (deaf′er).
2. A final syllable containing a long vowel sound is usually accented (en-ter-tain′, pa-rade′).
3. Affixes usually are not accented.

VOWEL SOUNDS IN SYLLABLES

The sounds of vowels in syllables are affected both by the content of the syllable and by the placement of accent. Some of the principles that work more often than not are the following:

1. When an accented syllable ends with a vowel, the vowel is usually long (ba'by, cli'mate).
2. When an accented syllable ends with a consonant, the vowel is usually short unless the following consonant is an *r* (prep'a-ra'tion, re-tract').
3. The vowels in many unaccented syllables are diminished to the point where their distinctive characters are almost completely lost, and they can be represented by the schwa (dis'ap-pear', tel'e-gram, hap'pi-ness).
4. The vowels in unaccented syllables are sometimes long vowels that are slightly reduced in duration and tend slightly toward the short sound (mu-si'cian, re-fuse').
5. When i takes the place of y before **er, es,** or **ed,** it keeps the sound the y had (dr*i*er, cr*i*ed, carr*i*ed).

Phonic Materials

Relatively complete phonic systems that are available commercially have been described on pages 261–263. The materials described below can be used as supplementary aids. This listing is intentionally restricted to items which we believe to be well designed and educationally useful.

CHARTS AND KEY CARDS

Phonics Key Cards. Wichita: McCormick-Mathers Publishing Co. A set of 78 cards, each with a line drawing, underneath which is printed the word represented by the picture, and the phonic unit for which this is the key card; includes single consonants, consonant blends and digraphs, short and long vowels, vowel digraphs, and diphthongs. This is a supplement (to the *Building Reading Skills* series) that can be ordered separately.

Hammond's ABC Sounds, Consonantal Blends, Vowel Blends. Maplewood, N.J.: C. S. Hammond Co. Three sets of key cards, printed in colors.

Webster Word Analysis Charts. St. Louis: Webster. Five wall charts, the first containing picture keys for all single letters.

PHONIC GAMES

Go Fish. Washington, D.C.: Kingsbury. Two sets, using cards played like rummy for practice with single and double consonants.

Vowel Dominoes. Kingsbury. Played like dominoes, but child has to match a vowel with a picture.

Consonant Lotto, by E. W. Dolch. Champaign, Ill.: Garrard. Phonic readiness practice with initial consonants, involving matching pictures whose names start with the same sound. Can be played by up to six children.

Vowel Lotto, by E. W. Dolch. Garrard. Another lotto game, involving matching pictures that have the same vowel sounds.

What the Letters Say, by E. W. Dolch. Garrard. A game to aid in association of sounds with letters.

Group Sounding Game, by E. W. Dolch. Garrard. Fifteen lotto-type games, each for six players, covering the phonic elements usually taught in the primary grades.

Take, by E. W. Dolch. Garrard. A card game involving matching cards that represent words with the same beginning sound, middle part, or ending.

The Syllable Game, by E. W. Dolch. Garrard. Contains three sets of cards going from two-syllable to four-syllable words.

Phonetic Quizmo, Milton Bradley. Phonic lotto game.

Grab. Dorothea Alcock, 324 East College St., Covina, Calif. Three sets of card games involving word matching that can be played with several variations.

Reading Laboratory 1: Word Games. SRA. Forty-four word games in individual packets.

Phonic Rummy. Kenworthy. Matching game with phonic elements. *Junior Phonic Rummy.* Kenworthy. Matching game using 110 frequently occurring words with short vowel sounds.

Phonics We Use—Learning Game Kit, Lyons and Carnahan. Ten separate games for teaching various phonic skills.

WORD WHEELS AND PHONIC STRIPS

Phono-Word Wheels, by R. A. Pulliam and U. A. Leavell. Steck. Five sets of word wheels, covering initial consonants; blends, digraphs, and endings; beginning blends; suffixes; and prefixes.

Webster Word Wheels. Webster. A set of 63 word wheels for practice with consonant blends, prefixes, and suffixes. Fourth grade and up.

Syllaboscope. Washington, D.C.: Woodcrafter's Guild, St. Alban's School. A wooden frame with wooden slides that can be used to mark a word off into syllables, and sets of word cards; two sizes, for group and individual use.

Embeco Word Builder. Milton Bradley. An inexpensive set of anagram letters printed on heavy cardboard, available in lower-case letters.

Embeco Phonetic Drill Cards. Milton Bradley. Word-family phonograms on large cards, each with hinged smaller cards containing initial consonants; by turning the hinges, different words are made.

Phonetic Word Analyzer. Milton Bradley. Wheel with interchangeable disks. Consonants and blends are matched with stems.

Word-Go-Round. Harper & Row. Three movable disks in a frame. Words can be formed by rotating disks.

APPENDIX

C

List of Publishers and their Addresses

The following list contains, in alphabetical order, the names and addresses of the publishers of the books and tests mentioned in the two preceding appendixes. Only one office is listed for each publisher. The abbreviation used in this volume is given first, then the full name and address.

Aladdin. Aladdin Books, *see* American Book Co.

Allyn. Allyn and Bacon, Inc., Rockleigh, N.J. 07647

American Book. American Book-Van Nostrand Co., 450 W. 33rd St., New York, N.Y. 10001

American Council on Education. 1 Dupont Circle, Washington, D.C. 20036

American Ed. American Education Publishers, Inc., 55 High St., Middletown, Conn. 06457. A Xerox company.

American Guidance. American Guidance Service, Inc., Circle Pines, Minn. 55014

American Library. American Library Association, 50 E. Huron St., Chicago, Ill. 60611

Appleton. Appleton-Century-Crofts, *see* Meredith Corp.

461

Association for Childhood Education International, 3615 Wisconsin Ave. N.W., Washington, D.C. 20016

Audio-Visual. Audio-Visual Research Co., 1509 8th St. S.E., Waseca, Minn. 56093

Barnell Loft, Ltd., 111 South Centre Ave., Rockville Centre, N.Y. 11570

Beckley-Cardy Co., 1900 N. Narragansett Ave., Chicago, Ill. 60639

Bell. Bell and Howell Co., Audio Visual Products Division, 7100 McCormick Road, Chicago, Ill. 60645

Benefic. Benefic Press, 10300 W. Roosevelt Road, Westchester, Ill. 60153. *See* Beckley-Cardy Co.

Bobbs. Bobbs-Merrill Co., 4300 W. 62nd St., Indianapolis, Ind. 46268

R. R. Bowker Co., 1180 Avenue of the Americas, New York, N.Y. 10036

Milton Bradley Co., Springfield, Mass. 01101

Wm. C. Brown Co., 135 South Locust St., Dubuque, Iowa 52001

California. California Test Bureau, a Division of McGraw-Hill Co., Del Monte Research Park, Monterey, Calif. 93940

Catholic University of America Press, 620 Michigan Ave. N.E., Washington, D.C. 20017

Center for Applied Linguistics, 1717 Massachusetts Ave. N.W., Washington, D.C. 20036

Chandler. Chandler Publishing Co., 124 Spear Street, San Francisco, California 94105

Chicago. See University of Chicago Press

Childrens. Children's Press, Inc., 1224 W. Van Buren St., Chicago, Ill. 60607

Council for Exceptional Children, 1201 16th St. N.W., Washington, D.C. 20036

Doubleday. Doubleday and Co., Inc., 277 Park Ave., New York, N.Y. 10017

The Economy Co., 1901 N. Walnut, Oklahoma City, Okla. 73105

EDL. Educational Developmental Laboratories, Inc., a Division of McGraw-Hill Book Co., 284 Pulaski Rd., Huntington, N.Y. 11744

ETS. Educational Testing Service, 20 Nassau St., Princeton, N.J. 08540

Educators. Educators Publishing Service, 75 Moulten St., Cambridge, Mass. 02138

Electronic Futures, Inc., 57 Dodge Ave., North Haven, Conn. 06473

Encyclopaedia Britannica Educational Corp., 425 N. Michigan Ave., Chicago, Ill. 60611

Essay. Essay Press, Box 5, Planetarium Station, New York, N.Y. 10024

Expression Co., P.O. Box 11, Magnolia, Mass. 01930

Fearon Publishers, 2165 Park Blvd., Palo Alto, Calif. 94306

Field. Field Educational Publications, Inc., 609 Mission St., San Francisco, Calif. 94105

Follett. Follett Educational Corp., 201 N. Wells St., Chicago, Ill. 60606

Funk. Funk and Wagnalls, a Division of Readers Digest Books, Inc., 380 Madison Ave., New York, N.Y. 10017

Garrard. Garrard Publishing Co., 1607 N. Market St., Champaign, Ill. 61820

Ginn. Ginn and Co., Waltham, Mass. 02154

Globe. Globe Book Co., 175 Fifth Ave., New York, N.Y. 10010

Golden. Golden Press, Publishers, 850 3rd Ave., New York, N.Y. 10022

The Gryphon Press, Highland Park, N.J. 08904

Hale. E. M. Hale and Co., 1201 S. Hastings Way, Eau Claire, Wis. 54701

C. S. Hammond and Co., Hammond Bldg., Maplewood, N.J. 07040

Harcourt. Harcourt Brace Jovanovich, Inc., 757 3rd Ave., New York, N.Y. 10017

Harper. Harper and Row, Publishers, Inc., 49 E. 33rd St., New York, N.Y. 10016

Heath. D. C. Heath and Company, 125 Spring St., Lexington, Mass. 02173

Holt. Holt, Rinehart, and Winston, Inc., 383 Madison Ave., New York, N.Y. 10017

Houghton. Houghton Mifflin Co., 2 Park St., Boston, Mass. 02107

Initial Teaching Alphabet Publications, Inc., 20 E. 46th St., New York, N.Y. 10017

International Reading Association, 6 Tyre Ave., Newark, Del. 19711

Iowa State University Press, Press Bldg., Ames, Iowa 50010

Kenworthy. Kenworthy Education Service, Inc., P.O. Box 3031, 138 Allen St., Buffalo, N.Y. 14205

Keystone. Keystone View Co., Meadville, Penna. 16335

Kingsbury. See Remedial Education Press.

Learning Through Seeing, Inc., 8138 Foothill Boulevard, Sunland, Calif. 91040

Lippincott. J. B. Lippincott Co., E. Washington Square, Philadelphia, Penna. 19105

Little. Little, Brown and Co., 34 Beacon St., Boston, Mass. 02106

Lyons. Lyons and Carnahan, Inc., 407 E. 25th St., Chicago, Ill. 60616

McCormick. McCormick-Mathers Publishing Co., Inc., P.O. Box 2212, Wichita, Kans. 67201

McGraw-Hill. McGraw-Hill Book Co., 330 West 42nd St., New York, N.Y. 10036

McKay. David McKay Co., Inc., 750 Third Ave., New York, N.Y. 10017

Macmillan. The Macmillan Co., 866 Third Ave., New York, N.Y. 10022

Meredith Corp., 440 Park Ave. South, New York, N.Y. 10016

G & C Merriam Co. 47 Federal St., Springfield, Mass. 01101

Merrill. Charles E. Merrill Books, Inc., 1300 Alum Creek Drive, Columbus, Ohio 43216

National Council for the Social Studies, 1201 Sixteenth St., N.W., Washington, D.C., 20036

National Council of Teachers of English, 508 S. 6th St., Champaign, Ill. 61820

Ohio State University Press, 2070 Neil Ave., Columbus, Ohio 43210

Open Court Publishing Co., Box 402, LaSalle, Ill. 61301

Oxford U. Press, Inc., 200 Madison Ave., New York, N.Y. 10016

Perceptual Development Laboratories, 6767 Southwest Ave., St. Louis, Mo. 63143

Phonovisual. Phonovisual Products, Inc., Box 5625, Washington, D.C. 20016

Pitman Publishing Corp., 6 East 43rd St., New York, N.Y. 10017

Pocket Books, Inc., *see* Simon & Shuster

Prentice. Prentice-Hall, Inc., Englewood Cliffs, N.J. 07632

Psychological. The Psychological Corp., 304 E. 45th St., New York, N.Y. 10017

Psychological Test. Psychological Test Specialists, Box 1441, Missoula, Mont. 59801

Random. Random House, 201 E. 50th St., New York, N.Y. 10022

Reader's Digest Services, Inc., Educational Division, Pleasantville, N.Y. 10570

The Reading Institute of Boston, 116 Newbury St., Boston, Mass. 02116

Remedial Education Press, Kingsbury Center, 2138 Bancroft Place, N.W., Washington, D.C. 20008

Ronald. The Ronald Press Co., 79 Madison Ave., New York, N.Y. 10016

Scarecrow Press, 52 Liberty St., P.O. Box 656, Metuchen, N.J. 08840

Scholastic. Scholastic Magazines and Book Services, 50 W. 44th St., New York, N.Y. 10036

Schoolhouse. Schoolhouse Industries, Inc., 170 Central Ave., Farmingdale, N.Y. 11735

Scott F. Scott, Foresman and Co., 1900 E. Lake Ave., Glenview, Ill. 60025

Selected Academic Readings, Associated Educational Services Corp., 1 W. 39th St., New York, N.Y. 10018

Simon. Simon and Schuster, Inc., 1 W. 39th St., New York, N.Y. 10018

Singer. L. W. Singer, Inc., a Division of Random House, 201 E. 50th St., New York, N.Y. 10022

SRA. Science Research Associates, Inc., 259 E. Erie St., Chicago, Ill. 60611

Steck. Steck-Vaughn Co., P.O. Box 2028, Austin, Texas 78767

Teachers. Teachers College Press, Columbia University, 1234 Amsterdam Ave., New York, N.Y. 10027

Teachers Publishing Corp., 23 LeRoy Ave., Darien, Conn. 06820

Teaching Technology Corp., 5520 Cleon Ave., N. Hollywood, Calif. 91601

University of Chicago Press, 5750 Ellis Avenue, Chicago, Ill. 60637

Viking. The Viking Press, Inc., 625 Madson Ave., New York, N.Y. 10022

Wagner. Harr Wagner, *see* Field Educational Publications

Walck. Henry Z. Walck, Inc., Publishers, 19 Union Square, New York, N.Y. 10003

Watts. Frederick Watts, Inc., 575 Lexington Ave., New York, N.Y. 10022

Webster. Webster Division of McGraw-Hill Book Co., Manchester Rd., Manchester, Mo. 63011

John Wiley and Sons, Inc., 605 Third Ave., New York, N.Y. 10016

Wilson. H. W. Wilson Co., 950 University Avenue, Bronx, N.Y. 10452

World. World Publishing Co., 2231 W. 110th St., Cleveland, Ohio 44102

Index

Abramowitz, J., 147, 399
accent, 245ff., 253, 457
Adams, R. B., 404
adapted reading program, 397
administrative arrangements, 134
affix, 233
age, and reading readiness, 24
Alcock, D., 228
Allen, R. V., 83
alphabet, 30
alphabetical order, 334
American College Dictionary, 208, 446, 448
American History Study Lessons, 399
American School Achievement Tests, 434
Ammons Full-Range Picture Vocabulary Test, 436
analogies, 288
Anastasiow, N., 38
Anderson, V. D., 56
Arbuthnot, M. H., 384, 389, 393
arithmetic, reading skills in, 346
Armstrong, L., 261
audience reading, 119, 196
auding, 302; *see also* listening comprehension
Audio Flashcard System, 227
audio-visual materials, 191
auditory acuity, 29
auditory blending, 237
auditory discrimination, 29, 236ff., 426; suggestions for teaching, 51, 239; sequence of development, 236; *see also* perception
auditory skills, 28
Austin, M. C., 106, 108

author, evaluating the, 318
author's plan and intent, grasping, 313

Bamman, H. A., 284, 293
Baratz, J. C., 427
Barbe, W. B., 22
Barnhart, C. R., 258
Barrett, T. C., 22, 56, 99, 182, 206, 305, 332, 393, 431
basal reader method: in first grade, 61ff.; in grades 2 and 3, 105ff.; in middle grades, 130ff.; variations in, 70, 132; comments on, 109
basal reader: approaches, 61ff.; materials, 61; instructional procedures, 65
basal reading materials: in first grade, 61ff.; in grades 2 and 3, 102ff.; in middle grades, 129ff.; in upper grades, 145
basal series, using different, 73
Basic Book Collection for Elementary Grades, A, 390
Basic English, 271
Basic Reading, Lippincott, 85
Basic Sight Vocabulary Cards, 227
Basic Sight Words, 271
Be a Better Reader, 283, 327, 351, 361
Beery, A., 22, 56, 99, 206, 332, 393, 431
Beginning Dictionary, 258, 271, 282
beginning reading instruction, 58ff.; historical overview, 58ff.; differences among, 59ff.; synthetic method, 60; whole-word method, 60, 61; basal reader approaches, 61; language-experience, 80; phonic, 84; lin-

guistic, 89; special alphabet, 90; programmed, 92; individualized reading, 95; comparison of approaches, 95ff.
begin-over approach, 410
Behavior Patterns in Children's Books, 391
Best Books for Children, 370, 390
Betts, E. A., 158
Bibliography of Books for Children, 390
bibliotherapy, 388
Bingham, A., 318
Biogeography Laboratory, 361
Bissett, D. J., 386
Blackman, M., 303
blend, 232, 451, 454
blending, 254; testing of, 175
Bond, G. L., 56, 96, 182, 216, 264, 293
Boning, R. A., 290, 328
Book B, Lippincott Basic Reading, 87
book clubs for children, list of, 441
book fair, 383
Books for Children, 390
booklists and indexes, list of, 442
book reports, 381
Book Selection Media, 390
book week, 383
boredom, freeing bright child from, 424
Bormuth, J. R., 377
Botel, M., 357
Botel Reading Inventory, 174, 436
brain-damaged children, 47
brain functioning, 4; see also neurology
Brake, R. G., 261
Branley, F. M., 361
Breaking the Sound Barrier, 261
Breen, L. C., 284
Bruner, J., 269
Bryant, N. D., 404
Buchanan, C. D., 94
Buckingham, B. R., 278
Building Reading Power, 291
Building Reading Skills, 242, 261
Burns, P. C., 183

Buros, O. K., 38, 433

California Achievement Tests: Social Studies, 176
California Reading Tests, 161, 435
California Tests of Mental Maturity, 436, 437
Can You Follow Directions, 314
Caroline, Sister Mary, 261
Carter, H. L. J., 276
categories, establishment of, 268
Catterson, J. H., 393
celebrating progress, 409
Chall, J. S., 243, 377
charts, reading, 348
check list for reading analysis, 177ff., 178, 179
child development, 2ff.; through reading, 8
children's books, learning about, 389
Children's Book Council, 383
Children's Knowledge of Words, 278
choral reading, 120, 196
chronological age, 24
clarity of perception, improving, 216
Clark, M. K., 68, 69, 105, 107, 255, 257, 303
class management and individualized reading, 202; see also grouping
class size, and individualized reading, 201
class survey, 153ff.
classics, 147
class test, on basal reader, 153
classification, 287
classroom library, 375
Clements, S. D., 404
closure, 209
clues, 214, 275; see also context
Clymer-Barrett Prereading Battery, 38
Clymer, T., 22
Cohen, S. A., 427
Cole, L., 198, 278, 339
Coleman, J. H., 325
College Discovery and Development Project, 359
color-blindness, 45

Colwell, E., 375
Combined Word List, A, 278
combining good procedures, 203ff.
comic books, 369
committees, 186
common words, 399
communication, 8
comparing different versions, 319
comparison of beginning reading approaches, 95ff.
competitors for children's time, 367
comprehension, development of, 293ff.; in first grade, 65; in grades 2 and 3, 105, 109; in middle grades, 132; in upper grades, 146; factors underlying, 300; building in primary grades, 303; models of, 305; levels of, 306; degrees of, 307; materials for practice in, 325ff.; assembling practice materials, 329
comprehension skills, in content areas, 338ff.; applying in content areas, 340
comprehension, and rate, 321ff.
Comprehensive Tests of Basic Skills, 176
computer-assisted instruction, 92
concentration, 358
concept development, 30, 266ff., 340
concepts, mathematics, 347; social studies, 347; scientific, 349
concluding paragraphs, 308
conferences, teacher-pupil, 199
configuration clues, 214
Consonant Lotto, 459
consonants, 448ff.; single, 449; double, 450; digraphs, 451; blends, 451; silent, 452
consonant substitution, 234
constitutional predisposition, 403
content areas, guiding independent reading in, 344; developing specialized skills in, 345; *see also* functional reading
content textbooks, teaching reading with, 341; helping those who can't read, 343

context, 121; deriving meaning from, 275; types of context clues, 276
context readers, 168
controlled reading, 220
Cooperative Reading Studies, U.S.O.E., 216, 243
corrective reading, 401, 402ff., 416
Courtis, S., 255
Crabbs, L. M., 323, 324, 328
Cramer, R., 318
Creekmore, M., 88, 89
critical reading, 317ff.
critical thinking, 317
Crosby, M., 391
cross-class grouping, 134
cross-grade grouping, 134
crossed dominance, 33
cue card, 239
cultural development, 7
cumulative records, 153
current events, 195
current news reports, 385

Dale-Chall Readability Formula, 377
Dale, E., 273, 278, 377
Dale List of 3,000 Words, The, 278
Dallmann, M., 127, 264
Davis, F. B., 305
Davis, O., 428
Dawson, M. A., 293
DeAngeli, M., 388
De Boer, D. L., 182
De Boer, J. J., 127, 264
decoding, 84
definitions, 281
Deighton, L. C., 286, 290
departmentalized instruction, 145
details, reading for, 311
determining learning needs, 152ff.
Detroit Beginning First Grade Intelligence Test, 437
developing specific reading skills, 66
developmental reading, 18; objectives of, 18–19; in first grade, 61ff., 79ff.; in grades 2 and 3, 102ff.; in middle grades, 129ff.; in upper grades, 144ff.; individualized, 199ff.

diagnosis, 402, 414ff.
Diagnostic Reading Tests, 161
Diagnostic Reading Workbooks, 325
diagrams, 348
dialects, 7, 427, 447
Diedrick, P. B., 305
dictionary, 334, 336; using as guide to pronunciation, 254; picture dictionaries, 254; use of in developing vocabulary, 281
difficulty of a book, 104, 130
digraph, 232, 446, 451, 454
diphthongs, 232, 446, 454
directional confusion, 33
directional orientation, 29
disabled reader, 302; motivating, 407; ensuring success, 407; celebrating progress, 409; making reading interesting, 409; considering the family, 413; teaching, 416ff.
Discovery Book to Accompany Better Than Gold, A, 308
discussion, 280
Dolch, E. W., 224, 227, 264, 271, 278
Dolch Basic Sight Words, 271
Dolch Basic Sight Word Test, 436
Doren Diagnostic Reading Tests, 174, 436
Duker, S., 203, 303
dullness, 396
Durkin, D., 56, 99, 265
Durr, W. K., 431
Durrell Analysis of Reading Difficulty, 164, 436
Durrell Listening-Reading Series, 166
Dykstra, R., 96, 216, 243
dyslexia, 403

Eakin, M. K., 390
Early, M., 312
early word recognition clues, 213
Earth's Atmosphere Laboratory, 361
EDL Reading Versatility Tests, 436
EDL Study Skills Library, 140
EDL Study Skills Library: Reference Skills, 360

EDL Study Skills Library: Science, 361
EDL Study Skills Library: Social Science, 362
Eichholz, G., 278
educational handicaps, and reading disability, 405
educationally disadvantaged, 32, 425ff.
Elementary English, 443
Elementary School Journal, 443
Ellinger, B. D., 318
Embeco Phonetic Drill Cards, 460
Embeco Word Builder, 460
emotional factors, and reading disability, 406
emotional maladjustment, and reading readiness, 54
emotional maturity, 33
Enchanted Gates, 105, 107
encyclopedia, use of, 337
endocrine problems, 403
energy, lack of, 403
English, standard, 7
enjoyment of reading, developing, 373
enrichment, 66
errors, in word recognition, 173
errors of measurement, 401
evaluation, 152ff.; of readiness, 36ff.; of reading level, 152ff.; of independent reading, 175ff.; of functional reading, 176ff.; of individualized reading, 203
evaluating what one reads, 317
Evertts, E., 243
Exceptional Children, 398
experience stories, 80ff., 81
experiential background, 30, 277
explanation and discussion, in vocabulary development, 280
expository material, 338
Eye and Ear Fun, 261
eye movements, 14, 117
eye-movement photographs, 14
eye-voice span, 120

family, and remedial reading, 411ff.
Farr, R., 38
Farrar, M., 291

Fernald, G. M., 217
Fields and Fences, 108
figure and background, 209
figures of speech, 285
finger-pointing, 116
first reader, 61
fixations, 14, 295
flash cards, 219, 225
Fleming, J. T., 31
Flesch, R., 216
following directions, 313
foreign language background, 7
Frackenpohl, H., 278, 360, 361, 362
Frost, J. L., 56
Frostig, M., 47
frustration level, 158
functional comprehension skills, developing, 338ff.; materials for, 360ff.
functional reading, 18, 333ff.; objectives of, 19; in first grade, 58; in grades 2 and 3, 123; in middle grades, 143; in upper grades, 148; evaluation of, 176; individualized, 197
Fun With the Family, 69, 71

Gainsburg, J. C., 146
Game of Ball, A, 93
games, reading, 225
Gans, R., 206, 364, 431
Gates, A. I., 314, 328
Gates-MacGinitie Reading Tests, 161, 435
Gates-MacGinitie Reading Tests: Readiness Skills, 38, 39, 434
Gates-McKillop Reading Diagnostic Tests, 164, 436
Gates-Peardon Reading Exercises, 328
Gateways to Readable Books, 391
general health, 33
gestalt, 208
Gillespie, J., 390
Gilmore Oral Reading Test, 164, 436
Gladney, M., 428
Go Fish, 459
goals, for every child, 394ff.
Goldberg, L., 91

Good Books for Children, 390
Goodman, K., 31
Good Reading for Poor Readers, 391, 442
Grab, 228, 459
Graph and Picture Study Skills Kit, 360
graphs, reading, 348
graphemes, 84, 232, 445
Gray, L., 127, 151, 393
Gray Oral Reading Tests, 164, 436
Greene, C. E., 284
Greenman, A., 88, 89
Greet, W. C., 257, 289
group assignments, 192
group efficiency, 185ff.; factors influencing, 188
group instruction, 185ff.; in first grade, 75ff.; in grades 2 and 3, 112ff., 114, 115; in middle grades, 134, 136, 137
group intelligence tests, 166
Group Sounding Game, 459
grouping, 110; kinds of, 185ff.
groups, number of, 186; size of, 188; flexibility, 188; names of, 189; types of, 185ff.; physical arrangement, 190; providing for needs, 184ff.; management, 112
Grover, C. C., 327
Growing Up with Books, 391
Growing Up with Science Books, 391
guessing, on tests, 163
guide to pronunciation, 131
guided reading, 65, 67, 70, 105, 108
Guiler, W. S., 325
Guralnik, D. B., 258

Hall, M. A., 83
Halvorsen, M., 261
Hammond's ABC Sounds, 458
Handbook of Technical Vocabulary, 278
handedness, 33
handicaps to reading progress, 395ff.; correcting, 406ff.
Harcourt, Brace School Dictionary, 258

Hargrave, R., 261
Harper Row Basic Readers, Strand II,
360
Harris, A. J., 22, 28, 43, 45, 56, 105,
107, 165, 171, 178, 183, 206, 235,
264, 278, 293, 322, 328, 332, 364,
373, 374, 379, 393, 401, 411, 421,
428, 431
Harris, T. L., 88, 89
*Harrison-Stroud Reading Readiness
Profiles,* 434
headings, 309
health problems, teacher's responsibility, 53
hearing defects, 4, 29, 32, 403
hearing vocabulary, 272
Heilman, A. W., 56, 99, 127, 151, 264,
332
helpers, 193
Hen in a Fox's Den, A, 91
Henmon-Nelson Test of Mental Ability, 437
Herber, H. L., 342, 364
Herold, C. P., 280
Herr, S. E., 262, 411
Hidden Persuaders, The, 317
Hildreth, G., 264
hobby groups, 186
Hodkinson, K., 291
Hogan, U., 284
home conditions, 142
homework, 149, 344
homograph, 236, 271
homonym, 236, 271
Horn Book, The, 391
Horn, T. D., 427
Hosier, M., 227, 262, 303
How to Study, 357
Hughes, A., 86
Hunnicutt, C. W., 377

imagery, 215
immaturity, and reading readiness, 47
important words, for primary reading,
221
independent reading, 111, 123, 376,
417; evaluation of, 175; for bright

children, 424; *see also* individualized
reading
independent reading level, 156
indexes, 442
index, use of, 336
individual differences, providing for,
110ff., 133, 184ff.
individual intelligence tests, 167
individualized practice materials, 146
individualized reading, 197ff.; in first
grade, 95; in middle grades, 140ff.;
recreational, 197; functional, 197;
practice on reading skills, 198; developmental, 199; factors influencing efficiency of, 201ff.; evaluation
of, 203
individualized word study, 281
individual needs, providing for, 184ff.
individual textbook test, 154
Individually Prescribed Instruction,
141
inferences, 316
inflectional ending, 232, 259
informal reading inventory, 154
information, location of, 334ff.
Ingalls, L., 261
initial sight vocabulary, 211
initial teaching alphabet, 90
In Other Words, Beginning Thesaurus,
288
In Other Words, Junior Thesaurus,
288, 289
inner speech, 12
instructional reading level, 158
intelligence, and reading readiness,
25ff.; and reading capacity, 166ff.,
395ff.
intelligence quotient, 5, 25
intelligence tests, 5, 36, 166ff., 436ff.
interest groups, 186
interest maturity, 385
interest questionnaire, 373, 374
interest range, 385
interest and readiness, 34, 53
Interesting Origins of English Words,
290
interests, building new, 373

interests, children's, 366ff.
interests, reading, 365ff., 370, 372, 398
Introducing Books, 390
introducing new ideas, to whole class, 194
introductory paragraphs, 308
Iowa Every-Pupil Test of Basic Skills, 435
Iowa Silent Reading Tests, 435
Iowa Test of Basic Skills, 161, 434
Iowa Test of Basic Skills: Work-Study Skills, 161, 176
i/t/a, 90
Iverson, W. J., 377

Jacobson, M. D., 278
James, W., 215
Jenkins, W. A., 289
Johnson, E. M., 325
Johnson, R. J., 31
Joplin Plan, 134
Journal of Reading, 443
Junior Crossword Puzzle Book, Series 1, 291
Junior Libraries, 391
Junior Phonic Rummy, 460
Junior Plots, 390
Junior Scholastic, 195

Karp, E., 227, 262, 411
Kephart, N. C., 47
Kerfoot, J. E., 99
Keys to Independence in Reading, 88
kindergarten, 46
Kindergarten Evaluation of Learning Potential, 42, 434
kinesthetic method, 217
King, M., 318
Kingsley, B., 262
Kircher, C., 391
Klare, G. R., 377
Kuhlmann-Anderson Measure of Academic Potential, 437
Kuhlmann-Finch Intelligence Tests, 437

Laird, H., 257
language, 8

language arts, 9
language development, 6, 31
language-experience approach, 48, 80
Language Master, 227
Larrick, N., 383, 384, 389
lateral dominance, 33
Latin roots, list of most common, 284
Learning Activities for Reading, 262
learning in reading, 3, 12–13
Learning to Read and Write, 86
Leavell, U. W., 297, 325
Leaverton, L., 428
Lee, D. M., 83, 318
Lee-Clark Reading Readiness Test, 434
left-to-right direction, 29, 33, 51, 52
Lembo, D., 390
Let's Look at Children, 42, 434
letter names, 30, 37
levels of comprehension, 306
library, 375
library books, 111; see *also* independent reading, recreational reading
library corner, 190
linguistic approaches, 89, 223
lip movements, 116, 137
Listen and Read Program, 303
Listen and Think Program, 303
Listening Aids Through the Grades, 303
listening comprehension, 166, 298, 301, 422
Listening Games, 303
Listening Skill Builders, 303
literary appreciation, 147
locating answers, 309
locating information, 334ff.
locational skills, 143, 334ff.
lockstep boredom, 424
Lorge, I., 222, 279
Lorge-Thorndike Intelligence Tests, 437

Macmillan Reading Program, The, 61, 66
Macmillan Reading Readiness Test, 38, 39, 42, 434

magazines for children, list of, 439ff.
Magic Box, A, 66, 68
Magnetic Card Reader, 227
main ideas, 307
maladaptive behavior, 54
Maleska, E. T., 291
Mann, H., 59
manuals for teachers, 64, 132
Map and Globe Skills Kit, 361
map reading, 348
Map Skills for Today, 361
Map Skills Project, 361
Maslow, P., 47
match, 224
materials: for comprehension practice, 325ff.; for individualized practice, 146; for differentiated program, 190; for individualized reading, 201; for functional reading, 360ff.; for recreational reading, 375, 388ff.; *see also* basal readers
mathematics, reading skills in, 346
maturation, 3
mature child, and reading readiness, 48
maturity of children and individualized reading, 202
maturity, in reading, 16
Mazurkiewicz, A. J., 93, 364
McCall, W. A., 323, 324, 328
McCracken, G., 87
McCullough, C. M., 56, 100, 127, 151, 272, 293, 301, 364
McCullough Word Analysis Tests, 174, 436
McDavid, R. I., Jr., 428
McGinnis, D. J., 276
McKee, P., 151
meaning, in reading, 10; *see also* comprehension
meanings, refinement of, 266; *see also* concepts, vocabulary
Meighan, M., 261
Melis, L., 368
mental ability tests, 436ff.
mental age, 5, 25, 166

mental development, 5; *see also* intelligence
mental grades, 397, 421
Mental Measurements Yearbooks, 433
mentally retarded, 46
Merritt, E., 442
metaphors, 285
Metropolitan Readiness Tests, 39, 40, 434
Metropolitan Reading Tests, 161, 435
Mills, Q. B., 52
Monroe, M., 257
Monroe Reading Aptitude Tests, 434
morpheme, 232
morphemic analysis, 121, 258ff.
Morrison, C., 269
motivation, 329, 373ff., 407ff.; creating motivation for improvement, 359; *see also* interests
Mower, R., 52
multi-cultural characters, 428
Murphy-Durrell Reading Readiness Analysis, 39, 434
My Puzzle Book, 228
My Self-Help Dictionary, 255
My Weekly Reader, 195

Naslund, R. A., 360, 361
Nelson Silent Reading Test, 435
neurological factors, 4, 32, 33, 403
New Basic Readers, 69
New Goals in Reading, 325
New Journeys in Reading, 297
New Phonics Skilltexts, 261
New Practice Readers, 327
New Reading Skill Builder Series, 327
New Reading Skilltest Series, 327
New Rochester Occupational Reading Series, 400
New Science Reading Adventures, 361
newspapers, 195
new words, 63, 212
New York Times, The, 391
non-English speaking children, 427
note-taking, 353

objectives, 17

Odland, N., 393
O'Donnell, M., 256, 257, 360
Ogden, C. K., 271
Olson, A. V., 63, 73
Open Court Basic Reader, 85
opposites, 287
oral language, 32
oral reading, in primary grades, 117ff.; in middle grades, 137, 138; class survey of, 153; evaluation of, 169ff.
organizing, skills in, 144, 349ff.
Organizing and Reporting Skills Kit, 360
Ornato, J. G., 291
Ortego, P. D., 427
Otis-Lennon Mental Ability Test, 437
outcomes, anticipating, 315
outlining, 350

pacing, 199
Packard, V., 317
paragraphs, 308; reading, 300; types of organization, 300
paraphrasing 353
parents, 382, 413
Parker, D. H., 147, 303, 327, 361
Peabody Picture Vocabulary Test, 437
Peardon, C. C., 314, 328
percentile score, 162
perception and imagery, 215
perception in reading, 9, 207ff.
perceptual-motor skills, 45
Perkins, R., 390
personal development, and reading, 387
personality traits, 33
Petty, W., 280
Phelps, E., 391
phoneme, 84, 232, 445
Phonetic Keys to Reading, 88
Phonetic Quizmo, 459
Phonetic Word Analyzer, 460
phonetics, 84
phonic accessories, 262
phonic approaches, 84ff., 223
phonic games, 459
phonic generalizations, 246ff.; deter-

mining which to teach, 252; simplified generalizations, 253
phonic knowledge, testing, 174
phonic materials, 122; list of, 458ff.
phonic principles, 232, 445; developed inductively, 233; developed deductively, 233
phonic programs, supplementary, 260ff.
Phonic Rummy, 460
phonic units, learning, 239ff.; when should be taught, 241
phonics, 84, 121, 216, 232ff.; concise summary, 444ff.; sequence in basal readers, 234, 244; combined with context, 235
Phonics Key Cards, 458
Phonics We Use, 240, 261
Phonics We Use—Learning Game Kit, 460
Phonovisual Method, 261
Phono-Word Wheels, 460
phrase reading, 295
physical development, 4, 32
physical factors, and reading disability, 403
picture clues, 214
picture dictionaries, 254
Picture Stories, 52
Picture Word Builder, 224, 228
Picture Word Cards, 227
picture word cards, 224
Pinter General Ability Tests, 437
Platt, H. G., 258
Poems and Verses About Animals, 386
Poems and Verses About the City, 386
Poems and Verses to Begin on, 386
poetry, 386
Poetry and Verse for Urban Children, 386
pointing with finger, 116
Pooley, R. C., 22
posture in reading, 117
Powell, W. R., 22, 56, 99, 206, 332, 393
Practice Exercises in Reading, 349

practice materials, assembling, 329; individualized, 146
Pratt, M., 261
prefixes, 232, 282, 284
preparation for reading, 65, 67, 69, 105, 106
preparatory book, 64
preprimers, 62
preprimer methodology, 66ff.
Preston, R., 357
primers, 62, 63
problems, reading of, 346
professional journals for reading teachers, 442
programmed approaches, 92
programmed reader, 92
Programmed Reading Book 1, 94
progress charts, 378
project approach, 344
project committees, 186
projects, 123
Pronouncing Dictionary of American English, A, 447
propaganda techniques, 319
psycholinguistic ability, 45
publishers, list of, 461ff.
pupil leaders, 193
puzzles, 191

questions, comprehension, 304

radio, 369
Ramsey, W. Z., 206
rapid readers, 168
rapport, 407
Rasmussen, D., 91
rate of reading, 14, 132, 147, 219, 328; in middle grades, 138; and comprehension, 321ff.; and life uses, 326
rating scale for reading readiness, 42ff.
reaction in reading, 11, 12
readability, 377; formulas, 338, 377
Reader's Digest Science Reader, 361
Reader's Guide to Periodical Literature, 338
readiness for higher levels of reading, 35

reading, importance of, 1; definition of, 13; nature of, 8ff.
reading achievement tests, 434
Reading Aids Through the Grades, 262
reading and personal development, 387
reading capacity, judging, 164ff.
reading check list, 177
Reading Comprehension, 327
reading corner, 376
reading disability, 394, 400ff.; identifying children with, 400, 402ff.; definition of, 165, 400
reading distance, 32, 117
reading expectancy, for slow children, 396ff.; for bright children, 421ff.
Reading Eye, The, 14
Reading for Meaning, 325
Reading for Understanding, 328
reading games, 191
Reading Games, 262
reading grade equivalent score, 162
reading instruction: objectives of, 17ff.; stages in, 20, 21; in first grade, 57ff.; in grades 2 and 3, 101ff.; in middle grades, 128ff., 129ff.; in upper grades, 128ff., 144ff.; with content textbooks, 341
reading interests, 365ff., 398; sex differences in, 141; opening up new, 385; development of, 373; children's, 370; studying, 372
Reading Laboratory 1: Word Games, 459
reading ladders, 386
Reading Ladders for Human Relations, 391
reading levels, determining, 152ff.
reading level groups, 185
reading, life uses of, 17
reading periods, duration of, 74, 113, 135
reading program, understanding, 383
reading rate, coordinating with comprehension, 168, 321ff.; flexibility, 168, 323
reading of problems, 346

reading readiness, 23ff.; definition, 23; and chronological age, 24; and sex differences, 25; and intellectual factors, 25; and relevant knowledge (concept development), 29; and letter names, 30; and language development, 31; and physical development, 32; and emotional and social maturity, 33; and interest in learning to read, 34; evaluation of, 36ff.; rating scale for, 42, 43ff.; development of, 45ff.
reading readiness tests, 37, 434ff.
reading-readiness first grade, 48
reading records, 180; keeping, 177ff.
Reading Research Quarterly, 443
reading retardation, 394
Reading Skills, 262
Reading Skills Four, 312
Reading Teacher, The, 443
reading tests, list of, 433ff.
Reading Tests and Reviews, 433
reading vocabulary, 272
receptive language, 31
recognition span, 14
record keeping, 177ff.; and individualized reading, 202
recording skills, 349
recreational reading, 18, 219, 373ff.; objectives, 20; in primary grades, 123; in grades 2 and 3, 111; in middle grades, 141; in upper grades, 147; individualized, 197
reference works, 337
regional dialects, 447
regression, 14
related practice, 342
remedial reading, 401; with individual child, 418; with a small group, 419
remembering what one reads, 320
repetition, limitations of, 213
rereading, 119
research reading, 123
return sweep, 14
reversals, 29, 403
Revised Core Vocabulary, A, 278
Richards, I. A., 271

rivalry, 417
Robinson, E. R., 393
Robinson, F. P., 342
Robinson, H. A., 360, 361, 362
Robinson, H. M., 70, 71
Robinson, L. A., 232
Roe, B. D., 338
root words, 259, 282, 284
Rosen, C. L., 427
Roswell-Chall Diagnostic Reading Test, 174, 436
Russell, D. H., 22, 227, 238, 262, 303, 304, 411
Russell, E., 238, 303
Russian reading instruction, 222

sample lesson, 41
Samuels, S. J., 31
Sanford, A. B., 327
Sartain, H. W., 206
Sawyer, R., 375
Schell, L. M., 183
schematic drawings, 348
Schiller, A., 289
Schnayer, S. W., 232
Schoolfield, L. D., 238, 261
Schoolhouse Key Lab, 227
schwa, 447
science, reading skills in, 348
seeking, 199
self-control, 34
self-reliance, 34
self-selection, 199
semantics, 270
semivowels, 446
sensory aspects of reading, 4, 9
sentences, reading of, 297
sequence of events, 311
Sequential Tests of Educational Progress, 435
Serwer, B. L., 83
Seuss, Dr., 387
sex and reading readiness, 25
Sheldon, W. D., 52, 106, 108, 151
Sheldon Basic Reading Series, 156
Shuy, R. W., 427
sight vocabulary, 211ff.; building a,

211ff.; materials for, 221ff., 224, 227
sight words, 211, 234; teaching, 212
signal words, 298
silent consonants, 452
silent reading, interpreting patterns in, 167ff.; in primary grades, 116, 137
Silent Reading Diagnostic Tests, 174, 436
silent reading performance, 168; teacher judgments about, 168
silent reading tests, on basal reader, 154; standardized, 433ff.
similes, 285
Simpson, E. A., 328
Sipay, E. R., 156, 243, 315
skill development, 66, 69, 70, 106, 109
skills practice, individualized, 198
skimming, 309, 310, 338
Skolnick, M., 171
sleep, lack of sufficient, 403
slow learning children, 395ff.; adapted reading programs, 397; reading goals for, 397; reading interests of, 398
slowness in reading, 168
Smith, H. K., 10
Smith, H. L., Jr., 427, 445, 446
Smith, J. A., 393
Smith, N. B., 22, 156, 206, 264, 283, 327, 332, 339, 351, 361, 364, 393
Snellen Chart, 32, 403
Snow, M., 390
social development, 7
social factors, and reading disability, 405
social handicaps, 405
social maturity, in reading readiness, 33
social studies, reading skills in, 347
socioeconomic conditions, unfavorable, 8, 30, 426ff.
Solar System Laboratory, 361
Solomon, D., 370, 390
Spache, E. B., 100, 127, 302, 346, 364
Spache, G. D., 100, 127, 302, 346, 364, 377, 391
Spache Diagnostic Reading Scales, 164, 436

Spache Readability Formula, 377
speaking vocabulary, 272
special alphabet approaches, 90
special needs groups, 185
specialized school personnel, 406
specific learning needs, analyzing, 167ff., 414ff.; preliminary testing, 153, 414
specific mental abilities, 27, 45
Specific Skills Series, 328
speech defects, and reading readiness, 31
SQ3R Formula, 342
SRA Achievement Series: Reading, 435
SRA Better Reading Books, 328
SRA Primary Mental Abilities Test, 437
SRA Reading Laboratory, 140, 147, 327
Stahl, S. S., 151
Standard American English as a second language, 427
standard error of measurement, 163
Standard Test Lessons in Reading, 324, 328
standardized oral reading tests, 163
standardized reading tests, 161, 434ff.; limitations of, 163
standardized reading test scores, 162
Stanford-Binet Intelligence Scale, 167, 437
Stanford Diagnostic Reading Test, 436
Stanford Reading Tests, 133, 161, 435
stanine scores, 162
Stauffer, R. G., 22, 264, 284, 293, 316, 318, 332
STEP Reading Tests, 161, 166, 435
Stoll, E., 280
Stone, C. R., 222, 244, 261, 327
Stotler, D. W., 361
Strang, R., 183, 243, 391, 431
structural analysis, 121, 258ff.
Studybook for Friends All About, 316
study habits, 355ff.
studying, physical conditions for, 358
Study Lesson in Our Nation's History, 399
study-type reading, 333

substitution technique, 234
subvocal reading, 11
success, ensuring, 408
suffixes, 232, 259, 260, 282, 285
summaries, one-sentence, 309
summarizing, in primary grades, 349; learning, 352
summertime reading, 384
superior reader, fostering continuing growth, 421ff.
supplementary materials, 104
supplementary phonic programs, 260ff.
supplementary reading books, list of leading series, 438
syllabication, 245, 253ff., 456ff.
Syllabiscope, 460
Syllable Game, The, 459
symbol-sound association, 239
synonyms, 287

tables, reading of, 348
tachistoscopes, 220, 228, 328
Tag, 88
Take, 459
Tanyzer, H., 93
tape recorder, for oral reading, 171; use with disabled retarded readers, 343
Taylor, S. E., 15, 278, 291, 360, 361, 362
teacher aides, 193
teacher competence, and individualized reading, 201
teacher enthusiasm, 376
teacher judgment, 41
teacher observation, 41, 356
teacher-pupil conferences, 199
Teacher's Handbook of Technical Vocabulary, The, 278, 339
teacher's manuals, 64, 132
Teacher's Word Book of 30,000 Words, The, 279
technical vocabulary, 148
television, effects of heavy watching, 273, 368
Terman, S., 216
testing, 152ff.
tests, alphabetical list of, 433ff.

textbook reading, 124, 143, 148, 341ff.; on whole-class basis, 195
textbook tests, 154ff., 340
thesaurus, 288
Thomas, N., 85
Thorndike, E. L., 222, 258, 274, 279
thought units, 295ff.; *see also* phrase reading
Thurstone, T. G., 328
Timberlake, J. B., 261
time allotments, 74, 135
timid children, 54
Tinker, M. A., 56, 100, 127, 151, 182, 272, 293, 301, 364
titles, 309
Tooze, R., 375
topic sentences, 300, 307
Townes, W., 256, 257
TQLR Formula, 303
Trace, A. S., Jr., 85, 222
tracing, 217
"transition" books, 104
transition class, 48
Traxler Silent Reading Test, 435
Treasure Under the Sea, 412
Turner Communications Series, 400
Turner-Livingston Reading Series, 400

under-achieving, 422
units, 123, 344
unstressed syllables, 447
Using Context Clues, 290

VAK, 217
VAKT, 217
Veatch, J., 206
verbal relationships, 287
verbalism, 269, 347
Via, B. D., 297
Vilscek, E. C., 100
vision, 9, 117
visual defects, 4, 28, 32, 403
visual discrimination, 28, 49
visual memory, 37
visual-motor method, 217
visual perception, 45
visual skills, 28
vocabulary, 221ff., 265ff.; development

of, 139, 265ff.; types of, 272; size of, 272; selecting words worth teaching, 221, 277; ways of teaching, 279ff.; materials for developing, 290
vocabulary control, 221ff., 274ff.
vocabulary, cumulative, 103
Vocabulary Development, 286, 290
vocabulary lists, 278
vocabulary load, 63, 73, 129, 221
vocabularies, specialized types of, 339
vocabulary, technical, 148
Vocational Reading Series, 400
vowels, 446ff.; long, 447; short, 447; diminished sounds, 447; single, 452; silent, 453; digraphs, 454; diphthongs, 454; followed by *r* and *l*, 455; sounds in one-syllable words, 456; sounds in syllables, 245, 458
Vowel Dominoes, 459
Vowel Lotto, 459
vowel phonemes, 253
vowel sounds in syllables, 458

Wagner, E. B., 56, 264, 293
Wagner, G., 227, 238, 262, 303
Walcutt, C. C., 87, 216
Walden, J., 31
Walters, G., 255
Weather and Climate Laboratory, 361
Webster's New World Dictionary, 258
Webster's Third New International Dictionary, 446
Webster Word Analysis Charts, 459
Webster Word Wheels, 460
Wechsler Adult Intelligence Scale, 437
Wechsler Intelligence Scale for Children, 167, 437
Wechsler Preschool and Primary Scale of Intelligence, 437
weekly newspapers, 195
Weintraub, S., 338
What the Letters Say, 459
Whipple, G., 426
White, C. E., 278
whole-class activities, 194, 195, 200

whole-word method, 60, 61
whole-word phonics, 233
Wilson, C. T., 399
Withrow, D., 391
Wittick, M. L., 100
Witty, P. A., 368, 373
Woelfel, S., 318
Wolf, W., 318
Word analysis, 232; *see also* phonics, structural analysis, morphemic analysis
word-by-word reading, 170
word cards, 225
Word Clues, 291
word games, 225
Word-Go-Round, 460
word list, 171; test, 172
Word List for the 1970's, 278
word meaning, 122, 266ff.; *see also* vocabulary
word origins, 288
word perception, 207ff.; speeding up, 219ff.
word recognition, 122, 207ff.; developing independence in, 121, 231ff.
word recognition errors, 173
word recognition tests, 171ff.
word study, 218, 281
word wheels, 460
Wordly Wise, 291
Words I Like to Read and Write, 256
workbooks, 64, 130, 325ff.; reading readiness, 49, 50, 52
work-study skills, 334
work-type reading, 333ff.
World History Study Lessons, 399
Wright, J. A., 299
Wright, W., 257
writing vocabulary, 272

Yoakum, G. A., 326

Zedler, E. Y., 238
Zintz, M. V., 427, 431